New Directions in Discourse Processing

Volume II in the Series

ADVANCES
IN DISCOURSE PROCESSES

ROY O. FREEDLE, *Editor*

Educational Testing Service

ABLEX Publishing Corporation
Norwood, New Jersey   07648

Printed in the United States of America

ISBN   0-89391-003-1   ISSN   0164-0224

ABLEX Publishing Corporation
355 Chestnut Street
Norwood, New Jersey 07648

This volume is dedicated with affection
to my sister
Joan
and her children
Laura,
Larry,
and
Cynthia

Contents

Preface to the Series   ix

Preface to Volume II   xi

Introduction to Volume II   xiii

1. A Schema-Theoretic View of Reading
Marilyn Jager Adams and Allan Collins **1**

Schema Theory and Language Comprehension   *3*
Schema Theory and Reading Comprehension   *7*
Conclusion   *20*
Acknowledgments   *21*
References   *21*

2. Event Chains and Inferences
in Understanding Narratives
William H. Warren, David W. Nicholas,
and Tom Trabasso **23**

A Walk Through the Inference Taxonomy   *38*
How Many Inferences: The Relevancy Hypothesis   *43*
Psychological Implications   *47*
Acknowledgments   *51*
References   *51*

**3. An Analysis of Story Comprehension
in Elementary School Children**
Nancy L. Stein and Christine G. Glenn **53**

The Story Schema   *58*
Episodic Relations   *67*
Experiment 1   *71*
Experiment 2   *101*
Conclusion   *115*
Acknowledgments   *119*
References   *119*

**4. Acquisition of New Comprehension Schemata
for Expository Prose by Transfer of a
Narrative Schema**
Roy Freedle and Gordon Hale **121**

General Introduction   *121*
Results and Discussion   *124*
Examples from Individual Subjects   *128*
Additional Distinctions in the Study of
   Expository and Narrative Competence   *129*
Appendix   *131*
References   *135*

**5. What's in a Frame?
Surface Evidence for Underlying Expectations**
Deborah Tannen **137**

Introduction   *137*
Data for the Present Study   *144*
Levels of Frames   *146*
Subject of Experiment   *146*
What's in a Film?   *151*
Film-Viewer Frame   *153*
Expectations About Events   *160*
Expectations About Objects   *165*
Evidence of Expectations   *166*
What's in a Theft?   *177*
Conclusion   *179*
Acknowledgments   *179*
References   *179*

6. Toward a Phenomenology of Reading Comprehension
Don Nix and Marian Schwarz **183**

Introduction *183*
Method *185*
Results *189*
Discussion *194*
Conclusion *195*
References *195*

7. Sociological Approaches to Dialogue with Suggested Applications to Cognitive Science
Roy Freedle and Richard P. Duran **197**

Some Cognitive Science Considerations
   vis-a-vis Sociocultural Rules *201*
Conclusion *206*
References *206*

8. Social Foundations of Language
Elinor Ochs **207**

The Cognitive Bias in Language Studies *207*
Social Foundations of a Syntactic Pattern:
   The Case of Left-Dislocation in Italian *211*
References *219*

9. Modes of Thinking and Ways of Speaking: Culture and Logic Reconsidered
Sylvia Scribner **223**

Cross-Cultural Studies on Verbal
   Reasoning *224*
Logical Thinking Versus Logical Error *228*
Empiric Versus Theoretic Explanations *229*
What Is Empiric Bias? Some Examples *231*
Empiric Versus Theoretic Explanations
   and Wrong Answers *233*
Empiric Bias: Task Dependent *236*
Schemas and Genres *239*
Acknowledgments *242*
References *242*

**10. Repetition in the Non-Native Acquisition
of Discourse: Its Relation to Text Unification and
Conversational Structure**
Deborah Keller-Cohen **245**

Introduction *245*
Part I *248*
Part II *259*
Conclusion *265*
Acknowledgments *269*
References *269*

**11. The Role of Adults' Requests for Clarification in the Language
Development of Children**
Louise J. Cherry **273**

The Request for Clarification *273*
Review of Other Work on the
    Request for Clarification *280*
The Role of Adults' Requests for
    Clarification for the Child's
    Language Development Process *282*
Acknowledgments *286*
References *286*

12. The Effects of Staging on Recall from Prose
P. Clements **287**

Discourse Analysis and Staging *288*
Experimental Evidence *304*
Summary and Conclusions *326*
Acknowledgments *330*
References *330*

Author Index 331

Subject Index 335

Preface to the Series

Roy Freedle
Series Editor

This series of volumes provides a forum for the cross-fertilization of ideas from a diverse number of disciplines, all of which share a common interest in discourse—be it prose comprehension and recall, dialogue analysis, text grammar construction, computer simulation of natural language, cross-cultural comparisons of communicative competence, or other related topics. The problems posed by multisentence contexts and the methods required to investigate them, while not always unique to discourse, are still sufficiently distinct as to benefit from the organized mode of scientific interaction made possible by this series.

Scholars working in the discourse area from the perspective of socio-linguistics, psycholinguistics, ethnomethodology and the sociology of language, educational psychology (e.g., teacher–student interaction), the philosophy of language, computational linguistics, and related subareas are invited to submit manuscripts of monograph or book length to the series editor. Edited collections of original papers resulting from conferences will also be considered.

Volumes in the Series

Vol. I. Discourse production and comprehension. Roy O. Freedle (Ed.), 1977.

Vol. II. New directions in discourse processing.
Roy O. Freedle (Ed.), 1979.

Preface to Volume II

This volume addresses several new directions in the study of discourse. In particular, two themes which are explored by a number of scholars from different disciplines are schema theory (largely from a psycholinguistic perspective) and a focus upon the most potent and far-ranging schemata yet available, that of culture. Cultural schemata are pursued in chapters addressing ethnographic factors affecting language, thought, and problem-solving activities, and in chapters addressing sociolinguistic aspects of language use. A more generalized discussion of schema theory is found in chapters which address language problems from a more psycholinguistic and/or developmental orientation. Finally, there are a number of chapters which broach quite new topics whose relationship to schema theory and culture, while not spelled out in detail, is nevertheless apparent. These chapters deal with the staging of propositions according to their topical importance to the discourse text at hand and the use of cohesion and turn-taking signals in the acquisition of a first and second language.

ROY FREEDLE
Princeton, N.J.
Feb., 1979

Introduction to Volume II

Roy Freedle
Educational Testing Service

Two broad theoretical orientations are beginning to emerge as potent organizers of the complex field of discourse—schema theory and cultural norms for using language. Both views, though seemingly separate, are intimately linked. For example, culture in some ways can be recast as a set of schemata for concretizing habitual ways to perform activities including those involving language. In addition, culture can be viewed as a set of interactive schemata for habitual ways in which interacting individuals can dynamically discover what each person intends to convey given the immediate context and shared presuppositions of the culture. Both views, though, deserve separate treatment in order to discern the special insights of each.

To achieve our ultimate goal of understanding how humans produce and comprehend discourse and how this interacts with communicative settings requires a multidisciplinary approach. Toward this end, the editor invited a number of experts in cognitive anthropology, ethnographic psychology, sociolinguistics, developmental psycho-social linguistics, education, linguistics, and cognitive psychology to contribute chapters dealing broadly with schema theory and/or the impact of culture on language use. In the early stages of bringing these several disciplines together, a common vocabulary was not sought—this being very much a future enterprise.

The first grouping of chapters highlights a variety of ways in which schema theory has been recently applied to the study of story recall, reading, and the transfer of story schemata to increase comprehension of expository prose. The first chapter by Adams and Collins provides a broad introduction to schema theory and then applies these concepts to clarify the process of reading. The next three chapters—by Warren, Nicholas, and Trabasso; Stein and Glenn; and Freedle and Hale—explore schema theory as it has been applied to characterize story structure and as it applies to the development of an internal template for guiding story comprehension and story recall. The chapter by Freedle and Hale also explores how such story schemata might be transferred to accelerate the development of an expository prose schema in children.

The next five chapters—by Tannen; Nix and Schwarz; Freedle and Duran; Ochs; and Scribner—focus more specifically on cultural schemata. Tannen explores a wide variety of frames (sometimes called scripts or themes) which are used by Greek and American adults in their perception and recounting of a "silent" film. Tannen analyzes the many ways in which these two populations use different interpretive frames to synthesize what they have seen and how these frames come to be variously realized in speech. Nix and Schwarz explore how differences in cultural experience of Black and White American children alters their interpretation of short written passages. Their method for zeroing in upon the precise nature of these covert frames is especially noteworthy. Freedle and Duran argue for introducing socio-linguistic and cultural insights into cognitive science by illustrating how dialogue involves scripts for managing social interaction in conversation. They further show how these concerns mesh with instantiations of scripts from lexical terms occurring in discourse.

Ochs offers cross-cultural evidence for the specificity of certain syntax rules (e.g., left-dislocation in Italian) which appear to be tied to certain social settings; thus she considers the possibility that language structure in part may reflect social processes and social structure. Scribner clarifies our under-standing of how culture and Western educational methods in particular may influence the manner in which individuals approach and solve logical problems from either a contextualized or decontextualized point of view. In other words some cultures instill decontextualization frames for treating language as a set of abstract propositions; Scribner further explores under what conditions such decontextualized frames may emerge in nonindus-trialized cultures.

The papers by Keller-Cohen and Cherry (now Cherry Wilkinson) give us a glimpse of how discourse theory can be used to study child language acquisition of a first and second language. Special request routines or schemata are examined by Cherry for their import in acquisition of a first language. Repetition requests are used significantly more often, and confirmation requests less often, for children of lower language development. It appears that primary caretakers may internalize an overall dialogue schemata (plan) for instilling language growth. The final chapter by Clements is an empirical investigation of Grimes' theory of how propositions are differentially staged so as to achieve varying degrees of textual importance or relevance to the total text. This represents a schema for conveying a speaker or writer's prior plan to a receptive listener who must also have internalized a similar schema in order to correctly decipher the staging signals.

It is evident that this second volume in the discourse series brings to the reader a wide array of topics, methodologies, and disciplines all of which are concerned with the analysis of discourse. This rich offering is purposely done in order to stimulate a more broadly based theory of discourse and thereby to encourage a more robust paradigm for future theorists and researchers to rely on. The particular themes explored in this volume—schema theory and cultural schemata—are in my opinion among the most broadly based and most potent influences on language structure and its processing. From these molar levels of orienting attitudes and routines for organizing social communication, social convention, knowledge categorizations and perceptual consistencies, we can draw our most accurate predictions concerning the more molecular language functions, such as how are propositions to be staged, what knowledge is presupposed of a particular listener, how much top-down vs. bottom-up processing should be engaged in for particular topics, settings, and participants, etc. While the details of this connection between the molar and molecular levels of language use are still very much a future enterprise, it is my expectation that, by bringing scholars together from ethnographic, psychological, educational, and linguistic backgrounds, we will eventually construct the necessary framework for a viable theory of discourse as a uniquely human adventure into the synthesis and transmission of knowledge.

1

A Schema-Theoretic
View of Reading

Marilyn Jager Adams
Allan Collins
Bolt Beranek and Newman

At one level, reading can be described as the process of translating graphemic strings into spoken words. However, what we really mean by reading is not the ability to decode words but the ability to extract the meaning, both explicit and implicit, from the written text. It depends on the intricate coordination of our visual, linguistic, and conceptual information-processing systems. If we are to understand reading, we must find a way to break it down into a set of more tractable subskills and to identify their interrelations.

The standard approach is to begin with the ultimate goal of the reader and then to determine its prerequisites. At the highest level, one has successfully read a passage if one understands it both as it was intended by the author and in terms of its impact on oneself. This presumes that one has extracted the information provided by the text, which, in turn, depends upon having comprehended the individual sentences, which depends upon having correctly processed the clauses and phrases of those sentences, which depends upon having recognized the component words of those units, which depends upon having recognized their component letters.

When reading is analyzed in this way, the component levels of processing appear to be organized hierarchically. The attainment of any given level presumes the execution of all subordinate or less complex levels; moreover, the converse is not strictly true. Whereas the reading of a written passage depends on the reading of its sentences, words, and letters, the dependency is, in some sense, unidirectional. An individual letter may be perfectly legible whether or not it is embedded in a word, a sentence, or a passage. Similarly, skilled readers are fully capable of reading individual words and sentences in the absence of a larger context. This asymmetry has been exploited by traditional analyses of reading. For teachers, it provides a rational structure for instructional programs: start at the bottom, with single letter recognition, and successively work up through the higher level skills. For researchers, it provides a means of empirically isolating the processes involved at any given level in the structure: the effects of higher order processes on the level in question are supposed to be null, and the effects of lower processes can be empirically identified and subtracted out.

The problem with this approach is that when one is reading a meaningful passage, one is not reading its component letters, words, and sentences in the same way as when they are presented in isolation. Rather, processing at each level is influenced by higher, as well as lower, order information. Thus, individual letters become more perceptible when they are embedded in words (Reicher, 1969; Wheeler, 1970). Individual words are recognized more easily when they are embedded in meaningful sentences (Schuberth & Eimas, 1977; Tulving & Gold, 1963). Unfamiliar words may be processed more easily if they are embedded in a familiar story (Wittrock, Marks, & Doctorow, 1975). Sentences that more coherently integrate the underlying semantic relations may be assimilated more easily than those that do not, irrespective of their syntactic complexity (Haviland & Clark, 1974; Pearson, 1974-75).

These sorts of interactions tremendously ease the task of the skilled reader. Because of them, one is not obliged to grind through every graphemic detail of the written representation. Instead one may opt to process lower order information only as is necessary for checking higher order hypotheses about the content of the passage. By contrast, these sorts of interactions greatly complicate the task of analyzing the reading process. They challenge the wisdom of bottom-up instructional strategies, and they all but nullify the generality of empirical findings based on "isolated" processes. Moreover, they leave us without a good working model of the reading process.

Recently, however, through the combined efforts of cognitive psychologists, linguistics, and specialists in artificial intelligence, a new set of formalisms for analyzing language comprehension has begun to emerge. These theories are, at core, related to the old notion of a schema (Bartlett, 1932; Kant, 1781; Woodworth, 1938). In the current literature, they are variously referred to as frames (e.g., Charniak, 1975; Minsky, 1975) and scripts (e.g., Lehnert, 1977; Schank & Abelson, 1975), as well as schemata (e.g., Becker, 1973; Bobrow & Norman, 1975; Rumelhart & Ortony, 1977). We would argue that schema theory, for the first time, provides a structure powerful enough to support the interactions among different levels of processing in reading.

In the remainder of this chapter, we will first provide a general description of schema-theoretic models and the way they work, and then examine some extensions of the models to the study of reading. A disclaimer is in order at this point. Many schema-theoretic models have been, are being, and will be developed, and there are some fundamental differences among them. In view of this, we have not tried to provide a faithful description of any one model. Instead we gloss over controversies and differences between models in the hope of providing a coherent tutorial glimpse of the overall effort.

SCHEMA THEORY AND LANGUAGE COMPREHENSION

A fundamental assumption of schema-theoretic approaches to language comprehension is that spoken or written text does not in itself carry meaning. Rather, a text only provides directions for listeners or readers as to how they should retrieve or construct the intended meaning from their own, previously acquired knowledge. The words of a text evoke in the reader associated concepts, their past interrelationships and their potential interrelationships. The organization of the text helps the reader to select among these conceptual complexes. The goal of schema theory is to specify the interface between the reader and the text—to specify how the reader's knowledge interacts with and shapes the information on the page and to specify how that knowledge must be organized to support the interaction.

Structural Organization of Schema-Theoretic Models

A schema is a description of a particular class of concepts and is composed of a hierarchy of schemata embedded within schemata. The representation at the top of the hierarchy is sufficiently general to capture the essential aspects of all members of the class. For example, if the conceptual class represented by a schema were "going to a restaurant" (Schank & Abelson, 1977), its top level representation would include such information as that a restaurant is a commercial establishment where people pay money to have someone else prepare their food and clean up after them. At the level beneath this global characterization are more specific schemata (e.g., going to a diner, going to a fast hamburger operation, and going to a swanky restaurant). In general, as one moves down the hierarchy, the number of embedded schemata multiplies while the scope of each narrows, until, at the bottom most level, the schemata apply to unique perceptual events. Each schema at each level in the hierarchy consists of descriptions of the important components of its meaning and their interrelationships, where these descriptions are themselves schemata defined at the appropriate level of specificity. The power of this structure derives from the fact that the top level representation of any schema simultaneously provides an abstraction of and a conceptual frame for all of the particular events that fall within its domain.

Because the top level description of a schema must pertain to every member of its class, many of its components may be but vaguely specified. For example, in the restaurant schema very few properties of *the place to be served* could be extended to all possible members of that class, be they any variety of booths, tables, or counters; accordingly, very few properties could be explicitly attached to its superordinate description. On the other hand, the most general schema for the place to be served in a restaurant effectively contains all of the service arrangements one has experienced, or, equivalently, the collective features of those service arrangements weighted in terms of their likelihood in different contexts. Thus, while no specific value is anticipated, a stereotype is defined; in the absence of further information, the concept is still meaningful.

Because the schema specifies the interrelationships between its underlying components, once any element is specified, it can be understood in the proper context. For example, if a counter is mentioned within the restaurant schema, it can immediately be understood as a place at which food can be served and not as an abacus or a parrying boxer's blow. Moreover, the introduction of a counter might be sufficient to eliminate swanky restaurants from consideration, thereby indirectly narrowing the probable range for other, as yet unspecified, components of the restaurant schema.

Any important element or schema within a schema may be thought of as a *slot* (Minsky, 1975) that can accept any of the range of values that are compatible with its associated schemata. The comprehension of a specific situation or story involves the process of instantiation whereby elements in the situation are bound to appropriate slots in the relevant schema. This process not only serves the purpose of filling out the details of the schema, but also of temporarily connecting it to characteristics of the bound schemata. Thus, if there is a nervous old man in the story who takes the order in the restaurant, he will be bound to the waiter role. If subsequently the waiter knocks over a glass of water, this fact will be related back ot the nervous quality of the old man currently assigned to the waiter role. Often, a text will not explicitly provide the element to be bound to a particular slot even though it is an integral component of some relevant schema. In these cases, the reader may assign *default* values. The default assignment will be determined by the values associated with its slot. The precision of the default description will depend on the specificity of those values. If one knew that the restaurant in the story was swanky, the default assignment might be that the customer sat at a table; if one also knew it was an authentic Japanese restaurant, the default assignment might be that the customer sat on cushions rather than a chair; if the story were about a particular, familiar Japanese restaurant, the default assignment might be very elaborate.

The Processing of Information

Within schema theory, the process of interpretation is guided by the principle that all data must be accounted for (Bobrow & Norman, 1975). Every input event must be mapped against some schema, and all aspects of that schema must be compatible with the input information. This requirement results in two basic modes of information processing. The first mode, *bottom-up processing,* is evoked by the incoming data. The features of the data enter the system through the best fitting, bottom-level schemata. As these schemata converge into higher level schemata, they too are activated. In this way, the information is propagated upward through the hierarchy, through increasingly comprehensive levels of interpretation. The other mode, *top-down processing,* works in the opposite direction. Top-down processing occurs as the system searches for information to fit into partially satisfied, higher order schemata.

An important aspect of a schema-theoretic account of reading comprehension is that top-down and bottom-up processing should be occurring at all levels of analysis simultaneously (Rumelhart, 1976). The data that are needed to instantiate or fill out the schemata become available through bottom-up processing; top-down processing facilitates their assimilation if they are anticipated or are consistent with the reader's conceptual set. Bottom-up processing ensures that the reader will be sensitive to information that is novel or that does not fit her or his ongoing hypotheses about the content of the text; top-down processes help the reader to resolve ambiguities or to select between alternative possible interpretations of the incoming data. Through the interactions between top-down and bottom-up processing, the flow of information through the system is considerably constrained. Even so, these processes are not, in themselves, enough to ensure apt comprehension.

The notion that the human mind is guided by a central, limited capacity processor is, by now, taken for granted within many psychological theories of information-processing. The general acceptance of this notion among psychologists has been principally due to empirical demands. Recently, however, Bobrow and Norman (1975) have argued that some such construct must be incorporated into any schema-theoretic type of system, be it person or machine, if its responses to its environment are to be rational and coherent.

Bobrow and Norman's argument is based on three observations. First, in order for a system that is so diffuse and receptive to maintain coherence, it must be imbued with purpose. In their words, "Without purpose, the system will fail to pursue a line of inquiry in any directed fashion" (p. 146). Moreover, too many purposes can be the same as none. Their second observation is related: individual purposes are, by definition, single-minded. In order to select among different, and possibly conflicting, purposes the system must have some more global self-awareness or, in Bobrow and Norman's words, "a central motivational process." Third, some mechanism which has access to all memory schemata must guide the interpretive process. This is necessary in order to decide when a schema has been adequately filled out for the current purpose, to evaluate the goodness of fit of the data to the schemata, and to detect and appropriately connect metaphorical or analogical references. These observations led Bobrow and Norman to conclude that the schemata must culminate in some central, omniscient processor—a grand self-schema, if you will. The primary responsibility of this processor is to adaptively allocate the limited resources for active processing among the various activities of the system.

Taking this notion back to the schema-theoretic model, we see that there are two basic ways in which the processing capabilities of the system may be limited (Norman & Bobrow, 1975). First, there may be some difficulty in mapping input data to the memory structure with the result that their normally automatic, bottom-up propagation through the system is obstructed; in this case, the system is *data-limited*. Second, the various, simultaneous demands for active control may exceed the system's capacity to cope; in this case, the system is *resource-limited* and the execution of some of the ongoing activities will be compromised. Both kinds of limitations are relevant to the reading process.

Norman and Bobrow (1975) have distinguished two types of data-limits on processing. The definitive characteristic of each is that no amount of effort on the interpreter's part will eliminate the problem. The first, *signal data-limits,* occur when the quality of the input confuses the mapping process, as, for example, when one is listening for a faint signal in a noisy environment. Examples of signal data-limits in the reading domain range from the deciphering of poor handwriting to the comprehension of a wholly incoherent passage. For the second kind of data-limits, *memory data-limits,* the quality of the input may be impeccable, but the mapping process is obstructed for lack of appropriate memory structures. Both of us would, for example, suffer from a memory data-limit in trying to understand a Japanese speech; since we know no Japanese, we could not, with any amount of effort, succeed. With respect to reading, problems related to memory data-limits are pervasive. For the beginning reader, they may occur at the level of single letter recognition. For more experienced readers, they may persist at the levels of word recognition, syntactic analysis, and, of course, in any dimension of semantic interpretation.

As an example of resource-limited processing, Bobrow and Norman describe the familiar situation in which one is simultaneously driving a car and carrying on a conversation. Both activities can be managed as long as they are proceeding as expected. If one, however, absorbs an inordinate amount of attention, it does so at the expense of the other. Surprising news may result in bad driving; a busy intersection may provoke a pause in the driver's speech or distract him or her from listening. The analogy exists in the reading situation—we can tolerate more or less distraction while reading, depending on the difficulty of our material or our reasons for reading it.

But, with respect to reading, the more critical problems related to resource-limited processing arise when activities subserving the same end compete for attention. If their respective demands cannot be met, the comprehension process breaks down. A good reader may encounter this problem when, for example, trying to read a legal document or a scientific paper that is outside of her or his area of expertise; the reader may devote a lot of energy toward understanding the words and sentences, only to find that she or he has not understood the meaning of the paragraph. For young readers, this kind of problem may be especially frequent since many of the subskills and concepts presumed by a text may not yet be well learned or integrated.

SCHEMA THEORY AND READING COMPREHENSION

A crucial idea for a schema-theoretic account of reading comprehension is that it involves the coordinated activity of schemata at all levels of analyses. As schemata at the lower levels (e.g., visual features) are activated, they are bound to and thus evoke schemata at the next, higher level (e.g., letters); as these schemata are activated, they, in turn, trigger their own superordinate schemata (e.g., words). In this way, through bottom-up processing, the input data are automatically propagated up the hierarchy toward more meaningful or comprehensive levels of representation. At the same time, schemata at higher levels are competing to fill their slots with elements from the levels beneath through top-down processing. Again, the theory is that, for the skilled reader, both top-down and bottom-up processing are occurring simultaneously and at all levels of analysis as he or she proceeds through the text (Rumelhart, 1976).

A necessary assumption here is that schemata exist at all levels of abstraction (Abelson, 1975; Rumelhart & Ortony, 1977). At the letter level, the schematic descriptions may be relatively concrete and specific. For example, the schema for an uppercase K might consist of three subschemata: (1) a vertical line on the left; (2) an oblique line extending upward from near the center of the vertical line to a point to the right of and perpendicular with the top of the vertical line; and (3) a second oblique line extending downward from somewhere along the bottom half of the first oblique line to a point directly beneath the top end of the first oblique line and perpendicular to the bottom of the vertical line.

At the other extreme, schematic descriptions may be very abstract and general. As an example, consider Rumelhart and Ortony's (1977) tentative version of the problem-solving schema. In it there are three variables: a Person P, and Event E, and a Goal G. The schema has a two-step structure:

1. E causes P to want G;
2. P tries to get G until P gets G or until P gives up.

Each of the elements like *cause, want,* and *try* in this schema are themselves schemata, just as the letters in the schemata for words are themselves schemata. Rumelhart and Ortony's version of the *try* schema has two variables which are bound in the problem-solving schema: a Person P, a Goal G. The proposed steps are:

1. P decides on an action A which could lead to G;
2. while any precondition A' for A is not satisfied, P tries to get A';
3. P does A.

The problem-solving and trying schemata reflect what Newell and Simon (1963) have called means–ends analysis. In means–ends analysis, whenever a goal cannot be obtained directly, an appropriate subgoal is set up. This subgoal may itself be recursively dissolved into sub-subgoals, until a stepwise means has been found to attain the original goal. We would argue, as have Newell and Simon (1963), that just such problem-solving pervades many human motivations and actions. It follows that a full understanding of many stories by and about people depends on being able to interpret their events in terms of something like the problem-solving and trying schemata that Rumelhart and Ortony (1977) have outlined.

The power of a schema-theoretic account of reading derives from the assumption that lower level schemata are elements or subschemata within higher level schemata. It is, above all, this aspect of the theory that allows perceptual elements to coalesce into meaning, that allows such abstract, higher order schemata as the problem-solving schema to be appropriately and usefully accessed. Moreover, it is this aspect of the theory which provides a structure for conceptualizing the interrelationships between levels of processing.

In order to give a more detailed description of what is theoretically happening as one reads, it is easiest to consider different levels of processing as if those levels were separable (which they are not). In the next four sections of this chapter, we will deal successively with letter and word processing, syntactic processing, semantic processing, and processing at the interpretive level. In each case, the basic argument in favor of a schema-theoretic explanation of these processes is that they cannot be explained in terms of bottom-up processing and that the top-down influences seem to be too automatic and too well structured to be attributable to simple guessing.

We will describe these processes in terms of how a skilled reader might arrive at an understanding of the following fable:

Stone Soup

A poor man came to a large house during a storm to beg for food. He was sent away with angry words, but he went back and asked. "May I at least dry my clothes by the fire, because I am wet from the rain?" The maid thought this would not cost anything, so she let him come in.

Inside he told the cook that if she would give him a pan, and let him fill it with water, he would make some stone soup. This was a new dish to the cook, so she agreed to let him make it. The man then got a stone from the road and put it in the pan. The cook gave him some salt, peas, mint, and all the scraps of meat that she could spare to throw in. Thus the poor man made a delicious stone soup and the cook said, "Well done! You have made a wonderful soup out of practically nothing."

—Aesop

Knowledge and Processing at the Letter and Word Levels

The first step toward understanding the Stone Soup story is that of recognizing the words. The processes involved in recognizing written words have been a topic of prolonged debate among educators and psychologists. On one side, there are those who argue that word recognition must be mediated by more elementary activities, like letter identification; on the other, there are those who argue that words are recognized wholistically.

The first position has many practical arguments in its favor. First, for example, the pattern analyzing mechanisms that must be posited would be far less cumbersome if the system worked on single letters or even their elementary features, than if it worked on whole word patterns. The importance of this argument is stressed when one considers the innumerable variety of type styles and scripts that are legible. Second, there must be some connection in the system between written and spoken language, and our alphabetic cipher provides a natural candidate for such a link. In addition, it provides a means by which unfamiliar written words that are familiar in their spoken expression can be "decoded." However, the potential advantages of an alphabetic language are denied if letters are not functional stimuli in reading. Third, thorough instruction in letter-to-sound correspondences has been shown to be an important component of early reading curricula (Barr, 1975; Chall, 1967); by implication these correspondences, or some aspect of the analysis they involve, must be useful to the reading process.

In support of the other contention—that people recognize words wholistically—is the fact that people act like that is what they do. Certainly skilled readers are rarely aware of reading in a letter-by-letter fashion. Moreover, experimental studies have shown that whole words can be perceived at least as quickly and accurately as single letters (Cattell, 1886; Reicher, 1969; Wheeler, 1970).

The most reasonable solution to this dilemma is that the process of recognizing written words involves analyses at both the letter and the word level, and that these analyses occur simultaneously and interact with each other. Recently, Adams (1979) ran a series of experiments comparing the visual processing of words, pseudowords, and orthographically irregular nonwords, which yielded direct support for this explanation. She then proposed a model which is very much in the spirit of schema theory.

The basic assumption underlying Adams' model is that any set of internal units or schemata that are repeatedly activated at the same time become associated such that the activation of one of them facilitates the activation of the others. The essential idea of the model is that the extraction of visual information proceeds in the same way for words, pseudowords, and orthographically irregular strings, and that their differential perceptibility is due to interactions between the schemata against which the visual information is mapped. These interactions are illustrated in Figs. 1 and 2.

The circles in Fig. 1 represent letter recognition schemata, the arrows represent associations between them. The full circles correspond to schemata receiving activation from both an external stimulus and other activated schemata while the broken circles correspond to those receiving activation from other schemata only. The degree of interfacilitation should be determined by both the strength of the external input and the strength of the association, where the latter is presumably a function of the letters' history of co-occurrence. The strengths of these interletter associations can therefore be estimated from transitional probabilities, as has been done in this figure.

This structure would predict a considerable perceptual advantage of words and pseudowords over orthographically irregular nonwords, especially given that the extraction of visual information proceeds in parallel. That is, interfacilitation between the component letters of words and pseudowords would be mutual and coincident with external input. With reference to the example in Fig. 1a, the T, the H, and the A would all be simultaneously receiving external activation from the stimulus and internal activation from each other. By contrast, the activation of the component letters of nonwords strings, as in Fig. 1c, would depend almost entirely on external input; since the transition probabiliites between the adjacent letters of irregular nonwords are quite small, their mutual facilitation must also be minimal.

In order to explain the perceptual advantage of real words over pseudowords a second, lexical level of analysis must be included in the model. This level is diagrammed in Fig. 2. The connections between the lexical schemata and the letter schemata represent the associations between them. The weightings of these associations are supposed to depend on lognormal word frequency. As the individual letter schemata receive input, they relay

STIMULUS

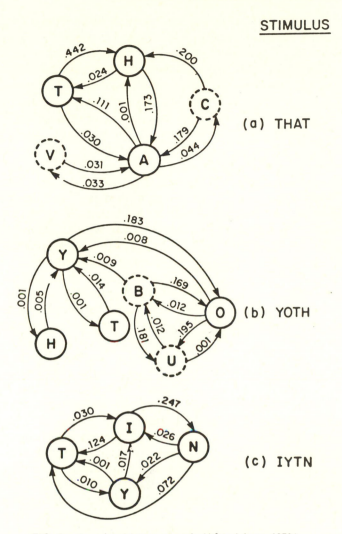

(a) THAT

(b) YOTH

(c) IYTN

FIG. 1.   Associated letter network. (After Adams, 1979.)

activation to all appropriate word schemata, and as a given word schema becomes active, it proportionately and reciprocally facilitates the letter schemata corresponding to its component letters.

In terms of schema theory, Adams is positing two kinds of interactive processes that take place simultaneously in recognizing words: the first depends on interconnections between schemata at the letter level, where one letter triggers an expectation for another letter; the second depends on the structure within schemata at the word level, where competing words are looking for letters to fill their respective slots.

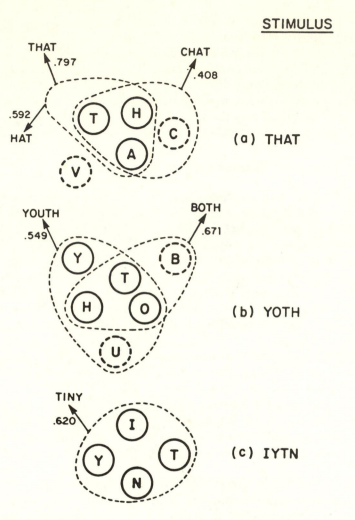

FIG. 2.   Associated lexical network. (After Adams, 1979.)

What happens concurrently at the feature, letter, and word levels as the reader scans through the Stone Soup story is something like this. The eye collects information about different visual features that are present. These are features that are automatically bound to slots that they fit in the letter schemata. Meanwhile, partially instantiated letter schemata are trying to find the appropriate visual features to fill their remaining slots. In addition, they are facilitating other letter schemata that correspond to likely neighbors and, finally, fitting themselves to slots in the word schemata. While all of this is happening, partially activated word schemata are trying to identify the appropriate letters for their own unfilled slots.

A natural extension of Adams' model would be that word schemata facilitate other word schemata that are likely to occur in the same sentence. This extension could explain the semantic priming effects that have been reported in the psychological literature (e.g., Meyer, Schvaneveldt, & Ruddy, 1974; Schuberth & Eimas, 1977; Tulving & Gold, 1963). But when a person is reading connected discourse, syntactic and higher order semantic knowledge must also be influencing the identification of words. As described below, words themselves are subschemata within these higher level schemata.

Knowledge and Processing at the Syntactic Level

Perhaps more than anything else, it was Chomsky's (1959) "Review of Skinner's Verbal Learning," that dealt the death blow to bottom-up theories of syntactic processing. Chomsky argued cogently that in building a descriptive model of linguistic behavior, the "...elimination of the independent contribution of the speaker and learner...can be achieved only at the cost of eliminating all significance from the descriptive system, which then operates at a level so gross and crude that no answers are suggested to the most elementary questions" (p. 30). In other words, top-down processes must be incorporated into models of syntactic processing if they are to have any explanatory power.

Recent experimental evidence not only supports the contention that syntactic analysis is guided by top-down processes, but, further, indicates that this happens in a way that is consistent with schema theory. That is, the syntactic processing of a phrase occurs not subsequent to, but in parallel with the processing of its lexical elements (Marslen-Wilson, 1973, 1975; Wannemacher, 1974). Moreover, the syntactic hypotheses interact with and thus facilitate the lower level processes (Marcel, 1974; Marslen-Wilson & Tyler, 1975).

One of the most powerful formalisms that researchers in artificial intelligence have developed for syntactic processing is the augmented transition network (ATN) grammar (Woods, 1970). Recently experimental evidence has been accumulating that ATN theory provides at least a plausible account of human syntactic processing (Stevens & Rumelhart, 1975; Wanner & Maratsos, 1975).

The ATN formalism is best explained in terms of a small network that can parse a subset of English. There exists an ATN grammar for most of English (Woods, Kaplan, & Nash-Webber, 1972), but it is complicated to understand. Figure 3 shows a sample network for analyzing English sentences (S) from Woods (1970), and associated networks for analyzing noun phrases (NP) and prepositional phrases (PP). The arcs (or pointers) in the ATN formalism act like slots in the schema formalism. Thus, going out from the S state in Fig. 3, any auxiliary (AUX) will satisfy the lower arc. "Auxiliary" defines the range

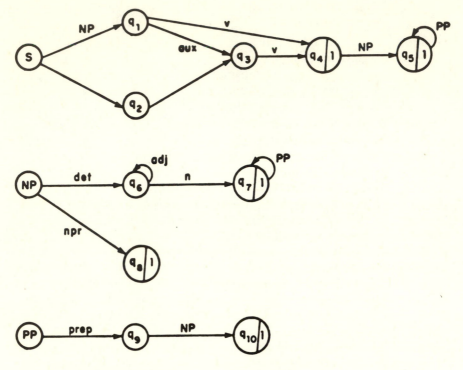

FIG. 3.   A sample transition network. S is the start state. q_4, q_5, q_6, q_7, q_8, and q_9, are the final states. (After Woods, 1970.)

of values that can satisfy that arc (or slot). The ATN formalism, however, has no notion equivalent to default values in the schema formalism. Like schemata, ATN networks are embedded: going along an NP arc in any network means jumping to the NP network to analyze a noun phrase. By allowing whole networks to replace arcs, the network for analyzing noun phrases need only be specified once. This is the same kind of power that comes from embedding in schema theory: one can have a schema for "trying" or a "restaurant" which can be referred to in a wide variety of different places by higher level schema, so it need only be specified once. ATN networks can in fact be viewed as procedural schemata for representing syntactic knowledge.

Woods (1970) describes how the ATN network in Fig. 3 analyzes sentences as follows:

> To recognize the sentence "Did the red barn collapse?" the network is started in state S. The first transition is the aux transition to state q_2 permitted by the auxiliary "did." From state q_2 we see that we can get to state q_3 if the next "thing" in the input string is an NP. To ascertain if this is the case, we call the state NP. From state NP we can follow the arc labeled det to state q_6 because of the

determiner "the." From here, the adjective "red" causes a loop which returns to state q_6, and the subsequent noun "barn" causes a transition to state q_7. Since state q_7 is a final state, it is possible to "pop up" from the NP computation and continue the computation of the top level S beginning in State q_3 which is at the end of the NP arc. From q_3 the verb "collapse" permits a transition to the state q_4, and since this state is final and "collapse" is the last work in the string, the string is accepted as a sentence. (pp. 591–592)

Most ATN parsers that have been developed to date have been top-down processors: the parser starts out looking for a sentence in the S network, and the parser will fail if the input is not a well formed string according to the grammar. But there is nothing about the ATN formalism that is inherently top-down. In fact, Woods (1976) has recently developed an ATN parser that proceeds in bottom-up fashion from the words first identified. This is important in speech processing, where the small function words that are crucial for top-down syntactic processing are the most difficult words to identify phonetically in the speech stream. In human comprehension, we envision both a top-down process, as most ATN grammars are currently designed, and a bottom-up process proceeding outward from the first words recognized to identify noun phrases, verb phrases, prepositional phrases, etc.

At the syntactic level, then, the reader's processing of the Stone Soup fable must be something like the following. From the top down the reader starts looking for a sentence. There is a high probability that a sentence starts with a noun phrase (i.e., arcs must have frequencies associated wtih them as in Adams' model in Fig. 1), and so the reader's initial expectation may be for a noun phrase, which "A poor man" satisfies. But different words in the sentence trigger expectations in a bottom-up fashion: "a" is usually followed by an adjective or noun; "man" is likely to be the final state in a noun phrase and therefore triggers expectations for determiners, adjectives, and possessives to the left and a verb phrase to the right. Thus, the nature of syntactic constraints is different from word and letter level constraints, but they operate in the same top-down and bottom-up patterns. Furthermore, they operate in conjunction with constraints at the other levels to determine what the reader comprehends.

Knowledge and Processing at the Semantic Level

In reading the Stone Soup fable the skilled reader fills in many details that are not in the text. For example, (1) that the man came to the house because he was hungry, and the maid sent him away because she didn't want to give away her master's food; (2) that the poor man asked to dry himself by the fire because he thought the maid might let him in, and he wanted to get into the house so he could get some food; (3) that the maid let him in because she felt sorry for him and did not realize his request was a ploy to get food; (4) that the man suggested making stone soup because he thought the cook might be fooled into thinking that a stone could be used to make soup, and, if so, she would throw in scraps of food as she normally does in making soup; (5) that the cook agreed because she thought the man knew about a novel dish, and she did not realize he had invented the dish as a ploy to get food; (6) that the cook did not realize that the man had contributed nothing to the soup; and (7) that the reason the soup tasted good was because of the ingredients the cook added. None of these motivations and causal connections is in the passage itself.

There is a large amount of the reader's world knowledge that must be invoked in order to construct such an interpretation for the Stone Soup fable. Table 1 shows what some of that information might look like in schema-theoretic terms.

The process of comprehending the passage at the semantic level must be something like the following. The fact that the man is poor triggers the notion that he does not have much money or wealth. The large house he comes to, therefore, must not be his own house. Begging is one means of obtaining food (see *How to obtain goods* in Table 1), and the fact that the man does not have money satisfies the precondition for begging. Because the reader tries to

TABLE 1
Some World Knowledge Schemata Needed for Stone Soup Fable

A maid
1. A woman servant P1 who cleans and takes care of residence 1 for master and/or mistress P2.
2. The goal of P1 is to please P2.
3. P2 pays P1 with money and/or by providing room and board.

How to please a master
1. A person P1 can please a master P2 by working hard, by being nice to P2, and by protecting P2's property.

How to obtain goods
1. If a person P1 has money M, P1 can buy goods G from a store 1 or person P2 possessing G.
2. If a person P1 has no money M, P1 can borrow M or P1 can steal goods G from a store 1 or person P2 possessing G, or beg for G from P2, or con P2 into giving G.

How to con somebody
1. If a person P1 has a goal G1, and
2. If another person P2 has a means M and a goal G2 to prevent P1 from obtaining G1, and
3. If P1 performs an action A which P2 thinks is directed toward a different goal G3 and which leads P1 to obtain G1 without P2 giving up either M or G2,
4. Then P1 cons P2 by doing A.

How to make soup X
1. A person P1 puts potable liquid in a pan.
2. P1 adds a large quantity of food X or a base for meat stock X like soup bones or scraps.
3. P1 adds spices and other bits of food F that are available.
4. P1 cooks over low heat for a long time.

interpret actions in terms of the problem-solving and trying schemata, she or he will bind the poor man to the person P in both schemata, and the begging of food to the action A in the trying schema that could lead to some goal G. Because no goal and no initiating event are specified in the story, the reader makes the default assumptions that the man is hungry (event E) and his goal G is to eat. It is the need to satisfy these slots in the problem-solving schema that forces these assumptions. Obviously they could be wrong; the man might be seeking food for his dog or casing the house to rob it, but the default values are assumed unless and until the reader is forced to revise them.

When the poor man is sent away with angry words, the reader similarly makes a default assumption that a resident of the house sends the poor man away, not because the poor man offended the resident but in order to preserve property (i.e., food). When the poor man comes back for permission to dry his clothes, this does not fit the earlier goal of wanting to eat, so the reader assumes that the poor man's goal has changed to getting dry from the storm mentioned in the first sentence. The reference to the maid in the last sentence of the first paragraph binds her to the resident who sent the poor man away originally. To fill the slots in the problem-solving schema, the reader assumes that the maid's goal in letting the begger come in is to make him happy, out of a general kindness to the poor. This is reconciled with her earlier refusal of food, because the action taken in this case does not violate the means by which she can please her master (see Table 1).

Inside, the man apparently adopts another new goal of teaching the cook how to make stone soup. The reader has no schema for making stone soup; it is news to the reader as well as the cook. But the reader, in order to understand the story, must have a schema like that in Table 1 as to how to make soup in general. One of the conditions for making soup is violated, namely, that the basic ingredients be edible or meat bones or scraps. This triggers the reader to look for another goal for the poor man's actions. The fact that the cook put a lot of scraps into the soup means that she has supplied the base for the soup. This suggests that the man's original goal of getting food might be his goal in making stone soup. There is nothing in the story that says he eats the soup, but the cook says the soup tastes good, which implies that it has been made. The default value when people perform some task together is that both share the fruits of the labor, so that the reader should assume the poor man gets to eat the soup. Therefore, the reader can make sense of this episode in terms of the man's reaching his original goal of obtaining food.

Furthermore, the clever reader will see that the number of independent goals for the poor man can be reduced to one, if the man's request to dry himself by the fire is interpreted as a subgoal to getting into the house, and getting into the house is, in turn, a subgoal to getting food . This interpretation works because an alternative to begging for goods is conning someone for goods (see Table 1). The way the con operates here is that the man has the goal to get food, which the maid wants to prevent. By asking to dry himself by the fire the man takes an action which leads to getting food, but which the maid thought was directed to getting dry. Thus, she misinterpreted his action and was conned.

A still more difficult inference is to see that the man conned the cook as well as the maid. To make this inference the reader must infer that the cook also would have refused the man food. In the case of the maid, this is revealed by her actions. In the case of the cook, it must be inferred from the fact that she too would want to please her master by preserving his property. Furthermore, the reader must infer both that the cook believed that the man's goal was to make soup from a stone, and that his real goal was to get her to give him some food. We saw how the reader could realize that the man's goal was to obtain food. The clue that the cook did not understand the man's goal is only indirect; she marvels at his having made a wonderful soup out of practically nothing, which implies she does not see that it was she who contributed all of the substantial ingredients to the soup and that he and his stone added nothing. Therefore, she too was conned by the poor man.

Thus, the skilled reader can make sense of the actions and motivations in such a story through a variety of inferences and default assumptions. This involves the use of a wide variety of world knowledge from the schema for problem-solving, to the schema for maids, to the schema for how to con somebody. Different readers may misinterpret the story in many different ways depending on which of these assumptions or inferences they fail to make or which they make incorrectly.

Knowledge and Processing at the Interpretive Level

An understanding of the interrelationships between the character and events in a story typically requires a host of complex inferences. But the goal of the skilled reader goes beyond that of following the story: in addition, the reader seeks to interpret or impose a structure on the passage as a whole. Processing at this level requires even more abstract knowledge and more complex inferences, since it depends less on the actual context of the text than it does on the goals of the reader and his or her perception of the author's intentions.

If the reader knows about fables, the Stone Soup story will be much easier to interpret. This is because fables are constructed according to a regular formula. A fable is a short story. Its characters, which are often animals, are stereotypes (e.g., maids are subservient, rabbits are frivolous, foxes are self-serving and cunning). Fables are generally based on the theme that life requires that we be flexible: individuals who are too nearsighted are liable to suffer ill consequences—their goals will be thwarted or they will be outsmarted; individuals who are adaptive and resourceful will be successful even in the face of adversity. Any particular fable is intended to convey a more specific lesson or moral within this theme. The moral is often summarized by the last line of the fable. All of this knowledge would presumably be organized in a general fable schema.

For purposes of interpreting the Stone Soup story, the reader's first task is that of recognizing that it is a fable. If this information is not explicitly given, it may be signaled in bottom-up fashion from the structure of the story or from the fact that it was authored by Aesop. Once the fable schema has been suggested, top-down processes will be initiated in the effort to satisfy its slots. Most importantly, the fable schema must (1) find either a flexible successful character or a rigid, foiled character, and (2) interpret the events leading to this character's success or failure in terms of some general lesson of conduct. If the moral were summarized in the last line, as is often the case with fables, the reader would be half-way there: he or she would only need to relate that synopsis back to the events in the story—the relevant characters would be brought out in the process. The moral is not summarized in the last line of the Stone Soup story, but the fable schema demands that there be one. The reader's task is therefore to use the event structure of the story to discover what the moral could be.

If the reader has made the inferences described in the previous section, then he or she should have constructed an event structure for the Stone Soup fable something like the following:

1. The goal of the poor man is to get some food.
2. The goal of the maid and the cook is to protect their master's goods.
3. The man's initial attempt to reach his goal is denied by the maid.
4. He devises a clever subterfuge to get part way to that goal.
5. He devises an even cleverer subterfuge to get the rest of the way to that goal.
6. The cook and the maid are conned into giving the man some food and, thus, betraying their master against their wills.

In this fable, Aesop seems to have filled two morals with one stone. While the poor man satisfies the flexible-and-successful description, the maid and cook satisfy the rigid-and-foiled description. Moreover, both the success of the poor man and the plight of the servants can be translated into general lessons of conduct. The generality of these lessons is evidenced by the fact that they can be captured by other maxims: for the man, "Where there's a will, there's a way"; for the servants, "Beware of Greeks bearing gifts." The reader who has recognized these lessons has understood the story in the fullest sense.

Since schemata at the interpretive level are not compelled by the text, one can enjoy and feel like he or she understands a story perfectly well without them. One might be fully satisfied with the Stone Soup story without drawing out its lessons. Or one might be entertained by the story of *Candy* without interpreting it as a spoof on *Candide*. But interpetive schemata add a level of understanding that may be enlightening and is often critical. We would argue that skilled readers have a variety of specialized schemata, like the fable schema, at the interpretive level that enable them to read such things as algebra problems, mysteries, political essays, allegories, recipes, contracts, and game instructions to their most useful ends.

CONCLUSION

The analysis of the Stone Soup fable at these four different levels illustrates how reading comprehension depends as much on the readers' previously acquired knowledge as on the information provided by the text. Moreover, comprehension depends on the readers' ability to appropriately interrelate their knowledge and the textual information both within and between levels of analysis. The power of schema-theoretic models of reading lies in their capacity to support these interactions through a single, stratified knowledge structure and a few basic processing mechanisms.

Top-down and bottom-up processing are fundamental mechanisms which apply at all levels of analysis. Bottom-up processing occurs when schemata that have been identified suggest other candidate schemata at the same level or the next level up. Examples of bottom-up processes at the four levels of analysis are:

(a) Letters that have been identified suggest neighboring letters and candidate words.
(b) A determiner such as "a" suggests that a noun or adjective will follow and that a noun phrase has been started.
(c) Reference to "begging for food" suggests the schemata for "obtaining goods" and "trying."
(d) The man's persistent, devious, and successful measures to get food suggest a candidate moral such as "Where there's a will, there's a way."

Top-down processing occurs when schemata that have been suggested try to find schemata from the same level or the next level down to fill out their descriptions. Examples of top-down processes at the four levels of analysis are:

(a) A candidate word such as MAN looks for M, A, and N to fill its three slots.
(b) A noun phrase looks for particular parts of speech, such as a determiner or a proper noun, to fill its initial slot.
(c) The problem-solving schema looks for a goal, such as eating, to account for the man's begging for food.
(d) The fable schema looks for a moral as the point of the story.

As top-down and bottom-up processes operate simultaneously at all different levels of analysis, they work to pull the various fragments of knowledge and information into a coherent whole.

Finally, neither the basic knowledge structure nor the processing mechanisms that have been described are supposed to be unique to a particular story or even to the reading process in general. Rather, within schema theory, the same knowledge structures and processes are supposed to underlie all cognitive processes. Clearly adults must have knowledge about maids, and stories, and problem-solving, and grammar like that described here. Such knowledge has many uses in addition to that of understanding text. Schema theory provides a way of integrating our understanding of text with our understanding of the world in general.

ACKNOWLEDGMENTS

The research reported herein was supported in part by the National Institute of Education under Contract No. MS-NIE-C-400-76-0116. The authors would like to thank Albert Stevens for his helpful comments on the manuscript.

REFERENCES

Abelson, R. P. Concepts for representing mundame reality in plans. In D. G. Bobrow & A. Collins (Eds.), *Representation and understanding: Studies in cognitive science.* New York: Academic Press, 1975.

Adams, M. J. Models of word recognition. *Cognitive Psychology,* 1979 (in press).

Barr, R. The effect of instruction on pupil reading strategies. *Reading Research Quarterly,* 1975, 10, 555–582.

Bartlett, F. C. *Remembering.* Cambridge, England: Cambridge University Press, 1932.

Becker, J. D. A model for the encoding of experiential information. In R. Schank & K. Colby (Eds.), *Computer models of thought and language.* San Francisco: Freeman, 1973.

Bobrow, D. G., & Norman, D. A. Some principles of memory schemata. In D. G. Bobrow & A. M. Collins (Eds.), *Representation & understanding: Studies in cognitive science.* New York: Academic Press, 1975.

Cattell, J.McK. The time taken up by cerebral operations. *Mind,* 1886, *11,* 220–242.

Chall, J. *Learning to read: The great debate.* New York: McGraw Hill, 1967.

Charniak, E. Organization & inference in a frame-like system of common knowledge. In *Proceedings of Theoretical Issues in Natural Language Processing: An Interdisciplinary Workshop.* Cambridge, MA: Bolt Beranek & Newman, 1975.

Chomsky, N. A review of B.F. Skinner's "Verbal Behavior." *Language,* 1959, *35* 26–58.

Haviland, S. E., & Clark, H. H. What's new? Acquiring new information as a process in comprehension. *Journal of Verbal Learning and Verbal Behavior,* 1974, *13,* 512–521.

Kant, E. *Critique of pure reason.* (1st ed. 1781, 2nd ed. 1787, Kemp Smith transl.). London: MacMillan, 1963.

Lehnert, W. Human and computational question answering. *Cognitive Science,* 1977, *1,* 47–73.

Marcel, T. The effective visual field and the use of context in fast and slow readers of two ages. *British Journal of Psychology,* 1974, *65,* 479–492.

Marslen-Wilson, W. Linguistic structure and speech shadowing at very short latencies. *Nature,* 1973, *224,* 522–523.

Marslen-Wilson, W. Sentence perception as an interactive parallel process. *Science,* 1975, *189,* 226–227.

Marslen-Wilson, W., & Tyler, L. K. Processing structure of sentence perception. *Nature,* 1975, *257,* 784–786.

Meyer, D. E., Schvaneveldt, R. W., & Ruddy, M. G. Functions of graphemic and phonemic codes in visual word recognition. *Memory & Cognition,* 1974, *2,* 309–321.

Minsky, M. A framework for representing knowledge. In P. H. Winston (Ed.), *The psychology of computer vision.* New York: McGraw-Hill, 1975.

Newell, A., & Simon, H. A. GPS, a program that simulates human thought. In E. A. Feigenbaum & J. Feldman (Eds.), *Computers and thought.* New York: McGraw Hill, 1963.

Norman, D. A., & Bobrow, D. G. On data-limited and resource-limited processes. *Cognitive Psychology,* 1975, *7,* 44–64.

Pearson, P. D. The effects of grammatical complexity on children's comprehension, recall, and conception of certain semantic relations. *Reading Research Quarterly,* 1974–75, *10,* 155–192.

Reicher, G. M. Perceptual recognition as a function of meaningfulness of stimulus material. *Journal of Experimental Psychology,* 1969, *8,* 275–280.

Rumelhart, D. E. Toward an interactive model of reading. In S. Dornic (Ed.), *Attention & performance, volume VI.* London: Academic Press, 1977.

Rumelhart, D. E., & Ortony, A. Representation of knowledge. In R. C. Anderson, R. J. Spiro, & W. E. Montague (Eds.), *Schooling and the acquisition of knowledge.* Hillsdale, N.J.: Lawrence Erlbaum Associates, 1977.

Schank, R., & Abelson, R. *Scripts, plans, goals, and understanding.* Hillsdale, N. J.: Lawrence Erlbaum Associates, 1977.

Schuberth, R. E., & Eimas, P. D. Effects of context on the classification of words and nonwords. *Journal of Experimental Psychology: Human Perception and Performance,* 1977, *3,* 27–36.

Stevens, A. L., & Rumelhart, D. E. Errors in reading: Analysis using an augmented transition network model of grammar. In D. A. Norman & D. E. Rumelhart (Eds.), *Explorations in cognition.* San Francisco: Freeman, 1975.

Tulving, E., & Gold, C. Stimulus information and contextual information as determinants of tachistoscopic recognition of words. *Journal of Experimental Psychology,* 1963, *66,* 319–327.

Wannemacher, J. T. Processing strategies in picture-sentence verification tasks. *Memory & Cognition,* 1974, *2,* 554–560.

Wanner, E., & Maratsos, M. An augmented transition network model of relative clause comprehension. Unpublished, Harvard University, 1975.

Wheeler, D. D. Processes in word recognition. *Cognitive Psychology,* 1970, *1,* 59–85.

Wittrock, M. C., Marks, C., & Doctorow, M. Reading as a generative process. *Journal of Educational Psychology,* 1975, *67,* 484–489.

Woods, W. A. Speech understanding systems. *Syntax and semantics, Vol. IV.* Bolt Beranek & Newman Report No. 3438, Cambridge, Mass., 1976.

Woods, W. A. Transition network grammars for natural language analysis. *Communications of the ACM,* 1970, *13,* 591–606.

Woods, W. A., Kaplan, R. M., & Nash-Webber, B. The lunar sciences natural language information system: Final Report. BBN Report No. 2378, Bolt Beranek & Newman Inc., Cambridge, Mass., 1972.

Woodworth, R. S. *Experimental psychology.* New York: Holt, 1938.

2 Event Chains and Inferences in Understanding Narratives

William H. Warren
University of Connecticut

David W. Nicholas
Yale University

Tom Trabasso
University of Minnesota

In two recent discussions, Schank (1975b, c) has argued that meaning rather than parsing of syntax is primary in natural language understanding. The derivation of meaning, however, requires two component processes: the application of knowledge and the making of inferences. Knowledge is crucial since one cannot understand an utterance unless one knows what is being talked about, and in order to grasp what the speaker intended, one must relate utterances to that knowledge and to one another (cf. Bartlett, 1932).

The problem of knowledge, for Schank, is essentially the problem of memory since memory is the repository of information about the world. Although we shall assume this to be the case, we shall focus on the second problem, that of making inferences, since so little seems to be known about what inferences are and how they operate. Our goal is to understand more about the procedures which enable us to take what is explicit in the text, apply our world knowledge to it, and come up with its meaning.

As a start, we found Schank's (1975b, c) functional definition of inferences useful. We assume, as does Schank, that the understander tries to represent the incoming textual information in a well-defined structure. In so doing, inferences serve two main functions: they (1) fill in missing slots in the structure and (2) connect elementary events in the structure with other events in order to provide a higher level organization.

In order to model the process of an understander making inferences, we place him or her at a moving point in an unfolding narrative. This point, at any given moment or locus in the narrative's progress, is termed the focal event in an event chain (Nicholas, 1976; Trabasso & Nicholas, 1977). Definition of this focal event allows us to determine the information available to the listener for making inferences at that moment in processing rather than assuming full retrospective knowledge. A further advantage is that inferences made from the focal event can be directed *backward*, linking it with previous events in the chain in a manner similar to Clark's (1975) concept of "bridging," or *forward,* predicting subsequent events (Nicholas, 1976; Trabasso & Nicholas, 1977; Rieger, 1974). These forward and backward directed processes may be viewed as the listener interrogating the text on the basis of the information he has in his possession at the time, asking Who? What? When? Where? Why? or How? in order to justify the focal event in relation to previous events, and What Next? in order to anticipate the coming events.

To begin matters and illustrate the event chain, consider the following brief story:

(1) It was Friday afternoon.
(2) Carol was drawing a picture in the classroom.
(3) David felt mischievous.
(4) David decided to tease Carol.
(5) When Carol was not looking,
(6) he tied her shoelaces together.
(7) Carol tripped
(8) and fell down.

As a convention for the analysis of narratives we have broken the story down into propositional units. Although one could do a microanalysis on the propositions, reducing further the ones listed above (Kintsch, 1974), we are satisfied to treat a proposition as an utterance that contains only one predicate relation and constitutes an event, in the wide sense of the term, in an event chain. The event chain, then, is represented as a string of numbered propositions, with a circle indicating the focal event. Figure 1 shows an event chain for the "shoelace" story above.

1   2   3   ④   5   6   7   8   FIG. 1.   An event chain for a story with eight
            focal   propositions. The focal event indicated is Proposition
            event   (4). The logical connections between propositions are
                                   as yet unstated.

In Fig. 1, imagine that the understander is at the focal event, Proposition (4). At this point in time, he can ask any of several inferential questions which are relevant to the progress of the story and which serve to incorporate the focal event into the chain. For example, he can ask:

(9) Why did David decide to tease Carol?

a motivational question, or

(10) When did he decide to tease Carol?

a temporal question, or

(11) Where was Carol?

which is a spatial question. The understander could try to predict in what manner David will tease Carol, making use of his knowledge about the act of teasing. Given the event chain depicted in Fig. 1 and the story content so far, however, there is very little information available at this point which would enable a prediction likely to be confirmed by subsequent events. Furthermore, the understander could continue to ask questions indefinitely but this is unlikely since most other questions are irrelevant to the narrative's development and would clutter the comprehension process. Some irrelevant questions are:

(12) What is the color of David's shirt?
(13) What was Carol drawing a picture of?

Some of the possible inferences will become relevant later in the text, but the comprehender's information at Proposition (4) is not sufficient to determine them in advance. This limits how many and what kind of inferences are made at each focal event. Some examples of future relevant inferences include:

(14) Is Carol wearing shoes? What kind of shoes are they?
(15) Was David sitting near Carol?

Once the comprehender has moved his focus from Proposition (4) to Proposition (6) in the shoelace story, other questions can be asked which permit text connections and the filling of slots:

(16) Why did David tie her shoelaces together?
(17) Whose shoelaces did David tie?

(18) How was David able to tie the shoelaces without being observed?
(19) Were Carol's shoes next to each other?

Inferences in Questions (16) , (17), and (18) are motivational, referential, and enablement types, respectively, all of which serve to connect propositions. Question (19) involves a spatial inference and is slot-filling in nature.

Now that the understander is at Event (6) in the chain, he has enough information to make specific predictions that are likely to be confirmed, e.g.,

(20) Carol will probably fall down.

This prediction is likely to be confirmed. Once the comprehender has moved to Proposition (8), the prediction becomes an explanation, namely, Carol's falling down was caused by her shoelaces having been tied together. Hence, backward inferencing is often the reciprocal of forward inferencing. While the direction of the inference depends on the location of the focal event, the link remains the same.

Two questions arise from this example: How can we classify the explanatory and predictive inferences that the understander makes? How can we usefully represent the relations of a narrative to reveal the inferences necessary for its comprehension? These are the questions to which we now turn.

THE INFERENCE TAXONOMY

Inferences in narratives are based mainly on three identifiable sources of information. The first source stems from the logical relations between the events specified in the text. Logical relations involve the causes, motivations, and conditions which enable events and are made in response to the questions Why? or How? The second source stems from the informational relations between events specified in the text. Informational relations involve the specific people, instruments, objects, times, places, and contexts of events, and these inferences are made in answer to the questions Who? What? When? and Where? The third source is that of the understander's world knowledge about the objects, actions, and events specified in the text. World knowledge is knowledge about the words employed, the things referred to, and the functional relations among them. This knowledge is derived from the understander's prior perceptual and verbal interaction with the world and it bears upon both the logical and informational relations. If any of these relations are not marked or specified directly in the surface structure of a proposition, then those relations necessary to the progress of the narrative must be inferred across the propositions if the narrative is to be understood.

The above distinctions lead to the following outline of an inference taxonomy. Our aim was to develop a usable set of mutually exclusive categories for the inferences systematically related to the event chain depiction of a narrative.

A. Logical inferences
  1. motivation
  2. psychological causative
  3. physical causative
  4. enablement
B. Informational inferences
  1. pronominal
  2. referential
  3. spatiotemporal
  4. world frame
  5. elaborative
C. Value inferences
  1. evaluative

The taxonomy is partially drawn from the work of Nicholas (1976), Trabasso and Nicholas (1977), Rieger (1974), and Trabasso, Nicholas, Omanson, and Johnson (1977).

Previously, Trabasso, Nicholas, and their colleagues have proposed an event chain structure with two dimensions: a forward–backward relation between events and a preventative–facilitative relation. The present taxonomy retains the forward–backward reciprocity but does away with the preventative–facilitative distinction on the grounds that the same inference must be made whether or not the projected outcome succeeds in the story itself. We found Rieger's (1974) list of inferences to be lacking on grounds that his categories were not mutually exclusive or well defined; they also were not related to the narrative structure. Another taxonomy, that of Clark (1975), has been recently developed for classifying inferences in spoken discourse. While Clark's categories are mutually exclusive, they are not related to text structure. Rather, they are based largely on rules of conversation, and depend upon a set of conventions that speakers/listeners agree upon in order to facilitate the comprehension of utterances in a social context. These conventions are still being identified and their correspondence to narrative structure and relationships is unclear.

Employing an architectural metaphor, we may indicate the role that the inferences in the taxonomy play in the construction of a representation of the narrative. Logical inferences are the joists and studs of the narrative, the scaffolding on which the story is hung and by which events are connected. There are four classes of logical inferences: motivation, psychological cause, physical cause, and enablement. They are the basic links in a causal chain and these causal links must be made above and beyond the simple specification of the objects and predicates involved, which is the domain of world knowledge.

Informational inferences determine the people, things, time, place, and general context of a given event. They are the floorboards and the paneling that logical inferences link together, and are necessary for the listener to know who did what. Elaborative inferences are the exception. They do not appear to be relevant to the progress of the narrative in this way but seem to serve the same purpose as drapery and wallpaper, namely, to merely flesh out objects and events. As a result, elaborative inferences are not reliably determined by the text itself. World-frame inferences define the edifice as a house, school, or office building. They can work "outside-in," or deductively, on a stated proposition or focal event, specifying the contextual constraints within which subsequent propositions are interpreted and made comprehensible. They can also work "inside-out," or inductively, determining a general context on the basis of clues given across several events or propositions.

Finally, the evaluative inferences are the comprehender's own judgments on the actions of characters or on the validity of the story itself, just as a building inspector evaluates the quality and compatibility of materials and the soundness of construction. These are based upon the understander's system of beliefs, values, and world knowledge of the situations portrayed.

Constraints on Inferences

The two operations of making inferences, connecting propositions and filling in slots, can now be illustrated. Text-connection occurs when two or more propositions are linked together. For example, the comprehender sees that a specified mental state motivates a specified goal when in the shoelace story he or she realizes that teasing Carol is a result of David's feeling mischievous. Slot-filling, on the other hand, occurs when, for example, an action is given but its motivation is unspecified and the listener attempts to fill it in. The inference that Carol is drawing a picture because artwork gives her satisfaction is such an inference and explains, in part, why she is not looking at David.

The two operations are actually quite similar. Text-connection becomes slot-filling when the alternatives are not explicitly stated in the text. In either case, the accuracy of the inference is determined by two factors: how the information given in the text bears on the inference, and the extent of the understander's world knowledge of the objects and events involved. These two factors jointly constrain the choice of alternatives and direct inferencing.

Consider the following two propositions:

(21) Joe killed Maria.
(22) Joe stabbed Maria.

In each case, what instrument did Joe use to do the deed? A slot-filling referential inference is required. In Proposition (21), the specified predicate *kill* leaves the choice wide open. Given one's world knowledge of the predicate and the appropriate instruments, anything from a bazooka to a ping-pong paddle is conceivable, although a peashooter is not. In Proposition (22), the inference is more tightly constrained by the form of the predicate *stab,* narrowing the alternatives to a knife or another sharp pointed instrument.

Consider a situation which requires a text-connecting referential inference:

> (23) a. Joe put a rose in his teeth.
> b. He held a gun in one hand,
> c. and a knife in the other.

Now examine four alternative endings:

> (24) Joe killed Maria.
> (25) Joe stabbed Maria.
> (26) Joe killed Maria, the escaped tiger.
> (27) Joe danced the tango with Maria.

Of the specified items, what instrument did Joe use in each case? In (24), the rose can be eliminated on the basis of one's world knowledge about the predicate, *kill*, about roses, and about Maria as a person. However, the information specified is insufficient to choose between the knife or the gun; he could have used either. In Proposition (25), the inference is strictly constrained to the knife. On the other hand, in Proposition (26), the knowledge that we have about tigers, the intimacy required for the use of knives, and the safer distance of guns, the inference is constrained to the use of the gun. Finally, in Proposition (27), the unexpected action implicates the rose as a central participant and directs a new connection between Propositions (27) and (23a). (See also "The Relevancy Hypothesis" below.)

THE EVENT CHAIN REPRESENTATION

The event chain represents directly the logical structure of a story (its "scaffolding"), depicting the causal inferences necessary for its comprehension.

Formal Components

We introduce this representation with an example, an event chain for the shoelace story in Propositions (1)–(8) above. Figure 2 depicts the shoelace story event chain with its logical relations. Note that, in Fig. 2, the events are

FIG. 2. An event chain for the shoelace story, with its logical structure specified from the protagonist's (David's) point of view by connections between the propositions. (See Tables 1 and 2 for identification of the event chain symbols.)

diagramed from the point of view of the protagonist, David. There are three formal components in the event chain representation: (1) the proposition types, (2) the connectives, and (3) the connection rules. We now discuss each of these components.

Proposition types. The seven proposition types are listed in Table 1. These categories are broad classes of events designed with reference to a chosen character in the narrative. The level of analysis is general and somewhat arbitrary but an attempt has been made to provide a useful set of identifying categories.

In Table 1, the basic dimensions of classification are trifold. There is a subjective/objective dimension, which means that an event may be classified with reference to the protagonist or to the external world. Second, the internal/external character of an event depends upon whether the event is inherently mental or physical. Finally, the voluntary/involuntary distinction indicates whether or not an event was under the protagonist's intentional control. In addition, we allow that a proposition may be caused by a stated proposition or an inferred proposition, or it may occur without apparent cause. These distinctions will become clearer with a description of each proposition type and its examples.

A STATE is an objective condition, a state of affairs which pertains to the physical world or to the physical condition of a character in the story. A STATE is a condition which may exist either prior to or as the result of a character's action. Some examples are:

(28) It was a Friday afternoon. (STATE)
(29) The dog was running fast. (STATE)
(30) John was breathing hard. (STATE)

An EVENT (here in the narrow sense) is similar but refers to occurrences or changes of state rather than to stative conditions per se. A division is made, however, between occurrences which are performed by a nonprotagonist and by the protagonist. Since the event chain is diagramed from the protagonist's point of view, a nonprotagonist's action appears to him as an objective

TABLE 1
The Types of Propositions Specified in an Event Chain Representation of a Story

	Type of Proposition	Description
	STATE	An objective condition of the world environment, of the protagonist, or of another character. STATES may exist either independently of or as the result of a protagonist's ACTION.
	EVENT	An objective occurrence or an action by another character. EVENTS may occur either independently of or as the result of the protagonist's ACTION.
"responses"	ACTION (ACT)	A voluntary external movement or behavior on the part of the protagonist.
(when motivated)	COGNITION (COG)	A mental act; a voluntary internal occurrence or self-induced state on the part of the protagonist. (Thought, remembered, imagined, perceived, judged, etc.)
"reactions"	DISPLAY (DISP)	An involuntary external movement or behavior on the part of the protagonist.
(when caused)	IMPULSE (IMP)	An involuntary internal occurrence or state of the protagonist. (Felt, intuited, dreamt, hallucinated, believed,,etc.)
	GOAL	A voluntary or involuntary internal goal held by the protagonist, a state of desiring that a certain occurrence should happen or condition exist. (Decided, planned, wanted, desired, etc.)

EVENT, while his own voluntary external movements—those movements under his control—are labeled ACTIONS. For example:

(31) The wind blew the tree over. (EVENT)
(32) a. The boy stepped on Jack's foot. (EVENT)
       b. Jack called the boy a jerk. (ACTION)

Often the distinction between a STATE and an EVENT is in the surface structure of the story. The difference between these two propositions may not be functionally important:

(33) The dog was running. (STATE)
(34) The dog ran. (EVENT)

Sometimes, however, the distinction may become functionally more important:

(35) The dog was running home. (STATE)
(36) The dog ran home. (EVENT)

Example (35) sets the stage for other events to occur *during* that STATE, while (36) indicates an EVENT that is complete and will be *followed* by subsequent events.

ACTIONS and COGNITIONS are *voluntary* activities on the part of the protagonist. They are referred to as responses when motivated by other propositions, but they may also occur spontaneously without explicit cause. A COGNITION is the internal counterpart of an ACTION, a voluntary cognitive act or voluntarily induced state which is often lexically marked by such words as *thought, perceived, wondered, remembered, imagined, meditated, saw, heard, noted, judged, pondered,* etc.

DISPLAYS and IMPULSES are called reactions, the involuntary counterparts to responses. They too may occur spontaneously. A DISPLAY is an involuntary external movement by the protagonist:

(37) a. The boy stepped on Jack's foot. (EVENT)
     b. Jack screamed and jumped up. (DISPLAY—caused)
(38) Mary's arm twitched. (DISPLAY—spontaneous)

An IMPULSE is an involuntary occurrence or state internal to the protagonist, and includes feelings, affects, beliefs, intuititons, dreams, and hallucinations, as in:

(39) a. The boy stepped on Jack's foot (EVENT)
     b. Jack got angry. (IMPULSE—caused)
(40) Paula felt on top of the world that morning. (IMPULSE—spontaneous)

(See Goldman, 1970, regarding the distinction between voluntary mental acts and involuntary mental occurrences.)

A GOAL is a special type of internal mental event which may be either voluntary or involuntary. It is an imagined condition or occurrence that the protagonist desires to achieve and may be lexically marked by such words as *decided, planned, wanted, desired, hoped,* etc.

The categories used here are readily translatable into those found in "story grammars" (Mandler & Johnson, 1977; Stein & Glenn, 1979; Thorndyke, 1977). For example, STATES often constitute story settings; they can also be outcomes or initiating events. COGNITIONS and GOALS are types of

TABLE 2
The Logical Connectives Between Propositions and
Their Event Chain Symbols

Connective	Symbol
Motivation	M
Physical cause	ϕC
Psychological cause	ψC
Enablement	E
Then (temporal succession)	T
And (temporal coexistence)	A

internal responses. ACTIONS are equivalent to attempts, DISPLAYS to simple reactions, and so on. The advantage of the present taxonomy is that it provides a set of nonhierarchical basic-level descriptors which are defined independently of presumed text structure, but can be linked to represent text structure. Such interpropositional links are called "connectives."

Connectives. The logical inference relations between propositions are specified in the event chain by labeled connective arrows, listed in Table 2. Informational inference relations could also be added to the representation, but this would not aid in determining their presence in the story and would detract from the clarity of the logical scaffolding.

Each logical inference type in the taxonomy is represented by a connective: motivation (M), physical causation (ϕC), psychological causation (ψC), and enablement (E). A single connective arrow indicates the reciprocity of that inference, in other words, the link maybe made forward or backward. In addition, the "then" connective (T) indicates a weaker temporal succession without causal force, and the "and" connective (A) indicates temporal coexistence. The distinction between motivation and psychological cause is related to the voluntary–involuntary dimension: voluntary activities are by definition motivated, while involuntary subjective activities are said to be psychologically caused.

(41) a. David liked Mary. (IMPULSE)
 b. David decided to tease Mary. (GOAL, M-caused)
(42) a. David liked Mary. (IMPULSE)
 b. David blushed when he saw Mary. (DISPLAY, ψC-caused)

A physical cause involves strictly physical or mechanical causality between objects, people and objects, or between people:

(43) a. John pushed Mary. (ACTION)
 b. Mary fell over. (EVENT)

An enablement denotes the link between one occurrence or state which is necessary but not sufficient to cause another one.

> (44) a. John took out his wallet. (ACTION)
>   b. John paid for the tickets. (ACTION)

Connection rules.   Before matters of specific content are involved, certain a priori rules constrain the permissible combinations of proposition types and connectives. For example, only external occurrences (ACTION, DISPLAY, and EVENT) have physical causal efficacy and only external EVENTS and STATES can be physically caused. On the other hand, only *internal* reactions can be psychologically caused. EVENTS are physical causally recursive: one EVENT can cause another. The enablement relation has a particularly complicated set of rules, limited for example by the fact that mental occurrences cannot enable others of a different type. In the mental domain, most apparent enablement relations are better understood as motivation relations. Generally speaking, however, there are few restrictions on connections between propositions.

Given the general restrictions of these connection rules, connections are further limited in any given case by the specific content of the propositions. A certain ACTION cannot be motivated by any and all EVENTS, but only by certain EVENTS in a given context.

Inferences in the Event Chain

The event chain representation can illustrate the operations of text-connection and slot-filling with logical inferences. A text-connection inference is represented by a connective arrow linking two classified propositions according to the connection rules. In Fig. 2, EVENT (6) ("Carol tripped") is linked by a physical cause connective to the protagonist's ACTION (5) ("He tied her shoelaces together."). The inference here is that David's tying of Carol's shoelaces caused her to fall down. A more complex example is given by explaining that ACTION (5): Why and how did he tie her shoelaces together? The immediate motivation, answering the "why" question, is provided by following the M arrow back to David's GOAL (3): "David decided to tease Carol." But in order for him to perform ACTION (5) successfully, a certain STATE of the world (4) had to be in effect: Carol's not looking. Thus, a GOAL (3) joins together with a STATE (4) to motivate and enable a certain ACTION (5).

If a certain ACTION is given in the text but no motivation connective links it to another proposition, then a slot-filling inference may be necessry. Suppose Propositions (2) and (3) were not given in the shoelace story. ACTION (5) is then unmotivated, and in this case cries out for some explanation: Why did David tie Carol's shoelaces together? On the basis of our world knowledge of ACTIONS and GOALS, we could fill this empty slot and infer that David performed this cruel ACTION (5) because he wanted to be mean to Carol, perhaps in revenge (in which case Carol's initial aggression would probably be specified) or because of a disposition (IMPULSE) toward meanness, teasing, or mischievousness.

In this case, a dangling ACTION would indicate an empty motivating-proposition slot. Other dangling propositions could indicate other missing connections: unspecified phsycial causes for events that do not just happen by themselves, enabling conditions necessary for given actions, and so on. The content of a proposition and our world knowledge of the specified occurrence determine whether the proposition is dangling or not, i.e., whether a given response or reaction may have occurred spontaneously. In any case, the presence of an unlinked proposition spurs an examination of its possible causes.

We would like to make a specific disclaimer about the psychological status of the event chain representation. Unlike the claims made for story grammars (Mandler, 1977; Stein & Glenn, 1979; Thorndyke, 1977), the event chain is merely a formalization of the story relations available to the understander, and *does not presume to model what is inside the understander's head.* It represents the logical inferences necessary for full comprehension of a particular story and we hope it will be used to help determine those inferential relations. Listeners' actual performances on these inferences may then provide the basis for a model of the understander proper.

Multiple Protagonists

The event chain representation offers yet another advantage over story grammars: it can be expanded to represent simultaneously the interaction of two or more protagonists. In working with the grammars, we noticed two things. First of all, we seldom ran across stories that involved only one, noninteractive character. In fact, stories presented as exemplars by the story grammarians frequently had several actors, and the choice of which character's actions to diagram was in some instances made on an arbitrary basis. However, the logical inference structure in such cases does not follow only one line of action. Second, we noticed that a proposition which is the *outcome* of an action for one character may serve as an *initiating event* for another. The interpretation of that proposition then depends on which character is viewed as the protagonist. The event chain provides for a dual representation of such propositions by diagraming multiple lines of action simultaneously.

A continuation of the shoelace story in which Carol takes her revenge on David is presented in Table 3, and its event chain diagramed in Fig. 3. In the representation, the string of story propositions is placed along the top of the page, while the protagonists are listed down the left-hand edge. Each

TABLE 3
A Continuation of the Shoelace Story

Propositions
1. It was Friday afternoon.
2. Carol was drawing a picture in the classroom.
3. David felt mischievous.
4. David decided to tease Carol.
5. When Carol wasn't looking,
6. he tied her shoelaces together.
7. Carol tripped
8. and fell down.
9. Carol got very angry.
10. She decided to get even with David.
11. She found David's bicycle outside the school
12. and let all the air out of the tires.

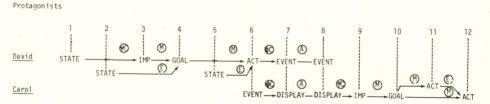

FIG. 3.   An event chain representation of a multiple-protagonist story, the shoelace story in Table 3. (See Tables 1 and 2 for identification of the event chain symbols.)

protagonist's line of action proceeds horizontally, with the proposition types and connectives being determined from that character's point of view.

In Table 3, Proposition (6), which is David's ACTION of tying Carol's shoelaces together, is an EVENT from Carol's point of view. That proposition and its two consequences (7) and (8) evoke IMPULSE (9) in Carol, and her anger in turn motivates the GOAL (10) of getting even with David. Thus, the progress of the story shifts from David's line of action to Carol's through the transition propositions (6), (7) and (8), which are dually represented.

A longer example with five protagonists, the Farmer Story (Mandler & Johnson, 1977; Throndyke, 1977), is presented in Table 4 and diagramed in Fig. 4. The Farmer Story is of particular interest because of its structure of nested episodes, each involving a new character and setting up the end of the story like a row of dominoes. This appears graphically as a "V" across propositions and characters in the event chain. The initial actions of the characters with GOALS, the cat and the cow, are essentially contracts with the farmer which motivate their final actions once the farmer fulfills the

TABLE 4
The Farmer Story, a Five-Protagonist Narrative[a]

Propositions

1. There was once an old farmer
2. who owned a very stubborn donkey.
3. One evening the farmer was trying to put his donkey into its shed.
4. First, the farmer pulled the donkey,
5. but the donkey wouldn't move.
6. Then the farmer pushed the donkey,
7. but still the donkey wouldn't move.
8. Finally, the farmer asked his dog
9. to bark loudly at the donkey
10. and thereby frighten him into the shed.
11. But the dog refused.
12. So then, the farmer asked his cat
13. to scratch the dog
14. so the dog would bark loudly
15. and thereby frighten the donkey into the shed.
16. But the cat replied,
17. "I would gladly scratch the dog
18. if only you would get me some milk."
19. So the farmer went to his cow
20. and asked for some milk
21. to give to the cat.
22. But the cow replied,
23. "I would gladly give you some milk
24. if only you would give me some hay."
25. Thus, the farmer went to the haystack
26. and got some hay.
27. As soon as he gave the hay to the cow,
28. the cow gave the farmer some milk.
29. Then the farmer went to the cat
30. and gave the milk to the cat.
31. As soon as the cat got the milk,
32. it began to scratch the dog.
33. As soon as the cat scratched the dog,
34. the dog began to bark loudly.
35. The barking so frightened the donkey
36. that it jumped immediately into its shed.

[a]After Thorndyke (1977) and Mandler and Johnson (1977).

conditional requirements. The cat's final actions (Propositions 29–32) do not make much sense in isolation:

(45) a. Then the farmer went to the cat
     b. and gave the milk to the cat.
     c. As soon as the cat got the milk
     d. it began to scratch the dog.

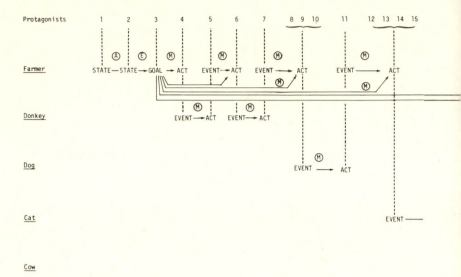

FIG. 4.   An event chain representation for the five-protagonist farmer story presented in Table 4.

Getting milk alone is insufficient to motivate the cat to take the particular ACTION of scratching the dog. But coupled with his earlier contract (Propositions 16–18 in Table 4), these events are adequate to motivate that ACTION. On the other hand, the initial and final actions of the characters without GOALS, the donkey and the dog, are not linked together with an M arrow but are consummated by simple one-step psychological causes and DISPLAYS. The farmer's initial GOAL of getting the donkey into the barn motivates all his ACTIONS until the contracts he has set up take over toward the end of the story.

This mode of representation thus captures the whole logical scaffolding of a story rather than the contributions of only one character. This permits us to trace the chain of inferences back through protagonist transitions, linking the whole story together.

A WALK THROUGH THE INFERENCE TAXONOMY

We now take a closer look at the specifics of the inference taxonomy. The examples below are written as text-connecting inferences. To make a slot-filling inference, for each example, read only Proposition (b) in each pair and ask Who? What? When? Where? Why? or How?

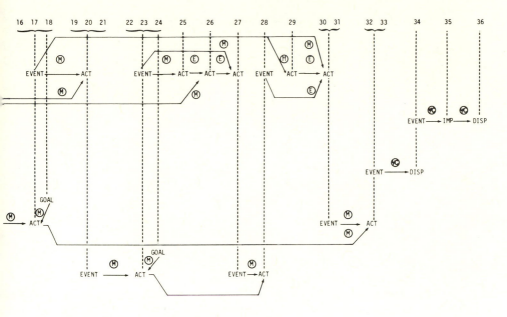

Logical Inferences (Why? How?)

Logical inferences have been discussed above at length in connection with the event chain representation. We provide a few examples here. Note that each class is bidirectional depending on the understander's location, moving either backward from the given focal event to infer its cause or forward from the given focal event to predict its plausible consequences. To make predictive inferences in the examples below, read only Proposition (a) in each pair.

Motivation.   Motivational inferences involve inferring the causes for a character's given voluntary thoughts, actions, or goals; or, reciprocally, predicting a character's thoughts, actions, or goals on the basis of stated causes.

      (46) a. Carol got very angry. (IMPULSE)
            b. She decided to get even with David. (GOAL)
      (47) a. Bob crashed Frank's new bike into a fire hydrant. (EVENT)
            b. Frank called Bob a moron. (ACTION)

Psychological cause.   Psychological causation involves inferring the causes for a character's given involuntary thoughts, actions, or feelings (or vice versa).

(48) a. Carol tripped and fell down. (DISPLAY)
    b. Carol got very angry. (IMPULSE)
(49) a. Tom dropped the hammer on his toe. (ACTION)
    b. Tom shouted in pain. (DISPLAY)

Physical cause.   Physical causation involves inferences about the mechanical causes for given objective events or states (or vice versa).

(50) a. David ties Carol's shoelaces together. (ACTION)
    b. Carol tripped and fell down. (DISPLAY)
(51) a. Lightning struck the old tree. (EVENT)
    b. The tree was burning all night. (STATE)

Enablement.   Enablement inferences determine the conditions which are necessary but not sufficient for a given event to occur (or determine the event that a given condition allows). World knowledge can be brought to bear on enablement conditions and inferencing can go on forever. Example (53) below is conditional upon Sam having a new kite, Sam being outdoors, it not raining, Sam not being a paraplegic, etc.

(52) a. Carol found David's bicycle outside the school (ACTION)
    b. and let all the air out of his tires. (ACTION)
(53) a. A good wind was blowing. (STATE)
    b. Sam flew his new kite. (ACTION)

Informational Inferences (Who? What? When? Where?)

Informational inferences enable the listener to understand who is doing what to whom with what instruments under what circumstances at what time and place, across propositions. They do not indicate the causes or consequences. Note that informational inferences are not bidirectional.

Pronominal.   Pronominal inferences specify the antecedents of pronouns such as *he, she, they, it, them, that one,* etc., in other propositions. World knowledge of gender names, plurality, social situations, and so on aids in resolving the antecedents.

(54) a. David decided to tease Carol.
    b. When Carol wasn't looking,
    c. *he* tied *her* shoelaces together.
(55) a. Chuck was late for Mark's party.
    b. *He* said he was sorry.

Referential. Referential inferences specify the related antecedents of given actions or events when the reference is not pronominally marked. whether or not they are explicitly stated in other propositions. The basic function of referential inferences is to clarify the roles of people and objects in related propositions. This includes, but is not limited to, specifying the contents of case roles for given predicates, as described by Fillmore (1968) and Meyer (1975); e.g., specifying instruments, agents, patients, vehicles, etc., when they are not given in the surface structure of a proposition. Text-connection involves selecting the proper antecedent from those given in the text; slot-filling requires the listener to supply an appropriate antecedent himself. Both 'kinds of inferences are performed on the basis of world knowledge about the objects and predicates involved (see "Constraints on Inferencing" above).

(56) a. Carol found David's bicycle outside the school
b. and let all the air out of the tires.

The text-connecting referential inference in Example (56) is that the tires belong to David's bicycle. This may involve the world knowledge that bicycles in general have tires.

(57). Carol was drawing a picture in the classroom.

A slot-filling referential inference about Example (57) is that Carol was using an instrument, probably a pencil, pen, or crayon since the predicate is *draw* and not *paint.*

(58) a. Ralph picked up his bat
b. and hit the ball over the fence.

In Example (58), the referential inference is that Ralph hit the ball *with his bat.*

Spatiotemporal. Spatial and temporal inferences locate a single or a series of propositions in place and time and determine their duration. Often place and time are specified in the setting of a story, and from then on apply to all subsequent propositions until a change is noted. Estimations of duration are often strictly based on world knowledge of similar events, or determined by using shorter simultaneous ("and"-connected) events as temporal markers.

In the shoelace story, time and place are established in the first two propositions:

(59) a. It was *Friday afternoon.*
  b. Carol was drawing a picture *in the classroom.*

This applies to all intermediate propositions until the location is changed later on:

(60) She found David's bicycle *outside the school.*

World-frame. World-frame inferences share some similarities with referential and spatiotemporal ones, but they serve a contextual or framing function. When working outside–in, they provide a context of place or general activity (e.g., playing baseball) within which subsequent propositions are interpreted and made comprehensible. In other words, they lay constraints on the possible interpretations of confusing or ambiguous propositions, eliminating some possibilities and specifying others. Consider the following:

(61) a. The wolves snarled at Sara,
  b. and the lions roared at her.
  c. But Sara wasn't scared.

The interpretation of this story is confusing unless the world-frame is specified:

(62) Sara was at the zoo.

A different world-frame would lend quite a different interpretation to these propositions and the source of Sara's confidence:

(63) a. Sara was on a safari in the jungle.
  b. She held a big elephant gun at the ready.

When working inside-out, a world-frame can be inferred on the basis of clues given across several propositions. The frame then embodies the concept which links the propositions together in a common activity.

(64) a. The kids were giggling in the dark.
  b. Jeff's mom lit the candles.
  c. When Jeff walked in the door,
  d. the lights went on
  e. and all the kids shouted, "Surprise!"

At some point in the story the light dawns: I get it, it's about a surprise party.

Elaborative.   Fleshing out the objects and events in a way that does not contribute to the logical process of the story comprise elaborating or elaborative inferences. Elaborations are usually straight additions of world knowledge, reasonable guesses about irrelevant aspects of the story. They can continue adding details almost indefinitely. In the shoelace story, elaborative inferences could answer the following questions:

(65) What kind of shoes is Carol wearing?
(66) What color is her hair?
(67) Is David's bicycle a racer or a chopper?
(68) What was Carol drawing a picture of?

Value Inferences

Evaluative.   The listener's judgments on the actions of the characters, the intentions of the author, and the validity of the story events themselves are value inferences. They involve judgments of morality, convention, and anomaly in characters' thoughts and actions or in story style and construction. They draw upon the listener's values and world knowledge of the situations mentioned. Evaluative questions about the shoelace story could include:

(69) Was David mean or nice to Carol?
(70) Was Carol justified in letting the air out of David's tires?
(71) Was letting the air out a good way of getting even with David?

HOW MANY INFERENCES:
THE RELEVANCY HYPOTHESIS

As we have pointed out, the interrogation of a text could conceivably continue indefinitely. Once the causal links for a given proposition have been fully established, all the pronouns have been specified, the context, time, and place have been determined, and the object roles have been clarified, inferencing could continue to enumerate enabling conditions, references, elaborations, and speculative predictions almost without limit. When does a listener *stop* making inferences?

This is not a new problem (see Meyer, 1975). Rieger (1974) has suggested that *all possible* inferences are made before the next proposition in the event chain is considered, but clearly this cannot be the case. The listener would be stuck on a line such as, "Once upon a time there lived a noble king," for several hours. Introspectively, it seems that we make very few of the myriad possible inferences and often hold the process completely in check until the important links become clear many propositions later. In Table 3, inferences about

David's mode of transportation are not made until reaching Proposition (11). Upon reading the previous line about the king, an understander infers very few of the conditions, such as wearing a seal ring or eating three meals a day, which might be the prerequisites for existing as a king.

One could, however, produce such inferences upon demand, or upon pausing to consider the passage for a few moments. A distinction thus arises: how many inferences *can* a listener make if forced, and how many inferences *does* a listener actually make when encountering at text? This "can/do" distinction becomes a serious dilemma for the experimenter attempting to test the inferencing process, for any probe question could evoke a retrospective inference instead of tapping an inference actually made during text presentation.

An hypothesis about the practical limits of inferencing is already implicit in this paper, called the "relevancy hypothesis." Formally, it states that *in understanding a narrative a listener makes only those inferences relevant to the progress of the narrative.* Beyond that, the number of detailed inferences made is probably a function of individual differences in reading or listening speed, the understander's goals and purpose in hearing the narrative, and the understander's imagination.

What makes an inference "relevant to the progress of the narrative"? Considering the previous discussion of logical and informational relations, we propose that *relevant inferences establish the information necessary to determine what happened and why.* This knowledge is essentially that necessary for comprehension of an event chain. "What happened" refers to physical events and character actions or responses; "why" refers to their causes and motivations. Other inferences are made when they become important to this basic thread of the story, for example, an unfulfilled enabling condition that could block a character's goal, a referential inference that specifies the murder weapon and provides a missing clue, etc.

Consider the following example:

(72) Joe danced the tango with Maria to a Fletcher Henderson tune under a darkening sky on Armistice Day with a rose in his teeth.

This sentence alone could prompt all sorts of detailed inferences. However, if it appeared in the context of a larger story, certain inferences would become relevant and others irrelevant. If Joe were a former member of Fletcher Henderson's orchestra, or an American soldier carrying on a wartime romance with a local girl, or a florist, or if hurricane warnings had been broadcast, very different connections to (72) would become important in order to understand how the story progresses via that sentence.

Four degrees of inferential constraint can be defined in this regard. The most unconstrained, first-order inferences are those that are consistent with but *undetermined* by information in the text. All elaborative inferences fall into this class, as do guesses at unindicated causes and motivations. They consist of straight additions of world knowledge detailing given objects, events, and logical relations. Hence, they cannot be text-connections. Consider example (73):

(73) The king knighted the courageous hero.

A listener might infer on the basis of world knowledge that the king was wearing a crown, red robes, holding a scepter, and so on. None of these inferences, however, is determined by the text. In other words there is nothing to indicate the color of the king's robes or if he is wearing robes at all. A listener is generally willing to relinquish such details if contradicted later in the text.

A tighter constraint is placed on second-order inferences which are *determined but irrelevant,* that is, indicated by the text but still not relevant to the progress of the story. They consist of interpreting given information on the basis of world knowledge, but are not important for determining what happened and why. Many referential, spatiotemporal, and enablement inferences, among others, fall into this category. In Example (73), world knowledge of knighting ceremonies permits the slot-filling referential inference that the king knighted the hero *with a sword,* and the slot-filling spatiotemporal inference that the hero was *kneeling directly in front of the king.* Such details are not easily contradicted in the text. If the king were using a hockey stick or the hero were kneeling a hundred yards away, the character of the ceremony would be significantly altered.

In third-order cases such inferences are both *determined and relevant* when indicated by the text *and* important to the thread of the story. They consist of interpreting given information on the basis of world knowledge to determine what happened and why. It is these inferences which the relevancy hypothesis proposes are necessary for event chain comprehension and suggests that listeners actually make. Consider the previous example placed in the following story.

(74) a. While the king was knighting the courageous hero,
     b. the marauders staged a sudden attack.
     c. The king rose from the hero's shoulder,
     d. and slew the Black Knight on the spot.

The instrument used in the knighting ceremony becomes critical to the king's survival in the next event, and a referential inference about the sword becomes relevant to the story. It is very difficult for the text to contradict such inferences except in extenuating circumstances; it would be hard to believe that the king slew the Black Knight on the spot with a hockey stick. (See "Constraints on Inferencing" above in connection with second- and third-order inferences.)

Fourth-order inferences are what we might call overconstrained or *redundant*. They duplicate information given or inferred which is already adequate to specify an event. Hence, they do not add anything new and are irrelevant to the progress of the story. For example, story listeners often fail to make inferences which interpolate a character's internal state (COGNITION and IMPULSE) in places where that state is redundant with the character's external actions.

> (75) a. Mary was petting her dog Ralph.
> b. Ralph suddenly bit Mary's arm.
> c. Mary's arm hurt terribly
> d. and she was furious at Ralph.
> e. Mary yelled
> f. and chased Ralph with a baseball bat.

In (75), Propositions (c) and (d) do not add anything we do not otherwise know. Mary's DISPLAY (e) and ACTION (f) are adequately accounted for by EVENT (b) alone. Mary yelling and chasing Ralph is equivalent to Mary being furious (Heider, 1958). Thus, the story is sufficient without the redundant interpolations.

Similarly, the proposition,

> (76) Jeff hit George.

does not require an inference about Jeff using arm muscles to be fully understood: the act of hitting is redundant with the act of using arm muscles. However, if it has been established that Jeff has a torn ligament, an inference about muscles would be relevant and might make an otherwise anomalous proposition comprehensible:

> (77) a. Jeff hit George.
> b. *Jeff* writhed in pain.

We suggest that, in recall, people are likely to delete or selectively forget redundant information (see Schank, 1975b). It is also possible that children omit many internal states from recall (Stein & Glenn, 1979), because actions and initiating events are redundant with them.

In summary, we can say that relevant inferences specify information about what happened and why. All classes in the inference taxonomy (except elaborative) may become important to this task. First- and second-order inferences are superfluous to the task, although they are consistent with given information and may add color to a story. Redundant inferences duplicate information which is already established.

The relevancy hypothesis is only an hypothesis and may or may not be an adequate portrayal of a listener's inferencing activity. Before this can be determined, the can/do distinction must be explored and a psychological definition of what constitutes a completed inference in the listener's head must be established. The notion of relevancy does, however, capture the information necessary for the understanding of an event chain.

PSYCHOLOGICAL IMPLICATIONS

We conclude the paper with some commentary on the psychological implications and the usefulness of the above analysis. The practical questions of interest are: What kinds of inferences can (or do) people make? and How do they make them? The event chain representation and the inference taxonomy could contribute to the study of these questions in several ways. Once the propositional types and their logical connectives have been identified in a narrative, one can construct inference questions that are theory based, identify which inferences are (or are not) text determined, decide which inferences call for what text information and world knowledge, and determine which inferences are proposition-connecting or slot-filling. The construction of test questions is aided by the association of the Who? What? When? Where? Why? How? questions with the inference classes.

Consider the following example:

(78) a. Chris wanted to help his mom. (GOAL)
     b. Chris picked some tomatoes from the garden. (ACTION)
     c. Chris finished in time for supper. (ACTION)

Suppose one asks:

(79) What did Chris do to help his mom?

The question (79) calls for a text-connecting inference about ACTIONS appropriate to a GOAL. Note that the text provides the required information content for inferences which are proposition-connecting in the form of subsequent ACTIONS.

Suppose we alter the example by deleting (78b). Then we would have a situation that calls for slot-filling. Clearly slot-filling should be more difficult and variable than text-connecting. The former requires information retrieval and is more open-ended than the latter, which makes the information available in the text and thus restricts the possibilities. To determine whether a slot-filling inference is plausible or acceptable still requires judgment on the part of the tester or experimenter. We have no formal way to make such decisions.

If the question asked of example (78) is:

(80) Why did Chris pick tomatoes?

we are asking for a motivational inference based on an ACTION. We have commented previously on this forward-backward reciprocity in logical inferences. It would be of interest to know if causes are as readily identified as consequences or predictions. It may be the case that causes are more likely or easier to infer since during natural language processing the understander is interpreting the focal event in terms of what preceded (caused) it more often than predicting what is about to occur. We also have commented that many predictions are not likely to be confirmed and that the information base is usually not there to direct clear expectations. Hence, the event chain analysis suggests that comprehension is more backward-directed than forward directed. Asymmetries in speed and accuracy in making backward as opposed to predictive inferences, where sufficient information is available, may shed light on this hypothesis of directionality in processing and the importance of the focal event in making inferences, interpreting the text, and determining the narrative's world-frame to facilitate further interpretation.

Suppose we modify example (78):

(81) a. Chris wanted to help his mom. (GOAL)
     b. Chris broke all the eggs in the refrigerator. (ACTION)
     c. Chris finished in time for supper (ACTION)

In Example (81) a GOAL motivates an ACTION, consistent with the logical constraints of the connection rules. However, an expected "helpful" ACTION does not occur, or is not specified. Instead, the content of ACTION (81b) is inconsistent at a semantic level with that of GOAL (81a) (See "Connection rules" above). This necessitates qualifying the story by making additional relevant inferences. An understander might devise a plausible rationale to relate (81a) and (81b). For example: Chris went to the refrigerator to take out the milk and he *accidentally* knocked over a carton of eggs. Alternatively, an understander might change the GOAL and infer that Chris was at heart angry with his mother. Such inconsistencies in a text require slot-filling inferences to establish the extenuating circumstances which make the story plausible. The kinds of inferences and their latencies that occur to fill out Examples (78) and (81) could demonstrate such effects empirically.

Another empirical question of interest is how close must events be in the chain in order to facilitate connection? In the farmer story of Table 4 and Fig. 4, some of the connections span nearly the whole story. In particular, the farmer's GOAL (Proposition 3) is connected to Propositions (6), (8)–(10), (12)–(15), (19)–(21) and (26). Suppose a series of Why? questions is asked about these propositions. What is the likelihood that Proposition (3) is given as the answer for each question? Are people equally fast in answering each question?

It is possible to create further modifications of Example (78) to study the effect of text distance:

(82)   a. Chris wanted to help his mom. (GOAL)
        b. Chris broke all the eggs in the refrigerator. (ACTION)
        c. Chris picked some tomatoes from the garden. (ACTION)
        d. Chris finished in time for supper. (ACTION)

If one again asks Question (79), "What did Chris do to help his mom?" one has in contrast to (78) placed an intervening proposition between the GOAL and the successful ACTION. In the development of reading and inferencing from text, young readers may be more likely to connect adjacent actions and goals than more distant ones, even though the semantic basis for the connection is inconsistent. Thus, in (82), they may incorrectly offer (82b) as an answer when it is adjacent to the GOAL. Alternatively, children may successfuly answer question (80) "Why did Chris pick the tomatoes?" more frequently when line (82c) is adjacent to the GOAL then when another proposition intervenes.

In Example (82) the interposition of semantically incongruous events between logically connected events may lead to inferences that were unintended by the writer or speaker. This possibility could lead to slower processing or even a disruption of a logically connected series of events in the chain. Note that such a disruption occurs at a very local level, essentially between adjacent pairs of events, and may underlie the loss in comprehension and recall found in a number of recent studies on study grammars. Kintsch, Mandel, and Kozminksy (1977), Thorndyke (1977), Bower (1976), Stein (1976), and Stein and Glenn (1977) have all shown that disordering of sentences in a text leads to lower levels of recall. Such findings are taken to support a particular story grammar and the idea that understanders possess prior "schemas" for assimilating story information. We would argue instead that the scrambling of sentences simply destroys the internal logic of the story and thereby inhibits the inferential connections necessary to determine the scaffolding of the event chain, rather than disrupting the "match" of the story to a preconceived story-grammar schema. The understander would be a more flexible processor of text if he were allowed to induce a structure rather than to apply a preconceived one. Knowing about stories amounts to knowing about the kinds of permissible connections between events rather than particular higher order structures.

The second question—How are inferences made?—remains elusive. it is unclear to us at this time whether or not different types of inferences require different processes. At the moment, we have no process model for how inferences are made. It is clear that such a model would require semantic interpretation as well as the retention of each given event long enough for connections to be made or slot-filling to be initiated. Models for the representation of text merely assume inferential processes. For example, in Kintsch's (1974) text analysis, proposition connections are often made in the representation of predicates and arguments. Likewise, in Schank's (1975a) conceptual dependency analysis, case-like referential inferences (specifying instruments, etc.) are made for verbs. These models, however, leave the procedures by which we make inferences an open question.

If people understand a narrative by determining all the information we have specified in the event chain, then the making of inferences which connect propositions or fill in missing events should promote comprehension and recall. One could promote connections and slot-filling explicitly in either of two ways. In the text itself, one could provide all of the critical events in a "well-formed" story and also make explicit, via lexical markers, the direct connections between the events. Both of these procedures reduce the amount of processing the understander has to do in order to arrive at a representation of the information specified in the event chain. Alternatively, one could promote the making of text-connecting inferences, as well as slot-filling or straight elaboration, by asking inference questions during the listening or reading of a text. Such questions would promote directed inferencing, analogous to what Craik and Lockhart (1972) have termed increased "depth of processing," which leads to better recall of lists of words, etc. Increased depth of processing (processing to the level of interpropositional meaning) and its relation to comprehension could thus be operationalized, helping the understander to learn and spontaneously use self-testing procedures for findings relations among events.

The idea that meaning involves knowledge about the relations of an event to other events is not new. The American philosopher and educator John Dewey (1963) defined meaning in a manner entirely compatible with the ideas about inferences and event chains proposed in this paper. We end our discussion with a quote on his definition of meaning:

> To grasp the meaning of a thing, event or a situation is to see it in its relations to other things; to note how it operates or functions, what consequences follow from it; what causes it, what uses it can be put to. In contrast, what we have called the brute thing, the thing without meaning to us, is something whose relations are not grasped. (p. 135)

ACKNOWLEDGMENTS

This research was supported by National Institute of Education Grant No. NIE-G-77-0018 to T. Trabasso, by National Institute of Mental Health Grants Nos. 19223 and 29365 to T. Trabasso, and by a National Institute of Child Health and Human Development program project grant (5 P01 HD05027) to the University of Minnesota's Institute of Child Development).

REFERENCES

Bartlett, F. C. *Remembering: A study in experimental and social psychology.* Cambridge, England: Cambridge University Press, 1932.

Bower, G. H. *Comprending and recalling stories.* APA Division 3 Presidential address, Washington, 1976.

Clark, H. H. Bridging. In R. C. Schank & B. L. Nash-Webber (Chairpersons), *Theoretical issues in natural langugae processing.* An interdisciplinary workshop in computational linguistics, psychology, linguistics, artificial intelligence. Cambridge, Mass., 1975.

Craik, F. I. M., & Lockhart, R. S. Levels of processing: A framework for memory research. *Journal of Verbal Learning and Verbal Behavior,* 1972, *11,* 671–684.

Dewey, J. *How we think.* Portions published in R. M. Hutchins & M. J. Adler (Eds.), *Gateway to the great books* (Vol. 10). Chicago: Encyclopedia Britannica, 1963. (Originally published by Heath, 1933, 1961.)

Fillmore, C. J. The case for case. In E. Bach & R. Harms (Eds.), *Universals in linguistic theory.* New York: Holt, Rinehart, & Winston, 1968.

Goldman, A. I. *A theory of human action.* Englewood Cliffs, N. J.: Prentice-Hall, 1970.

Heider, F. *The psychology of interpersonal relations.* New York: Wiley, 1958.

Kintsch, W. *The representation of meaning in memory.* Hillsdale, N.J.: Lawrence Erlbaum Associates, 1974.

Kintsch, W., Mandel, T. S., & Kozminsky, E. Summarizing scrambled stories. *Memory and Cognition,* 1977, *5,* 547–552.

Mandler, J. M., & Johnson, N. S. Remembrance of things parsed: Story structure and recall. *Cognitive Psychology,* 1977, *9,* 111–151.

Meyer, B. J. F. Identification of the structure of prose and its implications for the study of reading and memory. *Journal of Reading Behavior,* 1975, *7,* 7–47.

Nicholas, D. A. *Toward a taxonomy of linguistic inferences in children's story understanding.* Junior Project, Department of Psychology Library, Princeton University, 1976.

Reiger, C. J., III. *Conceptual memory; A theory and computer program for processing the meaning content of natural language utterances.* Unpublished doctoral dissertation, Stanford University, 1974.

Schank, R. C. *Conceptual information processing.* Amsterdam: North-Holland, 1975. (a)

Schank, R. C. The role of memory in language processing. In C. N. Cofer (Ed.), *The structure of human memory.* San Francisco: Freeman, 1975. (b)

Schank, R. C. The structure of episodes in memory. In D. G. Bobrow & A. Collins (Eds.), *Representation and understanding: Studies in cognitive science.* New York: Academic Press, 1975. (c)

Stein, N. L. *The effects of increasing temporal disorganization on children's recall of stories.* Paper presented at the Psychomic Society meeting, St. Louis, 1976.

Stein, N. L., & Glenn, C. G. An analysis of story comprehension in elementary school children. This volume.

Stein, N. L., & Glenn, C. G. *The role of structural variation in children's recall of simple stories.* Paper presented at the Symposium on the Develpment of Discourse Processing Skills, Society for Research in Child Development, New Orleans, 1977.

Thorndyke, P. W. Cognitive structures in comprehension and memory of narrative discourse. *Cognitive Psychology,* 1977, *9,* 77–110.

Trabasso, T., & Nicholas, D. W. *Memory and inferences in the comprhension of narratives.* Paper presented at the conference on Structure and Process Models in the Study of Dimensionality of Children's Judgments, Kassel, Germany, June 1977.

Trabasso, T., Nicholas, D. W., Omanson, R. C., & Johnson, L. *Inferences in story comprehension.* Paper presented at the Symposium on the Development of Discourse Processing Skills, Society for Research in Child Development, New Orleans, 1977.

3 An Analysis of Story Comprehension in Elementary School Children

Nancy L. Stein
Christine G. Glenn
Washington University, St. Louis

Recently, there has been a renewed attempt to describe the structures underlying the comprehension of complex linguistic information, such as story material (Mandler, Johnson, & DeForest, 1976; Rumelhart, 1975; Stein & Glenn, 1976). While knowledge concerning the cognitive structures which regulate single word and sentence processing are critical for a more complete understanding of story comprehension, this type of information is not sufficient to describe the results found in studying stories. The cognitive structures or schemas used during story processing may be quite independent of the structures used during single sentence processing. Accurate predictions concerning which parts of stories will be recalled, forgotten, or transformed cannot be made from data bases containing only knowledge of single word or sentence comprehension. Stories contain multiple cause–effect relations and descriptions of entire behavior sequences of events and actions. This necessitates the development of a model which defines the underlying structure used to comprehend the informational units in a story and the relations that occur between the units.

Bartlett (1932) was one of the first investigators who attempted to define the types of mental structures used during the encoding and retrieval of stories. Almost all of the recent studies on story recall or comprehension, including the present investigation, have adopted and attempted to refine some of the concepts used by Bartlett (i.e., Brown, 1975; Kintsch, 1976; Mandler et al., 1976; Paris, 1975; Stein & Glenn, 1976). In the process of collecting data on story recall, Bartlett arrived at several conclusions which diametrically opposed the available theories of memory at the time of his investigation. He argued that story recall is not an exact copy or reproduction of incoming information, as many trace theorists believed. Subjects did not remember the exact syntactic and semantic aspects of stories. The information underwent blending, omissions, inventions of new detail, and similar transformations. Bartlett felt that subjects tended to get an impression of the whole story and, on the basis of this mental "attitude," they would then reconstruct the details of the story. Subjects often based their reconstructions upon probabilistic estimates of what could have occurred rather than what actually did occur.

The fact that transformations occurred in recall led Bartlett to the conclusion that memory is constructive and is a product of the interaction between the incoming information and the strategies, mental operations, and structures used by the subject. The concept of a mental schema or structure influencing story comprehension is perhaps Bartlett's major contribution to theories of memory and is widely adopted by investigators studying the internal structure of stories (i.e., see Brown, 1975; Kintsch, 1976; Mandler et al., 1976; Paris, 1975; Rumelhart, 1975; Stein & Glenn, 1976).

A schema, to Bartlett (1932), represented "an active organization of past reactions and experiences which are always operating in any well-developed organism" (p. 201). These past experiences, although serially encoded and organized, operate as a unitary mass. Bartlett emphasized the reciprocal interaction which occurs between incoming new information and existing mental structures by stating that incoming information is actively integrated into a subject's existing mental structure but, at the same time, new information modifies the organization of preexisting structures. He described both the consistency and variability of story recall in terms of these structures. On the one hand, he felt that the broad characteristics of these schemas were stable over time and were shared by many individuals at least within a given culture. This would explain the consistency observed in recall over a period of repeated reproductions and across many individuals. However, he also argued that individual differences in attitudes, interests, and affectives states existed and influenced the variability that occurred in recall.

Although Bartlett's work covered a large number of theoretical problems, the application of his concepts requires the addition of major theoretical innovations. Bartlett never clearly defined the schemas which guide story processing. Furthermore, he was not concerned with the description of the external organization of stories and the variability that might exist between stories. Bartlett's stories, such as the *War of the Ghosts,* lacked a great deal of external organization; critical presuppositions were omitted, explicit references to the exact temporal occurrence of events were not included, and the social and cultural settings of the story were removed from those which were familiar to his subjects. Thus, it remains extremely difficult to make predictions concerning the processing of other stories from his results. In order to accomplish this task, a model which considers the relationship between the external organization of stories and the existing internal structures used by a subject must be developed.

Many investigators have been able to verify Bartlett's statements concerning the constructive aspect of memory by investigating the role of inferential thinking and prior knowledge on story comprehension (see Bransford & McCarrell, 1974, or Paris, 1975, for recent reviews of this research). However, a model or theory of story comprehension which formally defines the types of strategies, operations, and schemas used by a processor is also necessary to investigate the nature of story memory.

Two of the basic requirements for any model of prose comprehension are that it contain rules for defining the types of informational units contained in the material and that it defined the types of relations that exist between these units. These rules would permit a precise definition of the information contained in a passage and would enable an investigator to make specific predictions concerning the way in which this information would be encoded and internally represented by a subject.

The first step involved in developing a model, therefore, involves the choice of a unit of analysis. A unit is a measure of information and is a relative concept. The choice of unit will depend upon the questions asked by an investigator. When an investigator chooses a unit of analysis, several assumptions are generally made concerning this choice:

1. The unit is assumed to correspond to the types of categories processors use in structuring and remembering information.
2. The unit can often be described in terms of lower level units and the relations between these units.
3. The unit can be joined to other units of the same level by specified relations in order to form higher order units.

It is generally assumed that the unit chosen for narrative analysis must be larger than the individual word. The unit most widely used to date is the proposition (Fillmore, 1968; Kintsch, 1974). A proposition is defined as a predicator or relational word, usually the verb, and one or more arguments which stand in some specific relation to the predicator, e.g., the actor of a verb. A proposition roughly corresponds to a simple sentence.

The concept of a proposition (or a similar linguistic unit) can not completely describe a prose passage. An analysis of a passage into propositions does not provide information concerning the relative importance of individual propositions within the passage, nor does it indicate how these units are logically related to each other. A model of processing requires an analysis of the types of information that can occur in prose and of the types of relations that can exist between units. In order to do this, it is necessary to specify the kind of prose being examined. Different types of prose contain different types of information and different interunit relations. The present study is concerned with the comprehension of one type of prose: the story or folktale.

Rumelhart (1975) has recently developed a grammar which attempts to represent a processor's internal organization of story material. The grammar is composed of a set of rules that describe how a story can be broken down into units and how these units are related to one another. It is assumed that the organizational principles formalized in his grammar correspond to the organizational strategies used by subjects. In developing this grammar, Rumelhart analyzed the structure of folktales, fables, and myths. This type of narrative has two major characteristics: it is usually orally transmitted and its frequency of transmission is extremely high (for studies of folktales see Colby & Cole, 1973; Lord, 1965; and Propp, 1958). Even though there is variation in the production of a tale as it is retold, the end result is that a stable organization emerges. The type of logical sequence produced upon recall remains highly consistent despite variations in the specific content added to or deleted from the story.

In his schema for stories, Rumelhart's primary unit of analysis is defined as an informational node or category. Each category refers to specific types of information which serve different functions within the story structure. For example, almost all stories begin with information concerning the physical, social, or temporal context within which the remainder of the story occurs. The function of this information is to set the stage for the subsequent events. Rumelhart defines several different categories existing in a story structure, the information in any category containing one or several propositions. The number of propositions occurring is not the critical variable defining category membership. At times, information in an entire sentence may be classified into one or two different categories, depending upon the functional role of each portion of the sentence.

The categories can be described in terms of a hierarchical network in which a logical sequence is created among the categories and specific relations determine the degree of causality existing between any two categories. In describing the hierarchical network, Rumelhart assumes that each of the categories can be described in terms of higher order categories and that the hierarchy is basically a binary network. Thus, the internal representation of a story can be portrayed in schematic form as:

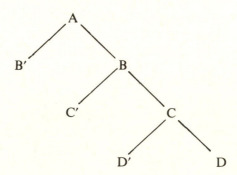

The highest order category in this network is A. A can be defined in terms of B' and B. B' is, in most instances, a primary category which cannot be further divided into other categories. A primary category can contain multiple elements but all of the elements have an underlying similar feature which makes them belong to category B'. Conversely, category B is a higher order category which can be defined in terms of C', a primary category, and C, another higher order category.

It should be noted that there are other types of representations which can be used. For instance, the informational categories could be represented as a linear sequence; A would then be diagrammed as follows:

B'————C'————D'————D

This type of representation does not postulate any higher order categories, and implies a rather simple model of processing. A set of informational categories is postulated which are joined by a set of relations. The choice between a linear and a hierarchical representation depends upon the interpretation of a hierarchical representation; at least two interpretations are possible. The least stringent is that the hierarchical network is used solely as a descriptive tool. The justification for its use is that it can describe a large number of individual cases, in this instance stories; presumably many stories can be more easily described if higher order categories are postulated. For instance, some stories might be described as containing several "B" sequences. If the hierarchical representation is interpreted in this way, the choice between a hierarchical and a linear representation depends on such criteria as convenience and ease and range of application; no differences in processing have been stated. A second interpretation of a hierarchical representation is that processing follows a hierarchical sequence. This interpretation obviously makes more assumptions about processing and about the psychological validity of a hierarchical model. The exact implications of this position have not been clearly developed. For example, one hypothesis that might be derived from the second interpretation is that the higher nodes are more central to the organization of the story and will be better recalled. There is at present no evidence which would support the second and more stringent interpretation and therefore no choice between interpretations and between the use of a linear versus a hierarchical representation can be made on the basis of data. Reasons for employing a hierarchical representation will be presented in the next section.

In an initial study (Stein & Glenn, 1975) Rumelhart's schema for stories (1975) was used to analyze story recall protocols from elementary school children. Several difficulties were encountered in an attempt to apply his original story schema to many of the stories in our collection of folktales and fables. The difficulties encountered in using Rumelhart's story schema and the subsequent changes made as a result of those problems are listed below:

1. Rumelhart used separate systems to describe semantic and syntactic relations occurring in stories. We found this distinction to be cumbersome and somewhat artificial. Therefore, the semantic and syntactic relations occurring in the story are combined into one structure.

2. Rumelhart's grammar did not specify the variety of causal links that occur within each category and between episodes of a story. Nor did he specify the structural variations that can occur within a single episode. Our story schema does both.

3. The third difficulty in using his grammar concerned the classification of story information into categories. His initial category distinctions were either too restrictive or did not encompass all types of information found in a variety of folktales. In our initial attempt to parse many children's stories, we found it necessary to delete some of his category distinctions, add new categories, and broaden the type of information classified in certain categories.

The next two sections include the presentation of the story schema that we used in analyzing the four stories presented in our two experiments. In addition, another 50 or more children's stories and fables were analyzed while constructing the schema. When examining the stories, it appeared that several major types of information could adequately describe the stories. The categories were an attempt to formalize these intuitive impressions. The final categories were chosen because they can be used to describe a wide range of stories. It is possible, however, that the category definitions will have to be changed or modified as data are collected. Furthermore, there may be significant differences between cultures in the types of distinctions used by processors. Nonetheless, these categories can be used as a first approximation in the attempt to delineate the distinctions people naturally use. The final sections of this paper present data from two studies that test some of the hypotheses derived from our schema for parsing stories.

THE STORY SCHEMA

Several assumptions are made concerning the analysis of stories. The first assumption is that story material has some kind of internal structure much like sentences (Rumelhart, 1975). The second assumption is that stories can be described in terms of a hierarchical network of categories and the logical relations that exist between these categories. It is further assumed that this network corresponds in some way to the way processors organize story information. This network defines a logical order which is assumed to exist between categories. The categories are types of information which recur in most folktales or fables. The intercategory relations specify the degree to which a category influences or logically precedes the occurrence of a subset category. The first section of the grammar presents the rules which define the category structures and the intercategory relations occuring in a simple story. Figure 1 summarizes all of the rules to be discussed in this section. Figure 2 presents both the internal structure of a simple story and an example which identically matches this structure. It should be noted that most story representations are more complex than the simple story. The structural variations and complexities that can occur are presented at the end of this section. However, the story, *Melvin, The Skinny Mouse,* should aid the reader in following the basic structural components of our schema.

A story consists of a setting category plus an episode system. These two categories are connected by an ALLOW relation. The rule for defining these categories is given by:

Rule 1:   Story →ALLOW (Setting, Episode System)

The first two lines in the Melvin story are each setting statements. The remainder of the information consists of an episode. The setting category serves two functions in the story. It introduces the main character(s) and it describes the social, physical, or temporal context in which the remainder of the story occurs. The type of information contained in this category is basically stative in nature and refers to long-term or habitual states of characters or locations, e.g., the mouse's name was Melvin, and he lived in a barn. However, an activity of a character may also be included in the setting if it describes habitual behavior patterns. The types of information in a setting statement are defined by:

Rule 2:   Setting → [$\begin{array}{c} \text{State(s)} \\ \text{Activity(ies)} \end{array}$]

Several states or activities can occur within the setting category and each is considered to be an exemplar of the category. Each exemplar can be referred to as a base level statement. In the Melvin story, there are two base level setting statements. The use of this term does not imply the existence of a hierarchy within the category. When more than one state or activity occurs, each is related to the other(s) by one of three types of relations: AND, THEN, and CAUSE. The AND relation describes the case in which two units co-occur in time. It can also describe the relation between two units in which there is no definite or apparent temporal sequence existing between the two statements. This is the case in the Melvin story (he was a skinny little mouse AND he lived in a barn). The THEN relation refers to the case in which one statement temporally precedes a second statement but does not directly cause the second although the first may create the necessary preconditions for the second statement to occur. The CAUSE relation refers to the situation in

Summary of Grammatical Rules

1. Story → ALLOW (Setting, Episode System)

2. Setting → State(s)
          Action(s)

3. Episode System → AND
                THEN   (Episode(s))
                CAUSE

4. Episode → INITIATE (Initiating Event, Response)

5. Initiating Event → Natural Occurrence(s)
                Action(s)
                Internal Event(s)

6. Response → MOTIVATE (Internal Response, Plan Sequence)

7. Internal Response → Goal(s)
                Affect(s)
                Cognition(s)

8. Plan Sequence → INITIATE (Internal Plan, Plan Application)

9. Internal Plan → Cognition(s)
               Subgoal(s)

10. Plan Application → RESULT (Attempt, Resolution)

11. Attempt → (Action(s))

12. Resolution → INITIATE (Direct Consequence, Reaction)

13. Direct Consequence → Natural Occurrence(s)
                Action(s)
                End State(s)

14. Reaction → Affect(s)
           Cognition(s)
           Action(s)

Intra-category connectors:
    AND: includes simultaneous or a temporal relation.
    THEN: includes temporal but not direct causal relations.
    CAUSE: includes temporal relations which are causal in nature.

FIG. 1.   Rules which define the internal representation of a story.

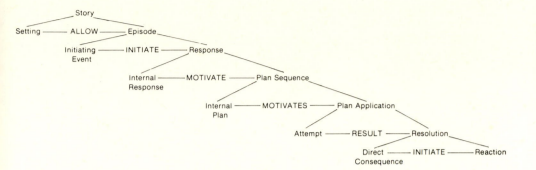

Melvin, The Skinny Mouse

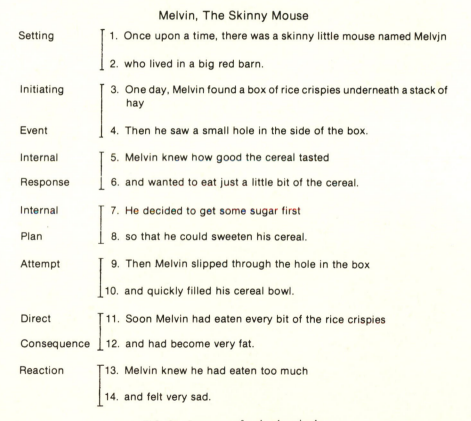

Setting	1. Once upon a time, there was a skinny little mouse named Melvjn
	2. who lived in a big red barn.
Initiating	3. One day, Melvin found a box of rice crispies underneath a stack of hay
Event	4. Then he saw a small hole in the side of the box.
Internal	5. Melvin knew how good the cereal tasted
Response	6. and wanted to eat just a little bit of the cereal.
Internal	7. He decided to get some sugar first
Plan	8. so that he could sweeten his cereal.
Attempt	9. Then Melvin slipped through the hole in the box
	10. and quickly filled his cereal bowl.
Direct	11. Soon Melvin had eaten every bit of the rice crispies
Consequence	12. and had become very fat.
Reaction	13. Melvin knew he had eaten too much
	14. and felt very sad.

FIG. 2. Structure of a simple episode.

which one statement directly influences the occurrence of the second statement. Within the category the relations between statements can be diagramed in a single logical chain similar to Schank's (1975) type of representation.

Although both the character introduction and the description of story context are considered to be setting statements, the two types of information may function differently in the organization of story material. It is almost impossible to begin the production of a story without including a character introduction. In stories in which there is no specific character introduction, many children construct their own introduction in order to begin story recall. This type of statement appears to act as a marker for the initiation of the recall schema (Stein & Glenn, 1975). Other types of information in the setting category may or may not assume a similar importance in the production of a story. In order to distinguish between these two types of setting information, we have labeled the character introduction as the Major Setting category and the other types of setting information as the Minor Setting category.

Setting statements generally occur at the beginning of a story, but they can occur almost anywhere in the sequence of the story schema when it is necessary to describe a new character or a new physical and social context.

The remainder of the story structure is described by an episode system. An episode system, like a story, is a higher order category and incorporates the entire story structure with the exception of the initial setting. An episode system consists of one or more episodes and is defined by the rule:

$$\text{Rule 3:}\quad \text{Episode System} \rightarrow \begin{array}{c} \text{AND} \\ \text{THEN} \\ \text{CAUSE} \end{array} \quad (\text{Episode(s)})$$

An episode is an entire behavioral sequence. The meaning of this term will become clearer below. Most stories contain two or more episodes which can be related to each other in several ways. Because of the complex interrelations that can exist among episodes, the schema of a simple episode will be described first.

An episode is the primary higher order unit of a story and consists of an entire behavioral sequence. It includes the external and/or internal events which influence a character, the character's internal response (goals, cognitions, plans) to these events, the character's external response to his goals, and the consequence resulting from his overt responses. Inherent in this sequence is a causal chain of events beginning with an initiating event and ending with a resolution. Thus, an episode is defined as:

Rule 4:   Episode → INITIATE (Initiating Event, Response)

which states that an episode consists of an initiating event plus a response. In the Melvin story, lines 3 and 4 are both base level initiating event statements. They mark Melvin's discovery of the box of rice crispies with a hole in it. These two statements serve to INITIATE (i.e., precipitate or lead to) the response which includes the remainder of the story. The INITIATE relation denotes a direct causal connection between the Initiating Event and Response categories.

The main function of an initiating event is to cause a response in the main character. The informational content of an initiating event can include three types of statements:

$$\text{Rule 5:} \quad \text{Initiating Event} \rightarrow \begin{array}{l} \text{Natural Occurrence(s)} \\ \text{Action(s)} \\ \text{Internal Event(s)} \end{array}$$

A natural occurrence is a change of state in the physical environment and, in most cases, is not caused by an animate being. Examples of these types of occurrences would be, "the chimney began to crack and fell on the roof." An action performed by either the major character or a minor character is also considered to be an initiating event if it evokes a response in a character. In one of our stories, *Epaminondas,* the boy's mother tells him to take a cake to his grandmother. The mother's action in this story is considerd to be an initiating event. An action originating in the main character can also be classified as an initiating event. For example, the little boy, Epaminondas, could have baked the cake. If he reacted to his own baking by deciding to share it, show it to his grandmother, etc., then his initial action is classified as an initiating event.

Internal events such as the perception of an external event are also classified as an initiating event, as in the Melvin example, i.e., Melvin sees the box of cereal. Changes in internal physiological states, such as hunger, pain, or sickness are also considered to be internal initiating events.

Setting and event statements can generally be distinguished because the former refers to habitual states or actions while the latter refers to changes in such states or to novel actions. Their major difference, however, is that they have different functions in the story. The setting provides the context for the story while the event is an immediate cause for a response on the character's part.

The initiating event category can contain several statements or exemplars. These statements are related by the same three relations which connect individual statements in the setting category: AND, THEN, and CAUSE. In the Melvin story the two event statements are joined by a THEN relation. (Melvin found the box of rice crispies, THEN he saw the hole in the box.)

The next higher order category, the response, consists of an internal response plus a plan sequence and is defined by:

Rule 6:   Response → MOTIVATES (Internal Response,
Plan Sequence)

The internal response refers to the psychological state of a character after an event. Lines 5 and 6 in the Melvin story are both internal responses. This category's main function is to MOTIVATE the character to formulate a plan sequence. The internal response category is defined in Rule 7 and contains three types of statements: affective responses, goals, and cognitions.

Rule 7:   Internal Response →
Affective Response(s)
Goal(s)
Cognition(s)

Affective responses include all types of emotional responses, such as happiness, sadness, despair, and indicate that a state of disequilibrium has occurred in a character. In the Melvin story, line 5, Melvin became very excited, is an affective statement. Goal statements refer to a character's desires or intentions. Line 6 in the Melvin story is a goal statement, i.e., he wanted to eat just a little bit of cereal. Cognitions are statements which refer to a character's thoughts. Most cognitions begin with phrases like—she knew, she remembered, she realized, she thought, etc. A possible cognition for the Melvin story would be, he knew the hole was just a little bigger than he was.

The internal response can contain one, two, or all three of these types of statements. There is no fixed order among these three types of statements, and they can be connected by AND, THEN, and CAUSE relations.

Many written stories do not contain the internal response category. The omission of this category can indicate that a character's feeling, goals, and thoughts are implicit either from the type of initiating event which has occurred or from the behavior which follows the initiating event. However, even when the written story does not contain a character's internal response, the internal representation of the story structure does.

The next higher order category, the plan sequence, can be divided into the internal plan plus a plan application:

Rule 8:   Plan Sequence → MOTIVATE (Internal Plan,
Plan Application)

The MOTIVATE relation again connects the internal plan to the plan application and implies a direct causal link between the two. The internal plan consists of a series of statements that define a character's strategy for obtaining a change in the situation. Lines 7 and 8 in the Melvin story constitute an internal plan. The function of an internal plan is to direct the character's subsequent behavior. It is composed of two types of information: subgoals developed in order to achieve the main goal, and cognitions about the situation, the hypothesized activity or the consequences of the behavior. It is defined by the rule:

Rule 9:   Internal Plan → (Cognitions, Subgoals)

The internal plan category is omitted from most children's stories because most characters have one major goal and use only one or two actions to obtain their goal. The internal plan usually occurs in stories in which the character perceives some difficulty in goal attainment and must think of a sequence of subgoals which are necessary if the major goal is to be obtained. A well developed internal plan is included in *The Tiger's Whisker,* one of the stories used in our two studies to be presented. If several statements occur in the internal plan, the three relations—AND, THEN, and CAUSE— can connect any two statements. The internal plan of the character MOTIVATES the plan application.

The plan application refers to both a character's overt attempt to attain his goal and the resolution of his conflict or disequilibrium:

Rule 10: Plan Application → $\begin{matrix} \text{RESULT} \\ \text{THEN} \end{matrix}$ (Attempt, Resolution)

The attempt includes statements referring to the character's overt actions to obtain a goal and the resolution includes the remainder of the story sequence. The attempt and resolution categories are connected either by a THEN relation or a RESULT relation. The RESULT relation signifies that the attempt directly causes the resolution. In many stories, however, the attempt is not a direct cause of the resolution but instead creates the necessary preconditions for the occurrence of this category. In the Melvin story, lines 9 and 10 are classified as attempt statements. Both of these statments are connected to the resolution by a THEN relation. The major function of attempt statements is to cause or lead to the resolution. The attempt is defined by the following rule:

Rule 11: Attempt → (Action(s))

Within the attempt category, base level statements can be connected by any of the three types of causal relations: AND, THEN, and CAUSE. In the Melvin story, the two base level attempt statements are connected by a THEN relation.

The final higher order category is the resolution which consists of the direct consequence and a reaction:

Rule 12: → INITIATE (Direct Consequence, Reaction)

The direct consequence INITIATES the reaction and implies a direct causal link between the two categories.

The main functions of the direct consequence category are: (1) to express the attainment or nonattainment of the character's goals, (2) to mark any other changes in the sequence of events caused by the character's actions, and (3) to INITIATE or cause a character's reaction to the direct consequence. Lines 11 and 12 in the Melvin story are base level statements classified as direct consequences. Line 11, "Melvin ate every bit of the rice crispies," marks the direct attainment of Melvin's goal (to eat some rice crispies). Line 12, "Melvin became very fat," marks an unforeseen result of Melvin's behavior.

The types of statements included in this category represent a broad spectrum of information. The three types of information included are: natural occurrences, actions, and end states.

$$\text{Rule 13: Direct Consequences} \rightarrow \begin{bmatrix} \text{Natural Occurrence(s)} \\ \text{Action(s)} \\ \text{End State(s)} \end{bmatrix}$$

Natural occurrences are included in this category because they can directly facilitate or impede the attainment of a character's goal. An example of this type of category appears in one of our stories, *The Fox and the Bear*. In one of the last episodes in this story, the roof begins to crack. This is a natural occurrence from the fox's perspective and it impedes his action. The roof and bear then fall in and trap both the fox and bear inside the henhouse. The natural occurrence of the roof falling in is part of the direct consequence because it influences the resolution of their behavioral sequence. Both actions and end states are also exemplars of the direct consequence category. In the Melvin story, line 11 is an action and line 12 is an end state. Several statements can occur in the direct consequence category and, again, any two statements can be connected by the AND, THEN, or CAUSE relation. In the Melvin story the two direct consequence statements are joined by the CAUSE relation.

The reaction is the final category that occurs in the structure of an episode. The types of statements which appear in this category are affective responses, cognitions, and action:

$$\text{Rule 14: Reaction} \rightarrow \begin{bmatrix} \text{Affect(s)} \\ \text{Cognition(s)} \\ \text{Action(s)} \end{bmatrix}$$

This category includes statements defining how a character felt about the attainment of his goal or what he thought about it. Lines 13 and 14 in the

Melvin story are reactions. A reaction can also include an action which results from an emotional response. A possible example for the Melvin story is, "Melvin began to cry." While reactions generally indicate how a character responds to a consequence, they can also specify how the attainment of an end state affects a second character in the story. An excellent example can be seen in two of our stories: *Epaminondas* and *The Tiger's Whisker*. In *Epaminondas,* the boy arrives at his grandmother's with a crumbled piece of cake. These statements are direct consequences. The grandmother reacts to the crumbled cake by telling the boy he's silly and then telling him how he should have carried the cake. The grandmother's response is defined as a reaction on her part. Her response contains an implied affective reaction and an overt action. The story does not explicitly state her affective response. However, in defining the story schema, it is hypothesized that an affective response is an inherent part of a reaction.

The reaction category is similar in content to the internal response category. However, there is one major difference. The reaction category contains no clear goal statements and does not lead to a plan sequence. In *Epaminondas,* the grandmother simply reacts to the boy bringing the crumbled cake. If a goal statement had been included in her response and if that goal had motivated a plan sequence, then her reaction would have been considered an internal response which then indicates the start of a new episode. The AND, THEN, and CAUSE relations are again used to connect individual statements in this category.

The reaction category usually occurs at the end of an episode, but it can also occur at other points in the episode. A character may have a reaction while he is involved in overt behavior. In some stories, characters pause to reconsider their goal but then proceed to complete their original plan sequence. If the consideration of a new goal does not cause a character to formulate a plan sequence, then the character's response is considered to be a reaction and not an internal response.

It is obvious from examining most folktales or fables that very few are as simple or straightforward as the structure given in a simple episode. Stories vary in terms of both their interepisodic complexity and in the number of episodes they contain. In fact, most stories include two or more separate episodes. The next section will consider the relations between episodes as well as some of the complexities that can occur within a single episode.

EPISODIC RELATIONS

Recall Rule 2, which defines the structure and relations of an episode system:

$$\text{Rule 2:} \quad \text{Episode System} \rightarrow \begin{array}{c} \text{AND} \\ \text{THEN} \\ \text{CAUSE} \end{array} \quad \text{(Episode(s))}$$

The rule states that an episode system consists of one or more episodes. We have not postulated a hierarchical structure to describe how two or more episodes are related in a story. This is because two episodes need not be combined to form a higher order category or unit of analysis. The relationships between individual episodes within an episode system are always represented as a logical chain, similar to the structure Schank (1975) uses to describe the structure of a single episode. The following section defines and illustrates the types of relations connecting episodes.

Any two episodes can be connected by the three relations AND, THEN, and CAUSE. The most common relations which connect episodes are the THEN and CAUSE relations. The THEN relation connects two episodes that occur in temporal succession; furthermore, the first episode does not directly cause the second to occur but may set up the necessary preconditions for the second episode. A good example of this relation is found in the classic folktale, *Goldilocks and the Three Bears*. When Goldilocks enters the Three Bears' home, two episodes occur in succession. The first episode recounts Goldilocks' discovery of the porridge, her desire to eat it, and the act of finishing the Baby Bear's porridge. The second episode describes her becoming fatigued, the discovery of the chairs, and her plan sequence of finding a suitable chair to sit in so that she might rest. The first episode does not directly cause her behavior in the second episode, but it may set the necessary conditions for its occurrence. The diagram below illustrates an episode system which contains two episodes connected by the THEN relation:

The second type of relation which connects two episodes is the CAUSE relation. The CAUSE relation implies a direct causal connection between two episodes. An example of this type of interepisodic relation occurs in *The Fox and the Bear*. The resolution of one episode occurs when the roof collapses and traps the fox and bear inside the henhouse. The next episode contains the behavioral sequence of the farmer who comes out to see what is the matter. Implied in this episode is the fact that the farmer must have heard some type of noise which then causes his investigation. This type of relation between episodes can be diagrammed as follows:

The diagram reads: a story consists of a setting plus an episode system. The episode system contains both Episode 1 and Episode 2; Episode 1 causes the occurrence of Episode 2.

Certain problems arise when the CAUSE relation is used to connect episodes. In many stories one episode does directly influence the behavioral sequence in the second. However, in many stories the processor must infer that there is a direct causal link between the two. Children below a certain age may not have the ability to make the types of inferences necessary to perceive the direct relationship between two behavioral sequences. Accordingly, their internal representation may be different from that of an older child's or an adult's organization of the same material. The Epaminondas story used in this study may, in fact, illustrate this point. Older children may immediately grasp the relationship between the grandmother's telling the boy how he should have carried the cake and the boy's subsequent action which states that he carried the butter in the way his grandmother told him to carry the cake. However, young children may not perceive the connection between the two. In the latter case, the two episodes in this story would not be causally related and would be connected by a THEN relationship.

The reverse phenomenon may be true when considering the representation for episodes connected by the THEN relation. The original story version may not specify a direct causal relation between two episodes. However, a subject, especially an older child or adult may infer a direct causal relation between the two episodes. Thus, in many instances, it is extremely difficult to represent the correct relation connecting episodes.

The third type of relation that can exist between two episodes is the AND relation. This relation describes the link between two episodes which occur simultaneously. Although none of our stories has two episodes occurring simultaneously, we have found a few folktales which do contain this type of episodic relation. The episodes occur in a temporal order in the story presentation but the type of connector which links the two episodes denotes simultaneity, i.e., meanwhile, at the same time, while the fox was doing this, etc. After two simultaneous episodes occur, both are usually related to a third episode by a THEN or CAUSE relation.

The number of relations that can exist between the two simultaneous episodes and a third episode varies. However, the next diagram illustrates the most common relationship between simultaneous episodes, and the type of structural organization between two simultaneous episodes and a third episode:

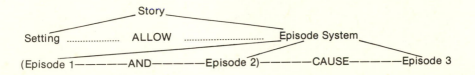

This diagram shows that the episode system is compose of three episodes. The first two are connected by the AND relation. The parentheses designate the fact that both Episode 1 and Episode 2 cause the third episode to occur.

In the fourth type of episodic relation, one episode is embedded or nested in another. An embedded episode is an episode which begins *after* a previous episode has begun and ends either before or at the same time as the previous episode. This type of relation occurs frequently when a story character's attainment of a goal is dependent upon the behavior of a second character. An example of this can be seen in our Judy story; it contains two embedded episodes which are nested in a third episode. The main character, Judy, wants something and depends upon another character for her goal fulfillment. When this occurs, an embedded episode for the second character is begun. This is necessary because the behavior sequence of the second character fulfills the requirements for the construction of an episode. In this story, Judy wants a hammer and a saw and asks her father to get them for her. The act of Judy's asking for these things is an attempt from her perspective but an event from the father's perspective. The event begins the embedded episode; it remains, however, an action from Judy's perspective. This also illustrates how one statement can serve two functions within a story. A second example of an embedded episode can be seen in *The Tiger's Whisker,* the second story used in the present experiment. The lady develops a plan or trick for obtaining a tiger's whisker. She begins her plan application by giving the tiger food and singing to him. The attainment of her goal, however, is contingent upon the tiger's behavioral sequences; his behavioral sequence consists of an embedded episode which is nested in the lady's behavioral sequence.

In addition to variations in the number of episodes found in stories, stories also differ in intraepisodic structure. The episodic structure which was defined by the grammar presents a very simple causal chain in which one type of information logically leads to the subsequent category. There are numerous ways, however, in which the basic sequence can be modified. The most common variation in single episode structures is the case in which an episode contains two or more higher order categories; for instance, a story could contain two responses or two plan sequences. A story would contain two responses if the main character fails to attain his primary goal on his first attempt and then formulates a different plan of attack in his second attempt. His primary goal, however, remains identical to the goal expressed in the first response. Therefore, both responses are considered to be part of the same episode. In addition, the same initiating event precipitates both responses. The fourth story used in this experiment serves as an example of this. In this story, Judy is going to have a birthday party. She decides that she wants a hammer and a saw. She proceeds to ask her father to get them for her but he does not fulfill her desire. She then tells her grandmother about her desire because she still wants to get the tools. Thus, the goal statements in Judy's second response is identical to that in the first response. There is no need for a new episode to describe her behavior in the second response.

The diagram below illustrates the organization of the Judy story in which one response causes the second to occur (the categories which constitute the response categories are not explicitly given).

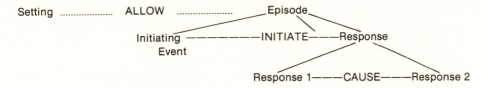

A second type of intraepisodic variation occurs when a setting or reaction appears at points other than their most common position. As stated before, setting statements can occur almost anywhere in the structure of an episode. They do not have to occur at the beginning of the story. When they appear within a single episode, the binary nature of the descending hierarchical structure is somewhat different.

An example of a setting statement occurring in the middle of an episode can be illustrated by an example from the story, *The Tiger's Whisker,* which was used in this study. A setting statement occurs immediately after an attempt statement:

(1) She (the lady) went to a tiger's cave   (Action, Attempt)
(2) where a lonely tiger lived   (State, Minor Setting)

The minor setting does not cause the attempt to occur but provides the necessary preconditions for its occurrence. The internal structure of this story variation is illustrated in the diagram below:

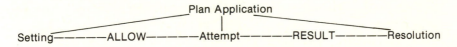

This indicates that the plan application consists of two primary categories, the setting and the attempt, plus a higher order category, the resolution. In these cases, the descending hierarchy of the story structure is not binary.

The final comment on the story grammar concerns the definition of an episode. In almost all folktales, one or two of the postulated categories are missing from each episode in the story structure. For example, many folktales do not include the character's internal response or his reaction at the end of an episode. Most tales do not include the internal plan. Some do not include an initiating event or an attempt. In order to be considered as an episode in our schema, a behavioral sequence must contain some reference to: (1) the purpose of the behavioral sequence, (2) overt goal-directed behavior, and (3) the attainment or nonattainment of the character's goal. Therefore, an episode must contain (1) an initiating event or an internal response which causes a character to formulate a goal-directed behavioral sequence, (2) an action, which can either be an attempt or a consequence, and (3) a direct consequence marking the attainment or nonattainment of the goal. If these three criteria are not met, the behavioral sequence is defined as an incomplete episode. An example of an incomplete episode occurs in one of our stories, *The Fox and the Bear.* In the last episode the resolution is omitted. The episode does not specify what the farmer did after he came out to see what happened. Thus, his behavioral sequence is incomplete.

The following sections present data from two studies completed on story recall and comprehension in first- and fifth-grade children. Study 1 examines the development of story recall. Study 2 investigates story comprehension by requiring children to answer probe questions concerning the type of relations they perceive between categories. In addition, Study 2 investigates the child's conception of the most critical elements occurring in story material.

EXPERIMENT 1

A set of hypotheses pertaining to the organization of story recall in children was derived from our story schema and from previous research findings on prose comprehension. The main goal of this study was not to systematically vary the structure of each story presented, but rather to collect recall data on several stories representative of those found in children's literature.

Research on adult memory for prose has shown that the information recalled in stories is not random. Bartlett (1932) found that the pattern of an individual's recall was highly consistent over a repeated number of story reproductions, and Johnson (1970) showed that certain informational units in a story are better recalled by all subjects than other units. Very little data exist in the developmental literature to compare the structure of story recall across age groups. Korman (cited by Yendovitskaya, 1971) and Stein and Glenn (1975) examined children's memory for stories. Korman has shown that children as young as five are capable of recalling the gist or central theme of a story. Thus, certain information assumes more importance in the structure of recall than other units. Similarly, Stein and Glenn (1975) found that the relative salience of story statements, as measured by their frequency of occurrence in recall, was highly consistent across grades (first and third) and over time (recall collected immediately after story presentation and again one week later). These findings indicate a high degree of similarity in the cognitive structures used by children during story encoding and retrieval.

In the present study, the consistency of organization, measured by the frequency of item salience in recall, was also examined. In the Stein and Glenn study, only one story was used. We felt that a greater number of stories had to be examined and that the age interval between the two groups of children had to be widened. However, we predicted that there would still be a high degree of similarity in the types of units recalled by the two different age groups of children.

In addition to examining the recall of individual statements, we examined story recall in terms of the informational categories specified in our story schema. If the concept of an episode described in our schema has any psychological validity, story information relating to the basic logical sequence of events should be retained by children. Furthermore, subjects should chunk information according to distinctions similar to those of our grammar, and certain categories should be structurally more important than others in the description of a story's logical sequence. In our initial study (Stein & Glenn, 1975), major settings, initiating events, and direct consequence statements were the most frequently recalled categories. The event and the consequence categories provide the basic cause–effect relations in a behavioral sequence. The major setting (the introduction of the main character) may act as a marker or signal for the beginning of story production. Thus, if the underlying logic of a behavioral sequence influences story recall, the saliency of categories in recall should vary. We further expected that the major setting, initiating event, and direct consequences statements should again be the most frequently recalled categories in all stories.

The next set of predictions pertain to the temporal sequence of information found in stories. To date, there is conflicting evidence concerning young children's ability to temporally organize story events. Both Piaget (1969) and Fraisse (1963) have maintained that young children lack the cognitive structures necessary to encode temporal relationships. Brown (1975), however, has shown that five-year-olds can reconstruct a sequence of events if the events are logically ordered. Additionally, in the Stein and Glenn study, most first-grade children had little difficulty recalling the correct temporal sequence of story events. The discrepancy among the findings in the above studies may be a function of the stories used. The ability to accurately order a sequence of events may be a function of the organization of the stories presented. If the stories told to children are well formed and match the order of events inherent in a child's internal schema, then the order of events in recall will match those of the story. Violations of the temporal sequence should force children to reorganize the story material or delete the disorganized information from their recall.

The last set of predictions involves the types of transformations occurring in recall. As Bartlett stated, the recall of stories contains numerous transformations of the original information. In attempting to construct his story grammar, Rumelhart (1975) proposed a set of summarization rules which would predict the type of deletions, integrations, and additions of new information occurring in story material. We have not attempted the construction of formal summarization rules for children's recall. However, several predictions can be made concerning the types of transformations which occur in recall.

If the concept of a behavioral sequence as defined in an episode is valid, we would expect that the recall protocols would contain information which defines the basic logical structure of the sequence. Information which is not directly related to that sequence or which only serves to elaborate the sequence will be omitted from recall. For example, adjectives, minor setting statements (e.g., information pertaining to locations, ancillary characters), and actions not directly related to the logical flow of the story should be omitted more frequently than information which is critical to the maintenance of the logical sequence of events. Additions of new information should occur when categories have been omitted from the external structure of story material or in places where the most probabilistic events of a behavioral sequence have not been included in the story.

Method

Subjects

Subjects were 48 children from an upper-middle-class school in St. Louis County. An equal number of first- and fifth-grade children participated in the study. Approximately half of the children in each grade were males and half were females. The mean ages in each grade were 6 years, 5 months for first grade and 10 years, 6 months for fifth grade.

Materials

Four stories were used in the study. One story was a classical folktale, *Epaminondas;* this story has many different versions and one was selected for use in this study. The other three stories were constructed by reading a variety of children's stories and then creating new versions of the tales. This procedure was followed because many of the initially selected stories were well known to the children participating in the study. The stories were selected as typical of children's stories. Without an ecological analysis of stories, it is not possible to give more specific guarantees of the typicality of these four stories. However, no attempt was made to make the stories correspond to the model, either by including all of the postulated categories in an episode or by equalizing the number of statements occurring in each category.

All of the statements in each of the four stories were parsed into the appropriate category specified by the grammar. The final parsings were completed by having three separate raters parse each story. When a disagreement occurred among the three raters, the statement was assigned to the category which had been used by two of the three raters. The initial interrater reliability for the four stories was 92%. There were very few disagreements and raters disagreed on no more than three statements per story.

Visual diagrams or tree structures of the stories were then constructed for each of the four stories. The original versions of the written stories and their tree structures are presented in Figs. 3 through 10.

Design

Children from each grade were randomly divided into two groups of 12 subjects each. Children in Group 1 at each grade level were told the first two stories; children in Group 2 at each grade level were told the second two stories. Stories were presented in a counterbalanced order.

	1st grade	5th grade
Stories 1 and 2	Group 1	Group 1
Stories 3 and 4	Group 2	Group 2

Children were told the stories rather than presented with recorded versions because pilot work had shown that young children had more difficulty sustaining attention with recorded versions. To control for bias in story delivery, two experimenters tested a random half of each group of 12 children at each grade level.

Procedure

At the beginning of each testing session, the subject was familiarized with the tape recording procedure. When the experimenter felt that the subject was relaxed, the session began. The experimenter told the child that he was going to hear a story. He was told to listen very carefully becase when the experimenter finished the story, he would have to tell the story out loud exactly as he had heard it. The experimenter then read the first story to the child. Immediately after the story presentation, fifth-grade children were asked to count backward from 50 by threes. First grades simply counted to 20. Then the child was asked to orally recall the story exactly as he had heard it. After he finished, the second story was presented in an identical fashion. All responses were tape recorded.

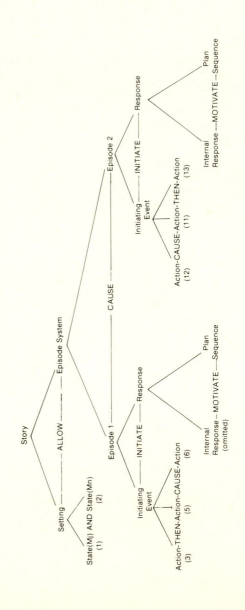

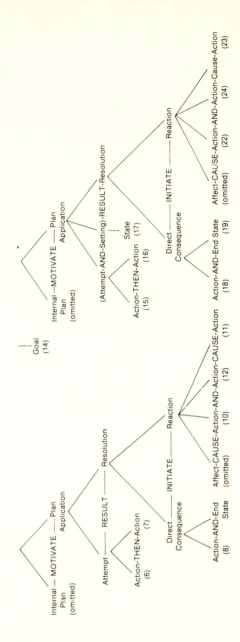

FIG. 3. Tree structure for Story 1: *Epaminondas.*

Category Type	Type of Information	Statement
Major Setting	State	1. Once there was a little boy
Minor Setting	State	2. who lived in a hot country
Initiating Event	Action	3. One day his mother told him to take some cake to his grandmother
Initiating Event	Action	4. She warned him to hold it carefully
Initiating Event	Action	5. so it wouldn't break into crumbs
Attempt	Action	6. The little boy put the cake in a leaf under his arm
Attempt	Action	7. and carried it to his grandmother's
Direct Consequence	Action	8. When he got there
Direct Consequence	End State	9. the cake had crumbled into tiny pieces
Reaction	Action	10. His grandmother told him he was a silly boy
Reaction	Action	11. and that he should have carried the cake on top of his head
Reaction	Action	12. so it wouldn't break
Initiating Event	Action	13. Then she gave him a pat of butter to take back to his mother's house
Internal Response	Goal	14. The little boy wanted to be very careful with the butter
Attempt	Action	15. so he put it on top of his head
Attempt	Action	16. and carried it home
Minor Setting	State	17. The sun was shining hard
Direct Consequence	Action	18. and when he got home
Direct Consequence	End State	19. the butter had all melted
Reaction	Action	20. His mother told him that he was a silly boy
Reaction	Action	21. and that he should have put the butter in a leaf
Reaction	Action	22. so that it would have gotten home safe and sound

FIG. 4. Text of Story 1: *Epaminondas.*

78

Category Type	Type of Information	Statement
Major Setting	State	1. Once there was a woman
Internal Response	Goal	2. who needed a tiger's whisker
Internal Response	Affect	3. She was afraid of tigers
Internal Response	Goal	4. but she needed a whisker
Internal Response	Goal	5. to make a medicine for her husband
Initiating Event	Natural Occurrence	6. who had gotten very sick
Internal Response	Cognition	7. She thought and thought
Internal Response	Goal	8. about how to get a tiger's whisker
Internal Plan	Goal	9. She decided to use a trick
Internal Plan	Cognition	10. She knew that tigers loved food and music
Internal Plan	Cognition	11. She thought that if she brought food to a lonely tiger
Internal Plan	Cognition	12. and played soft music
Internal Plan	Cognition	13. the tiger would be nice her
Internal Plan	Cognition	14. and she could get the whisker
Attempt	Action	15. So she did just that
Attempt	Action	16. She went to a tiger's cave
Minor Setting	State	17. where a lonely tiger lived
Attempt	Action	18. She put a bowl of food in front of the opening to the cave
Attempt	Action	19. Then she sang soft music
Attempt	Action	20. The tiger came out
Direct Consequence	Action	21. and ate the food
Attempt	Action	22. He then walked over to the lady
Direct Consequence	Action	23. and thanked her for the delicious food and lovely music
Direct Consequence	Action	24. The lady then cut off one of his whiskers
Direct Consequence	Action	25. and ran down the hill very quickly
Reaction	Affect	26. The tiger felt lonely and sad again

FIG. 5.   Text of Story 2: *The Tiger's Whisker*.

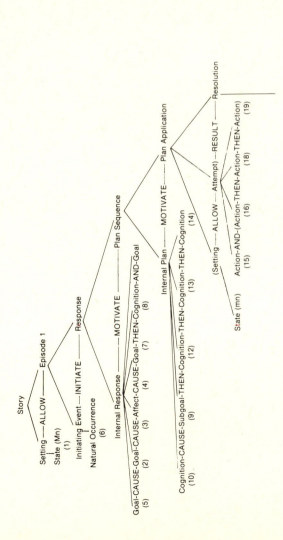

80

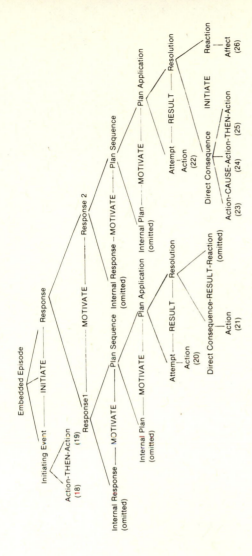

FIG. 6. Tree structure for Story 2: *The Tiger's Whisker.*

81

Category Type	Type of Information	Statement
Major Setting	State	1. There was a fox and a bear
Minor Setting	State	2. who were friends
Internal Response	Goal	3. One day they decided to catch a chicken for supper
Internal Response	Goal	4. They decided to go together
Internal Response	Goal	5. because neither one wanted to be left alone
Minor Setting	State	6. and they both liked fried chicken
Attempt	Action	7. They waited until night time
Attempt	Action	8. Then they ran very quickly to a nearby farm
Internal Response	Cognition	9. where they knew chickens lived
Internal Response	Affect	10. The bear, who felt very lazy
Attempt	Action	11. climbed upon the roof
Internal Response	Goal	12. to watch
Attempt	Action	13. The fox then opened the door of the henhouse very carefully
Attempt	Action	14. He grabbed a chicken
Direct Consequence	Action	15. and killed it
Initiating Event	Action	16. As he was carrying it out of the henhouse
Initiating Event	Natural Occurrence	17. the wieght of the bear on the roof caused the roof to crack
Initiating Event	Internal Event	18. The fox heard the noise
Internal Response	Affect	19. and was frightened
Minor Setting	State	20. but it was too late
Internal Response	Goal	21. to run out
Direct Consequence	Natural Occurrence	22. The roof and the bear fell in
Direct Consequence	Natural Occurrence	23. killing five of the chickens
Direct Consequence	End State	24. The fox and the bear were trapped in the broken henhouse
Attempt	Action	25. Soon the farmer came out
Internal Response	Goal	26. to see what was the matter

FIG. 7. Text of Story 3: *The Fox and Bear.*

Category Type	Type of Information	Statement
Initiating Event	Natural Occurrence	1. Judy is going to have a birthday party
Major Setting	State	2. She is ten years old
Internal Response	Goal	3. She wants a hammer and a saw for presents
Internal Response	Goal	4. Then she could make a coat rack
Internal Response	Goal	5. and fix her doll house
Attempt	Action	6. She asked her father
Internal Response	Goal	7. to get them for her
Internal Response	Goal	8. Her father did not want to get them for her
Internal Response	Cognition	9. He did not think that girls should play with a hammer and a saw
Internal Response	Goal	10. But he wanted to get her something
Direct Consequence	Action	11. So he bought her a beautiful new dress
Internal Response	Affect	12. Judy liked the dress
Internal Response	Goal	13. but she still wanted the hammer and the saw
Attempt	Action	14. Later she told her grandmother about her wish
Internal Response	Cognition	15. Her grandmother knew that Judy really wanted a hammer and a saw
Internal Response	Goal	16. She decided to get them for her
Internal Response	Cognition	17. because when Judy grows up
Internal Response	Cognition	18. and becomes a woman
Internal Response	Cognition	19. she will have to fix things
Internal Response	Cognition	20. when they break
Attempt	Action	21. Then her grandmother went out that very day
Direct Consequence	Action	22. and bought the tools for Judy
Direct Consequence	Action	23. She gave them to Judy that night
Reaction	Affect	24. Judy was very happy
Reaction	Cognition	25. Now she could build things with her hammer and saw

FIG. 8. Text of Story 4: *Judy's Birthday.*

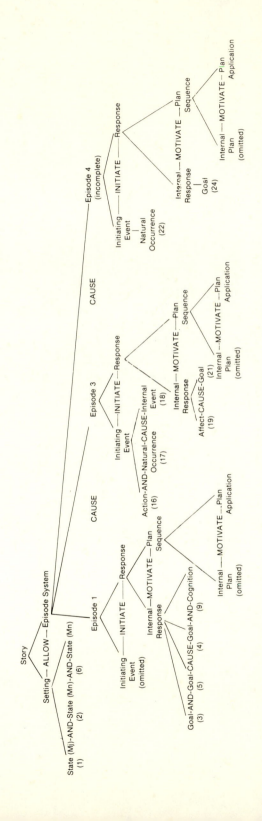

84

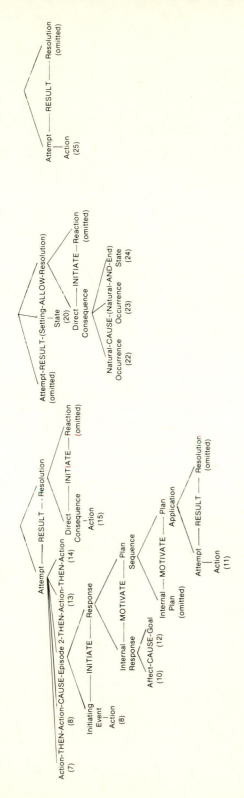

FIG. 9. Tree structure for Story 3: *The Fox and Bear*.

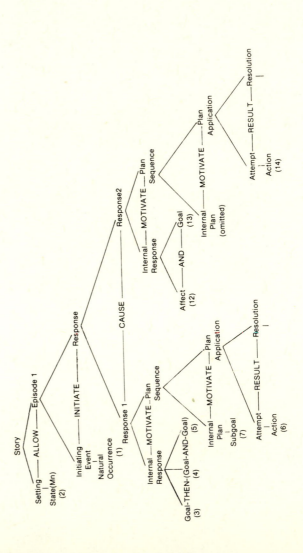

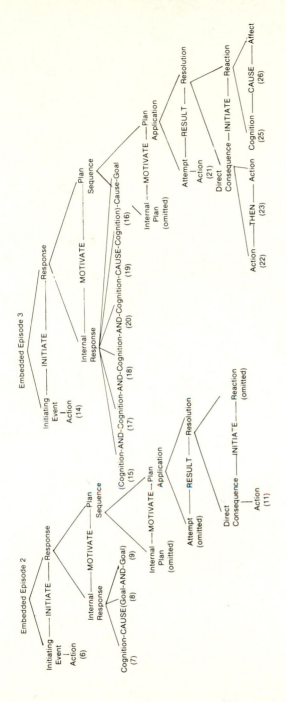

FIG. 10. Tree structure for Story 4: *Judy's Birthday*.

One week later, the child was tested again. He was asked to recall both stories he had heard in any order he could. This procedure was adopted so that the child would receive no information concerning either story.

Data Analyses

Each individual protocol was scored for the total number of accurately recalled units. The criterion for inclusion in the accurate recall measure was based on the semantic content of a base level statement. For example, in the Epaminondas story, many children said, "the sun was real hot and melted the butter." Credit was given for both base statements, "the sun was shining hard," and "the butter had all melted." Again, each protocol was scored by two people. Interrater reliability on scoring items as correctly recalled was above 93% on all four stories.

Results

Accurate Recall Performance

Because there was no a priori reason to predict story differences, each subject received a composite score by combining the total number of accurately recalled statements from both stories and then converting this to a proportion score. A three-way analysis of variance was then performed on this score with grade (1st, 5th) and story (Stories 1 and 2; Stories 3 and 4) as between-subject factors. Time (immediate, delayed) was the within-subject factor. All three main effects were significant. The interaction between time and story was significant, $F(1,44) = 9.46, p < .01$, and more importantly, the grade by time by story interaction was significant, $F(1,44) = 6.72, p < .02$, indicating that the stories were recalled differently as a result of grade and time conditions. Therefore, a separate two-way analysis of variance was completed on each of the four stories. In these analyses, grade was the between-subject variable and time was the within-subject variable. The mean proportion of accurate recall and significance levels for each story is presented in Table 1.

There were no significant grade by time interactions in three of the four stories. In these three stories, grade was a significant variable, with fifth graders recalling a greater proportion of statements than first graders. Time was also a significant variable for two of the three stories; more statements were recalled immediately after presentation than one week later.

In the fourth story, *Judy's Birthday*, time was also a significant factor. However, a significant grade by time interaction occurred. Newman-Keuls tests revealed a significant grade effect on immediate recall, with fifth graders

TABLE 1
Mean Proportion of Total Accurate Recall

A. Grade and Time

Story	Grade Comparisons			Time Comparisons		
	Grade 1	Grade 5	$F(1,22)$	Time 1	Time 2	$F(1,22)$
Group 1 n = 24						
Epaminondas	.47	.65	13.8[a]	.57	.51	ns
Tiger's Whisker	.48	.58	4.3[b]	.55	.50	6.8[a]
Group 2 n = 24						
Fox and Bear	.42	.51	6.0[c]	.51	.42	21.4[a]
Judy's Birthday	.47	.54	ns	.56	.45	27.2[a]

B. Grade by Time Interaction[d] for *Judy's Birthday* (n = 24)

	Grade 1	Grade 5
Time 1	.50	.62
Time 2	.44	.48

[a] $p < .001$.
[b] $p < .05$.
[c] $p < .01$.
[d] $F(1,22) = 5.6, p < .02$.

recalling more information on immediate recall than first graders ($p < .01$), and no grade differences on delayed recall.

In summary, all four stories showed a significant grade effect on immediate recall and three of the four stories showed this effect on delayed recall. Time was a significant variable for three of the four stories, with a greater proportion of units recalled in the immediate condition than in the delayed condition.

The recall data from each subject were then grouped according to the seven categories specified in the grammar: major setting statements, minor setting statements, initiating events, internal responses, attempts, direct consequences, and reactions. Each subject received seven scores, each signifying the proportion of statements recalled in each of the seven categories. Because only two stories contained internal plans, the internal plan statements were included in the internal response category for all analyses. A separate analysis of variance was completed for each of the seven category scores with grade as the between subject variable and time as the within subject variable. All stories were analyzed separately. The results were quite variable. The only category which showed significant grade effects in all four stories was the

TABLE 2
Mean Proportion of Accurately Recalled Internal Response
Statement for Each of the Four Stories

| Story | Grades | | Significance Level |
	1	5	
Epaminondas	.08	.35	$F(1,22) = 5.07, p < .05$
Tiger's Whisker	.28	.45	$F(1,22) = 10.09, p < .01$
Fox and Bear	.28	.44	$F(1,22) = 5.09, p < .05$
Judy's Birthday	.42	.54	$F(1,22) = 4.14, p < .05$

internal response category. Fifth-grade children recalled significantly more internal responses than first-grade children. The mean proportion of internal response statements recalled in each grade level is presented in Table 2.

The internal response category was also the only category which varied systematically over time. More internal responses were recalled at time 1 than at time 2 in three of the four stories. The mean proportion of internal responses recalled on immediate testing was .47 while the mean proportion on time 2 was .33. The level of significance for all three stories was at the $p < .05$ level. The recall of this category did not decrease significantly in Story 1, *Epaminondas*. The significance of this finding must be evaluated in terms of an increase in internal responses in the new information which children added to stories. The contrast in these two findings will be discussed in another section.

Relative Saliency of Each Individual Statement

The frequency of recall of each individual statment in each story was determined and a rank order of the items, proceeding from the best recalled item to the worst recalled item, was constructed for each grade level and each time condition. Spearman rank order correlations were then performed to assess the degree of relationship between grade levels and between time conditions. The correlations ranged from .84 to .98 for grade comparisons and from .91 to .99 for time comparisons. Although there was some degree of variation over the four stories, each correlation was highly significant, indicating that the extent to which an item is recalled is highly stable over time and between grade levels.

Relative Salience of the Informational Categories

Because the relative salience of the individual statements in a story did not vary significantly with either time or grade, the recall frequencies of each of the statements were collapsed across all four conditions. The combined recall scores for each story were then clustered according to category membership, producing a single frequency score for each category. The category frequencies were then converted to proportion scores. Rank orders for each story were then constructed with the best remembered category having the lowest rank and the worst remembered category having the highest rank. Table 3 presents the category ranks for each of the four stories.

The degree of similarity in the rank orderings was extremely high. A Kendall's coefficient of concordance was computed to assess the degree of relationship in the rank orders across all four stories; the coefficient is .84 which is highly significant ($p < .01$).

In all stories, the major setting category was the best remembered. Initiating events and direct consequences are always the next best remembered categories. The difference between the proportions of items recalled in these two categories was, for most stories, very small. The attempt category was fourth in all of the ranks except for one story, *The Tiger's Whisker*. In this story, the attempt category was fifth. Internal responses and minor setting categories were always recalled in the last three positions in the rank order. The exact position of the reaction category varied from fourth to seventh place. This category had a higher degree of variation than all other categories.

In order to more accurately assess the degree of recall variation in each category, the frequency distribution of statements within each category was examined. All of the informational items were divided into thirds according to how well they were recalled, from the third best remembered items to the third least well remembered items. The proportion of each category recalled in each third was then determined and these proportions are presented in Table 4.

TABLE 3
Rank Order of Categories for Four Stories[a]

Category	Story 1 Epaminondas	Story 2 Tiger's Whisker	Story 3 Fox and Bear	Story 4 Judy's Birthday
Major setting	1	1	1	1
Direct consequence	2	3	2	2
Initiating event	3	2	3	3
Attempt	4	5	4	4
Reaction	5	4	–	7
Minor setting	6	7	6	5
Internal response	7	6	5	6

[a]Ranks are integrated over grade and time conditions with best remembered items having the lowest ranks and worst remembered items having the highest ranks.

TABLE 4
Distribution of Category Variation for Four Stories[a]

Category	Top Third	Middle Third	Bottom Third	Number of Statements in Each Category
Major setting	1.00	0	0	3
Minor setting	0	.71	.29	7
Initiating event	.63	.13	.25	8
Internal response	.10	.31	.59	39
Attempt	.53	.16	.32	19
Direct consequence	.87	.13	0	15
Reaction	.22	.56	.22	9

[a]The proportion of each category recalled in the top third, middle third, or bottom third of the distribution.

Major setting statements and consequence statements were almost always found in the top third of the distribution. A few consequence statements were present in the second third of the distribution. The majority of initiating events are also in the top third of the distribution. There is a greater degree of variation in this category than in either the Major Setting or Consequence categories. This finding is also true for the Attempt category. The majority of Minor Setting statements and Reaction statements are found in the middle third of the distribution. The only category which is not well represented in the top two-thirds of the distribution is the Internal Response category. This category, however, contained 39 statements summed over the four stories and is the most diverse category in the grammar. It contains internal events, goals, affects, cognitions, and plans. The types of internal responses which were represented in the top third of the distribution were the major goal of the main character. In the three stories which contained major goals, these statements were extremely well recalled and were always in the top third of the rank orderings. This finding suggests that major goal statements may be remembered differently from other types of statements in the Internal Response category.

Transformations of the Original Story Material

Very few statements in the stories were recalled exactly as presented in the original story versions. Certain types of tranformations occurred regularly in all protocols. These transformations included substitution of words, deletions, and additions of information within statements. The most common transformations were verb substitutions. These substitutions occurred in 60% of all statements recalled in the four stories. Children substituted verbs such as went for ran, broke for cracked, told for warned, etc. In almost all cases, verb substitutions involved the replacement of the original verb with one that shared some meaning with the original but was semantically less complex.

Deletions and additions of information also occurred. The three types of information which were deleted most frequently were adverbs, adjectives, and prepositional phrases. For example, in *The Fox and the Bear,* children heard the statement, "they decided to catch a chicken for supper." Ninety-one percent of all children who recalled this statement deleted "for supper." Another example can be taken from *The Fox and Bear.* Children heard the statement, "the fox then opened the door of the henhouse very carefully." In over 50% of the protocols in which this unit was recalled, the children simply said, "the fox opened the door." They did not specify which door he opened or how he opened it. When "where," "how," or "when" information occurred in the stories, it was deleted from recall over 50% of the time. Adjectives like "new" and "beautiful" were also deleted consistently. However, additions did occur in the recalls and most involved new adjectives. For example, in *The Tiger's Wisker,* 32% of all subjects said that the tiger was not only lonely but that he was also old and poor.

One type of substitution occurred only in first-grade recalls. Ten percent of the children had difficulty remembering exactly who was the main character in a story. The two stories that presented the most difficulty in this regard were *The Fox and Bear* and *The Tiger's Whisker.* In *The Fox and Bear,* some children confused the actions of the fox and the bear or substituted another animal for the bear. In *The Tiger's Whisker,* the most common error was the substitution of a lion for the tiger. These character substitutions, however, did not detract from the production of a well organized story. In addition, these types of substitution errors were virtually absent from fifth-grade protocols.

One major type of transformation occurred in all of the protocols at both grade levels. Over 50% of all internal responses recalled were produced in an active form by changing the internal response of a character to an action on the part of the character. A clear example of this phenomenon is taken from the story, *Judy's Birthday.* This story had many statements which described the goals and thoughts of both Judy's father and grandmother. If children recalled these statements, they did so by having the father and grandmother tell Judy about their thoughts or feelings. An example from one protocol is:

> When Judy told her grandmother about what she wanted, her grandmother said to her; "I understand. I'll get them for you because you'll need them when you get to be a woman."

Thus, not only did this subject integrate and delete information but he also externalized the grandmother's thoughts by providing a conversational exchange between the two characters.

Additions of New Categories

The number of category additions was tabulated for each subject. In order to receive credit for including new category information, subjects had to add information which was not similar to the story content in any form. An example of entirely new information added is taken from two fifth-grade protocols. When these two subjects recalled *The Fox and Bear,* both children added new information at the beginning and at the end of the story. Both subjects stated that the fox and the bear were very hungry and had to find something to eat. Then they continued on with the remainder of the story. As they approached the end, both said that the farmer was very angry and was going to shoot the two animals. These two protocols each contained four new category additions.

An analysis of variance was completed on the total number of category additions with grade and time as treatment variables. Each story was analyzed separately. The mean number of additions per story is presented in Table 5. In three of the four stories, fifth-grade children included significantly more new category information in their recalls than first-grade children. In one story, Judy's Birthday, there were no differences between the two grades. Time was a significant variable for only one story, *Judy's Birthday.* In this story, all subjects added significantly more new information to recall in the delayed condition than in the immediate time condition. There were no significant interactions between time and grade for any story.

The inferences almost always made sense within the story; they provided logical links between information that had been explicitly given. For example, in *The Tiger's Whisker,* the character's main goal stated in the story was "to make a medicine for her husband." Many subjects, especially fifth-grade children, inserted the primary goal "to cure her husband" or "to make him feel better." In addition, the story did not include information about the lady's activities after she cut off the tiger's whisker. Almost all fifth-grade

TABLE 5

Mean Numbers of New Categories Added to Each Story by Grade Level and Time Condition

Story	Grade 1	Grade 5	Time 1	Time 2
1. *Epaminondas*	1.04[a]	2.75	1.75	1.91
2. *Tiger's Whisker*	1.02[b]	2.87	1.95	2.12
3. *Fox and Bear*	1.83[b]	3.79	2.45	3.16
4. *Judy's Birthday*	2.80	1.98	1.95[c]	2.58

[a] $p < .01$.
[b] $p < .001$.
[c] $p < .05$.

children completed the lady's episode by stating, "she cut off the tiger's whisker, ran home, and made the medicine for her husband."

The same type of additions were found in *The Fox and Bear*. In the original version, there was no initiating event in the beginning of the first episode. In the protocols, 33% of the first-grade protocols and 75% of the fifth-grade protocols included information that preceded the decision to kill a chicken for supper. Most children said, "the fox and the bear were really hungry." A couple said, "they hadn't eaten for days and they needed something to eat."

The categories most frequently added to the story recalls were internal responses and attempts. Forty-one percent of all new categories were internal responses and 37% were attempts. The next largest category added was the consequence category which consisted of 18% of the new responses. The remainder of the new information was distributed among the setting, initiating event, and reaction categories.

The fact that internal responses were consistently added to recall protocols is extremely important because in assessing accurate recall the internal response category was among the least well recalled categories. This discrepancy between the two findings indicates that chidren are very aware of characters' feelings, thoughts, and goals. The child's comprehension of exactly what these internal feelings or motives are may be different from the internal responses given in the original story versions.

The type of new information added to stories was fairly consistent across grade level in three of the four stories. The only story which contained grade differences in the type of new information added in recall was Story 4, *Judy's Birthday*. First-grade children added twice as many activity statements as fifth-grade children did. However, fifth-grade children added almost three times as many internal responses as did first-grade children. The addition of internal responses explains some of the decrease in fifth-grade recall during the delayed condition. Fifth graders did in fact recall significantly fewer accurate, internal responses on delayed recall. However, this type of category did not decrease in saliency when new information was assessed. The only thing that changed was the semantic content of the internal responses. In the original story, Judy asked her father to get tools for her. The father's response in the original version is given in the next four lines:

1. Her father did not want to get them for her.
2. He did not think that girls should play with a hammer and a saw,
3. but he wanted to get her something.
4. So, he bought her a beautiful new dress.

An example of a fifth grader's recall of the father's response was:

1. Judy's father couldn't get her the tools.
2. He didn't want her to get hurt,

3. because kids can get cut when they play with sharp things.
4. He knew she would be disappointed.
5. So he thought he'd get her something very special.
6. So he bought her a pretty dress.

Thus, children recalled as many internal responses as were in the original story version but added new information which they had inferred from the original story.

The fact that younger children added more new attempt categories than older indicates that first-grade children are capable of adding new information. Younger chlidren may have a more restricted range in terms of the amount and/or the types of new information which they can generate.

Temporal Sequencing Errors in Accurate Recall

The degree to which children were able to recall the story information in its original sequence was examined.

A rank order index was constructed in which the order of an individual subject's recall was compared to the order of the items in the original story structure. Three types of temporal reversals were classified as errors in this rank ordering: (1) intercategory reversals, (2) intracategory reversals, and (3) reversals occurring within a single statement. A Spearman rank order correlation was computed for each individual subject, and then subject means were tabulated for each grade level and each time condition. An analysis of variance was not performed on these data because the number of items recalled by each subject was extremely variable. The mean correlations were used simply as an index of temporal sequencing of story information. They are presented in Table 6.

All of the correlation coefficients were above .92 with one exception (.81). The relationship between the subjects' sequence of information and the

TABLE 6
Correlations for the Degree of Relationship Between the Temporal
Sequence of Statement in the Original Story Structure and the
Temporal Sequence Recalled by Children

	Time 1		Time 2	
Story	Grade 1	Grade 5	Grade 1	Grade 5
Epaminondas	.97	.99	.95	.99
Tiger's Whisker	.81	.99	.93	.99
Fox and Bear	.97	.95	.93	.96
Judy's Birthday	.92	.97	.97	.97

original story presentations was extremely high in all cases. The three types of temporal sequencing errors were then analyzed separately.

An intercategory error was defined as the temporal reversal of two statements from different categories. The percentage of intercategory errors for all four stories was minimal. Only 7% of all statements recalled in the four stories contained intercategory reversals. In addition, 75% of all reversals could be predicted from the proposed tree structures of each story diagrammed in Fig. 2 suggesting that the external structure matched the internal schema. Three of the four original story versions contained statements that were reversed when compared to their position in the tree structure. An example of temporal disorganization occurring in the presented version of a story can be seen in *The Tiger's Whisker*. The initiating event, which should occur immediately after the major setting statement, does not occur until the character's major goals are presented. The tree structure which represents the hypothesized internal structure of the subject in recalling the story reverses the order of the initiating event. Almost all intercategory errors in this story occurred when subjects recalled the initiating event before any of the internal response statements. A similar finding occurred in *The Fox and the Bear*. In the original story, the minor setting statement, "they both liked fried chicken," occurred between a goal and an action statement. Several children reversed the position of the minor setting statement in story recall and stated the information immediately after the major setting statement.

The remainder of intercategory errors occurred when two characters were interacting with one another. In *Epaminondas,* the major intercategory reversal occurred when children inserted the first action statement between the first two initiating events. An example of this reversal was: "the mother told him to take some cake to his grandmother. He put the cake in a leaf under his arm. Then she warned him to hold it carefully." The same type of reversal occurred in the fourth story, *Judy's Birthday*. Several children stated the direct consequence, "she gave them to Judy that night," and then stated, "she (grandmother) told Judy she would need them when she grew up." Thus, they reversed the order of the consequence statement and one statement from the internal response category.

The number of intracategory errors occurring in recalls was also measured. An intracategory error was defined as to the reversal of two statements within the same category. The two stories that produced the most intracategory errors were *Epaminondas* and *The Tiger's Whisker*. Only 5% of all the information recalled included intracategory errors. Two types of intra-category errors occurred. Children either reversed entire statements within a category or they deleted part of a statement and put the remainder after the second statement in the category. The second type of intracategory error occurred most frequently in *Epaminondas*. Children reversed the first two attempt statements by stating that the boy carried the cake in a leaf under his arm. This type of error is similar to a truncation error in which subjects delete information in order to make their productions less redundant.

The third type of temporal sequencing error, within statement reversals, occurred in 11% of the protocols. This error occurred primarily when children inverted the order of temporal markers included in a statement. One statement which contained consistent reversals was, "she (grandmother) went out that day." Subjects often stated, "that day she went out." With the exception of these types of reversals, subjects maintained the correct position of the information within statements.

Discussion

The first aim of the present study was to examine the effects of age and time on the recall and organization of stories. Significant developmental differences occurred on three measures: (1) total recall, (2) recall of internal responses, and (3) the number of inferences added to recall. Fifth-grade children included more of each type of information on recall than first graders did. These results were similar to the findings in our initial study (Stein & Glenn, 1975). The developmental increase found in the number of recalled internal responses is consistent with the results reported by Flappan (1968) in her work on children's understanding of social interactions. She found that older children stated more information concerning the intentions and motives of movie characters than did younger children. It may be that older children are more aware of the causal significance of intentional information and therefore include this type of information more systematically in the retelling of a story. However, the recall data in the present study do not indicate whether first-grade children encoded this information less often or whether they simply failed to include it in their recalls.

In contrast to the developmental differences found in the total amount of accurate information recalled, no significant age differences occurred in either the pattern of saliency or in the temporal organization of information in recall. The relative saliency of each informational statement was highly consistent across both grade and time conditions. This result is consistent with the findings from earlier studies on adult organization of recall (Bartlett, 1932; Johnson, 1970). This consistency in recall demonstrates that specific items clearly differ in terms of their importance in the organization and production of story material.

Developmental differences were not found when the temporal organization of story recall was examined. Children's sequencing of story information corresponded closely to the temporal sequence of items in the original stories. This contradicts the findings of Piaget (1960) who found that six- to eight-year-old children's recall of stories was poorly organized. In his studies of temporal sequencing errors were quite frequent, and several children were unable to produce the logical structure of a story. The differences between Piaget's results and ours may be due to differences in story complexity. While both his stories and ours were relatively short, our stories were more simply constructed in terms of the syntax of the sentences; the inclusion of temporal markers such as one day, later, then, and the logical organization of categories. Not surprisingly, the issue of story complexity is critical in the examination of temporal sequencing abilities. However, our results demonstrate that children as young as six are capable of organizing and temporally sequencing story information in simply constructed narratives.

Brown (1975) has examined young children's ability to temporally organize a series of pictorial events. She found that both five- and seven-year-old children experienced difficulty in reconstructing and recalling series of pictures when the descriptions of the pictures did not include specific causal relations relating the two pictures. However, when her verbal description of the items did include such relations, the ability to reconstruct the items improved significantly in both age groups of children. Although the younger children still had difficulty recalling the correct temporal order, recall greatly improved in the older chlidren. These findings further emphasize the importance of causal relations to constructing an accurate temporal sequence.

The effect of time was significant for three of the four stories. More accurate infromation was included in the immediate recall condition than in the delayed testing condition. In addition, the amount of new information added in recall significantly increased over a week's period of time in one of the four stories. This provides some support for one of Bartlett's original hypotheses. He argued that the listener develops a general idea of the whole story. Over time memory for specific details decreases. However the gist or theme of the story remains. The subject simply replaces the lost or nonretrievable information with inferred information which is consistent with the original story structure. A model of story comprehension will have to include rules which describe and predict the creation of new information occurring in recall. Certain types of inferences can be predicted from the rules described in our grammar. These predictions will be discussed in the final section.

The second aim of this study was to examine the category distinctions formulated in the grammar. The results from the present study were highly consistent with our original results (Stein & Glenn, Note 1). In all four stories, the seven categories differed in saliency of recall. The relative salience of each category was highly consistent across stories, grade levels, and time conditions. Major settings, consequences, and initiating events were the most frequently recalled categories. The remaining categories in terms of their recall frequencies were: attempts, reactions, minor settings, and internal responses. Although internal responses were frequently deleted, the primary goal of the protagonist was always well recalled. Furthermore, the majority of inferences were internal responses. This indicates that internal responses may be more important in the production of a story than their rank order suggest.

The fact that category membership did predict the saliency of an item indicates that listeners make distinctions between different types of information and that their distinctions correspond to some degree with the category distinctions made in the grammar. The differences in category saliency show that certain categories are structurally more important in the production of story recall. Subjects may use major settings, initiating events, major goals, and consequence statements as "markers" to generate story recall. Although these four categories may be critical in the production of stories, their saliency does not indicate whether or not other types of information are encoded less frequently.

Although category membership is predictive of item saliency, there was wide variation of item recall in certain categories and little in others. For example, attempt statements were scattered throughout the recall frequencies. This finding indicates that factors other than category membership influence how well an item will be recalled. One factor regulating the saliency of a particular item may be the degree to which the information in the item matches the subject's expectations of what should occur. For example, in Story 3, *The Fox and Bear,* one sequence of events occurring in the original story version was: the fox opened the door of the henhouse very carefully, he grabbed a chicken and killed it. The attempt statement of opening the door was not well recalled. Instead, most subjects inserted the statement, "The fox went into the henhouse." Apparently the act of going into the henhouse was more important in the structural organization of story production than was the act of opening the door. Therefore subjects readily inferred and stated the former action even though it was not present in the original story version.

A second variable which might regulate item saliency in recall is informational redundancy. If the information in a statement is implied by or is an elaboration of a previous item, there may be no reason for a subject to include both of these statements in recall. The rules which determine these summarization processes are not included in our grammar. However, they are an integral part of any model of story comprehension and the development of these rules should be pursued.

The types of relations occurring between the statments within a category may also be a critical factor in predicting how many statements from each category are produced in recall. Subjects may recall only item sequences that are connected by direct causal links. This hypothesis may be particularly valid when several statements occur within one category.

In summary, the results from this first study provide evidence for the usefulness of the story schema for defining the information contained in stories and for predicting the relative importance of various categories of information in recall. A more complete discussion of the use of the schema as a theoretical model will be presented in the conclusion section.

EXPERIMENT 2

The main purpose of Experiment 2 was to investigate aspects of story processing that could not be assessed with recall measures. Two tasks were used. The first concerned the types of information which children judge to be important or critical in each of the stories. The second task concerned the collection of data to determine the comprehension of causal relations both within episodes and between episodes. Probe questions were constructed to investigate children's perceptions of the reasons for the occurrence of certain events in each story. More specifically, the probe questions were used to assess children's comprehension of events connected by the CAUSE relation in each story. While both of these tasks force a child to rely on his memory for story information, they may require the use of different retrieval strategies than those found in recall. Therefore, certain types of information which were not included in recall may be produced during these tasks.

The purpose of the importance of judgments was twofold. The first was to determine the degree of correspondence between the information that children considered to be the most important and the information recalled most frequently in Experiment 1. When subjects are asked for the most important information in stories, the types of information they produce may be quite different from the information most frequently produced in recalling a story. Asking for judgments of importance may encourage more inferential thinking and may tap children's interpretations of the story events to a greater degree than the recall task does. The second purpose of this task was to examine possible developmental differences in children's criteria of importance information.

The probe questions focused on the types of causal relations children perceive between items. While the high accuracy of temporal sequencing found in the recall data indicate that both first- and fifth-grade children organize information in a consistent and similar fashion, the data do not indicate whether any developmental differences are present in the perception of the types of relations linking categories or episodes. By asking questions which focus directly upon the types of relations occurring in the story, developmental differences occurring in the perception of causality can be investigated.

Method

Subjects

Subjects were a group of 24 different children from the same upper-middle-class school used in Experiment 1. An equal number of first- and fifth-grade children participated in the study. The subject pool in each grade was divided equally by sex. The mean ages in each group were: 6 years, 3 months for first grade and 10 years, 5 months for fifth grade.

Materials

The identical four stories used in Experiment 1 were used in this study. A set of 12 or 13 probe questions was constructed for each story. The questions were written to assess children's comprehension of causal relations which either connect statements within an episode or statements that connect two episodes. The probes were phrased as a series of WHY questions. For example, the specific probe questions used for *The Tiger's Whisker* story were:

1. Why did the lady need a tiger's whisker?
2. Why was the lady afraid?
3. Why did the lady need to make a medicine?
4. Why did the lady decide to use a trick?
5. Why did the lady go to the tiger's cave?
6. Why did the lady sing a song and give the tiger food?
7. Why did the tiger come out of his cave?
8. Why did the tiger eat the food?
9. Why did the tiger walk over to the lady?
10. Why did the tiger thank the lady?
11. Why did the lady cut off the tiger's whisker?
12. Why did the lady run down the hill quickly?
13. Why did the tiger feel lonely and sad at the end of the story?

Design and Procedure

The 24 children were divided by grade level into two equal groups. All children were tested individually and each child heard all four stories. The stories were presented in a random sequence to each child. Before each story delivery, the child was told to listen very carefully so that he could answer questions about the story when the experimenter finished the delivery. The experimenter then proceeded to read the first story to the child. Immediately afterward, the 20-second delay occurred. During this time lapse, each fifth-grade child participated in a backward counting task. Each first-grade child simply counted to 20. Then the child was asked to tell the experimenter the one thing that happened in the story that was the most important thing to remember. After the child replied, the experimenter asked the child to recall the second most important thing and then the third most important thing. After the child answered the three questions, the experimenter proceeded to read the next story and then asked the child the identical questions for the second story. The identical procedure was employed until data had been collected on all four stories.

The decision to ask children for three important events was based on pilot data. First-grade children had great difficulty producing more than three pieces of information they considered to be important. In addition, we felt that the primary function of this task was to determine the types of information that were at the top of the hierarchy in terms of importance to the child.

After importance information had been collected on all four stories, the experimenter asked the child the probe questions for each of the four stories. The experimenter began with the first story the child had heard and proceeded until the data had been collected for all four stories. The probe questions for each story were presented in a random sequence. As in Experiment 1, two experimenters tested the children in each age group to control for experimenter bias.

Results

Importance Task

The importance judgments were first divided into informational statements. Fifth graders consistently produced more statements per importance judgment than the first graders did. First graders generally gave a single statement response while fifth graders gave an average of two statements per response. The difference between grade levels was significant for all four stories; the mean number of statements ranged from 1.0 to 1.17 for first graders and from 1.89 to 2.00 for fifth graders.

Fifth graders often connected their statements with causal or temporal connectors, such as: because, so that, and then, in order to, etc. These types of connectors almost never appeared in first grade responses. For example, in the Fox and Bear story, many children gave the "roof breaking" as one of the most important events in the story. When first-grade children produced this item, they generally gave it alone. However, when fifth-grade children mentioned this event, their statements included several other events. One fifth-grade response was "the bear made the roof cave in because of his weight and that killed some chickens."

The data from the three importance judgments were then divided into two groups: the information that actually occurred in the original story version and the information that was inferred from the original story content. Approximately 25% of the importance judgments from each grade level were inferred. There were no significant differences between grade levels nor were there any significant variations due to story.

The accurate importance judgments were then partitioned into single category statements and classified according to the categories postulated in the grammar. Each of the three judgments was analyzed separately. The data were collapsed across stories because the pattern of importance judgments did not vary significantly across the four stories. The total percentage of accurate responses per category for each of the judgments is presented in Table 7. The sum of the percentages in each column can exceed 100 because some responses included statements from two categories and were counted twice.

When the first importance judgments were examined, grade differences were found in the types of information children considered to be most important. First graders mentioned direct consequences proportionately more often than any other category. Internal responses were mentioned second and initiating events were mentioned third. Fifth graders gave proportionately more internal responses than any other category in their first judgments. Initiating events were mentioned second and consequences were mentioned third.

Proportion tests were completed to examine the differences between grades in each of the categories. Significant differences were found in the internal response and consequence categories. Fifth graders included significantly more internal responses than first graders in their first importance judgments

TABLE 7

Proportion of Accurate Responses Occurring in Each Category on Each of the Three Importance Judgments

Category	1st Judgment		2nd Judgment		3rd Judgment	
	Grade 1	Grade 5	Grade 1	Grade 5	Grade 1	Grade 5
Minor setting	.02	.08	.03	.02	.00	.06
Initiating event	.20	.21	.08	.04	.07	.04
Internal response	$.29^a$	.63	$.26^b$	.48	.26	.23
Attempt	.12	.06	$.13^b$	.31	.11	.27
Direct consequence	$.37^b$	.17	$.50^a$	.21	.44	.54
Reaction	.02	.04	.00	.06	.07	.13

$^a p < .01.$
$^b p < .05.$

while first graders included proportionally more consequence statements than fifth graders in their first importance judgments.

The same developmental differences were found on the second judgments. The only major difference between the first and second judgments was the increase in the number of attempt statements in the fifth-grade responses. It should be noted that when fifth graders included an attempt statement, it was generally causally related to either an internal response or to a consequence statement. There were no significant differences between first and fifth graders on the third judgments.

The accurate statements given in the three importance judgments were then compared to the information that was most frequently recalled in the stories in Experiment 1. The importance task was not a standard ranking task in which subjects had to rank order all information in the story according to their conception of importance. Therefore, the importance data were compared with the items in the top third of the frequency ranks from each of the four stories.

A slight grade difference was apparent in the degree of overlap between the two tasks. Approximately 60% of all items mentioned in the fifth-grade importance judgments appeared in the top third of the recall items, whereas 76% of all first-grade judgments appeared in the top third or recall. The differences between the two measures were primarily due to the fact that internal responses were mentioned proportionally more in the importance judgments than they had been in recall. This was particularly true of fifth-grade responses. In addition, major settings and initiating events which were almost always found in the top of the recall frequencies were included infrequently in the importance judgments. The discrepancies between the two measures show that neither recall nor importance judgments alone indicates the structural importance of a category in the organization of stories. Furthermore, although subjects may initially organize story information in a consistent fashion independent of the specific task demands, the task demands do alter the type of information retrieved by subjects at both grade levels.

The last analysis on the importance judgments focused on the inferences that were included in the judgments. The new information was classified into two types of responses: those responses that included the moral lesson of the story and those responses that were simple category additions or elaborations.

In Story 1, *Epaminondas,* 95% of the additions referred to either the moral lesson of the story or to a summary statement of the entire story. Examples of moral lesson statements were "different things should be carried in different ways" or "he should always cover the butter if the sun was shining." In Story 4, *Judy's Birthday*, 61% of the additions were moral lessons such as: "the important thing to remember is that her grandmother really understood her feelings." The inferences in the other two stories were primarily category additions such as new goals explaining a character's behavior in more detail or new consequence statements. For example, in *The Tiger's Whisker,* some children said that the most important thing was that "she got back to her husband safely," or that "the tiger didn't get mad at the lady because he understood her."

Analysis of Probe Questions

The responses to probe questions were first classified into three categories: nonresponses, errors, and correct responses. Children's answers were classified as errors when they clearly contradicted the original story information. Both the error rate and the number of nonresponses were extremely low in both age groups. In the first grade, 12% of the responses were classified as errors and 7% were classified as nonresponses. Only 2% of the fifth-grade responses were erroneous and 4% of the probes remained unanswered. The majority of erroneous responses occurred in Story 3, *The Fox and the Bear;* 72% of all first-grade errors and 59% of all fifth-grade errors were found in this story.

The number of accurate statements that were given in response to each probe question was then tabulated. Fifth graders gave significantly more statements per probe question than did first graders (1.56 for fifth graders versus 1.06 for first graders, $p < .01$). The multiple statement responses were generally linked by either CAUSE or AND relations. An example of a multiple response from the Judy story occurred in response to the question, "why did the grandmother buy Judy the tools"; several fifth graders replied, "she bought them because she knew Judy wanted the tools and because it was her birthday." The first reason is an internal response and the second is an initiating event. The two statements are related to each other by an AND relation and both are causally related to the grandmother's behavior, which is classified as a direct consequence. In contrast to this type of reply, first-grade responses generally contained only one reason for the occurrence of a specific event.

An analysis was then performed on the types of information given in response to probes. First, each probe question was classified according to the categories of the model. Then the responses to each of the questions were classified according to category type. Two separate analyses were performed: the first concerned the probe questions constructed to measure perceived causality between two episodes; the second concerned probe questions designed to measure perceived causality between statements within an episode. Each type of relation will be considered seprately.

Relations Between Episodes

In the four stories used in this experiment all of the interepisodic relations were causal. There were two types of episodes in the stories; embedded episodes and nonembedded episodes. Questions were constructed to elicit the types of connections which children perceived between both embedded and non-embedded episodes.

Three stories contained embedded episodes. Both *The Tiger's Whisker* and *The Fox and the Bear* contained one embedded episode; *Judy's Birthday* contained two such episodes. In both *The Tiger's Whisker* and *Judy's Birthday*, the embedded episodes occurred as the direct result of the characters' attempts to obtain his or her goal. In both of these stories the main character was dependent upon a second character to achieve his or her goal. In the Fox and the Bear story, an embedded episode was the result of the bear formulating a second goal before the resolution of his primary goal. In all three stories the embedded episode occurred as a result of one of the character's attempts. Therefore, the responses to the probe questions should contain an attempt as the causal factor. The proportion of responses which contained the correct causal event for the occurrence of each of the embedded episodes is presented in Table 8.

All children in both grades produced the correct reason for the occurrence of three of the four embedded episodes. The only embedded episode which caused any difficulty was the bear's behavioral sequence in Story 3, *The Fox and Bear*. Only 58% of the fifth graders and 42% of the first graders gave correct responses in reply to the probe question, "Why did the bear feel lazy?" Correct responses to this question included replies such as "he was tired from running so fast" or "he was lazy because he didn't sleep enough before he ran."

TABLE 8
Proportion of Subjects Who Produced Causal References in
Reply to Probe Questions Concerning the Relationship
Between Episodes

	Grade 1	Grade 5
Embedded Episodes (N = 4)		
Tiger's Whisker (N = 1)	1.00	1.00
Fox Bear (N = 1)	.58	.42
Judy's Birthday (N = 2)	1.00	1.00
Nonembedded Episodes (N = 5)		
Epaminondas (N = 2)	.37[a]	1.00
Fox and Bear (N = 3)	1.00	1.00

[a] $p < .001$.

The remainder of the children at each grade level did not know why the bear felt lazy.

The remaining questions concerned the perception of causality between nonembedded episodes. Three nonembedded episodes were present in Story 3, *The Fox and Bear,* and two were present in Story 1, *Epaminondas.* The proportions of correct responses concerned the causal relations between each of two episodes are also presented in Table 8. All fifth graders gave correct responses to all probe questions. First graders had more difficulty with the first story *Epaminondas.* This story accounted for all of their errors. Two questions were asked to investigate the perception of causality between the Epaminondas episodes. The first was, "why did the boy want to be very careful with the butter?" and the second was, "why did he put the butter on top of his head?" In response to the first question, 16% of the first graders stated that Epaminondas didn't want to ruin it like the cake, 8% said he didn't want it to melt, 59% stated that he either wanted to eat something with it or that his mother wanted to make something with it, and 16% did not know why. Thus, 75% of the first-grade children gave no explicit causal reason which could be linked to any behavior in the previous episode. When responses to the second question were analyzed, 50% of the first graders responded by saying that he put the butter on top of his head because his grandmother told him to do that. The remainder of the children stated that he either wanted to get it home safely or that he did not know the sun was shining. Thus, 50% of the first-grade children did indicate that the grandmother's previous reaction caused the boy's subsequent behavior. However, these children remained convinced that the grandmother actually told the boy how to carry the butter rather than the cake.

The results from these two probe questions indicate that many of the first-grade children may not have perceived the relationship between the grandmother's reaction to the crumbled cake and the boy's subsequent attempt. Thus, for these children the two episodes would be linked by the THEN relation which implies no direct causality between the episodes, but indicates that one episode contains the necessary preconditions for the next episode to occur. In addition, the results indicate that the percentage of younger children who did perceive some type of causal relationship between the two episodes based their interpretation on incorrect data. This misperception was also reflected in the types of value judgments and inferences some children made at the end of the testing session. For example, one first-grade child commented on the story after task completion by saying that his mother shouldn't have called him a silly boy because he carried the butter the way his grandmother told him to. This comment indicates that the semantic content of the reaction was transformed to fit the child's expectations of what should have occurred in the story.

Intraepisodic Relations

The remainder of the probe questions concerned the perception of causal relations within an episode. The questions contained statements from four categories described in the grammar. These categories were: internal responses, attempts, consequences, and reactions. The one question concerning an internal plan was grouped with the internal response questions. An example of each type of probe question is listed below:

1. Internal Response: Why did the lady need a tiger's whisker?
2. Attempt: Why did Judy tell her grandmother about her wish?
3. Consequence: Why did the fox kill the chicken?
4. Reaction: Why did the tiger feel lonely and sad again?

Probe questions concerning the cause for major settings and initiating events were not included in these analyses. The major setting category has no causal event preceding it; therefore, the WHY question is inappropriate. Probes concerning initiating events in the beginning episode of each story were inappropriate for the same reason. Probe questions were constructed for initiating events occurring in the second and third episodes of stories, but these were used to assess the comprehension of causal relations between episodes.

The probe questions and the responses were classified according to category type. The data are presented according to the four types of probe questions asked.

(a) Internal Responses   In the story grammar, an internal response is caused by either an initiating event or another internal response. If a probe question is asked about the cause of an internal response which is logically preceded by another internal response, subjects' responses should include the statement of the immediately preceding internal response. In these types of questions the inclusion of an initiating event as a causal factor may depend upon the ability of the child to proceed in reverse fashion through a causal sequence. If, however, an internal response follows an initiating event, subjects' responses should include the event. Of the probe questions focusing on internal responses, 43% contained statements that directly followed the initiating event in the original story version. The remainder of the questions concerned internal responses which followed other internal response statements. The proportion of responses occurring in each of the categories is presented in Table 9. In this table, a distinction was made between responses containing only one informational category and those containing two

TABLE 9

Proportion of Correct Responses Occurring on Probe Questions: Responses Are Grouped by Informational Category

Categories Occurring in Responses	Categories Occurring in Probe Questions							
	Internal Response		Attempt		Consequence		Reaction	
	Grade 1	Grade 5	Grade 1	Grade 5	Grade 1	Grade 5	Grade 1	Grade 5
Minor setting	.08	.07	—	.01	.07	.13	—	—
Initiating event	.18	.10	.26	.19	.27	.09	—	—
Internal response	.63	.40	.67	.55	.39	.30	—	—
Attempt	—	—	—	—	.05	—	.20	.04
Consequence	—	—	—	—	.12	.13	.62	.52
Reaction	—	—	—	—	—	—	.07	.15
Initiating event + internal response	.01	.16	.03	.10	.01	.06	—	—
Internal response + internal response	.10	.23	.03	.12	.05	.20	—	—
Consequence + attempt	—	.04	.01	.03	.01	.03	.11	.29
Internal response + setting	—	.04	—	—	—	.02	—	—
Attempt + setting	—	—	—	—	.03	.04	—	—

categories. The former are presented first in the table while the combination responses are given below them.

When the responses were analyzed, internal responses and events were the most frequently included categories. Sixty-nine percent of the fifth-grade responses and 74% of the first-grade responses contained internal responses; event statements were found in 19 and 26% of the fifth- and first-grade responses, respectively. Event statements were included less often than would be expected. There may be two reasons for this. First, the original story versions did not contain the highest order goal which was the immediate result of the event. Subjects often gave a higher order goal rather than an initiating event. An example of this occurred in *The Tiger's Whisker*. When subjects were asked why the lady needed to make a medicine for her husband, only 30% of the first-grade children and 75% of the fifth-grade children gave the initiating event, i.e., her husband's illness, as the reason. The remaining children in each grade responded to this question by giving a higher order goal, e.g., the lady wanted to cure her husband. A second and related reason is that the higher order goal may directly imply the event. For example, curing a person implies an illness. Thus by stating this goal, many children may have felt it unnecessary to explicitly refer to the initiating event. However, most of the fifth-grade children who included a higher order goal also included the initiating event. Furthermore, in questions which could have included an internal response from the story, many fifth graders responded by giving two internal responses as the cause for the internal response given in the probe question. The overall proportion of multiple responses was .11 for the first grade compared to .49 for the fifth grade. The proportion tests completed on this data showed the difference to be significant ($p < .01$).

Although significant developmental differences were present in the number of statements included in the responses, none of the younger children had difficulty in producing higher order goal statements of other types of internal responses in reply to the probe questions. Furthermore, many of the internal responses that were poorly recalled in Experiment 1 were frequently produced in response to these questions by children from both age groups.

(b) Attempts   In the structure of an episode, an attempt is part of a plan application. The attempt is directly caused by an internal plan which in turn is caused by an internal response. Therefore, most attempts should be directly caused by an internal plan, if it is contained in the story, and/or an internal response. Because the internal plan category was well developed in only one story, responses which contained internal plan statements were grouped with replies which contained internal responses. Furthermore, only one attempt probe question elicited any type of internal plan statement. When children were asked why the lady sang a song and gave the tiger food, 50% of the fifth

graders and all of the first graders responded with a goal statement that was not included in the plan.

The majority of the reasons given for attempt statements were internal responses. Internal response statements were given in 73% of all first-grade responses and 77% of all fifth-grade responses. Initiating events were given in 19% of the first-grade responses and 26% of the fifth-grade responses. This type of response generally occurred when an internal response was not included in the original story version and the initiating event immediately preceded the attempt statement. Fifth-grade children again gave more multiple responses in reply to attempt questions than first-grade children. The few instances in which children responded to attempt probes with attempts or consequences occurred in Story 1, *Epaminondas,* and Story 4, *Judy's Birthday.* Some children responded to the question, "why did Judy tell her grandmother about her wish?" with the statement, "because her father got her a dress." These children omitted the internal response, which occurred immediately before Judy's attempt and gave a consequence statement instead. However, these types of responses occurred infrequently.

(c) Direct Consequences The responses to direct consequence probes were the most varied of all types of responses. Five of the six categories were represented in response to these probes. However, the most frequently mentioned category was the internal response which was included in 45% of the first-grade responses and 58% of the fifth-grade responses. Children in both age groups regarded the character's intentions and motives as the major locus of causality. The actual attempt was not as psychologically important in causing the consequence. Initiating events were linked to consequence statements in response to a few probes. When asked why the fox killed a chicken, many children simply said, "because he was hungry;" similarly, when asked why the cake crumbled, some children said, "because his mother didn't tell him how to carry it."

Direct consequence probes occasionally elicited consequence responses. This occurred when there was more than one direct consequence statement and the first caused the second to occur. For example, when children were asked why the fox and bear were trapped, most children replied, "because the roof fell in on them." Minor setting statements occurred in responses referring to the butter melting in Epaminondas. Almost all children said, "because the sun was shining" or "because the sun was hot."

Thus many different categories are perceived to cause the end result of an episode. The goal statement, however, remains the predominant cause of the consequence.

(d) Reactions The majority of reactions were perceived to be caused by the previous direct consequence or by an attempt plus consequence. Seventy-

three percent of all first-grade responses and 81% of all fifth-grade responses included at least one consequence statement. An example of an attempt plus consequence response occurred in Epaminondas; when asked why the grandmother told the boy he was silly, many children replied, "because he carried the cake on his head and it broke."

Discussion

The first purpose of this experiment was to compare the types of information judged to be most important in stories with the information subjects recalled the most frequently in Experiment 1. A high degree of overlap was found, indicating that the structural importance of certain types of information may be a relatively stable aspect of processing. Specific statements appear to be central to the organization of information independent of task demands, at least as long as the task focuses on the semantic content of the story. However, the results also show that task demands do influence the types of information that are retrieved. The major difference between the types of information given on the two tasks involved the internal responses. When asked for the most important information, subjects stressed the motives, feelings, and thoughts of the characters to a greater degree than subjects did on recall. This kind of information appears to be more central to what can be considered the meaning of a story than the recall data indicate. The importance of internal responses was particularly prominent among fifth graders. Older children gave significantly more internal responses than younger children. While the majority of first graders included some reference to the characters' intentions or feelings, they focused on the outcomes more frequently than on the internal responses. The reason for this developmental difference in importance judgements is unclear. It is evident from the probe questions that both first and fifth graders were aware of the internal responses of story characters. In addition, previous research (Bearison & Isaacs, 1975; Berndt & Berndt, 1975) has shown that when motives and intentions of characters are explicitly stated in stories, children as young as six or seven years will use intentions rather than outcomes to make judgments concerning the relative "goodness" or "badness" of a character's behavior. Thus, first-grade children do comprehend intentions and motives. In our stories, the character's goals, desires, and thoughts were explicitly stated. Thus, we would have predicted that younger children as well as older children would stress similar types of information in their judgments. As is evident from the results, this was not the case. Young children may simply not spontaneously attend to motivational factors as consistently as older children do.

The fact that 25% of the children in each age group included inferences or moral lessons in their importance judgments supports the contention that inferences are an integral part of the comprehension process. While there were no differences between grades in the number of such inferences, there did seem to be a change in the type of information given; this was particularly evident in the Judy story. Many of the fifth-grade inferences were attempts to draw a general interpersonal moral or lesson from the story. Examples of this are "The most important thing is that her grandmother really understood her feelings" or "the most important thing is to have parents who understand you." The lessons given by first graders tended to focus on a more personal event or statement in the story; for example, "She should not get her dress dirty," or "she should be careful because hammers and saws are dangerous." It is evident that more data must be collected before these hypotheses can be confirmed. Nonetheless, the examination of children's conceptions of importance may provide useful information on children's processing of stories and the types of inferences they make.

The second purpose of this experiment was to investigate children's perceptions of cause–effect relationships in stories. Children had little difficulty answering the probe questions. The responses to the questions generally indicated that children perceived the cause–effect relations postulated in the story grammar; the results give some support to the proposed relations linking categories. However, the preponderance of replies that included internal responses was greater than would be predicted by a simple inspection of the grammar. Internal responses were perceived as the immediate cause for most internal response, attempt, and consequence statements. This clearly indicates that internal responses are perceived as the principle locus of causality in a story and parallels the central importance attributed to them by older children on the importance judgments. Variations in the responses also showed that factors other than the logical organization proposed in the grammar determine the perception of causality. The semantic content of the statements appears to be critical in determining which two statements children will perceive as being causally related.

A major developmental difference in the amount of information produced was found on both the judgment task and the probe question task. Fifth graders consistently gave more information in their responses than first graders. While first graders typically gave one statement responses, fifth graders gave more multiple statement responses. One possible reason for this difference is that older children may be more aware of the informational needs of a tester than younger children are. They may understand that another person will not assume that they are aware of many reasons for the occurrence of an event unless they explicitly state the multiple reasons. However, the overall results indicate that this reason may not be the most appropriate one. Fifth graders did not give multiple responses to all probe questions. Additionally, when first graders were asked if there were any more reasons for the occurrence of an event, most of them could not produce additional information. Thus older children may make spontaneous causal inferences more readily than younger children and chunk more story information into larger units than younger children.

CONCLUSION

This study has presented and partially validated a schema for stories. The experimental results answer certain fundamental questions about children's organization of story information. This section will further explicate the theory of processing inherent in the grammar. The theory is based on the assumption that incoming information is encoded in relationship to already existing psychological structures or patterns of information. These existing structures determine the information encoded and inferences generated in the process of comprehension. When reading or listening to a story subjects expect certain patterns of information, attend to informational sequences that match these patterns, and organize incoming information into similar patterns. Task requirements may influence both the type of information retrieved from a structure and the particular structure used to encode information. If the grammar corresponds to the internal structures used by subjects during story comprehension, several predictions concerning both the organization of incoming information and the generation of new information can be made.

Temporal Sequencing of Story Information

The first set of predictions concerns the variables which regulate children's ability to produce the correct temporal sequence of a given story. Two sets of predictions can be made. The first concerns the skills necessary to organize statements within an episode. The second concerns the skills necessary to order entire episodes in the correct temporal sequence.

If the temporal organization within an episode in any given story corresponds to the structure represented in the grammar, subjects should have little difficulty organizing the information and maintaining the original temporal sequence. The results from our recall study support this hypothesis. The stories used in the recall experiment did correspond (for the most part) to the logical sequence specified in the grammar. The proportion of temporal ordering errors was small for both age groups. However, an adequate test of the postulated episodic structure requires the examination of stories which violate this structure. If subjects do organize story information according to the rules of the grammar, then any deviation from the proposed structure should require some type of reorganization of the incoming information. One method of creating deviations in the temporal sequence of an episode is to manipulate the positions of each of the seven categories. If this procedure is carried out, then reorganization should occur by: (1) changing the order of the presented categories to correspond to the logical order postulated in the grammar, (2) adding logical relations which directly connect the relocated category with surrounding categories, (3) adding both new categories and relations to create a logical sequence, or (4) deleting inconsistent or poorly organized information.

The type of reorganization which a subject will use may be a function of the distance a category is moved from its original location and the relation of the moved category to the new surrounding categories. For instance, an analysis of the linguistic forms used to mark logical relations indicates that cause–effect orders and effect–cause orders are easily interchangeable. The sentences, "her husband was sick so she needed to make a medicine" and "she needed to make a medicine because her husband was sick" are inter- changeable and both linguistically acceptable. If a story is disorganized by simply reversing two categories, subjects may supply the causal connection between the two categories. If the category is moved more than one location away from its original position, there may be no plausible direct connection between the moved category and the surrounding categories. In this situation, the subject should either reorganize the story by placing the mislocated category in its original position or generate new information and relations to logically link the misplaced category with surrounding categories.

The type of category manipulated may influence the reorganizational strategy used. For instance, the probe question data showed that the internal response category was perceived as the major locus of causality for both attempts and consequences. If the temporal organization of the episode is changed so that the internal response is placed after either the attempt or the consequence, subjects may only need to generate the appropriate causal connection between the displaced internal response and the surrounding categories. The movement of other categories may require a greater amount of reorganization.

The above predictions were based on the logical structure of an episode. It is also important to examine the temporal sequencing of episodes in a story and of statements within a single category. A factor which may influence children's ability to retain these sequences is the types of logical relations between episodes and between statements. We would expect the temporal sequencing of information joined by a CAUSE relation to be well retained. Conversely, the temporal order of information joined by the AND relation may be highly variable; sequential reversals should be more common. Sequences joined by the THEN relation may fall between the two; to the extent that the first unit is perceived as creating the necessary preconditions for the second, the order should be well retained.

Two critical factors may influence all types of story reorganization. The first is the availability of critical cognitive operations necessary to perform the transformation on information. The second is the ability to apply the appropriate strategy, given that the subject has the cognitive operations available to transform the data. Both Brown (1976) and Piaget (1960, 1969) argue that the preoperational child lacks operational reversibility, i.e., the ability to retrace a logical sequence or argument in reverse order. Brown (1976) argues that although preoperational children can construct logical sequences in a forward order, they cannot construct the sequence in a reverse order, e.g., from effect to cause. Thus for preoperational children any temporal disorganization which occurs in the structure of a story should decrease the amount of accurately recalled information. The young child may recall only those sequences which have a direct forward cause-effect relationship. However, older children who have the operational structures to proceed through a logical sequence in a reverse order may be able to reorganize a disorganized story without deleting information. As Brown notes, the type of logical relation between items as well as the child's operational level will influence performance significantly.

Inferences

Inferential thinking is another critical issue related to story comprehension. The production of inferences is a normal product of story comprehension. The grammar can be used to predict many of the kinds of inferences which occur. As subjects process a story, they may form hypotheses about the kinds of information which are appropriate or likely to occur; the inferred information may then become a part of their internal representation of the story. This type of constructive thinking is presumably the result of knowledge about the structure of stories, namely, the informational categories and relations, knowledge concerning the specific kinds of events portrayed in stories, and the developmental level of the child.

Knowledge about the structure of stories should be apparent in at least two ways. First, the deletion of one or more categories should increase the number of inferences made. That is, if one or more of the categories proposed in the grammar are missing from the original story version, the subject may generate new information to construct a logical sequence. For example, if the initiating event is deleted from the original story version, subjects should generate information which would make the internal response in the story more meaningful. Generally, the inferential information should be of the same category as the deleted information; this is the most obvious way to maintain the logical sequence. However, the additions may not correspond to the deleted category. For instance, when an event is deleted, an individual may create an appropriate event or he may include a higher order internal response, as both events and internal responses are perceived as causing other internal responses.

A second way in which structural knowledge may influence inferential additions concerns the types of categories added. Some categories are structurally more important than others. Major settings, initiating events, major goal statements, and consequences are the most salient categories in recall; if these types of information are missing in a story, subjects may tend to add them more frequently than they would add minor settings, other internal responses, attempts, or reactions, if the latter categories were missing.

An additional factor which may affect the production of new information is a subject's prior knowledge about the specific situation or events of a story. In our recall data subjects often substituted new information for information that occurred in the original story. The new information belonged to the same category as the original information but was probably more consistent with the subject's knowledge of similar situations. Substitutions consisting of more probable events may help the processor maintain the structural and semantic cohesiveness of the story.

Developmental differences should occur when certain types of categories are deleted from a story. Children below the age of six or seven have a great amount of difficulty in spontaneously generating the cause of a subsequent behavior or in proceeding in reverse fashion through a logical chain (Brown, in press). Therefore, when the first category in an episode is deleted, young children may have more difficulty adding information to the story than older children.

Construction of Stories

The final issue to be discussed is the spontaneous construction of new stories. It is assumed that the structures that influence the comprehension of stories also influence the spontaneous generation of stories. Thus, the type and sequence of categories generated in spontaneous stories should be similar to the proposed internal representation.

From our initial inspection of stories generated by children in school situations, there appear to be critical differences between story comprehension and spontaneous story production. Children in first and second grade frequently generate stories that include only major and minor setting statements, e.g., descriptions of characters' physical states, activities, and recurrent desires. Older children begin to generate behavioral sequences defined in an episode but omit critical categories and relations which are critical in the development of a logical sequence of events. Some stories contain several episodes in succession which have no relation to one another. Even in our examination of adult story production, irrelevant themes often pervade the story sequence; the storyteller often forgets what type of information he already generated and begins an entirely new behavioral episode. One of the critical differences between the comprehension of stories and the spontaneous construction of stories is that in the former the complete logical sequence is inherent in the story, i.e., the items are prearranged. When a subject spontaneously constructs a story, the logical relationships between categories and/or episodes are often not apparent to the subject until after he has begun production. In order for the story to contain a logical flow of events, many subjects may have to rework the information they have generated in order to develop all possible productions.

These predictions were all generated from the model of processing inherent in our schema. However, they remain to be tested. They are presented to define the types of organizational processes used during story encoding and retrieval. While the studies presented in this paper offer support for the category distinctions and the interrelations between categories, the validation of the schema as a reliable construct for predicting more general aspects of story comprehension remains a long-term goal.

ACKNOWLEDGMENTS

We thank Lois Orchard, Sally Rude, and Patti Schwartz for assistance in data collection, and express our gratitude to Merlynn Bergen, Lois Orchard, Tom Ludwig, and John Stern for helpful comments on an earlier draft of this manuscript. We are extremely grateful to Mr. Elmer Schweiss, principal of Spoede School, and Mr. Joe Brown, principal of Old Bonhomme School, for their continuing patience and support of our research.

REFERENCES

Bartlett, F. C. *Remembering: A study in experimental and social psychology.* Cambridge, England: Cambridge University Press, 1932.

Bearison, D. J., & Isaacs, L. Production deficiency in children's moral judgments. *Developmental Psychology,* 1975, *11,* 732–737.

Berndt, T. J., & Berndt, E. G. Children's use of motives and intentionality in person perception and moral judgment. *Child Development,* 1975, *46,* 904–912.

Bransford, J. D., & McCarrell, N. S. A sketch of a cognitive approach to comprehension: Some thoughts about what it means to comprehend. In W. B. Weimer & D. S. Palermo (Eds.), *Cognition and symbolic processes.* Washington, D.C.: Winston, 1974.

Brown, A. L. The development of memory: Knowing, knowing about knowing, and knowing how to know. In H. W. Reese (Ed.). *Advances in child development and behavior,* Vol. 10. New York: Academic Press, 1975. Pp. 103–152.

Brown, A. L. The construction of temporal succession by preoperational children. In A. D. Pick (Ed.), *Minnesota symposium on child psychology,* Vol. 10. Minneapolis, Mn.: University of Minnesota, 1976.

Colby, B., & Cole, M. Culture, memory and narrative. In R. Horton & R. Finnegan (Eds.), *Modes of thought: Essays on thinking in Western and non-Western societies.* London: Faber & Faber, 1973. Pp. 63–91.

Fillmore, C. The case for case. In F. Bach & R. Harms (Eds.), *Universals in linguistic theory.* New York: Holt, Rinehart & Winston, 1968.

Flappan, D. *Children's understanding of social interaction.* New York: Teacher's College Press, 1968.

Fraisse, P. *The psychology of time.* New York: Harper & Row, 1963.

Johnson, R. Recall of prose as a function of structural importance of the linguistic unit. *Journal of Verbal Learning and Verbal Behavior,* 1970, *9,* 12–20.

Kintsch, W. *The representation of meaning in memory.* Hillsdale, N.J.: Lawrence Erlbaum Associates, 1974.

Kintsch, W. In comprehending stories. Paper presented at the Carnegie Symposium on Cognition, May, 1976.

Lord, A. B. *The singer of tales.* New York: Atheneum, 1965.

Mandler, J. M., Johnson, N. S., & DeForest, M. A structural analysis of stories and their recall: from "Once upon a time" to "happily ever after." Center for Human Information Processing Technical Report, April, 1976.

Paris, S. G. Integration and inference in children's comprehension and memory. In F. Restle, R. Shiffron, J. Castellan, H. Lindman, & D. Pisoni (Eds.), *Cognitive theory,* Vol. 1. Hillsdale, N.J.: Lawrence Erlbaum Associates, 1975.

Piaget, J. *The language and thought of the child.* London: Routledge & Kegan Paul, 1960.

Piaget, J. *The child's conception of time.* London: Routledge & Kegan Paul, 1969.

Propp, V. *Morphology of the folktale.* Bloomington, Indiana: Indiana University Research Center in Anthropology, Folktale and Linguistics, 1958, P. 10.

Rumelhart, D. E. Notes on a schema for stories. In D. G. Brown & A. Collins (Eds.), *Representation and understanding: Studies in cognitive science.* New York: Academic Press, 1975. Pp. 211–236.

Schank, R. The structure of episodes in memory. In D. G. Brown & A. Collins (Eds.), *Representation and understanding: Studies in cognitive science.* New York: Academic Press, 1975. Pp. 237–272.

Stein, N. L., & Glenn, C. G. A developmental study of children's recall of story material. Paper presented at the Society for Research in Child Development. Denver, 1975.

Stein, N. L., & Glenn, C. G. An analysis of story comprehension in elementary school children: A test of schema. *Resources in Education,* Vol. 11, No. 8, August, 1976.

Yendovitskaya, T. V. Development of Memory. In A. V. Zaporazhets & D. B. Elkonin (Eds.), *The psychology of preschool children.* Cambridge, Mass.: MIT Press, 1971. Pp. 89–110.

4

Acquisition of New Comprehension Schemata for Expository Prose by Transfer of a Narrative Schema

Roy Freedle
Gordon Hale
Educational Testing Service

GENERAL INTRODUCTION

In the typical school setting, children are exposed to discourse as a primary means of instruction. Such discourse often consists of *expository* and *descriptive* forms. Yet while children of about five and six years of age reveal poor ability in understanding expository and descriptive forms, they do have the ability to understand and recall *narrative* discourse. The pilot study which we will present below investigates one way to *transfer* the comprehension schema for narratives so as to expand children's comprehension and recall of expository and descriptive prose. The practical implications of this research for education are clear: classroom learning often requires comprehension of expository and descriptive passages (whether presented in oral or written form). Since first graders and kindergarteners do not yet have facility in comprehending such passages, the facilitation of at least expository comprehension by means of narrative schema transfer should accelerate the rate at which such materials can be introduced to children in the early school years.

Schema theory will form the background for developing our ideas on transfer effects at the level of discourse. Schema theory has had a profound effect on recent work in discourse theory (Shank & Abelson, 1977; Chafe, 1977; Anderson, Spiro, & Montague, 1977; Freedle, Naus, & Schwartz, 1977; Kintsch, 1977; Rumelhart, 1975; Mandler & Johnson, 1977; Mandler, 1978; Stein & Glenn, 1979, this volume). A good deal of this recent work has centered on the structure and recall of stories. It has been proposed that a grammar for narrative (story) discourse structure helps to clarify and define

the internal representation of the information contained in a story *schema.*
Such information provides a kind of template which aids the language user in
both comprehending and recalling stories.

By implication, if the language user fails to have a schema for a certain type
of discourse, he/she should do poorly in both comprehending and recalling
the information in this discourse. Our pilot study below suggests one way to
instruct children of about five years of age to transfer the knowledge they
already have of story structure and apply this knowledge in the comprehension and recall of a previously unfamiliar discourse type—namely, expository
prose. Work underway by author Roy Freedle (see footnote 1, p. 129) extends
this transfer to descriptive prose using a variety of methods. The best way to
convey how this can be accomplished is to begin by presenting examples of
narrative and expository texts which clearly reveal the differences as well as
the similarities between these two genre:

Expository "Farmer" passage	Narrative "Farmer" passage	Category label for story information
Here's how a farmer	Once there was a farmer	Setting.
can get his stubborn	who wanted to get his stubborn	Response-goal.
horse into the barn.	horse into the barn.	
The farmer can go into the barn	The farmer went into the barn	Beginning.
and hold out some sugar	and held out some sugar	Attempt.
to get the horse to come and eat.	to get the horse to come and eat.	
But if the horse does not like sugar,	but the horse did not like sugar	Response
he will not come.	and he did not come.	Outcome.
Here's another thing he can do.	The farmer tried something else.	Beginning.
Suppose the farmer has a dog.	The farmer had a dog.	Setting.
He can get the dog to bark at the horse.	He got the dog to bark at the horse.	Attempt.
This may frighten the horse	This frightened the horse	Response.
and make him run into the barn.	and made him run into the barn.	Ending.

The middle column labeled narrative "Farmer" passage is typical of the
types of narratives studied by Mandler, Stein and their colleagues. To the left
of the narrative is an expository prose passage which uses *almost the identical
semantic content* as the narrative. Given this similarity, one is immediately
struck by the following question: If children do so well comprehending and
recalling narrative structures (Mandler & Johnson, 1977; Stein & Glenn,
1979) why shouldn't they do about equally well in comprehending and
recalling these *expository* passages?

Early work by Piaget (1955) suggests that they do *not* do well; even children
of 7 or 8 years of age do poorly at recalling and answering questions about

non-narrative prose. But Piaget did not control semantic content across discourse types; hence Piaget's results are equivocal without this necessary control for difficulty of the semantic content. This is a very important variable to control (if not within the individual subject, at least across groups) because in general, story material tends to consist of "easy" semantic content, whereas expository prose typically consists of "difficult" thematic material. By controlling the semantic content across discourse genre, as illustrated above, one is in a position to determine whether expository prose *is* inherently more difficult than narrative. Pilot data, which will be presented in more detail below, indicates that without special aids, five year olds *do* experience considerable difficulty in comprehending and recalling material in the expository form. If the expository type is presented to them first, five year olds give very fragmented and disorganized free recalls. But if five year olds receive a narrative passage first (with different content, but of about the same difficulty level as the "Farmer" passage) and next receive the expository "Farmer" passage, then they show a significant *increase* in the amount of information recalled from the expository passage. In addition, they tend to recall the expository material in a form that sounds oftentimes more like a narrative. The challenge of these data is to explain why the *order* in which these discourse forms are presented makes such a difference (to the young subjects) in performance, and why the narrative form (signalled primarily by the verb's present/past tense indicative form) tends to be used in recalling the expository forms.

Before presenting an account of the results in terms of schema theory, let us anticipate and dismiss a possible objection that may be raised—that one reason the expository recall is better as a second task is due to practice. The pilot results, within the limits studied, rather clearly indicate that practice alone with a particular genre does *not* invariably improve performance (when different semantic content is used for each repetition of the genre). Instead the observed improvement in expository recall as the second task must depend upon something else; as more data is presented, it will be clear that that something else is schema transfer.

The two narrative passages that were used in the study (entitled "farmer" and "raft") were constructed prior to writing the expository versions. The narrative passages structurally reflected all the aspects required by a story grammar (see Rumelhart, 1975; Mandler & Johnson, 1977, for a detailed account of this grammar)—hence such categories as Setting, Episodic Beginnings, Attempts, Outcomes, and Endings were employed. A corresponding expository passage was constructed by faithfully following the sequence and content of the narrative propositions—the changes that were introduced were primarily verb structure changes which were necessary to produce a well-formed exposition. Hence the expository version had *all* the basic categories (or at least near replicas of the basic narrative categories) that ordinarily are associated with a narrative structure. In designing the pilot study, we reasoned that if the narrative form was presented first, one could say that the story *schema* was still "foregrounded" (see Chafe, 1972, for a discussion of foregrounding) in the child's memory after he/she had recalled its contents. Then, if the child got an expository passage of basically the same kinds of categories that typically signal a story schema (even though the semantic content is different across the narrative and expository forms received by the child), the child would be very likely to *discover* this similarity. He/she would then use the schema in which he/she is already competent (the story schema) to aid in comprehending this new expository form, and finally, would demonstrate the consequences of that discovery by recalling the expository material as though it had been presented in narrative form. Since such a result occurs for many subjects the data suggest that *schema transfer* has taken place. That is, the knowledge employed in comprehending narratives is employed in a novel setting to aid in comprehending a new discourse form, the expository.

RESULTS AND DISCUSSION

The data reveal that when expository is presented first (to kindergarteners), the average percent of present–past tense usage (appropriate to a story schema) is 23%, but this average percentage jumps to 59% ($p < .025$) when the expository passage *follows* the narrative passage. Thus this significant tense structure shift is one piece of evidence for the hypothesis of narrative schema transfer. In addition the number of *propositions correctly recalled* (ignoring verb tense in the scoring of content correctness) is clearly greater for all six categories of exposition (setting, beginnings, etc.) when expository is the second task than when it is the first task (the non-transfer condition). The greater recall in the transfer condition is explained as follows: when the subject fails to "have" a schema to aid in comprehension and recall, it is more difficult to organize, label, store, and retrieve the propositional content of a text. But *with* such a schema (due to the effect of schema transfer), the amount of propositional content comprehended and recalled should and does increase. This is because the newly acquired schema-for-exposition helps the subject to organize, label, store, and retrieve the propositional content. For kindergarteners, the increase is about evenly distributed across the category types, as illustrated in Fig. 1.

It is also evident upon examining the results for the fourth graders, that the position of the expository task for these older children has only a slight effect on recall of four of the six categories, with performance in the "Ending" category being the most affected by task position. The reason these older children are not much affected by task order is that they already possess

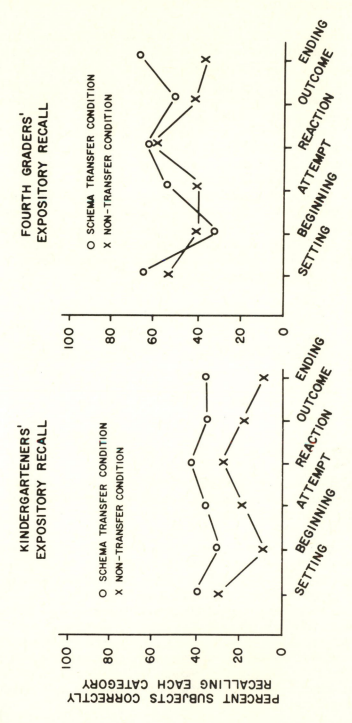

FIG. 1. Results of the schema transfer and non-transfer conditions for kindergarteners and fourth graders. See appendix for further discussion of the category labels.

schema competence for both narrative and expository genre, hence there is nothing to be gained by attempting schema transfer across tasks. This is evident too when one examines the verb tense and mood structure; the older subjects tend to use primarily the correct subjunctive mood when recalling expository material regardless of task position, and they tend to use primarily the correct present/past tense indicative when recalling the narrative passages, regardless of task position. Comparing across age groups, it is evident in the above figures that the fourth graders in general do better in recalling each of the six category types than the kindergarteners.

The category results for the narratives are given in Fig. 2.

We can see from scanning the recall data for each of the six categories of the narrative across and within age groups, that task order (i.e., practice per se) has very little influence on the results. Certainly the degree of improvement across the six categories for the kindergarteners' recall of narratives is nowhere near the degree of improvement in recall observed when comparing their gain scores for responding to expository content. The *fourth* graders' narrative results show no systematic improvement according to task order; hence practice per se cannot be used to explain the total pattern of the results presented—instead the concept of schema transfer seems most consistent with all the results.

Another result of significance in comparing all narrative recalls with expository recalls is that the category "Reaction" is much higher for expository than narrative. This could be important for the following reason. Mandler, Stein and their colleagues typically find the "Reaction" category for narratives to be poorly recalled—we find it also tends to be low just for our narrative recalls. Is it possible then that the *function* of the "Reaction" category for expository passages is very different from its *function* in narratives? The following reasoning suggests that the "reaction" category does seem different in the time genre functions; saying "Something *may* frighten the horse" in an expository passage can be said to imply that "Something may *not* frighten the horse" is also possibly true. This is due to the use of subjective mood which makes heavy use of modals as "may, can, should, could, ..." The corresponding propositions from the narrative version "Something frightened the horse" by no means carries the added implication that "Something did *not* frighten the horse," hence expository and narrative clearly differ in this logical implicational aspect. Presumably facts such as these must be implicated in explaining why the "reaction" category was more salient and memorable in the expository passage than in the narrative passage.

In general this pilot study indicates that it is possible to improve children's ability to grasp the meaning of a previously unfamiliar genre—the expository. This is accomplished primarily by transferring

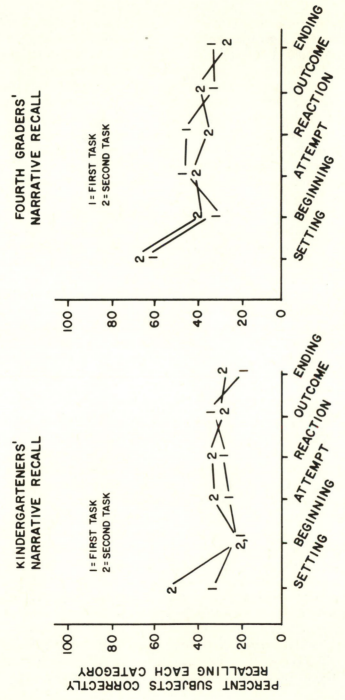

FIG. 2. Results of narrative recall by kindergarteners and fourth graders.

competence from one genre (the narrative) in one of two ways: (a) by schema *assimilation* or (b) schema *accommodation*. Schema assimilation takes place when the child totally adapts the expository material to fit a narrative schema. This occurred for a few young subjects who *totally* used present/past indicative in recalling their expository passage in the transfer condition. In this case the new genre structure (exposition) was totally assimilated by the old schematic structure (the narrative schema). Schema accommodation, though, is the more frequently occurring schema change that takes place during transfer. This manifests itself primarily by the subject's *mixing* present/past tenses along with subjunctive mood within the same recall protocol (the expository recall). In this case the narrative schema has only *partially* been adapted to aid in comprehending and recalling the new expository structure. Thus the discourse transfer results provide support for Piaget's dictum that new structures (exposition) are first learned using old contents (the 6 categories of narrative), while new contents (subjective verb mood) are first used within old familiar structures (the narrative schema). Continual re-exposure to the transfer condition could very well show a gradual weakening of the confusion between verb mood and tense within the same recall protocol with a full-blown expository schema finally emerging in its own right after much practice in the transfer condition. One should then be able to see (in expository recalls) the gradual schema accommodation changes that eventuate in the birth of this new schema, without disruption of competence in the old narrative schema which can coexist with the newly acquired schema.

EXAMPLES FROM INDIVIDUAL SUBJECTS

Here are a few examples illustrating, first, schema transfer (kindergarten subject) by a process of *total assimilation* in which recall of the *expository* "farmer" passage shows total use of a tense/mood structure appropriate to a narrative schema: "A farmer . . . a farmer *put* some sugar in the barn and . . . he *did*n't eat it . . . he *did*n't eat . . . The horse *did*n't eat the sugar. He *had* a dog. He *barked*. So, . . . So the horse *goes* in the the barn." Our focus here is on the tense structure. Nowhere in the recall protocol has the subject used the subjunctive mood as in "The farmer *could go*. . . ." Also highly evident in this recall is considerable distortion of the semantic relations of the original text concerning "who might do what to whom." We also see a rather incoherent stringing together of propositions and incorrect use of, and/or an ambiguous use of, referential pronouns. Such matters of proper "staging" (see Grimes, 1972; Clement, 1979, in press) of information by use of cohesive ties (Halliday & Hasan, 1976) are taken up in studies currently underway by author Roy Freedle.

Here is an example (also from a kindergarten subject) which Freedle[1] called *schema accommodation* in which narrative schema (judging by present/past tense structure) is only partially used to recall the expository "farmer" passage: "The dog *will* frighten the horse and make him go into the barn. And ... since the horse *does*n't like sugar he *wouldn't come* in. And ... and the horse *is* too stubborn. And ... the farmer *got* his dog out and *brought* him in." While most of the verbs are in the present or past tense indicative the example of Aux+verb (*wouldn't come*) is a very interesting attempt on the subject's part to try to accommodate part of the expository "grammar" within the time frame of the narrative schema. As before, the recall of the expository is awkwardly "staged."

Another example of schema accommodation (also a kindergarten subject) is cited below primarily for its uniqueness—typically we have found that past/present versus subjunctive mood scoring reflects most clearly the dynamics of the schema transfer effect. The recall which follows shows, though, that there are other ways, albeit infrequent ones, of demonstrating schema accommodation: "How do you get a stubborn horse into the barn? The farmer *goes* into the barn and holds out some sugar. What happens if the horse doesn't like sugar? Does he have a dog? (long pause) That *will* scare the horse and make him run into the barn." This child uses rhetoric questions to try to merge the hypothetical events of the expository form with the real-time events of the narrative schema.

ADDITIONAL DISTINCTIONS IN THE STUDY OF EXPOSITORY AND NARRATIVE COMPETENCE

Several definitions must be advanced.

(a) We shall distinguish two kinds of expositions: expo–type–1 and expo–type–2 which will be presented as stimulus texts in some of the experiments. They differ as follows: Expo–type–1 is the kind we have been concerned with up to now and is captured, at the sentence level, by the following form *"The farmer can take the cow."* Expo–type–2, on the other hand, uses the indefinite "you" as the sentence actor: *"You can take the cow."* Expo–type–2 will sometimes be referred to as a "2nd person exposition" in what follows. Notice that expo–types 1 and 2 differ only with respect to the "actor" feature. Otherwise the pairwise sentences from their respective discourses share two elements: the verb structure is the same and they share

---

[1]Freedle, R. Children's transfer of a narrative schema to other discourse types: acquisition of new comprehension schemata for expository and descriptive prose. Manuscript submitted to and funded by National Institute of Education. Manuscript dated Nov. 11, 1977.

the same direct objects. Expo–type–1 differs from its corresponding narrative sentences in *one* element—verb structure. Expo–type–2 differs from its corresponding narrative sentences in *two* elements—verb structure and "actor" (3rd person versus 2nd person as actors). Thus expo–type–2 is more "distantly" related to narrative than is expo–type–1. The pilot data suggested that transfer most readily occurs between narrative structure and expo–type–1 structure. An experiment now underway by author Roy Freedle investigates some implication of this distinction.

(b) One measure we have found useful is the percent of present/past tense usage (future tense was measured separately). If a recall protocol reads as follows: "The farmer *could go*. He *went* into the barn and *gets* the horse." The percent of present/past tense usage is 66.7% because there are three main verbs in the recall and two of them are either in present or past tense. Correctness of recall does not enter in here.

(c) The narrative requires the assumption of a *real time frame,* whereas expository (of the type we consider) does *not* assume that the propositions advance along some time frame—only hypothetical events are assumed, not real ones. While many other characteristics would be mentioned concerning differences in genre structures, those of verb-structure and time-line suffice for our current set of studies.

(d) Rumelhart, Mandler, and Stein have each suggested very elaborate coding systems to describe the events in narratives. The appendix includes a rather abbreviated discussion of the many concepts needed to describe narrative structure; the appendix also suggests ways to label the corresponding semantic categories for expository discourse of the types we have been discussing here.

Appendix

This appendix is based on Freedle's (Footnote 1) suggestion of the similarities and differences between several discourse types.

A very brief characterization of the narrative categories used primarily by Mandler and Johnson (1977) will be helpful as a starting point.

A setting usually consists of stative information about one or more characters (e.g., "Mary lives in Kansas City.") The setting is followed by at least one episode. An episode consists of three basic parts—a beginning, a development and an ending or outcome.

A beginning may be any sort of event. The listener clue that setting information is complete and that the beginning node has been entered is usually signified by a shift from a state description to an event description. (E.g. "Mary lives in Kansas City. One day she went for a walk in the park and saw a robin....").

A development represents a shift to a reaction of a story character. (E.g., "...She was overjoyed at seeing the robin...."). The shift is from an external to an internal event with some implicit connection to a causal relation. For example, seeing the robin and being in the park made her joyous. The reaction makes the character the central "protagonist" in the episode.

The reaction typically consists of two parts—a simple reaction which specifies an emotional response or the thoughts of the protagonist, and a goal. For the goal, the protagonist formulates a plan to deal with events as they unfold. A pathway to reach the goal completes the development section. A goal pathway consists of an attempt to reach the goal and the outcome of that attempt. The attempt may consist of a series of actions which the protagonist engages in to reach the goal. The outcome category indicates whether the attempt was successful or not. Other complications in goal path are also described in Mandler & Johnson.

Several options are available for the ending category. The ending may have an 'emphatic' character which resolves or wraps up a series of events. (E.g., "Finally after all her troubles of the day, Mary returned home to a warm bed.") An ending may also refer back to one or more nodes in the episode, and may include a reaction on the part of another character.

As a very rough first draft, we'll now suggest a highly tentative set of categories for expository type-1 to show the type of structure that is eventually needed to guide a more detailed generation of experimental predictions for future studies. The existence of such a set of formal categories (much in the spirit of Rumelhart-Mandler-Stein categories) for expository prose will help to state more clearly what type of knowledge is embodied in saying that a person "knows" or "has" an expository-schema as opposed to "having" a narrative-schema.

The key elements for narrative schema were said to be: (1) a setting, (2) a goal, a development section having a (3) beginning, (4) a simple reaction, (5) an attempt, (6) an outcome, and (7) an ending. The corresponding labels which we propose to attach to very similar information for expository type-1 prose is as follows: (1') a setting or hypothetical setting (e.g., "*Suppose* a farmer wanted to get his horse in the barn.") (2') a problem or hypothetical problem (e.g., "Suppose you had the following problem and wanted to know how to solve it.") A hypothetical "solution" section ("solution" is the higher-node label for the concepts which follow) which consists of (3') a list of recommended instruments or conditions necessary to begin the solution, (5') the suggestion of at least one procedural-attempt to reach the desired problem-solution, (6') an indication of probable tests to be used in deciding whether a solution has been found, and (7') some closing comments which put the problem in perspective or somehow indicate that the hypothetical time-frame has come to an end. I have not yet quite decided whether a node corresponding to narratives' "simple reaction" has a clear representation in expository-type prose considered here; but for the sake of completeness let us add it as follows: (4') a possible difficulty of an emotional or probable-thought-path type to be anticipated on the part of the characters or things which enable the pathway to the solution to be effected.

It is perhaps useful to think of these expository category labels as applying to a RECIPE IN A COOKBOOK with which we are all familiar. The setting (1') is typically a cook in his/her kitchen. The problem (2') is the desired or hypothetical goal (e.g., to bake a cake). One can imagine the recipe reading:

"Here's how you go about baking a chocolate cake." Notice that the recipe does not assert that such and such an action has taken place or is taking place; it merely asserts that this is what you can do or should do if you want to achieve the end-goal, a baked cake. It is therefore a hypothetical set of actions that will follow. The instruments (3′) are obvious in a recipe—they are all the utensils and ingredients needed to perform the recommended actions. Oftentimes the instruments occur first in a recipe following the title. Thus there are special subtypes of expository forms (here the printed cookbook) which alter the sequential flow of the category information—this is merely one of the matters that must be dealt with more formally in a projected theory of expository grammars. Notice that the instruments are not asserted to be necessarily present as they would be in a narrative. Instead they are asserted to be what you will need if you follow out the recommended solution. In this sense the reading of the recipe (using a procedural-schema-expository-type to comprehend the recipe) must be distinguished from the actual doing or carrying out of the actions when it comes time to actually follow the recipe in a step-by-step manner in real time. Thus we are still dealing with hypothetical states rather than actually occurring states which have a real time line associated with them. This is clearly different from the time-line in narratives.

The procedural-attempts are very much like narrative attempts except that again they are not asserted to have been done but are merely recommended procedural attempts. One may also call the procedural-attempts "recommended-preparatory-actions" (e.g., "Heat the oven for 5 minutes to 350 degrees; then remove batter from mixer...."). These preparatory assertions again have not occurred in any real time frame, they are merely recommended acts. We retain the term 'attempts' in the label, though, to show its similarity to its corresponding term in the narrative grammars.

Tests correspond closely to narrative outcomes. They are like expected results from each set of subroutines that one goes through in making the final product—the chocolate cake (e.g., "The frosting is now ready. Now return to oven and remove...."). The statement about the frosting is an anticipated outcome from a sequence of prior procedural steps. The sentence about returning to the oven initiates another procedural subroutine. Finally the anticipated ending of the exposition is typically some statement such as "Now your cake is ready for serving."

There is an important difference between expository and narrative prose that must be noted. In a recipe-exposition, one must not list procedures that are *likely* to fail, they can be legitimately mentioned only if nothing better is available as a recommended procedure—but even if so mentioned, they must be *marked* by their anomolous character of "not-likely-to-succeed-if-tried". To illustrate this imagine your outrage if in reading a recipe you came across a statement such as "... Now you have finished the second part. Of course, this is not likely to give you the desired result. Instead you should try...." Your annoyance stems from a violation of a presupposition of how recipes should be constructed—that is, it violates your schema of what a well-formed recipe should consist of. This suggests that in its unmarked states of procedures, instruments, tests, etc., an expository passage typically will consist of steps that have a substantial guarantee of success. In narrative episodes, in contrast, this constraint typically doesn't apply—an episode can end badly and unexpectedly and yet one feels no sense of well-formedness having been violated. This difference can be important, especially when testing older subjects who surely have internalized this higher-order constraint that the procedural-attempts have a high likelihood of success in solving the problem at hand. (Author Roy Freedle has begun studies devoted to this difference.) If an expository form violates this presupposition, then the recall protocols should be less coherent, or less accurate due to the fact that an extra information-processing step has to be engaged in—namely, noticing that a presupposition has been violated and tracking down what the error is; this in turn can affect the subsequent comprehension steps which would be reflected in less accurate information in recalling the text or could also be reflected in more poorly organized ("staged") text recall.

REFERENCES

Anderson, R. C., Spiro, R. J., & Montague, W. F. *Schooling and the acquisition of knowledge.* Hillsdale, N.J.: Lawrence Erlbaum Associates, Inc., 1977.

Chafe, W. Discourse structure and human knowledge. In R. Freedle & J. B. Carroll (Eds.), *Language comprehension and the acquisition of knowledge.* Wash. D.C.: Winston, 1972.

Chafe, W. Creativity in verbalization & its implications for the nature of stored knowledge. In R. Freedle (Ed.), *Discourse production and comprehension.* Norwood, N.J.: Ablex, 1977.

Clements, P. Experimental investigations of the staging of discourse. This volume.

Freedle, R., Naus, M., & Schwartz, L. Prose processing from a psychosocial perspective. In R. Freedle (Ed.), *Discourse production and comprehension.* Norwood, N.J.: Ablex, 1977.

Grimes, J. *The thread of discourse.* Ithaca, N.Y.: Cornell University Press, 1972.

Kintsch, W. *The representation of meaning in memory.* Hillsdale, N.J.: Lawrence Erlbaum Associates, Inc., 1974.

Longacre, R. Sentence structure as a statement calculus. *Language,* 1970, *46,* 783–815.

Mandler, J. A code in the node: the use of a story schema in retrieval. *Discourse Processes, a multidisplinary journal,* 1978, *1,* 14–35.

Mandler, J. & Johnson, N. S. Remembrance of things parsed: story structure and recall. *Cognitive psychology,* 1977, *9,* 111–151.

Paris, S., & Lindauer, B. The role of inference in children's comprehension and memory for sentences. *Cognitive psychology,* 1976, *8,*

Piaget, J. *The language and thought of the child.* N.Y.: Meridian books, 1955.

Rumelhart, D. E. Notes on a schema for stories. In D. Bobrow & A. Collins (Eds.), *Studies in Cognitive science.* N.Y.: Academic Press, 1975.

Shank, R., & Abelson, R. *Scripts, plans, goals, & understanding.* Hillsdale, N.J.: Lawrence Erlbaum Associates, Inc., 1977.

Stein, N., & Glenn, C. An analysis of story comprehension in school children. This volume.

Thorndyke, P. Cognitive structures in comprehension & memory of narrative discourse. *Cognitive psychology,* 1977, *9,* 77–110.

Waugh, N., & Norman, D. Primary memory. *Psychological review,* 1965, *72,* 89–104.

5 What's in a Frame?
Surface Evidence
for Underlying Expectations

Deborah Tannen
University of California, Berkeley

INTRODUCTION

I have been struck lately by the recurrence of a single theme in a wide variety of contexts: the power of expectation. For example, the self-fulfilling prophecy has been proven to operate in education as well as in individual psychology. I happened to leaf through a how-to-succeed book; its thesis was that the way to succeed is to expect to do so. Two months ago at a conference for teachers of English as a second language, the keynote speaker explained that effective reading is a process of anticipating what the author is going to say and expecting it as one reads. Moreover, there are general platitudes heard every day, as for example the observation that what is wrong with marriage today is that partners expect too much of each other and of marriage.

The emphasis on expectation seems to corroborate a nearly self-evident truth: in order to function in the world, people cannot treat each new person, object, or event as unique and separate. The only way we can make sense of the world is to see the connections between things, and between present things and things we have experienced before or heard about. These vital connections are learned as we grow up and live in a given culture. As soon as we measure a new perception against what we know of the world from prior experience, we are dealing with expectations.

The notion of expectations is at the root of a wave of theories and studies in a broad range of fields, including linguistics. It is this notion, I believe, which underlies talk about frames, scripts, and schemata in the fields of linguistics, artificial intelligence, cognitive psychology, social psychology, sociology, and anthropology at least (and I would not be surprised if similar terms were used in other disciplines I do not happen to know about). In this chapter I will illustrate a way of showing the effects of these "structures of expectation" on verbalization in the telling of oral narratives. Before I proceed, however, it will be useful to give a brief sketch of the various ways in which these terms have been used in the fields I have mentioned.

Because of the infinite confusion possible as a result of the great number of authors and contexts we will need to discuss, I will categorize the main theorists first according to the disciplines they work in, and then according to their choice of terms.

In the field of psychology we need to consider the work of Bartlett (1932), Rumelhart (1975), and Abelson (1975, 1976). Rumelhart is a cognitive psychologist and Abelson a social psychologist, but both have become increasingly associated with the field of artificial intelligence. In the latter field, Abelson works closely with Schank (Schank & Abelson, 1975). The second major researcher in this field is Minsky (1974). Linguists we will consider are Chafe (1977a, b) and Fillmore (1975, 1976). In anthropology, the names of Bateson (1972) (his work was originally published in 1955) and Frake (1977) must be noted, as well as Hymes (1974) who may more precisely be called an ethnographer of speaking (to use the term he himself coined). In sociology the theorist is Goffman (1974).

Let us now consider the above scholars in groups according to the terms they prefer to use. The term "schema" traces back to Bartlett (1932) in his pioneering book, *Remembering* (Bartlett himself borrows the term from Sir Henry Head). This term has been picked up by Chafe as well as Rumelhart, and by others, as for example Bobrow and Norman (1975), who are also in the field of artificial intelligence. The term "script" is associated with the work of Abelson and Schank. The term "frame" is associated most often with the anthropological/sociological orientation of Hymes, Goffman, and Frake, and with the artificial intelligence research of Minsky. Their use of the term stems from Bateson. "Frame" is also used by Fillmore, who notes that he came to it by a different route, that of the structuralist notion of syntagmatic frame.

To complicate matters further, a number of these writers use more than one term (Fillmore: scene-and-frame; Chafe: schema, frame, and categorization), or express dissatisfaction with the term they use (Bartlett writes that he would really prefer "active developing patterns" or "organized setting"; Fillmore says he would prefer "module").

To uncomplicate matters, however, all these complex terms and approaches amount to the simple concept of what R. N. Ross (1975) calls "structures of expectations," that is, that, based on one's experience of the world in a given culture (or combination of cultures), one organizes knowledge about the world and uses this knowledge to predict interpretations and relationships regarding new information, events, and experiences. Bartlett (1932), the earliest of the theorists discussed here and the first psychologist to use the term "schema," in effect said it all:"...the past operates as an organized mass rather than as a group of elements each of which retains its specific character" (p. 197).

Bartlett's concern, as his title indicates, is "Remembering"; he relies heavily on Head's notion of "schema" (quoting extensively from a book entitled *Studies in neurology*) (Head, 1920) in order to support his theory that memory is constructive rather than consisting of the storage of all previously perceived stimuli. Bartlett contends that an individual "has an overmastering tendency simply to get a general impression of the whole; and, on the basis of this, he constructs the probable detail" (p. 206). One more aspect of Bartlett's work that is particularly significant, in his estimation as well as mine, is the "whole notion, that the organized mass results of past changes of position and posture are actively *doing* something all the time; are, so to speak, carried along with us, complete, though developing, from moment to moment" (p. 201). This is the aspect of schemata which he felt was lost in that term, and it is for this reason that he preferred the terms "active, developing patterns." Bartlett's apprehensions about the term "schema" were obviously justified, for in most of this work, the notion of constant change has been lost. For example, Charniak (1975), an AI investigator who follows Minsky, states, "I take a frame to be a static data structure about one stereotyped topic..." (p. 42).

Perhaps the most direct descendent of Bartlett is Chafe (who, although he does not specifically emphasize the dynamic nature of schemata, does not imply a necessarily static notion of them either, perhaps because as a linguist he is not so much subject to the computer metaphor). In fact, as Bartlett investigated the nature of memory by reading passages to groups of subjects and having them recall them at later intervals, so Chafe (1977a, b) has been studying the recall of events by showing a film to groups of subjects and having them retell what they saw at later intervals (in fact, these data are the basis of the present paper).

As a linguist, however, Chafe (1977a) is interested in verbalization. He posits the question: after witnessing or experiencing an event, "What kinds of processes must this person apply to convert his knowledge, predominantly nonverbal to begin with, into a verbal output?" (p. 41). The first element in this process, he hypothesizes, is the determination of a schema, which refers to the identification of the event; the second is the determination of a frame, which refers to the sentence-level expression about particular individuals and their roles in the event; finally, a category is chosen to name objects or actions which play parts in the event. For all these choices, one must "match the internal representation of particular events and individuals with internally represented prototypes" (p. 42).

Since we are encountering the term "prototype" here, it is as good a time as any to note that this is another currently popular term which is inextricably intertwined with the notion of expectations. As Fillmore (1975) notes, the "prototype idea can be seen in the color term studies of B. Berlin and P. Kay (1969) and in the 'natural category' researches of E. Rosch (1973)" (p. 123). Fillmore lists a number of other related concepts as well from a variety of disciplines. The prototype, like the frame, refers to an expectation about the world, based on prior experience, against which new experiences are measured and interpreted.

Returning to our discussion of the uses of the term "schema," we may note the work of Rumelhart (1975), who devises a schema for stories in the interest of developing an automatic "story parser" for artificial intelligence consumption. Rumelhart acknowledges his debt to Schank as well as Propp (1958).

To give one final example of how the notion of schemata has been used in AI, we refer to Bobrow and Norman (1975), who "propose that memory structures [in a computer] be comprised of a set of active schemata, each capable of evaluating information passed to it and capable of passing information and requests to other schemata" (p. 148). Their association of schemata with automatic processes seems to reflect faithfully the function of expectations: "Any time there is a mismatch between data and process or expectations and occurrences, conscious processes are brought in" (p. 148). This reflects, then, the way in which a person's perception of the world proceeds automatically so long as expectations are met, while s/he is stopped short, forced to question things, only when they are not.

Abelson's interest in scripts spans three fields: ideology, story understanding (that is, for the purpose of computer simulation), and social behavior (talk at UC Berkeley, March 1977). Abelson's broad interests render his work on scripts particularly interesting. He became interested in scripts, he explains, in connection with the predictability he discerned in Goldwater's belief system! Among the most interesting of the perspectives Abelson (1976) investigates is the relationship between scripts, attitudes, and behavior: "In our view, attitude toward an object consists in the ensemble of scripts concerning that object" (p. 16). He notes, therefore, that it is interesting to talk about scripts when there is a clash between how people behave and how you might expect them to behave. An understanding of their scripts, then, explains the link between attitudes and behavior.

In the area of story understanding, Abelson has worked alongside Schank. They note that their notion of script is like Minsky's notion of frames, "except that it is specialized to deal with event sequences" (Schank & Abelson, 1975). In fact, for Schank and Abelson, *script* is only one form of knowledge structure; it is their aim to define others as well. Their latest book (Schank &

Abelson, 1977) differentiates between scripts, plans, goals, and themes, which, they note, are explained in descending order of clarity. It should be noted, perhaps, that earlier papers make other distinctions. In Abelson (1975), there are script, theme ("a conceptual structure which accounts for a number of related scripts..."), and dreme ("a conception of the possibility that one or more themes are subject to change") (p. 275). In Abelson (1976), "The basic ingredient of scripts we label a *vignette*" (p. 2). Finally, Schank and Abelson (1975) distinguish two kinds of scripts: situational and planning scripts. Planning scripts are said to "describe the set of choices that a person has when he sets out to accomplish a goal" (p. 154), and therefore seem identical to what they now define as a separate knowledge structure called a plan. The situational script seems to be what they now simply call "script," that is, a familiar, causally connected sequence of intentional (goal-oriented) events (Abelson talk, UC Berkeley, March 1977).

Schank and Abelson's (1975) notion of script is best characterized by their example of the restaurant script. They illustrate the existence of scripts in knowledge structures by presenting the following sort of story:

> John went into the restaurant. He ordered a hamburger and a coke. He asked the waitress for the check and left.

One might ask how the story can refer to *"the"* waitress and *"the"* check "just as if these objects had been previously mentioned." The fact that they can is evidence of the existence of a script which "has implicitly introduced them by virtue of its own introduction" (p. 4.)

It remains now for us to examine the notion of *frame*. As mentioned above, this term has probably the widest distribution, occurring in the work of Bateson and Frake in anthropology, Hymes and Goffman in sociology, Minsky in artificial intelligence, and Fillmore in linguistics.

Bateson introduced the notion of *frame* in 1955 to explain how individuals exchange signals that allow them to agree upon the level of abstraction at which any message is intended. Even animals can be seen to use frames to interpret each other's behavior, by signaling, for example, "This is play." Bateson (1972) insists that "frame" is a psychological concept, but to characterize it, he uses "the physical analogy of the picture frame and the more abstract... analogy of the mathematical set" (p. 186).

In his work on the ethnography of speaking, which seeks to analyze language as it is used by people in specific cultures, Hymes (1974) includes frames as one of the "means of speaking." In order to interpret utterances in accordance with the way in which they were intended, a hearer must know what "frame" s/he is operating in, that is, whether the activity being engaged in is joking, imitating, chatting, lecturing, or performing a play, to name just a few possibilities familiar to our culture. This notion of frames as a culturally determined, familiar activity is consonant with the term as used by Goffman (1974) and Frake (1977).

Frake traces the cognitive anthropological use of "frame" to structural linguistics and credits his field with having broadened the concept from its linguistic application to isolated sentences to a sequence of conversational exchange. Frake goes on to complain, however, of the very misconception that Bartlett cautioned against and which we have noted in the work of the artificial intelligence theorists, that is, the idea that people have in their heads fully-formed "cognitive ideolects" which can be described and which add up to "culture." In other words, he is opposing a static notion of frames in favor of an interactive model. He notes that anthropologists had come to refer to "eliciting frames," as if they were there and had merely to be tapped. Frake suggests instead, and this is an approach basic to the work of John Gumperz and other ethnographers of speaking, that the key aspect of frames is what the people are *doing* when they speak. He discusses the notion of *event* which seems to correspond to what Gumperz (1977) calls an *activity* as the unit of study: an identifiable interactional happening that has meaning for the participants. Thus the anthropological/sociological view stresses *frame* as a relational concept rather than a sequence of events; it refers to the dynamic relationship between people, much like Bartlett's (1932) "organized mass" of past experience which is "actively *doing* something all the time" (p. 201, italics his). Frake (1977) ends his paper with the extended metaphor of people as mapmakers whose "culture does not provide a cognitive map, but rather a set of principles for mapmaking and navigation," resulting in "a whole chart case of rough, improvised, continually revised sketch maps" (pp. 6–7). This metaphorical chart case seems awfully like a set of overlapping, intertwining, and developing scripts.

In contrast with the anthropological/sociological characterization of frames as an interactional unit with social meaning, Minsky's (1974) is a static concept, rooted in the computer model of artificial intelligence. Acknowledging his debt to Schank and Abelson, Bartlett, Piaget, and others, Minsky propounds the notion of frame as an all-inclusive term for "a data-structure for representing a stereotyped situation" (p. 212). For Minsky, this term denotes such event sequences as a birthday party (corresponding to Schank and Abelson's restaurant script), but also ordered expectations about objects and setting (for example, a certain kind of living room). Minsky distinguishes between at least four levels of frames: surface syntactic frames ("mainly verb and noun structures"), surface semantic frames (seemingly corresponding to Fillmore's notion of case frame), thematic frames ("scenarios"), and narrative frames (apparently comparable to Schank and Abelson's scripts). Although Minsky's explication of the frame theory, which appeared in 1974 as a memo from the MIT AI Lab does not constitute much theoretical innovation beyond the work of Bartlett and others we have seen who followed him, yet it represents a particularly coherent, complete, and readable formulation of the theory, and perhaps for this reason it has had resounding impact on the field of AI as well as on many other disciplines.

Fillmore, too, has chosen the term "frame," and it is perhaps fitting to end with his treatment of this material, for his short paper (1975) brings all these ideas into focus in connection with linguistics. He begins with a listing of theories of Prototype and Frame from a variety of disciplines. Fillmore uses nearly all the terms we have discussed somewhere in his paper (except "scripts"). His thesis is that a frame-and-scene analysis of language can elucidate hitherto fuzzy areas of linguistics. He uses "the word *frame* for any system of linguistic choices...that can get associated with prototypical instances of scenes" and the word *scene* for "any kind of coherent segment of human beliefs, actions, experiences or imaginings" (p. 124). Furthermore, "people associate certain *scenes* with certain linguistic *frames*" (p. 2). Fillmore then shows how this approach to meaning is useful in three areas: (1) analysis of discourse, (2) acquisition of word meaning, and (3) the boundary problem for linguistic categories.

These, then, have been the major theories making use of notions of frames, schemata, and scripts. They may all be seen, in some sense, to be derived from Bartlett. It may be useful, before proceeding to our data, to consider one more research tradition which also can be seen to derive from Bartlett, and to be related to the concept of structures of expectation, even though it does not employ the specific terms we have been investigating. This is the work of the constructive memory theorists in cognitive psychology.

Research in this tradition has demonstrated the effect of context on memory performance tasks. The first of these was Pompi and Lachman (1967) who showed the superior performance on memory tasks of subjects who had read a passage in coherent order over those who had read a scrambled version of it. Even more striking, however, is the research of Bransford and his co-workers (Bransford & Franks, 1971; Bransford & Johnson, 1973). They showed that subjects were unable to recall well a passage which contained only pronouns and described a series of actions. When the same passage was read, however, under the title which identified the sequence of actions as, for example, someone washing clothes, subjects were able to recall it well. In the terms we have been considering, we might say that the title identified the sequence of events as a familiar script, or that it fit the activity into a known frame.

Similar evidence lies in the research of Anderson and Ortony (1975). They presented subjects with sentences like, for example, "The woman was waiting outside the theater." After reading a list of such sentences to subjects, they tried to elicit the sentences by using one-word cues. It was found that context-associated words which did not actually appear in the sentences were better cues than context-free words which actually were in the sentence. In other words, in the sentence given, "actress" was a better cue than "woman," even though the word "woman" actually was in the target sentence while "actress" was not. This is reminiscent of the Schank and Abelson restaurant script hypothesis, which pointed to the fact that a waitress could be treated as given when no waitress had been mentioned.

What unifies all these branches of research is the realization that people approach the world not as naive, blank-slate receptacles who take in stimuli as they exist in some independent and objective way, but rather as experienced and sophisticated veterans of perception who have stored their prior experiences as "an organized mass," and who see events and objects in the world in relation to each other and in relation to their prior experience. This prior experience or organized knowledge then takes the form of expectations about the world, and in the vast majority of cases, the world, being a systematic place, confirms these expectations, saving the individual the trouble of figuring things out anew all the time.

At the same time that expectations make it possible to perceive and interpret objects and events in the world, they shape those perceptions to the model of the world provided by them. As Bartlett put it, one forms a general impression (we might say, one labels something as part of a certain scene, frame, or script) and furnishes the details which one builds from prior knowledge (that is, from the script). Thus, structures of expectation make interpretation possible, but in the process they also reflect back on perception of the world to justify that interpretation.

All these theories have referred to frames and other structures of expectation, but they have shown no way of discovering what those structures consist of, for they have been mainly concerned with language comprehension. In this chapter, I would like to consider how expectations affect language production, and, in the process, show a way of discovering what constitutes them—that is, to show how we can know what's in a frame.

DATA FOR THE PRESENT STUDY

In connection with a project directed by Wallace Chafe, a movie was shown to small groups of young women who then told another woman (who they were told had not seen the film) what they had seen in the movie. The film was a six-minute short, of our own production, which included sound but no dialogue. It showed a man picking pears from a tree, then descending and dumping them into one of three baskets on the ground. A boy comes by on a bicycle and steals a basket of pears. As he's riding away, he passes a girl on a bike, his hat flies off his head, and the bike overturns. Three boys appear and help him gather his pears. They find his hat and return it to him, and he gives them pears. The boys then pass the farmer who has just come down from the tree and discovered that his basket of pears is missing. He watches them walk by eating pears.

This film was shown and this procedure followed in ten different countries. I oversaw the administration of the experiment in Athens, Greece and have studied the Greek narratives.[1] In describing the events and people in the movie, subjects organized and altered the actual content of the movie in many ways. The ways in which they did this are evidence of the effect of their structures of expectation about objects and events in the film. The comparison of narratives told by Greek and American subjects makes it possible to see that these structures are often culturally determined, as one would expect.

On the basis of this hypothesis, I have isolated sixteen general types of evidence which represent the imposition of the speakers' expectations on the content of the film. These are not absolute categories, and certainly this is not a definitive list, yet they cover a broad range of linguistic phenomena, and they represent a way in which structures of expectation can be characterized.

Labov (1972) discusses a series of surface linguistic phenomena in oral narratives which he calls "evaluative." They are "the means used by the narrator to indicate the point of the narrative," or to answer in advance the question, "So what?" Since the point of a narrative is directly related to the expectations of people in the culture in which it is told, it is not surprising that Labov's evaluative elements are closely related to my notion of evidence of expectations. I will note these similarities as they arise in the following discussion.

---

[1]No attempt was made, in gathering our narratives, to find "equivalent" or "comparable" subject populations from the point of view of socioeconomic status or other external variable besides age and sex. Our interest was in exploring *different* approaches to verbalization of events in the same film. While it is tempting to hypothesize that the differences are culturally-based, this need not be the case to demonstrate that there are consistent differences in the way these two groups of subjects approached the verbalization task. It may be noted briefly, however, that the twenty American subjects were students at the University of California, Berkeley, while the twenty Greek subjects were attending evening classes in the English language at the Hellenic American Union in Athens. Seven were university students, two were university graduates, six were high school students, and four were employed high school graduates. The American subjects were slightly older, ranging in age from 18 to 30 with a median of 23, while the Greeks ranged in age from 16 to 26 with a median of 19. Virtually all the American subjects had been raised in cities, and most of the Greeks had been born and raised in Athens, except for one from Istanbul and four from Greek towns. It might be noted, however, that a typical Athenian has closer ties with rural life than do American city-dwellers, as Athenians often make "excursions" to the villages and most have relatives living in the countryside whom they visit regularly.

LEVELS OF FRAMES

Any speech event represents the overlapping and intertwining of many relations concerning the context as well as the content of communication. In the case of the oral narratives under study here, the larger context is the one in which the speaker is the subject of an experiment, and the context in which that experiment is being carried out is an interview mode, in which the speaker knows that her voice is being tape-recorded. Clearly, the speaker's expectations about being the subject of an experiment in an academic setting, and her feelings about having her voice recorded, affect her narrative performance.

The content of the story, furthermore, is the narration of events in a film, so the speaker's expectations about films as well as her expectations of herself as a film viewer also come into play. Finally, the events, objects, and people depicted in the film trigger expectations about similar events, objects, and people in the real world and their interrelationships. All these levels of knowledge structures coexist and must operate in conjunction with each other to determine how the events in the film will be perceived and then verbalized. In the following discussion, I will consider these various levels of expectation structures in turn, in order of scope (that is, from the overriding context, subject of experiment, to the relatively narrow object level) and in each case I will demonstrate how the expectations are revealed in surface evidence of the types I have been looking at. In cases in which there are significant differences between Greek and American responses, that will be noted. After expectations have been seen to operate on these various levels, I will list the sixteen types of evidence used in the preceding discussion and explain and exemplify each. In a final section, I will discuss the elements of one specific set of expectations, that is, parts of the narratives relating to the occurrence of a theft.

SUBJECT OF EXPERIMENT

The broadest level of context operating in the film narratives relates to the situation in which the speakers find themselves. As subjects of an experiment, they are telling a story to a person they have never met before.[2] They do not know the purpose of the experiment, so they do not know what elements in their story will be of interest to the hearer. This is clearly an unnatural context for storytelling. The fact that it is an experiment situation may well affect

---

[2]The interviewer was of the same sex and similar age, to minimize the discomfort caused by this situation.

every aspect of the telling, although it is also likely that the speakers have told stories and told plots of films so often that they lapse into a habitual narrative mode. It is, nonetheless, a context in which the speakers are subjects of the experiment, and they reveal expectations about that situation in their talk.

On the average, the American narratives are longer and more detailed than the Greek ones. It is possible that this is a function of the Americans' assumptions about the experiment situation. That is, not knowing the purpose of the experiment, they may feel that the more details they give, the more likely they will include what is wanted. Moreover, they may have an instinctive feeling that it is a memory test. A number of American subjects overtly express their discomfort about how much detail to include (some repeatedly), while a few Greeks ask at the beginning but do not return to the issue. For example, S34 says

> S34 (45)   ...and then-- UM...just..how..I mean how picky do you want.[3]

Another American subject expresses regret that she does not remember more details:

> S49 (55)   ...That's all I remember. You should have caught me
> ...ten minutes ago when I remembered...Who passed the
> ...the man before the kid on the bicycle, I don't remember.

The use of a *negative statement* is one of the clearest and most frequent indications that an expectation is not being met. As Labov (1972) puts it, "What reason would the narrator have for telling us that something did not happen since he is in the business of telling us what did happen?" He explains, "...it expresses the defeat of an expectation that something would happen" (pp. 380–81). I have demonstrated this in a natural narrative (Tannen, 1977) elsewhere, and numerous examples will be seen in this paper as well. In the above example, the negative statement "I don't remember" indicates the

---

[3]The number following S (in this case S34) refers to the subject number. The number in parentheses refers to a "chunk" number, in accordance with a process of chunking utterances developed in the Chafe project. Other conventions of transcription:

...is a measurable pause, more than .1 sec. Precise measurements have been made and are available.

.. is a slight break in timing.

. indicates sentence-final intonation.

, indicates clause-final intonation ("more to come")

-- indicates length of the preceding phoneme or syllable.

Syllables with ˇ were spoken with heightened pitch.

Syllables with ˆ were spoken with heightened loudness.

/ / enclose transcriptions which are not certain.

[ ] enclose phonemic transcriptions or nonverbal utterances such as laughter.

speaker's expectation that she should have remembered the characters in the film in order to tell about them.

The fact that the speaker is wondering about the purpose of the experiment shows up in another narrative in this way:

> S39 (169) ... If this is for gestures, this is a great movie for gestures.

The non-syntactic anaphora (Gensler, 1977), "this," refers to the experiment, indicating that this "frame" has been in the speaker's mind even though she has not mentioned it overtly. Moreover, twelve Americans begin their narratives with "Okay," and three others with "All right" or "Sure," implying that they are agreeing to fulfill a request.[4] Two American subjects and one Greek indicate that they have kept this frame in mind, for they end their narratives by asking "Okay?" (Greek: *endaxi?*), which seems to be asking, "Is that what you wanted?"

Even though the storytelling is occurring in an experiment situation, it is an interaction between two people, both women, of roughly the same age and class. Thus it is inevitable that the speakers' habitual conversational expectations come into play. This can be seen in the following example. S37's storytelling mode is automatically triggered, but it conflicts with the interview conventions which require that the subject answer questions rather than the interviewer, and that the subject, moreover, conform to the rules established by the addressee. S37 has just made a statement which is a *judgment* about the sounds in the film. Since a judgment is clearly a comparison of the events of the film to her own expectations, she instinctively wants to check out her judgment with the addressee, who she knows has heard about the film from other speakers as well.

> S37 (24) ... has anybody told you that before? Or r you're not supposed to tell me that.

S37 acknowledges the constraint of the interview situation by her negative statement, "you're not supposed to tell me that." Two more sorts of evidence of expectations can be seen here: the appearance of the *modal,* "be supposed to," lexically measures the addressee's actions against expected norms (Labov discusses modals as "evaluative" as well). Finally, the false start is a frequent occurrence in oral narratives which indicates the operation of expectations. The false start in this example, "r," is minimal, but it seems that the aborted "r" was intended to begin the phrasing, "Are you allowed to tell me?" The speaker's decision to switch to a negative statement seems to be evidence that she recalled the interview situation and its attendant constraints.

---

[4]Nine Greek subjects began by saing *Nai,* "Yes." The others simply launched into their narratives. This coincides with my findings (Tannen, 1976) that *nai,* commonly translated "yes," in fact is often used more like the English "okay" or "yeah" than the English "yes."

STORYTELLING FRAME

For some subjects, awareness of the experiment situation seems less overriding than for others. For example, S4 gives the following reason for including details in her narrative.

> S4 (52)   ... I'm giving you ăll these details. I don't know if you want them. ... UM-- ... the ... rěason I'm giving you the details is cause I don't know what the point of the movie was. ... Okay? So maybe yŏu can see something that I didn't. ... Okay?
> /laugh/

S4 apparently feels that when telling about a movie, she should know and communicate what "the point" was. Her inability to do this creates enough discomfort for her to mention it as a reason for telling details. She seems to feel, moreover, that it is odd for her to tell details without fitting them into some structure or "point." Her statement about the interviewer's ability to make sense of the details (note again the modal, "can") indicates that she is operating on a cooperative model in which she assumes her purpose is to communicate to her hearer. This is somewhat different from the expectation of a purpose of furnishing data for an unidentified researcher.

A similar expectation about the reasonableness of the hearer shows up in S39.

> S39 (124)   don't say yes, because you don't you've never seen that /??/. All right. Okay.

All subjects had been told that the person they were telling their story to had not seen the film. Therefore, S39 expects the hearer to act like an ignorant addressee. Similarly, S47 asks:

> S47 (20)   ... AH-- would you like to know what ... the goat looked like? [thiyə]? I hate to take away the suspe̎--nse or anything.

This statement reveals the expectation that limits the amount one ought to tell about a film to someone who has not seen the film and intends to, since part of film-viewing involves not knowing any more than the film itself has shown you, or "suspense." Thus S47 is approaching the telling task from a "film-telling" frame rather than from an "interview-for-experiment" frame, such as the one which causes S34 to ask, "how picky do you want?"

There are a number of ways in which subjects reveal that they have expectations about how to tell a story. For example, it is clear that they feel they should tell only important elements. However, since they are not sure what they are telling the story for, they cannot always judge whether elements are important. This discomfort is verbalized, making that expectation overt.

S4 (15)   .. he's wearing like an apron with huge pockets. .. But I don't think you see the apron at first. I don't know if that's important or not.

S4 (152)   ... Who looks like a Mexican-American if that's important?

S34 (79)   ... And I don't know if this--... really is important, it's not important it's just something I noticed,

The word *just* frequently functions to underplay a statement to block criticism on the basis that it is not more, therefore revealing the assumption that others might expect more. This function of *just* is discussed at length elsewhere (Tannen, 1977). In the above example, S34 says that the point she has made is "just something I noticed"; the *just* follows a negative, as it often does: "it's not important." Both these traces reveal the expectation that anything worth mentioning in the narrative is important.

A number of subjects reveal the expectation that events be related in the story in the temporal order in which they occurred.[5]

S4 (33)   ... Let's see is it while he's up in the ladder? or .. or before. ... UM--... anyway,

The *anyway* is a common type of evidence that an expectation is violated.[6] In this case it functions as an admission of defeat, at the same time that it marks the fact that an attempt was made to get the temporal order right. This speaker uses "anyway" in the same way later, and expresses the same expectation when she gives an excuse for putting something out of its temporal order. Like many other subjects, she mentions later in her story that a rooster was heard in the beginning of the film. Then she explains,

S4 (67)   Anyway. ... I just remembered that. ... Anyway,

She seems to be saying, "I'm breaking the rules of storytelling a bit, but be indulgent. I tried." Another subject shows a similar concern with getting the temporal order of events right.

S39 (105) ... Came dow .. oh no, that didn't happen yet. ... So--... the sequence is funny... if you don't really... remember.

Moreover, the strength of this constraint is evidenced in the striking accuracy in all our narratives, both Greek and American, with regard to temporal sequence.

---

[5]We know from the work of Alton Becker that this is not so for members of Balinese or Javanese society.

[6]"Anyway" was investigated in an elicitation-of-interpretations format. Results are discussed in Tannen (1976) under the subheading taken from one respondent's apt characterization, "Sour Grapes Anyway."

WHAT'S IN A FILM?

The narratives in this sample constitute a special kind of storytelling; they are about events in a film. At least one subject commented about how it felt to be talking about a film in this setting.

> S39 (22) ...so...it's very funny to make this telling.

We may assume that others felt "funny" about it as well, even if they did not say so, since when we tell each other about films we have seen, we usually do so for internally-generated reasons. Still, talking about films is a common practice in American and Greek society, and in these narratives, expectations about being subjects of an experiment clearly interplay with expectations about telling about movies.

The narratives of the American women contain more evidence of expectations about films as films than the Greek narratives. For example, nine Americans mention that the film contains no dialogue. As usual, the negative statement indicates that its affirmative was expected. Another way in which this film clearly did not adhere to subjects' expectations about films is with regard to its sound effects. Six American speakers mention the sounds in the film. For two of them, the sound track of the film is the theme which unifies their narratives, about which they adduce details, and which they return to repeatedly. Another subject, in fact, telling about the film a year after she first saw it, recalled this as the most salient feature of the film, even though she had not mentioned the sound at all the first time she told about it.

Three Americans devote a considerable amount of attention to this aspect of the film. One introduces it this way:

> S37 (20) but there..is...a lot of sound effects.   ...Which are nŏt...totally UM--...consistent.

The *but* is another important kind of evidence of expectations. It marks the contrast with the expectation established by the preceding statement about there being no dialogue in the film.[7] Two other Americans say:

> S44 (13) and the soŭnd is just...is...is really intensified /well/... from what..it..usually..would be, I think.

> S46 (22) ...And what I noticed...first off...was that all the noises in the movie,...were UM--...out of proportion.

The fact that these three subjects were particularly uncomfortable about the violation of this expectation about film sound tracks is marked in a number of ways. First of all, they continue to devote large portions of their narratives

---

[7]"But" as a denial of expectation signal is discussed in Lakoff (1971); its function in discourse is discussed in Tannen (1977).

to discussing it. Second, their statements are broken up by numerous pauses. Finally, and most obviously, judgment is implied in their choice of adjectives: "not consistent," "intensified," "out of proportion." Other subjects, however, mention this aspect of the film without implying judgment:

S4 (65)   ... And the movie had a sound track. ... It's important.

S12 (2)   The movie seemed very ... sound oriented.

S4, still concerned with making it clear that she is adhering to the expectation that what she tells be important, notes that the sound track is "important" because it is unusual. Otherwise, one would assume that a movie has a sound track, and it would not be reportable. (Schank and Abelson would say that it is known by virtue of its inclusion in the "film script.")

American subjects reveal other expectations about verisimilitude in films. For example, one speaker comments on the quality of the color:

S24 (9)   ... Something that I noticed about the /movie/ particularly unique was that the colors .. were ... just ... vêry strânge.... Like ... the green was a ... inordinately bright green, ... for the pears, .. and ... these colors just seemed a little ... kind of bold, almost to the point of ... being artificial.

S24 assumes that the colors are not supposed to be "artificial," and she is making a judgment about the fact that they were. This is, again, a significant verbal act, and her raised amplitude reveals her emotional investment in the process ("very strange"), as well as the hedges ("just," "a little ... kind of," "almost to the point of ... being"). Another subject makes a similar judgment about the costumes.

S39 (45)   ... And the pẽople looked very funny, because they were suppõ--sed, ... to be-- ... far--mer--ish, ... and really just had ... clothes like a person with like ... store levis, and ... a ñ--ew red bandana around his neck and a ... things like

S39 expects the film to be realistic in its effects and considers it noteworthy that the characters' clothing seemed inauthentic to her. She is maintaining a "film-viewer" point of view, reporting the costumes as artifacts of the film, rather than simply describing them as clothes worn by people involved in the events she is reporting, as all the others who talk about clothing in fact do. Increased pitch and amplitude as well as elongated sounds and pauses also contribute to the denial-of-expectation implication of her statement; they connote surprise.

Films are expected to be internally consistent with regard to concrete details. Thus S34 was very troubled because she thought she detected a contradiction; she recalled seeing two baskets on the ground before the boy stole one, and then she recalled seeing two remaining. In fact, she made an error. There were actually three baskets in the first place. However, her sense that the film was inconsistent was so disturbing to her that she spent a great deal of time talking about it in her initial narrative, and when she was asked to retell the narrative six weeks later, she again devoted a large portion of her story to discussing this detail.

Another expectation about films revealed in our narratives is related to its pace. Two subjects comment, with reference to a scene in which a man is picking pears,

> S34 (29)   .. There's nothing... doesn't seem to be very hurried. ... In the movie. It's fairly... slow,

> S50 (21)   ... A--nd... he's... it... the.. cămera spends a lot of time watching him... pick these pears,

Again, they comment on the pace as an artifact of the film, not as a comment on the way the man is behaving, indicating that the speakers are in a film-description frame.

A final observation about film expectations entails that any character introduced in the film must play a role in the plot. Three Americans comment about a man who passes by with a goat, to the effect that he does not figure in the action. S24, for example, says that the man and goat

> S24 (28)   ... and just kind of walk off. They don't really seem to have too much to do,... with.. what's going.. on.

Again, the word *just* (in fact the almost formulaically common qualification-plus-hedge "just kind of") marks the expectation that MORE was expected. The implied judgment in the second part of the statement is again signaled by the clutch of hedges ("really," "seem," "too much") which soften the impact of the negative statement. Similarly, in another scene, a girl on a bicycle passes the boy on his bicycle. Two Americans indicate that the appearance of the girl had less significance than they expected of a character introduced into the film. In one case this is shown by the statement,

> S39 (135) ... That was all that.. you saw of her in the movie.

In another it takes the form of a report of the viewer's thoughts:

> S6 (78)   ... a--nd UH--... you wonder how she's going to figure in on this.

FILM-VIEWER FRAME

This last example is an indication of another level of frame, closely related to that of the "film frame" we have been discussing. The speaker, S6, reports the events of the movie from her own point of view and therefore is characterizing herself as a film viewer. She reveals her expectations of herself and how she interacts with the film. In the above example, she shows herself anticipating the events of the film before they occur, trying to "psych out" the strategy of the plot. This speaker does this a number of times in her narrative. Another instance is:

> S6 (69)   ..and you think "Aha. ... UH ... Are we gonna go back to the man over there" but no.

Thus the interplay between her expectations and the events of the film are part of her narrative content. Her experience as a viewer is part of her story which therefore becomes a story not only of the movie but of her viewing of it as well.

This can be seen in another subject's conclusion of a particularly short and straightforward narrative:

> S8 (59)   And ... yŏu're left with this dilemma, ... what does this guy [laugh] you know what does this guy really think.

S8, like nearly all our subjects, assumes that the pearpicker's thoughts are significant. She expresses this in terms of the expectation that the film should make clear the character's attitude toward the events of the film, so that uncertainty about that attitude becomes a "dilemma" for her as a viewer.

A similar point of view can be seen in S34:

> S34 (24)   I don't know what ... I wasn't sure at first if they were apples, or if they were pears, but ... UM ... he's picking pears,

If the task is to describe what happened in the film, and if the speaker's conclusion is unquestionably that the man was picking pears, why does she report her initial uncertainty as to whether they were apples or pears? Her inclusion of this internal process of interpretation reflects her telling not only the story of the film, but the story of her experience watching it.

There are other examples of the "film-viewer frame." Perhaps one more aspect of it will suffice to indicate its function in the narratives. When a speaker reports her interpretation of the film, she necessarily characterizes herself as a film viewer. Therefore, for example, a speaker who reveals her expectation that an event in the film will have significance by saying that she thought the goat would eat the pears, follows this up with,

> S39 (69)   That's .. I don't know whether you're supposed to think that or not.

Her *false start,* the *negative statement* about her own knowledge, and the *modal* all indicate her insecurity about the image she has presented of herself as a film viewer. The expectation is revealed that an adept viewer correctly interprets the actions of a film.

Strikingly, preoccupation with the film as a film and oneself as a film viewer is absent from the Greek narratives. No Greek speaker criticizes the film or comments on it as a film in any way. The Greek narratives include no comment about the sound track, and no discussion of the speakers' anticipation of what would happen. In fact, fully half of the Greek subjects tell their entire narratives without ever making reference to the film as a film. Rather, they tell about the events directly. This is particularly noticeable in the beginning and end of their narrations, where there is the greatest likelihood in English narratives for the film to be mentioned as a film. For example, a typical beginning of a Greek narrative is:

G1 (1)   ...e...to proto praghma pou eidha, ..itan ena pra--sino kataprasino topio,
          ...e...the first thing that I saw, ..was a gree--n verygreen landscape,[8]

This narrative ends:

G1 (77)   etsi...menei aporimenos o--
          thus...(he) remains wondering the--

This is in contrast to such openings as "The film opened with..." or "The first scene showed...." While ten of the twenty Greek subjects make no reference at all to the fact that the events they are telling about occurred in a film, all twenty Americans make some allusion to it somewhere in their narratives, and most make much more than passing reference, as has been seen.

Of the ten Greek subjects who make some reference to the fact that they are talking about a film, only three actually mention the word "film" directly. Two of these mention it only once, in the first line of their narratives, and the third mentions it in both the first and the last lines. The other seven Greeks refer to it indirectly, generally through the verb edheichne or dheichnei, "(it) showed" or "it shows," in which the deleted subject is "the film."

This unmistakable difference between the points of view or frames of the Greek and American subjects seems to indicate that Americans are media-wise, or media-conscious, so their expectations about films and film-viewing are more developed and more salient to them. This tendency, however, to view the film as a film (or, put another way, to be conscious of the frame "film-watching") may be related to another striking difference between Greek and American narratives: the tendency of Greeks to interpret and make judgments about the events and people portrayed. While a number of Americans develop their narratives into extensions of the theme that the film had a strange soundtrack, a number of Greeks develop their narratives into extensions of some theme about the signicicance of the events in it. Thus,

---

[8]Greek transliteration will reflect Greek spelling as closely as possible. Translation will reflect syntax in the original whenever possible without making the meaning incomprehensible. The G# represents the subject number for Greek subjects.

Greeks are also seeing the film as a film, but they are interested in its "message" rather than its execution.

In order to illustrate this characteristic of the Greek narratives, I will translate the entire narrative of one speaker, eliminating pauses and other details of transcription so that the events can be followed easily. Although this is an extreme case, it dramatizes a tendency which is present to some extent in nearly all the Greek narratives. First of all, it is full of *interpretations* and *judgments*. Second, it is interesting to note which of the events of the film this speaker chooses to include in her story, and which she *omits*.

> G12 From what I understood, it was an episode, it happened in Mexico. I suppose, the people seemed Mexican to me, and it showed the how a person was gathering pears, and it insisted that which he did, he was living. The in other words that he cultivated the earth, that he gathered these the harvest, was something special for him . . . it was worth something. He lived that which he did, he liked it. And it showed a scene-- it must have been the agricultural life of that region, someone who passed with a goat, a child a child with a bicycle, who saw the basket, with the pears, and took it, and then as he was passing, he met in the middle of the field, another girl with a bicycle, and as he looked at her, he didn't pay attention a little, and fell from him fell from him the basket with the pears, and there again were three other friends of his, who immediately helped him and this was anyway something that showed how children love each other, they have solidarity, they helped him to gather them, and and as he forgot his hat, there was a beautiful scene where he gave them the pears and returned it back again. In other words generally I think it was a scene from the agricultural life of the region it showed. That's it.

A vast array of interpretive devices are operating here to support G12's main idea: an all's'-right-with-the-world, romantic view of the meaning of the film. She discusses at length the pearpicker's attitude toward his work, as if it were known to her, yet it is clearly her own interpretation, as is her comment that the interaction between the boy and the three others who help him shows "how children love each other." These interpretations seem to be motivated by her own expectations about farmers and children. Similarly, her use of the adjective "beautiful" to describe the scene in which one boy gives the others some pears constitutes a judgment about the events. A process I have called *interpretive naming* can be seen in her reference to the three boys as "friends of his," without overtly marking that this is an interpretation, which it clearly is. Finally, to support her interpretation, G12 omits parts of the film that would suggest a less rosy picture of the world. For example, she is the only one who actually omits to mention that the boy fell off his bicycle. She also omits the entire last scene in which the three boys pass by the tree where the man has discovered that his pears are missing. Moreover, she underplays the fact of the theft. Thus, the use of *interpretation* shapes this entire narrative in a way that it never does for our American subjects' narratives.

Such free use of interpretation first of all reveals a different attitude toward the activity of film-viewing and/or of being the subject of an experiment. It also yields an especially clear insight into the speaker's expectations. G12's idiosyncratic interpretation of the pearpicking film indicates her pastoral view of or expectations about farmers and children, which are part of a larger expectation about the romantic message of the film.

The tendency to approach the film for its "message" can be seen in other Greek narratives as well. For example, G6 ends by saying,

> G6 (50)   ... *allo an /dhinei/ tora--* ... *o kathenas alles erminies.*
> ... other if / gives/ now-- ... each (one) other interpretations.
> [it's something else again if each person gives different interpretations]

Another subject indicates her expectation that she should be able to interpret the film by a negative statement which she in fact *repeats.*

> G9 (107)   ... *tora to topio vevaia itan orai--o.* ... *alla dhen xero na to exighiso.*
> ... now the landscape certainly was lovely. ... but (I) don't know (how) to explain it.

After saying a few more sentences about the landscape, she says again, "but I don't know how to-- how to explain it."

Furthermore, while G12 was an extreme example of interpretive narration, other Greeks showed similar tendencies. For example, G11 says (again I will simply write the English translation to facilitate reading):

> G11   ... (there) was a perso--n ... a person of the earth. ... one of those who labor. ... a farmer, ... (he) was gathering-- ... (he) had worked-- the whole year, ... and (he) wanted to take his fruits. ... (he) was going up, (he) was going down, (he) was sweating, (he) was looking at .. EH with a devo--tion you know the pear ... (he) was taking it (he) was putting it in the basket, ... (it) was falling down from him (he) was going down (he) was grasping it (he) was putting it back in the basket [sigh] ... very devoutly.

That the man was a farmer is *interpretive naming*; that he worked all year is an *inference* which contributes to the romantic interpretation of the farmer's relationship to his fruit. The speaker used the *katharevousa* word for "fruit," *karpous,* which is a more literary word, suggesting the notion "fruits of his labor" rather than simply "fruit" in the sense of "pears." She also *generalizes* the actions which occur once in the film and reports them as if they were done repeatedly, contributing to the interpretation of the farmer as a hardworking person. Even the speaker's intonation and her slow rate of speech conspire to create this effect. This personal view of the pearpicker surfaces at the end as well, where G11 reports his reaction to discovering that a basket is missing, from his point of view:

> G11 (117).. *to allo ghemato pou einai?*
> .. the other full (one) where is (it)?

Finally, she infers his emotions at that point and repeats her inference, and switching to his point of view without marking the switch overtly.

> G11 (119)... *TSK alla... moirolatrika to pire dhen boro-- na kano*
> *tipota tora pia. ... EH-- vlepei tous.. treis bobires pou*
> *troghane to--... achladhi,.. tous koitaze moirolatrika-- alla*
> *dhen boro na kano tipota allo*
> ... TSK but... fatefully (he) took it (I) can't-- do anything
> now anymore. ... EH-- (he) sees the.. three kids who were
> eating the--... pear,.. (he) was looking at them fatefully-- but
> (I) can't do anything else

"He took it fatefully" means something like, "He was philosophical about it." The speaker, however, seems to be characterizing her own view of life, or her expectation about farmers, rather than reporting what was actually dramatized in the movie.

Another Greek subject also interprets the pearpicker's actions at the end, although her interpretation is somewhat different. She also makes her identification with the man more immediate by assuming his point of view:

> G16 (80) ... *dhen-- UH-- anti na tou pi-- na t na tou pi paidhia--einai*
> *ap ta achladhia ta opoia-- pithanon na echete pari eseis, ... ta*
> *vlepei, kai--... ta koitaei etsi me ... choris na tous pi tipota,*
> *evg evghenika as poume tous ferthike, ... UH koitaxe, kai--*
> *eidhe as poume oti-- troghan ta achladhia, kai--sa na*
> *efcharistithike/??/ kai dhen eipe tipota oti einai dhika mou ta*
> *achladhia afta,*
> ... (he) didn't--UH-- instead of telling them-- of of telling
> them children-- (they) are from the pears which-- possibly you
> have taken, ... (he) sees them, and--... (he) looks at them
> thus with ... without telling them anything, ki kindly let's say
> (he) treated them,, ... UH (he) looked, and-- (he) saw let's say
> that-- (they) were eating the pears, and-- as if (he) was
> glad/??/ and (he) didn't say anything that these pears are
> mine,

G16 thus has interpreted that the man picking pears is glad to see the boys enjoying his pears, and that he treats them "kindly." The fact that she believes she should evaluate the film's message is seen, finally, in her following and last comment:

> G16 (93) ...ghenikos echei stoicheia etsi anthropias /alla/ synedh-
> iazmena kai me--...me ti...tha borouse perissotero na
> eiche as poume stin archi--
> ...generally (it) has elements thus of humanism /but/
> combined also with--...with what...(it) could have had
> more let's say in the beginning--

Thus G16 makes it explicit that her inferences about the pearpicker's attitude contribute to an interpretation of the message of the film. Her complaint about "what it could have had more," that is, "the more meaning it could have had" in the beginning, seems to refer to her dissatisfaction with the film's moral viewpoint at first. This may be related to her rather complex and clearly emotionally tinged complaint that the boy who had fallen off his bicycle should have thanked the three boys who helped him by giving them pears right away, instead of doing so only when they returned his hat to him, after he had been on his way already. In addition, it may refer to her interpretation of the same motions and expression of the pearpicker in the opening scene which led G12 to interpret that he revered his pears. G16 said,

> G16 (3) ... TSK kai-- ta mazevei-- etsi me--...me poli--...e-- sa na
> ta thelei dhika tou. me poli etsi-- /s/ idhioktisia dh dheichnei
> mesa.
> ...TSK and-- (he) gathers them-- thus with--...with a lot--
> ...EH-- as if (he) wants them (to be) his own. with a lot thus--
> (of) /s/ proprietariness (it, he) sh shows inside.

With an equally free stroke, G16 interprets the pearpicker's motions as indicating possessiveness. These interpretations come from the same slow motions which led Americans to comment on the pace of the film.

Another example of the kind of interpretation found in the Greek but not the American narratives is G2's comment about the three boys' appearance:

> G2 (46) ... TSK...en to metaxi pros ironia...e pros ironia tis tychis
> ... TSK...in the meantime by irony...EH by irony of luck

Like her judgment about the boy's failure to thank his helpers (a comment made by a number of other Greeks as well), her comment about luck's irony indicates she is regarding the events of the film as intrinsically significant rather than as events to remember for a memory task.

Finally, a number of Greek subjects show a pronounced inclination to philosophize about the film and its meaning after they have told it. G16 goes on after the interviewer has indicated satisfaction:

G16   It has such elements as, of course, and the young man who took
the basket, I believe that he shouldn't have taken it, he took it at
first, but then with the young men's deed who called to him and
didn't ask, he gave them pears. And in the beginning the
gentleman who was gathering pears took great care of them, this
shows that man to be, that is, there are many contrasts in the
film. Although in the beginning you believe that the child will
give (them) pears, he goes away. But then after they give him
the hat he changes his mind and gives them again. And the
gentleman who was harvesting in the beginning and you thought
that he was collecting them for himself and it shows a man but
when he sees the children going away each holding a pear and
sees that they are his and doesn't call them you see a conflict and
you think it wasn't as I thought. It has many conflicts in it and--

Just as this speaker goes on and on about the conflicts in the film, another one
continues interminably about the pessimism of the film because it had a lot of
falls in it!

It is clear then that the way in which the subjects talk about the film is
shaped by their notion of what constitutes appropriate comment about a film.
Americans tended to operate from a film-viewer frame and criticize the film as
a technical product; Greeks tended to operate from a film-interpreter frame
and expected the film to have a "message" which they proceeded to explain.[9]

EXPECTATIONS ABOUT EVENTS

We have seen many ways in which speakers reveal expectations about the
context and activity in which they are taking part. In addition, the way they
describe the events in the film indicates their expectations about specific
events portrayed in it.

Personal Encounters

When a man with a goat walks by the tree where the man is picking pears, S6
typically reports,

S6 (20)   And the man up in the tree doesn't even notice,

Similarly, when the boy comes by and takes a basket of pears, she says,

---

[9]It is tempting to hypothesize that this reflects a more general tendency of Greeks to
philosophize—an observation which coincides with my impressions during several years'
residence in Greece.

S6 (65)   and the man up in the tree doesn't even... doesn't notice anything.

The negative statement, as has been seen repeatedly, indicates that an expected action failed to take place. The use of *even* intensifies this effect; it implies that "at least" this was expected and indicates surprise that it did not occur. In this case, the expectation is that when two people cross paths in a setting in which they are the only people present, they will notice and probably acknowledge each other. This shows up in another narrative this way:

S34 (43)   .. And there doesn't seem there's no communication between the two of them, ... or anything,

Comments like these are frequent in both Greek and American narratives. They are even more frequent with regard to the passing of the boy on his bike than about the man passing with the goat. In the case of the boy coming by, the expectations about interactions dovetail with expectations about the theft. That is, in addition to an expectation that the man and the boy would interact, there is an assumption that in order for the boy to steal the pears, he must not be noticed by the man. Thus, mentions of the fact that the man did not notice the boy both mark a denial of expectation based on an interaction frame and also make explicit an element of a theft frame. For example, one subject says,

S44 (54)   and the man doesn't know that the little boy is there.
(60)   ...And like.. so the man didn't hear the little boy,.. you know... being there, ...and-- he--.. ended up.. UM--... swiping.. one of his baskets of pears,

By juxtaposition, it is clear that the theft of the pears is seen as a consequence of the man's inattention. S6, the American who habitually verbalizes her expectations about the movie and plays them off against what actually happens, puts it this way:

S6 (30)   ...At least.. it seems to me that.. you know he would notice this boy

The same idea is operating more subtly in the following statement:

S50 (67)   ...But he's very brazen. I mean there's [o].. they're only about three feet apart.

The use of the *evaluative adjective* "brazen" and the word "only" both allude to the expectation that the man would notice the boy. These are two kinds of evidence of expectations. The second statement is, in effect, an explanation of the first. In fact, *adjectives* nearly always represent an interpretive or evaluative process on the part of the speaker at least in these narratives and probably in any storytelling event.

Confrontation

A related expectation about encounters between people which also overlaps with the theft frame can be seen in the way speakers describe the last scene in the film, in which the three boys pass the man who has just discovered that his pears are missing. S53 says,

> S53 (66) ...and he just kind of looks at them and...doesn't do anything.

There are a number of indications that the speaker expected a confrontation of some sort between the man and the passing boys. Once again, the word "just" and indeed the combination "just kind of," implies that MORE was expected. The increased pitch on "looks at them" also indicates surprise. Furthermore, the negative statement, "doesn't do anything," as has been seen so often, indicates that its affirmative was expected: he should have done something when the boys passed eating pears.

Another subject reveals the same expectation in this way:

> S49 (49) for sŏme reason he didn't stop them or ask them where they got the pears.

Again, the negative statement indicates what S49 expected the man to do. Also, an increase in pitch and amplitude indicates surprise that this did not happen. Another example of the same expectation is in S50's account:

> S50 (171) and I thought maybe that there was going to be a big dramatic moment, where...he's going to accuse the little boys who'd actually been like..good Samaritans, of stealing the pears. ...But he just sort of watches them, ..as they walk by, and they don't pay any attention to them...to him, he's..they're just eating their pears,

There are numerous other similar examples in both the Greek and American narratives, all showing roughly the same pattern of evidence that a confrontation was expected when the boys passed the man. This is a good example of how structures of expectation overlap, for there are at least three contexts operating in this scene. For one thing, there is the situation of people passing each other in the country, and in this way this scene is similar to the ones already discussed in which the man passes with a goat and the boy passes on a bicycle. Second, the expectation of confrontation arises since the man has had his pears stolen, and the boys pass holding pears. Finally, this is a movie, and there is an expectation of a "climax" at the end of a film, as well as the expectation that something startling should happen somewhere in the film. This is what the subject seems to have in mind when she says "a big dramatic moment."

Accident Frame

A scene in the film that lends itself to interpretation is one in which the boy falls off his bicycle. Two sets of expectations come into play here: those about accidents and additionally and contrapuntally those about causality. There are noticeable differences between Greek and American narratives with regard to this scene.

The scene in which the boy falls off his bicycle is intentionally ambiguous. In the film, the following events are seen in the following order:

1. The boy is riding his bike.
2. A girl is riding her bike.
3. The boy and girl pass each other on their bikes.
4. The boy's hat flies off his head.
5. The boy turns his head backward.
6. A bicycle wheel is seen hitting a rock.
7. The boy is on the ground under his fallen bike.

The conclusion that the boy has fallen off his bicycle is drawn by everyone seeing this film. This is interpretive in some sense, since the boy is not actually seen falling off, but it is the only rational conclusion to be drawn from the juxtaposition of events in which the boy is riding his bike and is then seen on the ground under it. However, the reason for the boy's fall can be interpreted in a number of ways.

Some interpretation about the causality of the fall is made by all subjects in our sample. Theoretically, they could have simply reported that the boy fell without explaining why, but in fact no one does this. In keeping with the interpretive penchant of Greeks already noted, six Greek speakers explain the boy's fall from his bicycle by reference to events that did not actually appear in the film. In fact, they make *incorrect statements* in their explanations; the hypothesis, then, is that their interpretations came from their own expectations about what might cause a boy to fall off his bicycle.

Four Greeks say that the boy fell because the bicycles collided, and two others say that he fell during the "meeting" of the two bikes, implying but not stating that the bikes collided. No American makes such a statement. In general, the Greek explanations for why the boy fell are more varied than the American explanations. There is striking unanimity among Americans that the boy fell because his bike hit a rock. Fifteen say that he turned and hit a rock, while four say simply that he hit a rock. Only one makes an incorrect statement, saying that he fell because he was tipping his hat to the girl. By contrast, two Greeks say he fell because he was looking at the girl; four say he tripped on a rock; eight say he turned and then hit a rock; one says he was rushing; six, as we have seen, attribute the fall to a collision. Such explanations as "rushing" and "collision" clearly come from an accident

TABLE 1
Number of Subjects Mentioning Person and/or
Objects

	English	Greek
Girl only	0	7
Rock only	0	2
Girl and hat	0	1
Girl, rock, hat	13	4
Girl and rock	7	6

frame, that is, the expectation that a bicycle accident might be caused in this way. The "tipping hat" explanation comes from the coincidence of an accident frame (not paying attention causes accident) and a greeting frame (boy meets girl and tips hat). Two Greeks but no Americans opt for the boy-meets-girl frame by itself as a cause (he fell because he was looking at the girl).

A pattern of interpretive omission can be seen here as well for the Greek subjects. Table 1 shows who and what got mentioned in the narratives. Thus, American subjects mentioned all three objects or two of them. Even if they did not include the girl in their explanation for the fall, yet they noted that she had appeared in the film. Greeks, however, more often than not, failed to mention all three objects which were portrayed in the fall sequence. It may be that their tendency to interpret events led them to a commitment to one interpretation of causality, and as a result to ignore objects or people that did not contribute to their interpretation. A total of nine Greek subjects (nearly half) mention only the person or object to which they are attributing causality.

While no Americans actually make the incorrect statement that the bikes collided, they are aware of this expectation. Two subjects make this overt:

S6 (84)   and you think "U?." You know "Are they going to collide,
S24 (58) and you wonder if there's going to be a collision.... But.. instead they just.. kind of.. brush.. by each other

S24 exhibits the by now familiar set of cues marking denial of expectation: the use of "but," "just kind of," and the negative implied in "instead." "You wonder" is a variant of a negative for it states something that did not happen.

Another aspect of the accident frame has to do with the boys' emotions. Such elements as the characters' emotions and thoughts are necessarily interpretive, for the film does not represent these directly. S6 reports,

S6 (109)   .. He's kind of crushed, and I don't know... you know... I think his ego was hurt.

The hedges are a clue to the fact that she is stating something that is different in kind from a report of events directly witnessed.

Reaction to Theft

In the end of the film, the man discovers that a basket of pears is missing. Americans, even more than Greeks, tell what his emotions were when he made this discovery. Sixteen Americans and eleven Greeks mention the man's reactions, either by describing his actions or inferring his emotions.

Ten Americans and three Greeks report the man's actions; eight of these Americans and two of these Greeks mention that he counts the baskets (one Greek, by *generalization,* says that he "counts and counts again," generalizing the gesture of counting which was portrayed once in the film and thereby creating an effect of great perplexity on the part of the man). Most of the subjects in both groups who report the man's feelings say that he was puzzled or wondering (seven Americans, five Greeks). There is a difference, however, in what the others say. Two Americans say that he was angry or upset, while three Greeks say that he was surprised. That is, the deviant responses go in different directions; the Americans opt for a more intense negative reaction, and the Greeks go for a less negative one.

Then the three boys pass eating pears. Seventeen Americans and twelve Greeks report the man's reaction in some way. An equal number, roughly, say that he was puzzled or something similar (eight Americans and nine Greeks). One American and one Greek say that the man does not do anything (revealing the expectation that he would). Four Americans say that the man "just looks" at the boys, indicating by the "just" that they expected him to do more. Five Greeks say that he "doesn't say anything to them," implying that they expected him to say something.

These interpretive adjectives about the man's reaction when the boys pass with pears can only come from the expections of the speakers about how he should react, for the film does not show feelings.

EXPECTATIONS ABOUT OBJECTS

It has been seen that expectations can reflect assumptions about broad context and actions. In addition, we have expectations about specific activities and even objects. For example, the film shows a man in a tree picking pears. The film was shot in Briones Park, where there happened to be a single pear tree. Three Americans, in the beginning of their narratives, state that the film was set in an orchard. They *generalize,* it seems, based on their expectations that a pear tree would be in an orchard. In one case, we can practically see the inferential process by which one tree becomes an orchard:

> S37 (3–6) ...the-- landscape is like U--H a f--...sort of peasant landscape but it isn't really farmland, it's like an orchard. ... It's a small orchard,

From the approximation "like an orchard" comes the conclusion "it is an orchard." In a fourth narrative, the speaker reveals the same expectation by her *negative statement.*

    S24 (6)   it wasn't a pear orchard, ... or anything like that.

As usual, her statement of what it was not is evidence of an expectation that it should have been. This expectation operates for Americans but not for Greeks.

A similar pattern can be seen in mentions of the road in the film. Four Americans refer to it as a "dirt road," and a fifth calls it a "gravel path." Again, a negative statement and the use of "just sort of" are familiar signals:

    S50 (72)   this road that's... UH it's not paved, it's just sort of a dirt road,

Thus we have evidence that Americans expect roads to be paved. By contrast, only one Greek refers to the road as *"chomatodhromos,"* "a dirt road." It seems reasonable to attribute this difference to the greater likelihood of a road being unpaved in Greece. This pattern of evidence indicates again how the use of adjectives tends to be evaluative (in Labov's sense), that is, to reveal some expectations.

EVIDENCE OF EXPECTATIONS

Thus it has been shown that structures of expectation are constantly mediating between a person and her/his perceptions, and between those perceptions and the telling about them. These expectations operate on all levels, from the broad level of context and activity (interview, subject of experiment) to ideas about episodes and actions, to objects and people. The kinds of evidence that have been seen to reveal the existence of these expectations (or scripts or frames or schemata) will now be listed and exemplified briefly. The types of evidence I have looked at, listed roughly in order of the degree to which they depart from the material in the film, are[10]: (1) omission, (2) repetition, (3) false starts, (4) backtrack, (5) hedges and other qualifying words or expressions, (6) negatives, (7) contrastive connectives, (8) modals, (9) inexact statements, (10) generalization, (11) inference, (12) evaluative language, (13) interpretation (14) moral judgment, (15) incorrect statements, (16) addition.

---

[10]It is clear that paralinguistic and prosodic features such as raised pitch and amplitude and drawn-out vowels also function as expectation evidence, and I have considered them in my discussion. However, I have not studied these in depth and therefore limit this list to strictly linguistic features.

1. Omission

A narrator cannot recount every detail. Some things are necessarily omitted. However, omissions can indicate expectations, especially when contrasted with what is included by other speakers. This was seen in the narrative of G12 who omitted events that would have contradicted her optimistic interpretation. One more example can be seen in the way in which reference is made to the man who passes with a goat. All Americans who mention this man refer to him as a man with a goat. In contrast, three of the fourteen Greeks who mention this man omit to mention that he had a goat with him. The conclusion suggested is that it is less remarkable, less unexpected, for Greeks that a passing man should be leading a goat. In Schank and Abelson's terms, the goat is in the Greeks' script for passing country person. For Americans, however, the goat is unexpected and therefore reportable. We may say that the Greeks omitted to mention the goat and thereby revealed something about their expectations.

2. Repetition

Repetition is another element that does not violate the reality of the events in the film but is nonetheless a departure from straight narrative syntax. Labov (1972) has shown that repetition can be an effective device in making "the point" of a story.

There are at least three different types of repetition: false starts (which will be discussed under that heading), linking (which seems to be a time-filler), and repetition of complete statements. The third type, which we will be concerned with, can take the form of (a) identical or changed wording and (b) immediate or later restatement.

An immediate repetition, like a linking repetition, can be a stalling mechanism, especially when it is uttered at a slowed pace, with elongations of syllables and pauses, and with clause final intonation at the end:

> G18 (106) *kai ta paidhakia synechisane to dhromo. . . . synechisane--*
> *. . . to dhromo,*
>
> and the children continued the road. . . . (they) continued--
> . . . the road,

When a repetition comes after some intervening commentary, however, it generally underlines a key phrase or idea which constitutes a kind of frame evidence:

> G11 (119)   *. . . TSK alla . . . moirolatrika to pire*
> (124)   *tous koitaze moirolatrika--*
> (119)   . . . TSK but . . . fatefully (he) took it
> (124)   (he) looked at them fatefully--

This reemphasis indicates the speaker's main interpretation of the film which, as has been seen, comes from her own expectations about the pearpicker's point of view. Repetition, then, is closely related to the phenomenon of reportability which is a direct function of unexpectedness.

3. False Starts

There are a number of types of false starts; the most significant in terms of discovering frames is a type I have dubbed "contentful." That is an instance of a statement being made or begun and then immediately repudiated or changed. For example, G11 said of the boy,

> G11 (113) *synantise ... ochi dhen synantise tipota allo,*
> (he) met ... no (he) didn't meet anything else,

The speaker began to say, incorrectly, that the boy met someone else, revealing her expectation that the story would continue with another meeting.

An expectation about conversational coherence can be seen in a false start in which "and" is switched to "but."

> G14 (20) *... kai-- alla-- meta to-- /s/ kaloskeftike,*
> ... and-- but-- then (he) thought better of it--,

The fact that G14 began by saying "and" indicates the expectation that the following statement would be consonant with the preceding one, a basic assumption about narrative connections.

4. Backtrack

A backtrack represents a break in temporal or causal sequentiality, a disturbance in the narrative flow. A temporal backtrack returns to an event that occurred earlier than the one just stated. A causal backtrack is an interruption for the purpose of filling in background information.

An example of a temporal backtrack can be seen when a Greek subject introduces her narrative, tells of the pearpicker, and then says,

> G9 (9) *... /a/ stin archi archi omos EH-- lalisan kati-- koko--ri.*
> ... /a/ in the beginning beginning however EH-- crowed some-- roo--ster.

The co-occurrence of a falst start, elongations of sounds, and a filler (EH--) with a backtrack is frequent. A mistake has been made, and the backtrack constitutes a correction. Therefore there are numerous traces of the speaker's discomfort. In the above example, the backtrack reflects the realization of a violation of the expectation that the narrative adhere to temporal constraints, at the same time that it reflects the speaker's subject-of-experiment expectation that she tell as much as she can recall.

A causal backtrack supplies information that was not included at first (we might say it was assumed as part of the script) but is later considered needed.

> G18 (57) *kai-- epese-- m-- meta to paidhi opos pighaine brosta dhen eidhe kala, ... kai tou epese-- m-- TSK tou pesane ta frouta kato.*
> and-- (he) fell-- m-- then the child as (he) was going forward didn't see well, ... and (from) him fell-- m-- TSK (from) him fell the fruit down.

G18 apparently began to say that the child fell, but then she felt that it was appropriate to explain why he fell, and finally she decided that the important fact was that the fruit fell to the ground. The backtrack shows her awareness of the expectation that causality be explained. The beginning of her utterance, "and-- (he) fell--" constitutes a false start, but in this case it is the content of the replacing statement rather than the content of the repudiated statement which is of interest.

5. Hedges and Hedgelike Words or Phrases

There are numerous words and phrases that may be classed as hedges or hedgelike. By qualifying or modifying a word or statement, hedges measure the word or idea against what is expected. They caution: "not so much as you might have expected." To consider all hedges would be a mammoth study in itself. They include such expressions as: really, anyway, just, obviously, even, kind of. Examples discussed in the preceding text are such words as "anyway" and "just."

Let us look at one other example. Following are the sentences from one narrative that contain the word "even."

> S6 (20) And the man up in the tree doesn't even notice.
> (65) and the man up in the tree doesn't even ... doesn't notice anything.
> (142) He doesn't .. he doesn't even notice that the pears are stolen yet.

(20) refers to the pearpicker not noticing the goatman go by. (65) refers to his not noticing the boy make off with the pears. In all three cases, there seems to be an element of surprise that the man did not notice what was happening. "Even" implies that this would be the least one might expect. The frame, then, calls for people to notice what is happening around them. "Even" intensifies the effect of the negative statement. As with "just kind of," "doesn't even" seems to be almost formulaic, as is seen in (65) where it contains a false start as well.

6. Negatives

Numerous examples of negatives have been discussed (p. 147). In general, a negative statement is made only when its affirmative was expected.

One of the most consistently reappearing negative statements refers to the fact that the man picking pears is not watching the boy who steals a basket from him. Ten American subjects make some negative statement about this, such as was seen in the previous example from S6 (65). As stated above, this reflects an interaction frame. However, it is stated by so many speakers because it is also a necessary part of the theft frame: that is, there is a scenario for a theft that includes the thief not being noticed by the victim. The theft frame will be investigated in detail in the last section of this chapter.

7. Contrastive Connectives

I have shown (Tannen, 1977) that an oral narrative uses the word "but" to mark the denial of an expectation not only of the preceding clause (Lakoff, 1971) but of an entire preceding set of statements or of narrative coherence in general. Thus in Greek, the word *alla* ("but") is often used to introduce a new scene in the narratives, in accordance with the expectation that things continue as they are unless otherwise marked. There is also an expectation that when people turn to leave, they continue on their way: a leaving frame. Thus when in the film the three boys interrupt their departure and turn back because they found the bicycle boy's hat on the ground, the fact that they found his hat is introduced by the word *alla* in the narratives of eight Greek subjects. Thus it has been seen that the word "but" often introduces a negative statement or, as in the following example, follows a negative.

> G18 (46) ...*kathondas*...*kai-- mallista dhen kathise sti thesi tou*, ...
> *alla kathise-- m--*...*brosta brosta sto podhilato.*
> ...sitting...and-- indeed (he) didn't sit in his seat, ...but (he) sat-- m-- way up front on the bicycle.

A bike-riding frame leads one to assume that a boy sits on the seat of his bike. This subject pointed out a departure from the frame: the boy did not sit on the seat. No one else made this observation, perhaps because the same frame led them to make an inference. I, for example, assumed that although the film showed the boy standing on the pedals and leaning forward as he mounted the bike, that he would immediately sit down on the seat when he got out of camera range. My own expectations about bike riding led me to assume that.

8. Modals

Modals are relatively infrequent in narratives since they make statements which are not directly narrative. "Must," "should," and Greek *prepei* reflect the speaker's judgment according to her own standards and experience. "May," "can," and Greek *borei* measure what happened against what is possible. The most frequent modal construction in the present data is the type that marks inferences of the form "must have been."

> G13 (3)   ... *tha prepei na epine krasi ghiati itan poli kokkinos,*
> ... (he) must have drunk a lot of wine because (he) was very red,

The use of *prepei* ("must have") overtly marks the fact that G13 is making an inference. It has already been seen that inferences represent evidence of structures of expectation.

Two other instances of modals reflect the judgment that the boy should have given the three helpers pears earlier than he did. Two others indicate interpretation of the future, which can only be based on expectations (that is, that the farmer will fill the third basket with pears). Finally, "can" is used twice to describe ability, which must be an inference since it cannot be observed from the outside.

> G14 (17)   ... *borouse na to sikosi aneta aftos o mikros.*
> ... this little boy could lift it easily.

The mention of the boy's ability indicates that G14 did not expect him to be able to lift a whole basket of pears.

9. Inexact Statements

Inexact statements are not like interpretations and inferences, for they relate what was in fact shown in the film, but they do not report events precisely as they occurred. Rather, they are fuzzy or slightly altered.

The greatest number of inexact statements about a single episode are about the fall (pp. 163–165), as, for example, when the boy is said to have fallen during his meeting with the girl.

Another common type of inexact statement represents a kind of collapsing of events into a significant kernel. For example, in the film the boy gives three pears to one of the three boys who helped him, and that boy then distributes one pear to each of this friends. Some subjects explain this in just this way. However, some others say something like,

> G2 (45)   *tous edhose ta tria achladhia*
> (he) gave them the three pears

That is, the events are collapsed to convey the significant outcome: the three boys ended up with the pears. The mechanics of their distribution is not seen as significant, since the entire event is grouped under the heading of a giving frame. The frame, by its definition, operates as a selection process, determining which details are significant.

Finally, by the same process, the "name of the frame" can influence the categorization of actions within it, causing them to be represented inexactly. For example, since the film about the pears has no dialogue, when the boys wish to get the attention of the other boy who is walking away with his bike in order to return his hat to him, one of the threesome is seen to whistle, and the sound of a whistle is heard. Yet one subject reports,

> G14 (59) ... *kai-- tou-- fonaxe enas-- o allos*
> ...and-- (to) him-- called a-- the other [and the other one called to him]

Thus the action of "whistling" becomes "calling." The word "called" is used automatically to describe the action of getting the boy's attention because an attention-getting frame is thought of as "calling." Put another way, it may be said that calling is the prototypical way of getting someone's attention.

10. Generalization

Closely related to inexact statements is the process of generalization or multiplication by which one object or action is reported as more than one. This may reflect the nature of art, in this case the movie, in which a single instance is understood to represent multiple instances. It is furthermore intriguing to speculate that the phenomenon supports Bartlett's hypothesis of constructive memory, by which memory is seen as a process of storing individual images and recalling them as representative of numerous instances, based on structures of expectation.

Generalization has been seen in the tendency for the lone pear tree to be recalled as being in an orchard (pp. 165–166), and for activities depicted once in the film to be recalled as repeated actions. For example, the man in the tree is shown climbing down the ladder. The single descent is taken to represent repeated descents:

> G14 (8)   ... *kai katevaine kathe toso,*
> ...and (he) was coming down every now and then,

Another subject makes the same generalization and creates the effect of repeated actions through her intonation combined with the past continuous tense:

> G11 (8)   ... *anevaine, katevaine, ydhrone,*
> ...(he) was going up, (he) was coming down, (he) was sweating,

The knowledge that fruitpicking necessitates numerous trips up and down clearly triggered this generalization.

11. Inferences

Inferences are statements which could not be known simply from observation of the film, as for example when subjects report characters' thoughts, feelings, and motivations. Thus when G10 said that the man on the ladder "was afraid of falling," she was saying more about her own expectations of what a man on a ladder would feel than about what the film showed.

Inferences about why the boy fell off his bicycle have been discussed at length (pp. 163–165). That the boy loses his hat and turns his head back is a fact, but that he turns to look at the girl is an inference. While six Greek subjects make this inference, two Greeks and three Americans say that he turned to look at his hat, and two Greeks and four Americans say that he looked, without saying at what. One subject makes both inferences:

> S24 (62) he's .. UM ... kind of looking back ... at her .. and the hat,

In general, speakers state inferences as categorically as they state things they actually saw. In other words they believe they saw what they expect to have been the case, based on what they saw combined with what they know of the world.

12. Evaluative Language

I have so far distinguished three types of evaluative language: (a) adjectives, (b) adverbs, and (c) adverbs whose domain is an entire episode.

Adjectives are used to describe setting, people, and objects. They actually occur rather infrequently in narrative (cf. Labov). When they do occur, however, the fact that the speaker chose that quality to comment upon is significant, and more often than not, the quality expressed reveals some comparison with what might have been expected. For example, a Greek woman calls the pearpicker *psilos* ("tall") while no American does. This may well reflect some framelike notion of how tall a person ordinarily is. Similarly, a Greek subject calls the setting,

> G1 (2) *ena pra--sino kataprasino topio*
>   a gree--n verygreen landscape

The second adjective, "verygreen," seems to reflect an impression that the landscape is greener than might be expected (it is, in comparison to Greek landscapes). In general, the assignment of values like "tall," "big," and "very" anything are the result of some evaluative process on the part of the speaker. First, these qualities are not absolute in the sense that a man can be called a man or a tree a tree, and second, the fact that they are singled out for mention must be accounted for.

Adverbs describe the way in which something was done, and such description reflects a distinctly evaluative process. For example, one Greek subject says that the three boys at the end walk past the pearpicker in this way:

G8 (61)   *kai troghane amerimna ta achladhia min xerontas oti itan klemmena.*
and (they) were eating carelessly the pears not knowing that (they) were stolen.

The comment that the boys were eating the pears "carelessly" (or "indifferently") indicates some contrast with another way they might have been behaving: in particular, that those who are in possession of stolen goods would be nervous. The inclusion of the adverb measures the boys' behavior against expected behavior for people in their position.

Adverbs such as "suddenly" or "luckily" are often used to introduce new episodes. They indicate the speaker's attitude toward the event about to be reported and how it relates to those that have already been told. For example, in Greek, *etyche,* which corresponds to English "(he) happened to," is used a number of times. This word is related to the word *tychi,* "luck," so that its meaning is something like, "as luck would have it."

G3 (42)   *etyche ekeini tin ora na katevainei o-- erghatis apo ti-- skala,*
(at) that time the-- worker happened to come down from the ladder,

Etyche comments on the unexpectedness of the event, that is, for the victim to cross paths with the possessors of the goods stolen from him.

13. Interpretation

Interpretation is similar to evaluation and inference, but it is a bit further removed from the events depicted in the film. It has already been seen (pp. 156–160) that in our sample, Greek subjects exhibited more inclination to interpret events than Americans.

Interpretive naming is the process by which a noun is used for a character or object which represents more information than the film presented. This was seen (p. 156) when the three boys were called "friends" of the other boy. In a more frequent example, if a speaker calls the man who is picking pears simply "a man," she is not imposing any more information about him than that which is obvious to anyone. However, if she calls him a "farmer" or "worker," she is imposing her knowledge of the world and expectations about picking activities and the people who engage in fruitpicking.

A final example of interpretation can be seen in the exchange of pears scene, in which the boy with the bicycle gives three pears to one of the other boys after that boy has returned his hat to him. Generally, Americans tend to report the exchange without comment while Greeks tend to interpret the giving of pears as a gesture of thanks. This interpretation depends upon expectations based on a helping frame. One Greek does not mention the exchange as such but indexes it for its significance alone, saying simply that the boy "thanked" the threesome. Thus interpretation can substitute for events.

14. Moral Judgment

Moral judgments are the first of the last three types of evidence which come entirely from the speaker's frames or knowledge of the world and are imposed on the events of the film. A number of Greek subjects, for example, comment that the boy should have given some pears to the three boys who helped him earlier than he did. One American does this as well:

> S6 (122) ... UM--... I thought why didn't he think of it before.

A moral judgment is often emotionally charged, sometimes accompanied by much verbal fussing, as can be seen in G16's account:

> G16 (40) *kai-- tote to paidhi, ..katalavainei stin /a/ eno eprepe kanonika-- otan to voithisan na dhos na-- ton voithisan na ta-- dhos ta achladhia pa na ta vali sti thesi tous, eprepe kanonika...na dhosi na prosferi EH--na--...se ol se osa paidhia itane na prosferi-- ligha achladhia, kai dhen prosfere. ...alla otan eidhe na tou xanapighan ton fonaxan ghia na-- tou pane to kapello, ...tote sa na katalave oti-- eprepe na prosferi stin archi, ...kai prosfere meta ap afti ti cheironomia pou to xanafonaxan ghia to-- na tou dhosoun to kapello tou. ...kai-- archizei kai moirazei apo ena achladhi sto kathe paidhi.*
>
> and-- then the child, .. realizes in the /beg/ while (he) should have ordinarily--when (they) helped him to give to-- (they) helped him to give the-- them the pears (he) goes to put them in their place, (he) should have ordinarily... given offered EH-- to--...to al to as many children as there were to offer-- a few pears, and (he) didn't offer. ...but when (he) saw them bring him back (they) called him to-- give him the hat, ... then as if (he) realized that-- (he) should have offered in the beginning, ...and (he) offered after this gesture that (they) called him back for the-- in order to give him his hat. ...and-- (he) starts to distribute one pear each to each child.

The passage is confusing because of the plethora of interruptions, backtracks, false starts, hesitations, elongations of sounds, and repetitions. All of these evidence the speaker's strong feelings about her moral judgment.

A moral judgment can be much more subtle, as for example when an American commented that the pears the boy gave to the three helpers "weren't the best of the bunch," implying a negative judgment about his character.

15. Incorrect Statement

Incorrect statements represent false recollections. For example, one Greek subject refers to the boy among the threesome who is the most prominent in the action as the tallest. In fact he is not the tallest. Her incorrect recall seems to reflect her preconception about "leaders" (the very idea that this boy is the "leader" is an interpretation which is made overt by at least one other Greek subject who calls him *archighos*).

A number of incorrect statements were seen in connection with the boy falling off his bicycle (p. 163). Another expectation shows through the incorrect statement by a number of subjects that the boy remounts his bike after the accident. This recollection can only come from the speakers' expectations, for in the film the boy walks off with the bike. One subject even extends the image of the three boys helping:

> G20 (42) *to voithisane na anevi-- pali sto podhilato,*
> (they) helped him to get up-- again on the bicycle,

Sometimes the speaker is aware that there is something wrong with her recall; sometimes she corrects herself, and sometimes she opts for the incorrect version.

> G1 (46) *... UH ... kai n'anevi pali sto po.. ochi ... nai.*
> ... UH ... and to get up again on the bi.. no ... yes.

Two other strikingly similar accounts illustrate that the incorrect statement is simply a more extreme manifestation of the operation of expectations which in other cases result in negative statements.

> G9 (79) *... EH-- kai anevike to aghoraki pano s ochi dhen anevike sto podhilato,*
> ... EH-- and the littleboy got up on no (he) didn't get up on the bicycle,

> G18 (89) *kai anevike to paidhi epano sto ochi dhen anevike sto podhilato,*
> and the child got up on the no (he) didn't get up on the bicycle,

16. Addition

The most extreme evidence of a speaker's expectations lies in the process of addition: the mention of a character or episode that was not in the film at all. For example, one Greek subject introduced the three boys this way:

G21 (83)   ... e--keini tin ora, edheixe-- ... TSK mia ghynaika, ... itan
dhyo ghynaike ... mia ghynaika me tria paidhia,
... (at) tha--t time, (it) showed-- ... TSK a woman, (there) were two wome, ... a woman with three children,

There was no woman in the film. The appearance of the woman, therefore, evidences an expectation on the part of G21 that children in the road would be accompanied by a woman—or two!

In some cases, as with incorrect statements, the speaker questions her recollection, but she may still opt for the incorrect one:

G18 (11)   ... EH-- sto dhromo omos, ... E--M ... pou pighaine, synantise ... ochi dhe synantise tipota allo, ... nai. epighe ekei, kai-- m-- ... TSK itan aftos o-- meta pighe ena koritsaki, ... sto dhromo pou pairnousan ta dhyo podhilata, synantise ena allo koritsaki,
... EH-- on the way however, ... E--M ... where he was going, (he) met ... no (he) didn't meet anything else, ... yes (he) went there, and-- m-- ... TSK (it) was this-- then a littlegirl was going, ... on the road where the two bicycles were passing, (he) met another littlegirl,

As with previous examples, there are numerous verbal cues that the speaker is unsure of what she is saying. Yet once she commits herself to the assertion that the boy met another girl, she repeats it, as if to reassure herself. Through the process of generalization, that is, of reduplicating what was a single instance, G18 builds upon what she did see to add something she did not, based on her expectations of what would have been likely, had the film contained more. In fact, as will be seen in the final section, she goes on to say that the second girl was going to steal pears.

WHAT'S IN A THEFT?

In the discussion so far I have indicated a number of levels of expectations, ranging from interactional context to objects, and I have shown various kinds of linguistic evidence for these expectations, ranging from omissions and additions to false starts and raised pitch. Another way to approach frames or

TABLE 2
Number of Mentions of Actions Relating to Theft by Greeks
and Americans

Action	Greeks	Americans
Thief enters	19	20
Thief stops	4	12
Victim not paying attention	6	10
Thief sees victim's inattention	10	8
Thief decides to take goods	3	14
Thief takes goods	19	16
Thief puts goods on vehicle	14	12
Thief leaves	15	17
Victim returns to scene	16	18
Victim discovers theft	14	19
Victim reacts	11	18

sets of expectations may be to look at which elements in a set of actions are chosen for mention by a large number of speakers. In order to see how this operates for one set of events, I noted all mentions of all activities relating to the theft. In all, thirty different actions were mentioned by at least one speaker. Of these, only eleven actions were mentioned by more than ten speakers in either group (Greeks or Americans). A list of these eleven (see Table 2), then, constitute a profile of the most salient parts of a theft frame. The number of subjects who mentioned each action gives an indication of the relative salience of each action. Only 16 Americans directly state that the boy takes the pears. The four others say this indirectly by stating he decided to take them and leaving it at that.

OTHER EFFECTS OF THEFT THEME

The fact that the film centers around a theft has effects on how other events in it are told; in a way, the theft theme diffuses. For example, after telling that a man passed (the goatman), one Greek subject said,

G16 (9)   *dhen vazei dhen--... ...thelei tipota na k pari apo afta.*
(he) doesn't put (he) doesn't--... ...want to st take from them.

The negative statement, as usual, prompts the question why she would tell what the man did NOT want. She even begins, apparently, to say "he doesn't want to *steal* any," as she utters the false start "k," probably from "*klepsi*," "steal". It seems likely that she had in mind the subsequent act by the boy. Similarly, the Greek speaker who added a second girl passing on the road after the accident scene, then inferred from her own false recall that this girl also wanted to take some pears.

G18 (120) *synantise ena allo koritsaki, ..to opoio pighaine-- ekei fainetai na pari kai afto-- ...frouta.*
(he) met another littlegirl, ...who was going-- there (it) seems to take fruit too.

More subtly, another Greek describes the boy leaving the place where the farmer was up in the tree "quickly" (*ghrighora*). Again, the adverb attributes a quality to the boy's action which is furnished by the speaker's expectations about how a person leaves the scene of mischief.

CONCLUSION

I have shown that the notions of script, frame, and schema can be understood as structures of expectation based on past experience, and that these structures can be seen in the surface linguistic form of the sentences of a narrative. Furthermore, the structures of expectation which help us process and comprehend stories serve to filter and shape perception. That is why close analysis of the kinds of linguistic evidence I have suggested can reveal the expectations or frames which create them.

ACKNOWLEDGMENTS

Research for this study was supported in part by NIMH Grant 25592 to Wallace Chafe. In addition, I am grateful to the University of California, Berkeley, for a travel grant which contributed to the cost of my airfare to Greece, and to Bruce Houston for graciously making available to me the facilities as well as the students of the Hellenic American Union in Athens. I wish most of all to thank Wallace Chafe for his untiring encouragement and guidance. In addition, I want to thank Louis Gomez for directing me to and talking to me about the relevant constructive memory research, and David Levy for doing the same with artificial intelligence research.

REFERENCES

Abelson, R. P. Representing mundane reality in plans. In D. G. Bobrow & A. M. Collins (Eds.), *Representation and understanding.* New York: Academic Press, 1975. Pp. 273–309.
Abelson, R. P. Script processing in attitude formation and decision-making. In J. S. Carroll & J. W. Payne (Eds.), *Cognition and social behavior.* Hillsdale, N. J.: Lawrence Erlbaum Associates, 1976.

Anderson, R. C., and Ortony, A. On putting apples into a bottle: A problem in polysemy. *Cognitive Psychology,* 1975, *7,* 167–180.

Bartlett, F. C. *Remembering: A study in experimental and social psychology.* Cambridge: Cambridge University Press, 1932.

Bateson, G. A theory of play and fantasy. Reprinted in *Steps to an ecology of mind.* New York: Ballantine Books, 1972. Pp. 117–193.

Bobrow, D. G., & Norman, D. A. Some principles of memory schemata. In D. G. Bobrow & A. M. Collins (Eds.), *Representation and understanding.* New York: Academic Press, 1975. Pp. 131–149.

Bransford, J. D., & Franks, J. J. The abstraction of linguistic ideas. *Cognitive Psychology,* 1971, *2,* 331–350.

Bransford, J. D., & Johnson, M. K. Consideration of some problems in Comprehension. In W. G. Chase (Ed.), *Visual information processing.* New York: Academic Press, 1973.

Chafe, W. Creativity in verbalization and its implications for the nature of stored knowledge. In R. O. Freedle (Ed.),*Discourse production and comprehension.* Norwood, N.J.: Ablex, 1977. Pp. 41–55.

Chafe, W. The recall and verbalization of past experience. In R. W. Cole (Ed.), *Current issues in linguistic theory.* Bloomington, Indiana: Indiana Univ. Press, 1977. Pp. 215–246.

Charniak, E. Organization and inference in a frame-like system of common sense knowledge. In R. Schank & B. L. Nash-Weber (Eds.), *Theoretical issues in natural language processing: An interdisciplinary workshop in computational linguistics, psychology, linguistics, and artificial intelligence.* Cambridge, 1975. Pp. 42–51.

Fillmore, C. J. An alternative to checklist theories of meaning. In *Proceedings of the first annual meeting of the Berkeley Linguistics Society,* Institute of Human Learning, University of California, Berkeley, 1975. Pp. 123–131.

Fillmore, C. J. The need for a frame semantics within linguistics. In *Statistical methods in linguistics.* Stockholm: Skriptor, 1976. Pp. 5–29.

Frake, C. O. Plying frames can be dangerous: Some reflections on methodology in cognitive anthropology. *The Quarterly newsletter of the Institute for Comparative Human Development,* The Rockefeller University, 1977, *1,* 1–7.

Gensler, O. Non-syntactic anaphora and frame semantics. *Proceedings of the third annual meeting of the Berkeley Linguistics Society,* Institute of Human Learning, University of California, Berkeley, 1977. Pp. 321–334.

Goffman, E. *Frame analysis.* New York: Harper & Row, 1974.

Gumperz, J. Sociocultural knowledge in conversational inference. In M. Saville-Troike, *28th Annual roundtable,* Monograph series on languages and linguistics. Georgetown: Georgetown Univ. Press, 1977.

Head, Sir Henry. *Studies in neurology.* Oxford: Oxford Univ. Press, 1920.

Hymes, D. Ways of speaking. In R. Bauman & J. Sherzer (Eds.), *Explorations in the ethnography of speaking.* London: Cambridge Univ. Press, 1974.

Labov. W. The transformation of experience in narrative syntax. In *Language in the inner city.* Philadelphia, PA.: Univ. of Pennsylvania Press, 1972.

Lakoff, R. If's, and's and but's about conjunction. In C. J. Fillmore & D. T. Langendoen (Eds.), *Studies in linguistic semantics.* New York: Holt, Rinehart & Winston, 1971.

Minsky, M. A framework for representing knowledge. P. H. Wintson (Ed.), *The psychology of computer vision.* New York: McGraw Hill, 1975. Pp. 211–277.

Pompi, K. F., & Lachman, R. Surrogate processes in short-term retention of connected discourse. *Journal of Experimental Psychology,* 1967, *75,* 145–157.

Propp, V. *Morphology of the folktale,* 2nd ed. Austin: Univ. of Texas Press, 1958.

Ross, R. N. Ellipsis and the structure of expectation. *San Jose State Occasional Papers in Linguistics,* Vol. 1, 1975, 183–191.

Rumelhart, D. E. Notes on a schema for stories. In D. G. Bobrow & A. M. Collins (Eds.), *Representation and understanding.* New York: Academic Press, 1975, Pp. 211–236.

Schank, R. C., & Abelson, R. P. Scripts, plans and knowledge. *Advance papers of the Fourth International Joint Conference on Artificial Intelligence, Tbilisi, Georgia, USSR.* Cambridge, Mass.: Artificial Intelligence Lab, Vol. 1, 1975, 151–157.

Schank, R. C., & Abelson, R. P. *Scripts, plans, goals, and understanding: An inquiry into human knowledge structures.* Hillsdale, N.J.: Lawrence Erlbaum Associates, 1977.

Tannen, D. An indirect/direct view of misunderstandings. Manuscript. University of California, Berkeley, 1976.

Tannen, D. Well what did you expect? *Proceedings of the third annual meeting of the Berkeley Linguistics Society,* Institute of Human Learning, University of California, Berkeley, 1977. Pp. 505–515.

6 Toward a Phenomenology of Reading Comprehension

Don Nix
IBM, Yorktown Heights

Marian Schwarz
Columbia University

INTRODUCTION

The goal of the work reported here is to eventually provide a means for diagnosis and remediation for interference difficulties that exist for minority persons when interacting with majority reading materials. Although such difficulties are both pervasive and debilitating, there is little information available regarding the types of factors that are systematically relevant to describing and overcoming the difficulties. This paper presents an experimental technique being developed to directly investigate sources of interference, along with preliminary results of an application of the technique. The intention is to sketch an approach that differs from other current approaches, and that appears promising, based on preliminary results.

The following general orientation provides a background for the approach. An individual can be thought of as interacting with the world in terms of a system of relevances (Schutz, 1967, 1970) which constitute reality in such a way that certain configurations are perceived as problems for which solutions are available. One's system of relevances, acquired in cultural, peer, and familial encounters, determines those features of the world that will be attended to—for example, which features will be constituted as typical, which as problematical, which as irrelevant, and which as invisible. Multiple realities arise to the extent that significant cultural, peer, and familial experiences exhibit patterned differences. Thus, if I am expected to perform a task in your reality, but my reality does not recognize it as a task, or as the same task, then I am literally a stranger with regard to what is required of me.

Standardized reading comprehension situations are an expression of a language performance system of relevances shared by the majority culture. As such it is to be expected that minority persons will be in the role of strangers with regard to various aspects of the situation, including both the social interaction and the language-use dimensions, and will accordingly have problems. The interest here is in characterizing differences that occur in language use and which are partly responsible for situating minority persons as strangers with regard to a standardized testing situation.

More specifically, the focus is on the interactive and constructive aspects of reading comprehension—the relationship between what the text contributes and what the reader contributes. These interests are formulated in terms of a comparative technique, in order to look at points of diversity between minority readers' strategies and strategies required by majority-based materials, and in order to systematically characterize such variation.

It has been hypothesized (Baratz, 1969) that surface syntactic and morphological features are a source of interference in reading comprehension. However, empirical evaluation does not tend to confirm this (see review by Hall & Turner, 1974). In fact there seems to be little reason to expect such surface features to be a main source of difficulty, when one considers the complexity of interaction between a reader and a text.

An area of investigation to which the current approach is more closely related is the "constructivist" literature in psychology (Bransford & Johnson, 1973) which focuses on demonstrating that a person comprehends language in terms of what he or she already knows. Prior knowledge is used to determine among other things what is important in the text, how it relates to the rest of the text, and how it relates to the knowledge of the reader or listener. So far, relatively little effort has been made to specify in detail the particular constructive processes that are important, although certain theoretical (Clark, 1975; Rieger, 1975 a, b) and empirical (Bransford & Johnson, 1973; Haviland & Clark, 1974; Kintsch, 1974, Chapter 8; Kintsch & von Dijk, in press) exceptions indicate that such an effort may be fruitful. These studies (which predominantly involve listening comprehension, and do not consider minority–majority differences) in varying degrees use the concept of inferences that relate antecedents to consequents in terms of normative relationships in the perceived world of the reader or listener. These "natural" inferences are links between elements of the text, as well as between the text and the reader/listener's prior knowledge of the world.

Although the above studies provide a heuristic basis for the study to be reported here, the methodology used (by the empirical ones) is not appropriate for the purposes of this paper. That is, standard experimental design requires precise definitions of the variables of interest, operationalized in such a way that other variables are systematically precluded (constituted as invisible). However, it is of particular importance to minimize the imposition of a given system of relevances on the possible outcome of the research (e.g.,

Circourel, 1964; Garfinkel, 1964; Jennings & Jennings, 1974.) Since little is known about reading comprehension in general, and minority–majority differences therein, it seems premature to use a methodology which assumes the significant variables are already known.

Therefore, the current approach is based on an interview procedure and a special representational technique for describing expectancies and results. In order to investigate the strategies and norms of interpretation used by minority readers, we asked each participant to read aloud various paragraphs and then to answer comprehension-type questions. We then discussed the chosen and alternative answers with the reader, in an attempt to isolate important strategies used. As it is clear that interviewing introduces certain methodological problems, such as asking too much and too little, as well as not knowing what to ask, we used the representational technique for depicting the semantic network—both the one implied by a majority reader's processing of the text as well as the one implied by the participant in our study. This representational technique was intended to clarify what inferences we (as majority readers) deem relevant to our answers to the questions, and what inferences the participants in the study (being minority readers) deemed relevant to their answers, as well as the systematic differences between the two systems of relevance. Thus, interviews were used in order to avoid the restrictions of statistical designs, and a special representational technique was used in order to be more clear about what we were doing in the interviews and in their interpretation.

Clearly, the answers a participant gives in responding to interview questions for reading material do not directly indicate what was done during reading. However, we have assumed that information produced by the participant during the interview gives insight into the system of relevances triggered by the material in the paragraph. The question is not about what the participants actually do during reading and comprehending a paragraph, but rather is about what the participants deem relevant to answering questions about what the paragraph means.

METHOD

Participants

Participants in the study were 10 tenth-graders, 6 females and 4 males, from a federally funded reading center in East Harlem, New York City.

Materials

1. Comprehension Items   Five items from the SRA Junior RFU series (SRA, 1963) were used with slight modifications to certain content words and

"Sally" passage

(a) Sally loved animals. She brought home every stray animal that she could find, no matter what it looked like. Her mother declared that she adopted any animal as long as it was

    A. lively B. alive C. large D. lame

"Summer" passage

(b) That summer we bought electric fans, drank gallons of ice water, and spent most of our time by the river, but nothing worked. We simply had to resign ourselves to being

    A. hot B. tired C. poor D. sick

"Postman" passage

(c) The postman always comes, regardless of the weather. We can always

    A. write to him B. pay him C. depend on him D. hear him

FIG. 1. Comprehension items (a), (b), and (c).

expressions. The particular items were chosen in part because of their stress on inferencing. Each item consists of a brief two- or three-sentence paragraph with the last sentence to be completed from a choice of four words. Figure 1 contains the items to be discussed in the Results section.

2. Target Networks A target network (TN) was constructed for each paragraph (Nix, in press), consisting of the propositional content of the paragraph and the inferential ties between the propositions. The network represents a target in the sense that it is consistent with the answer expected by the test designers. The TN was intended to represent certain salient features of the semantic network relevant to completing the paragraph according to the majority reader's perspective. Features not represented in the TN may or may not be involved in comprehension. The intention is simply to include only those features which can provide a minimum set needed for making comparisons. Further research based on this representational scheme will provide more firm guidelines on what to include in a given TN.

Figure 2 contains an abbreviated version of the TN for item (a) in Fig. 1. The complete TN is more detailed than necessary for the present purposes. Briefly, the numbers in parentheses in Fig. 2 indicate propositions underlying the text, and the connecting lines indicate either linguistic (straight lines), embedded (straight lines with arrows), temporal (double lines—Fig. 4 only), or conceptual (arched lines) ties between the propositions. Figure 3 contains a list of the propositions indicated in Fig. 2. Each proposition consists of a

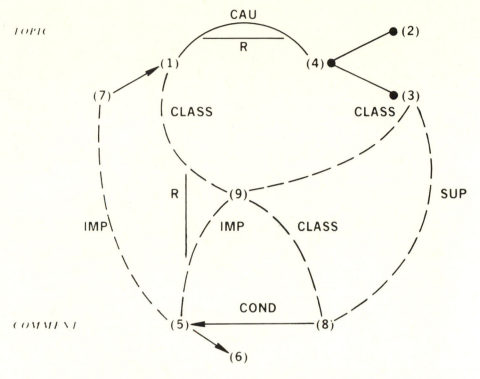

FIG. 2.   Target Network (TN) for "Sally" passage (Passage (a) in Figure 1).

predicate (in this example a verb from the sentence) or special relator (here either POSIT which POSITs something, or LINK which indicates that its arguments are to be considered as a unit in some subsequent relationship) followed by arguments which stand in a certain role with regard to the predicate or relator. For brevity the arguments have not been labeled here. It

(01) LOVE: Sally, animals
(02) bring home: she, animals
(03) POSIT: animals, stray, findable, any appearance
(04) LINK: (2), (3)
(05) declare: mother, (6)
(06) adopt: Sally, animals
(07) discuss: mother, (1)
(08) POSIT: animal; alive
(08') POSIT: animal; lively
(09) POSIT: (); unusual
(10) want: mother, Sally, (6)
(11) prefer: reader's mother, (8')
(12) LINK: (10), (11)

FIG. 3.   Proposition list for "Sally" passage (Passage (a) in Figure 1).

should be clear what the roles in Fig. 3 are. For example in Proposition 6 "(06) adopt: Sally, animals," it is Sally who is doing the adopting and the animals are being adopted. Note that a proposition can be an argument as in Propositions 4, 5, 7, 9, 10, and 11. The blank proposition in argument 1 of Proposition 9 is variable, indicating that any proposition tied to Proposition 9 becomes 9's first argument.

Figure 2 may be interpreted as follows. (1) and (4) are connected by a causal inference (CAU). In addition (1) and (3) can be classified (CLASS) as unusual situations, cued by such surface features as "love," "every," "that she could find," and "no matter." Further, no time sequence is implied. This section of the TN, the introduction of a recurrent, descriptive situation, is referred to as the Topic, in contrast, for example, to the beginning of a time-sequenced narrative. In accord with this, the Comment section consists of Sally's mother's evaluation of the topic, rather than a continuation of a plot. Proposition 5 (with its embedded proposition, 6), implies, based on the use (e.g., "illocutionary force," Searle, 1969) of "declare," that Mother is discussing or making observations about Sally's behavior(Proposition 7). Another implication (IMP) of using "declare" is that what is declared is unusual or noteworthy, thus (5) is tied to (9). Also, (8) serves as the condition (COND) for (5), since (5) is both unusual and thus in consonance with the import of the paragraph, and also it is a superordinate (SUP) of (3), which none of the other choices is. Finally, the straight lines labeled "R" are anaphoric references signaled by surface linguistic elements (i.e., pronouns). Dotted lines indicate covert inferences rather than overt—for simplicity, this distinction will not be made in the following discussion.

This paragraph, then, introduces information regarding the unusualness of a certain situation, and an observation that such unusualness is indeed the case. The TN indicates this by the two propositional clusters (1, 2, 3, 4, and 5, 6, 8) and the interrelationships between them (Propositions 7, 9, and the SUP ties). The TN is an attempt to focus on features that cue a majority reader to include certain lines of inference and exclude others without having to leave perceived features unaccounted for, and without having to assign idiosyncratic attributes to the text in order to do this.

Similar networks were constructed for the other paragraphs in the study. The purposes of the TNs were to aid in the clear formulation of the presumed majority-relevant aspects of the paragraph and in the development of interview questions and the interpretation of interview responses.

Procedure

Each participant was interviewed individually, and was told the interviewer was interested in how people understand paragraphs and answer questions. For each paragraph, the participant read and completed the paragraph aloud, getting help on specific words if necessary. Next the interviewer asked various general questions (e.g., "How did you get that?," "Why is it better than this?," "What in the paragraph tells you this?"), and more specific questions relating to the TN and to the participant's ongoing responses. For each participant the five paragraphs were completed in one session lasting approximately 30 minutes. All sessions were tape recorded and transcribed. From this data Participant Networks (PNs) were then created for each participant–paragraph interaction. The PNs are parallel to the TNs in that each PN schematically represents the salient features of the semantic network apparently used by a given participant in selecting the "answer." The procedure is designed to enable systematic comparisons between strategies employed by different readers for a given item (an example of a PN appears in Fig. 4 below).

RESULTS

The results of using the paragraph in Table 1 will be presented in terms of the TN and the network exemplified by the participants' response. These results, together with the results of the paragraphs in Table 3 and 4, will then be discussed at a somewhat more general level. Further, the various participants will be grouped together, with exceptions noted where important. The discussion will thus be based on a collage (rather than an average). Each collage is based on a discussion (by the authors) in TN-like detail of each participant's responses to each paragraph. Two paragraphs used in the study but not yet adequately analyzed will not be presented.

The participant network for item (a) is presented in Fig. 4, based on the proposition list in Fig. 3. The answer normally picked was "lively," that is, Proposition 8′ (two participants picked "alive" according to the TN, and one participant picked "alive," but according to the PN). The choice of "lively" was based on an implication (IMP) of "declare" to the effect that declaring involves wanting or instructing someone to do something—thus Proposition 5 implies Proposition 10. This implication, together with the participant's statement that his or her own mother prefers lively dogs (rather than, for example, lame or large dogs), Proposition 11, form a link, Proposition 12, that infers via a personal (PER) inference that therefore Sally's mother is instructing Sally to bring home lively dogs (Proposition 8′).

In general, the PN in Fig. 4 shows a different network of salient features than the TN in Fig. 2, for the same paragraph. Whereas in the TN the answer is knit relatively closely into the context of the rest of the paragraph, in the PN the answer is knit into a portion of the paragraph plus a personal set of experiences of the participant (the participant who picked "alive" according to the PN did so because his mother did not want dead animals to be brought

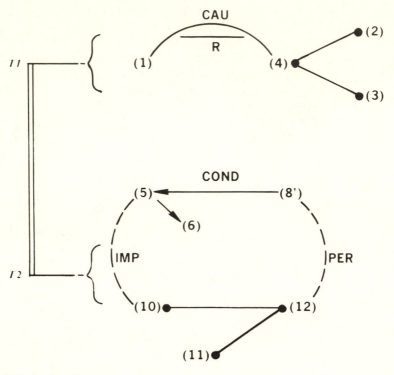

FIG. 4.   Participant Network ("PN") for "Sally" passage (Passage (a) in Figure 1).

home). Whereas in the TN the propositions form a Topic–Comment set with "declare" referring back to earlier propositions, in the PN the propositions comprise a time-sequential (labeled T1, T2) plot with "declare" referring outside the propositions in the paragraph. In general, then, the two systems of relevance here represented by the TN and PN appear to have certain characteristic differences, in terms of the contextual features they select as being salient factors related to the task of completing the final sentence in the paragraph.

This is further supported by participant explanations for rejecting certain alternative answers, in particular "lame" and "alive." Rejections of these alternatives were based, again, on a personalized context (e.g., "Why adopt a lame animal if you're going to have to pay money for it?," "Who would want to adopt a dead dog?")—the TN did not provide a relevant set of criteria.

In both the target network and the participant network the use of context and knowledge-of-the-world-based inferencing are important in picking an answer. The differences seem to be in terms of what context and what inferences are selected as relevant to the task. This is further suggested by responses to the other paragraphs. We will outline this from a somewhat more general perspective (not using TNs and PNs). Basically PNs have been grouped into two or three alternative strategies and generalizations have been made to capture the differences between these strategies.

Figures 5, 6, and 7 refer, respectively, to the "Sally," "Summer," and "Postman" passages that are shown in Fig. 1. Each vertical column represents an answer choice made by one or more participants, Alternative 1 in each case representing the target choice, and Alternatives 2 and 3 representing participant choices. The other information in the vertical columns represents components of the solution strategy (apparently) used to arrive at the answer

Discourse Features (alternative perceptions of)	Alternative 1 (resulting in choice of "alive")	Alternative 2 (resulting in choice of "lively")
A. DISCOURSE FRAMING (and its effects)	topic → comment	action → reaction
B. SYNTAX BENDING		
1. Verbs	"loved", "brought", "declared", "adopt" are in habitual mode—no specific time frame, no chronology.	"loved" and "brought" are part of action; "declared" and "adopt" are part of reaction. Three specific time frames in chronological sequence.
2. Intensifiers (function of)	"every", "no matter", "any" cause focus on enlarging the class of animals Sally would adopt, establishing the trend that "alive" fits into, as descriptor of largest class.	intensifiers focus on necessity of mother's impending reaction—her need to restrict Sally's adopting behavior.
3. "declare" (choice of usage)	mother describing Sally to the outside world	mother talking to Sally to limit her actions.
C. KNOWLEDGE ACTIVATING	bringing home disabled animals is humane behavior sanctioned by the community	bringing home lame animals necessitates expenditures of money and is not done by sensible people
D. LANGUAGE NORMING (way of speaking)	one of hyperbole and exaggeration in which "alive" would be consistent.	"alive" would represent a truism or redundancy and thereby does not make sense in this situation.

FIG. 5.   Tentative classification for the "Sally" passage (Figure 1).

Discourse Features (alternative perceptions of)	Alternative 1 (resulting in choice of "hot")	Alternative 2 (resulting in choice of "poor")	Alternative 3 (resulting in choice of "tired")
A. DISCOURSE FRAMING (and its effects	implicit problem → effort to overcome it → result	statements of the symptoms of an underlying condition— statement that the condition remains unchanged	3 actions → result of the 3 actions
B. SYNTAX BENDING	"nothing" and "worked" are cohesive ties referring to the 3 actions (bought, drank, spent) and their implicit purpose anaphorically	"nothing worked" is an exophoric reference to some outside force that might have counteracted poverty	"nothing worked" is an exophoric reference to some outside force that might have prevented fatigue
C. KNOWL-EDGE ACTI-VATING (as a source of seman-tic orientation)	"fans", "icewater", and "going to the river" are things that are intended to overcome heat	"fans", "icewater", and "going to the river" are symptoms of poverty	"buying fans", "carrying water", and "going to the river" all the time are activities that are tiring
D. LANGUAGE NORMING	"we simply had to" is a culture specific way of saying "in spite of", reinforcing tendency to bind second sentence to initial sentence	"we simply had to" perhaps meaning "in a simple way" (this is a conjecture)	

FIG. 6. Tentative classification for the "Summer" passage (Figure 1).

FIG. 7. Tentative classification for "Postman" passage (Figure 1).

Discourse Features (alternative perceptions of	Alternative 1 (resulting in choice of "depend on")	Alternative 2 (resulting in choice of "pay him")
A. DISCOURSE FRAMING	general statement → emphasis by restatement using synonymy	topic → characterizing detail (perhaps influenced by a language norm that says it's better to bring in new information rather than just restate old information)
B. KNOWLEDGE ACTI—VATING (as a source of semantic orientation)	postmen are in fact dependable	postmen need to be paid off like everyone else in uniform

192

choice specified at the head of the column. This information either was inferred from statements made by participants during elicitation or is a paraphrase of such statements. The horizontal columns are organizing concepts developed in an ad hoc way to fit the patterning of behaviors that seem to emerge from the data. They represent an attempt to develop descriptive terminology for classes of constructive behavior activated in a reader by a text. They are a set of organizing labels for future research.

Discourse framing refers to the reader's allocation of an underlying intersentence structure to the text. It cannot be determined when or with what influence or on what evidence a framing decision is made in the solution process. However, it can be seen that framing is consistent with behaviors in the other three categories. For example, in Fig. 6, the framing of the text as a statement of the underlying conditions of poverty rather than a personal narrative about solving a particular problem is consistent with the choice of "poor" as the best answer. In Fig. 7, the frame, "topic-characterizing detail," precluded the choice of "depend on him" which would have been a restatement of the first sentence in the item.

Syntax bending does not refer to the imposition of dialect syntax on the text, or to the inability to process certain structures. Rather this category refers to ways in which grammatical constructions were enlisted to support an extremely wide range of text interpretations. In Fig. 5, the verbs, "loved," "brought," "declared," and "adopt" have a perfective, completive aspect assigning them to the specific time frames of the narrative as opposed to their habitual timeless quality in Alternative 1. In Fig. 6, Alternative 2, "nothing worked," is seen as an exophoric reference to some outside force that might have counteracted poverty in contrast to its anaphoric reference function in Alternative 1.

Knowledge activating refers to the use of personal knowledge cued by a word or concept to create a context that will make sense to the reader. In Fig. 6 the fans, ice water, and going to the river are seen as symptoms of poverty, the participant asserting that anyone who was not poor would have an air conditioner, drink soda, and go to a swimming pool. Another example is in Fig. 7, Alternative 2, in which the postman was described as someone who needed to be paid, since in the experience of the participant uniformed persons frequently needed to be "paid off."

Language norming is a function of beliefs about appropriateness of language use: conventions controlling the collocation of language forms and perceived utterance function. In this data, the target answer choice violated the language norms of several subjects as in Fig. 5 where "alive" was considered a truism, too obvious to qualify as a sensible statement, particularly in a test situation.

There is no way to determine from these data the relative potency of any of these behaviors in the construction of a solution by a reader. We cannot know whether the activating of a body of experience or knowledge, such as the fact that fans are a sign of poverty, causes a certain framing decision or whether a framing decision causes a certain semantic interpretation. All we can say is that readers use their knowledge of discourse frames, the world, syntactic flexibility, and language norms to make sense of text.

DISCUSSION

Several general implications of the results of this study may be drawn. First, the results tend to support the idea that a reader's system of relevances interacts with how she or he processes text. Various features of the text and the reader's personal experience are selected as relevant to the task and the answer is constructed from this nexus of features.

Second, as intended, the study has provided evaluation of the methodology used—TNs, PNs, and interviewing. It is expedient, so far, to characterize aspects of the comprehension process in terms of Target and Participant networks—especially with the networks represented in fuller detail and subjected to an ongoing interactive process of modification. The networks provide a means for bringing a reader's knowledge-of-the-world into an operationalized description of how that reader processes a text and how such processing may or may not differ from other readers. Although there are many questions to be resolved regarding the representational scheme used, it is promising as a style of investigation.

Third, as a result of this study we feel that an interviewing approach, which has been used effectively in other areas (e.g., Labov, 1972), can be used as a method in the study of reading comprehension. As was expected, various problems must be overcome to make the approach as reliable as possible. For example, in the present study the TNs were intended to be of use in structuring or at least being aware of certain features in the interviews. However, at times they were not actually used and at other times, especially in the development stage of the study, they could not be used because they did not adequately focus on what emerged as important. It is necessary, then, to develop this use of the TNs.

In terms of the specific implications of the results of this study (answers given, explanations given, inferences made, context used) it is not possible to generalize to other participants reading and discussing other materials with other interviewers. Our study shows what certain readers did under certain circumstances. It will be necessary, at this level, to simply do more of this to determine, for example, more clearly what types of inferences are used and how they differ from a majority-oriented TN.

It is also necessary, given our goal stated at the beginning, to determine what types of cues in the comprehension situation cause a reader to use one context rather than another. What types of words encourage the use of a given type of context? What types of discourse structure, particularly ones that are difficult or not perceived at all, encourage the use of a personalized context (see Pichert & Anderson, 1976, for an example of the comprehension effects of a macrostructure)? How does the reader's view of what is required determine what is to be selected as relevant to the task—how, for example, is this related to the reader's view of language use? These and other questions must be addressed in order to relate particular participant-produced strategies with specific types of textual features.

CONCLUSION

Clearly the approach described above (multiple realities, the representational scheme, interviewing, the labels) is in a preliminary stage. There are at least two good reasons for presenting it at this time (Spring, 1975). First, the results obtained were encouraging in that they conformed to the approach without being restricted to it. And second, there is little if any work within the paradigm of experimental methodology that illuminates the phenomeno- logical nature of reading comprehension, even if the minority/majority focus is omitted. The work here is tentatively presented as an outline of a new approach to an old problem, rather than as a solution to the problem itself.

In summary, minority dialects have been and still are treated as random or inconsistent deviations from so-called correct English, and thus there was no point in studying systematic interference between the two with regard to language comprehension. Recently linguists, among others, have altered this view to the extent that minority English is treated (by many people) as a consistent linguistic system, and has accordingly been hypothesized to be a source of interference in comprehending majority English materials. Whether or not the interference hypothesis is signficiant enough to provide diagnostic and remediation information (and, as mentioned earlier, this seems unlikely), certain aspects of this change from one paradigm to another bear on what we are proposing. That is, rather than typifying as restricted certain cognitive strategies minority persons use to process language, it seems more productive to view the strategies as functioning as a system of relevances which has patterned differences from majority strategies. The techniques of context- situated inferences and interviewing sessions appear to be a productive way to study these differences.

REFERENCES

Baratz, J. C. Teaching reading in an urban Negro school system. In J. C. Baratz & R. Shuy (Eds.), *Teaching black children to read*. Washington, D. C.: Center for Applied Linguistics, 1969.

Bransford, J. D., & Johnson, M. K. Consideration of some problems in comprehension. In W. Chase, (Ed.), *Visual information processing*. New York: Academic Press, 1973.

Circourel, A. V. *Method and measurement in sociology*. New York: The Free Press, 1964.

Clark, H. H. Bridging. In R. Schank & B. L. Nash-Webber (Eds.), *Theoretical issues in natural language processing*. Washington, D.C.: Center for Applied Linguistics, 1975.

Garfinkel, H. Remarks on ethnomethology. In D. Hymes, (Ed.), *Languages in culture and society*. New York: Harper & Row, 1964.

Hall, V. C., & Turner, R. R. The validity of the "Different Language Explanation" for poor scholastic performance by black students. *Review of Educational Research, 1974, 44,* 69–82.

Haviland, S. F., & Clark, H. H. What's new? Acquiring new information as a process in comprehension. *Journal of Verbal Learning and Verbal Behavior, 1974, 13,* 512–521.

Jennings, K. H., & Jennings, S. H. M. Tests and experiments with children. In A. V. Circourel, K. H. Jennings, S. H. M. Jennings, K. C. W. Leiter, R. Mackay, H. Mehan, & D. R. Roth, (Eds.), *Language use and school performance*. New York: Academic Press, 1974.

Kintsch, W. *The representation of meaning in memory*. New York: Wiley, 1974.

Labov, W. *Language in the inner city*. Philadelphia: University of Pennsylvania Press, 1972.

Nix, D. H. Toward a systematic description of some experiential aspects of children's reading comprehension. In R. Farr & S. Weintraub (Eds.), *Alternative approaches to reading comprehension research*. Newark, Delaware: International Reading Association, in press, 1979.

Pichert, J. W., & Anderson, R. C. Taking different perspectives on a story. Center for the Study of Reading Technical Report No. 14. Urbana-Champaign: University of Illinois, 1976.

Rieger, C. Understanding by conceptual inference. Computer Science Department Technical Report TR-353. College Park, Maryland: University of Maryland, 1975. (a)

Rieger, C. Conceptual overlays. Computer Science Department Technical Report TR-354. College Park, Maryland: University of Maryland, 1975. (b)

Science Research Associates, *Reading for understanding*. Chicago: SRA, 1963.

Schutz, A. *The phenomenology of the social world*. Evanston, Ill.: Northwestern University Press, 1967.

Schutz, A. *Selected writings* (H. R. Wagner, Ed.), Chicago: University of Chicago Press, 1970).

Searle, J. R. *Speech acts*. Cambridge: Cambridge University Press, 1969.

7 Sociolinguistic Approaches to Dialogue with Suggested Applications to Cognitive Science

Roy Freedle
Richard P. Duran
Educational Testing Service

In this chapter we shall quickly review how various findings in sociolinguistics reveal important aspects of dialogue behavior which are often ignored or treated in an ad hoc fashion in many current systems for modeling discourse behavior from a cognitive science viewpoint. Many of the phenomena we will cite below are already quite familiar to sociolinguists but have not received much systematic attention on the part of researchers interested in computer models of dialogue behavior.

We begin by listing and defining several of the major categories of variables which sociolinguistics have isolated and then go on to present examples of these variables which affect speech in dialogue settings. The chapter ends by discussing how these various findings might affect the design of dialogue systems in cognitive science, with special attention paid to the Schank–Abelson theory which has been, to date, largely restricted to discourse comprehension.

Ervin-Tripp (1964) has suggested five major classes of variables of concern to sociolinguists (these are based in part on a more elaborate system developed by Hymes, 1962):

1. attributes of *participants* engaged in speaking to each other in a given context; e.g., sex, age, social status, cultural roles, kinship relations;
2. the particular *topic* under discussion in a communication;
3. the *setting* in which communication occurs, including the time, place, and social situation;
4. the *forms* used to carry out communication, be it written messages or spoken dialogue; or the particular language code employed to generate

content—such as the use of Black dialect or signed English, for example; and

5. the *functions* or goals served by the communication, such as a *request* for goods or services or information; a request for social recognition; interpretation of information; expressive uses of language; use of routines such as greetings or apologies.

We shall suggest several examples of how these five attributes of concern to sociolinguists occur in dialogue. The reader should pay particular attention to the ways in which clusters of the five variables interact.

The social relationships of *participants* can alter what is considered to be a socially well-formed dialogue. Consider the following pair:

(a) "Honey, hand me the paper."
(b) "Mr. Jones, please hand me the paper."

If a mother is speaking to her child she can use "familiar" forms of address as given by (a). If she used (b) it would be socially ill-formed. However, if she were addressing a teacher, option (b) would be the socially well-formed choice of realizing the speech act of a request form. The interactions here involve relative status, familiarity, kinship, and how it affects the form of the speech act.

The *topic* selected by the social participants is sometimes restricted to what will be socially well-formed given the role relationships of the participants. Thus, a husband and wife may readily talk about sexual problems together but a grandmother with her grandson may find this topic to be a taboo subject.

The particular social *setting* can alter the selection of a topic depending upon the social relationships among the participants. For example, a husband and wife can discuss their sexual problems most readily in the privacy of their own bedroom (if they live with others), but may consider it sociall unacceptable to verbally discuss the same problem when attending a funeral.

To elaborate further, using the same example, the particular *forms* used to carry out the dialogue may interact with the setting, participants, and topic. For example, the husband and wife may find a verbal exchange about their sex problems more compatible than a written form of exchange when in the privacy of their bedroom. But this same topic may be discussed in written form even when they are at the above-mentioned funeral. In other words, some topics are taboo in certain settings only when verbal communication is insisted upon. The topic may be acceptable if the form of the communication is changed to that of writing.

The particular communicative *function* which is to be served can also be restricted by participants, setting, mode, and topic. A request is a special language function. But making a verbal request of a dead person who lies before us in a casket to help us understand the meaning of life may or may not be appropriate depending upon what the religious-cultural beliefs are of the participants who are gathered together. Indeed, the same individuals who object to a verbal or prosaically rendered written request may find a poetic rendering of this request quite acceptable and even obligatory, especially when the person making the poetic request is a minister.

While all five of the above variables represent a very complex system of interactions, the sociolinguists must be given their due when it comes time to model significant aspects of real-life dialogues. Ignoring their discoveries seems to lead to ad hoc remedies when difficulties of a social nature crop up in the modelling process. (Some of the concerns we are raising here have also been broached by ethnoscientists such as Werner (1966). Some cognitive considerations of Werner's theory were discussed in Freedle (1972, pp. 203–205). The interested reader is referred to those articles.)

A useful technique for detecting the occurrence of different interactions of sociolinguistic variables is to focus on major classes of surface cues or "contextual cues" (Gumperz & Tannen, 1978) in real dialogue which signal their interactions. The four classes of surface cues to be considered below—code-switching, paralinguistic devices, sequencing, and message form—are mentioned in the work of Gumperz and Herasimchuk (1975). These cues are far from exhaustive but are exemplary of the kinds of phenomena studied by sociolinguists which are rarely if ever treated in the cognitive science literature to date.

1. First the phenomenon of *code-switching* carries important information. Alternating between English and Spanish, for example, or between Black dialect and so-called standard English is one aspect of code-switching. Such alternations are more likely to occur when the *participants* identify themselves as members of a particular ethnic group, and when the setting, functions, and topics of a discourse are *informal*. But code-switching tends not to occur when the setting is more formal, say in a classroom, and when the function and topic of discourse serve to convey factual information, and when the receiver of the information is a monolingual adult. Thus code-switching, when it occurs, signals important information about the intentions and social perceptions of the participants.

2. A second way in which sociolinguistic variables affect conversation is in terms of *paralinguistic devices* such as intonational shifts or prosodic cues as might occur for example when a mother repeats a request to a child in the presence of an honored guest, as in saying:

"Johnny, didn't I tell you to take out the garbage"
(spoken in a soft and "even" intonation)

as opposed to the same request made after the visitor has left, but this time using a high-pitched and dramatically intoned register.

In this example the social setting and social roles of the parent and child undergo a shift from conditions demanding polite intonation to one signaling dominance of the mother over the child. Notice, too, that this relationship is asymmetric in the sense that the child does not have the same degrees of freedom to address the mother with impolite intonation, unless he wants to invite some form of punishment. Hence the *range* of use of intonational registers is differentially distributed among the members of a cultural community. Social dominance and status is the social factor that best accounts for these varying degrees of freedom across different participants in a dialogue.

3. A third manner in which speech in dialogues may reflect the interaction of sciolinguistic variables is in the *sequencing* of comments or in the allocation of turns to speak in conversation. Consider the following exchange between a doctor and a patient who intends to lose weight (see Weiner & Goodenough, 1977):

> DOCTOR: Have you been successful with that (fluid reduction)?
> PATIENT: Well, it didn't seem like I was losing, to me, I mean. Sometimes I may lose 5–6, that's all.
> DOCTOR: That's about as much as you've lost.
> PATIENT: Mmhumm.
> DOCTOR: What's the highest that you—Is the most you have ever weighed?

The second comment of the doctor offered with *falling intonation* is described as a repetition pass by Weiner and Goodenough and is characterized by the addition of no new information on the part of the speaker. Note that in the next comment, the patient acknowledges control of the conversation and signals no new information to add in the topic being discussed. In the next turn, the doctor (who represents the socially dominant role, given the medical setting) introduces a *new* request for more detailed information. That is, his higher status provides him with more lattitude in introducing new topics.

4. A fourth manifestation of interacting sociolinguistic variables on discourse is in choice of message *form* or speech event as it occurs, for example, in deciding how to address a large audience as opposed to delivering a lunch-time talk to a few colleagues. In the first case the setting, participants, and function of communication restricts one to the discourse genre of "formal" speech while in the latter case the realization of these same three variables would suggest information conversation with less marked dominance on the part of the main speaker. That is, the few colleagues may feel it appropriate to interrupt the speaker without feeling that they had violated a social rule.

SOME COGNITIVE SCIENCE CONSIDERATIONS
VIS-A-VIS SOCIOCULTURAL RULES

The considerations mentioned above are suggestive of ways humans speak to each other in highly particularized ways so as to honor social and cultural norms as they are realized in real-world situations. Many of these phenomena seem to be rather crucial in developing more adequate and flexible models of dialogue behavior within cognitive science. In particular, the sorts of phenomena cited indicate that many interacting and overlapping cognitive frames or cognitive schemata representing sociocultural knowledge are governing choices of phonetic (see Labov, 1973), lexical, and discourse genre forms as well as topic realizations. In particular Gumperz (1977) has used the term *conversational inference* to refer to how speakers understand each other while making assumptions or inferences about each others' intentions, communicative purposes, social history, and so on. According to Gumperz, meaning in a communication evolves dynamically in the course of conversation and can extend well beyond the immediate contents of utterances; he states (Gumperz, 1974):

> We first process talk to derive the general perspective or interpretive frame in terms of which we judge what is going on and then in turn use this interpretative frame to decide on what is intended at any one point in the event and on how to respond. (p. 4)

To a great extent Gumperz's overview of dialogue is at the core of most cognitive science analyses of purposeful speech. Yet is has not been until recently that cognitive scientists such as Schank and Abelson (1977), Bruce (1977), and Schmidt (1976), to cite just three, have begun to systematicaly elaborate knowledge structures of social relations in computer models of natural language.

Schank and Abelson's current research into the interrelationships of such concepts as vignettes, scripts, plans, goals, and themes (to be defined below) seems to overlap in many respects with the phenomena studied by the sociolinguists. While the Schank–Abelson theory primarily focuses on story *comprehension* and while the sociolinguists often focus upon language *production* restrictions, we nevertheless feel that there exist many possible avenues by which the two types of theories can be merged. To aid the reader in this discovery process we now introduce some very brief definitions of the Schank–Abelson theory.[1]

---

[1]In the Schank–Abelson theory, knowledge is represented in terms of the seven levels of representation: conceptual dependency networks, vignettes, scripts, plans, goals, roles, and themes. No attention will be given here to the conceptual dependency level as it is not as valuable to consider with regard to social information as the other levels.

A vignette is defined as a labeled action and a series of vignettes, clustered into separate scenes, comprise a script. At higher levels, scripts may occur in order to realize plans, which, in turn, are a series of projected actions used to satisfy goals. A theme is described as a family of goals that tend to occur together because of attributes of actors. A goal is a realization of a component of a theme.

Following Schank and Abelson (1977), scripts may be thought of as structured in the more detailed way outlined below (with several liberties taken on our part for descriptive convenience):

SCRIPT: Name (e.g., restaurant script)
TRACK: a particular version of a script (e.g., a French restaurant)
PROPS: objects
ACTORS: actor names
ROLES: actor name, role name (e.g., Dr. Schank, father of Hana)
SCENES: name, partial order sequence (e.g., in restaurant script, entering, examining menu, ordering, eating, paying, and leaving are six scenes which occur usually in the order stated)
ENTRY   } predicates on actors (e.g., the person entering restaurant is
CONDITION   } hungry)
RESULTS: predicates on actors (e.g., the person's hunger is satisfied)

Before we proceed further, we should point out that Schank–Abelson define a script as nonlinguistic knowledge of a stereotypic sort. At first glance this definition may appear to rule out the possibility of merging sociolinguistic rules about dialogue with script theory simply because dialogue is realized in linguistic forms. But this would be a misinterpretation of what kinds of knowledge the sociolinguists have studied. From our viewpoint socio-linguistic rules mainly represent *scripts for how to use speech acts;* they are *stereotypic routines which employ social knowledge* which just happens to be manifested largely by language in dialogue, but can also involve the use of gesture, physical placement of individuals, paralinguistic signals such as intonation, and so on. That is, scripts for using speech acts are another *kind* of stereotypic knowledge that incorporates many but not all of the concepts which Schank and Abelson use to define their idea of scripts. This similarity can be seen by setting up the following approximate correspondence between terms from sociolinguistics and terms from the Schank–Abelson theory:

Function = track, entry conditions, results
Setting = props
Participants = roles, actors
Form = particular track of a script

We claim that the rules for dialogue represent scripts about how to linguistically convey knowledge of scripts. That is, dialogue instantiates the Schank–Abelson scripts typically by *naming* them. But dialogue also has been argued above to include *rules about how to organize ways to speak about these verbally instantiated scripts.* This particular way to speak is itself a higher-order script of how to use scripts. It represents stereotypic (culturally normative) knowledge of the social rules. Its cognitive representation may also be nonlinguistic in the strict sense (e.g., "themes" in the Schank–Abelson theory), but its communicative realization most noticeably takes the form of speech.

Perhaps the easiest way to see this distinction we are making is by selecting excerpts from the *dialogues* which Schank and Abelson (1977, pp. 223–224) use to illustrate their script theory.[2] We shall select those parts of the dialogue which signal the kinds of stereotypic knowledge of a sociolinguistic nature which represents how people negotiate meaning and intentions by a subtle interplay of language and the immediate context. In presenting these excerpts we have taken liberties by making assumptions about possible intonational patterns which the two speakers probably used (in particular we have assumed that "..." in the dialogues represents either a long pause and/or the absence of a falling intonation contour).

Hana is Schank's daughter. The dialogue immediately below was recorded when she was age three years and four months.

PARENT: Tell me a story—what happens in a restaurant? What happens— you go inside the restaurant....

(*Note:* we assume that the dots indicate a long pause or absence of falling intonation; this can be interpreted, given the context, as a social signal *take-possession-of-the-floor* and *complete* the script that was lexically signaled in the last clause.)

HANA: You sit down, and you uh, eat food.

(*Note:* Hana appears to be able to comprehend the social cue correctly since the parent does not interrupt or correct the child; had an inappropriate response been made the parent might well have repeated the social cue or might have taken the script (the restaurant script) one step further and left off again with a nonfalling intonation in the hopes that the child will "catch" his intentions for her to complete the script.)

PARENT: And then what happens after she gives you the food?
HANA: She gives you dessert.
PARENT: And then what happens?
HANA: And then you leave.
PARENT: And then you leave? Just like that?

---

[2]Schank and Abelson's examples were intended to exemplify how knowledge of scripts *develops* and how this is evidenced in speech. It should be noted that their aim was *not* to convey an exposition of scripts for *speech acts* and that this latter form of exposition is introduced by us here to show how knowledge of scripts interacts with sociolinguistically based discourse rules.

(*Note:* the last clause would be cryptic in its meaning unless it represents a finely tuned negotiation of how words and intonations are used to compute intended meaning and intended activities to be engaged in next in terms of the content to be expressed in the next turn.) Hana takes up the challenge of the parent's intended meaning of saying "Just like that?" and responds correctly with the following:

HANA: No, the waitress gives you some money and you pass some money...."

Because the parent does not interrupt the additions which Hana makes, she can *assume* that she correctly comprehended the parent's intentions which were weakly signaled by his cryptic clause.[3]

Another example of negotiated social meaning and intentions is covered when Hana is slightly older, at age four years and two months.

PARENT: Now, I want you to tell me what happens when you go to a restaurant.

(*Note:* again the restaurant script has been lexically instantiated; also a "telling" script has been instantiated, and it has been instantiated by a sociolinguistic speech act taking the form of a request.)

HANA: OK.

(*Note:* Hana interprets the request for beginning the script as merely a request for whether she wants to comply or not; she fails to enter directly into a description of the restaurant script—see Weiner and Goodenough, 1977, for a further classification of this type of turn-taking signal; in other words Hana did not instantiate both scripts in giving her response; she appears to have comprehended the information about the restaurant script but failed to instantiate the "telling" script.)

PARENT: What happens in a restaurant? Start at the beginning.

---

[3]In their research, Schank and Abelson have devoted much attention to different levels of knowledge that people possess about the world including awareness of social and cultural experiences. To date, however, the Schank–Abelson theory does not give much attention to systematizing knowledge about how speakers signal social meaning in language when they have something to say. Instead most of the emphasis has been on how one understands stories about people based on the narrator's point of view. That is to say, no attempt is made at modeling the social attributes (be they permanent or fleeting) of speakers as revealed by the precise ways in which they communicate to each other. Yet as we point out, the social attributes of actors within a narrative *are* quite often inferrable from the form and content of each of the actors. This is the type of information which has been systematized by the sociolinguists.

(*Note:* because the parent repeats his request, this indicates to the child that she failed to give a totally adequate interpretation of what he expected her to do—hence, we see again the moment-by-moment interplay of how meaning and intentions are subtly signaled given the immediate context by employing sociolinguistic knowledge which is displayed by use of turn-taking signals and repetitions of other clausal information). Hana then responds with a very well-developed description of a restaurant script which suggests that she now has correctly interpreted the last request. It perhaps also suggests that she realized that she made an "error" in not responding earlier with a direct entry into the description of a restaurant script.

The above two excerpts illustrate how sociolinguistic information interacts with lexically instantiated scripts of the Schank–Abelson types.

A third and final example of this subtle interplay between dialogue information, social turn-taking signals, and scripts is again taken from Hana at age four years and two months.

PARENT: What happens when you take an airplane trip? Tell me from the beginning.
HANA: OK, you go to the airport, and then...do you think I should tell...you might get hungry and there's a restaurant?

(*Note:* She interrupts the airport script with a higher-level interpretive *frame* that can be designated here as a special kind of sociolinguistic script which deals directly with questions concerning covert cognitive-social intentions—exactly how much information did the parent expect her to provide; that is, did the parent want just the main outline or many of the subplots that could occur in the airplane script? Hana here uses dialogue and an intonational device (probably of nonfalling intonation signaled by the three dots just prior to her use of the frame) for "stepping out" of the script that she had just entered moments before. Tannen (1979) has discussed language frames of this type in greater detail.)

The parent follows Hana's special request with the following:

PARENT: No, let's just tell about the airplane. Or is that what happens when you're in an airplane?
HANA: No, once that happened in New York, when we picked you up.

(*Note:* the parent signaled his expectations of what he wanted his daughter to say in a highly compact but essentially cryptic way—his statement "...or is that what happens..." *indirectly* requests whether the normative airplane script alawys contains a restaurant scene; in the context of what has been already said, it is possible for the child to "compute" the intended meaning. Because she gives an appropriate reply this indicates that she did compute the intended meaning.)

CONCLUSION

In summary, while many correspondences can be seen between the Schank–Abelson theory and sociolinguistic rules about ways to speak, we believe that a case can be made for considering sociolinguistic rules to be special kinds of higher-order scripts—scripts which help to produce and comprehend information at all levels of the Schank–Abelson knowledge structure theory. In particular dialogue rules to us represent higher-order nonlinguistic knowledge scripts about *how* to organize what to say and *how* to comprehend verbally instantiated concepts, be they vignettes, scripts, plans, goals, or themes.

REFERENCES

Bruce, B. Plans and social actions. University of Illinois at Urbana, Center for the Study of Reading, 1977.

Ervin-Tripp, S. An analysis of the interaction of language, topic and listener. *American Anthropologist,* 1964, *66,* 86–102.

Freedle, R. Language users as fallible information-processors: implications for measuring and modeling comprehension. In R. Freedle & J. B. Carroll (Eds.), *Language comprehension and the acquisition of knowledge.* Washington, D.C.: Winston/Wiley, 1972.

Gumperz, J. J. The role of dialect in urban communication .Unpublished manuscript, 1977.

Gumperz, J. J., & Herasimchuk, E. The conversational analysis of social meaning: A study of classroom interaction. In M. Sanches & B. G. Blout (Eds.), *Sociocultural dimensions of language use.* New York: Academic Press, 1975.

Gumperz, J. J., & Tannen, D. Individual and social differences in language use. In W. Wang and C. Fillmore (Eds.), *Individual differences in language ability and language behavior.* New York: Academic Press, 1978.

Hymes, D. The ethnography of speaking. In T. Gladwin & W. Sturtevant (Eds.), *Anthropology and human behavior.* Washington, D.C.: Anthropological Society of Washington, 1962.

Labov, W. *Sociolinguistic patterns.* Phil., Pa.: Univ. of Pennsylvania Press, 1973.

Schmidt, C. F. Understanding human action: recognizing the plans and motives of other persons. In J. S. Carroll & J. W. Payne (Eds.), *Cognition and social behavior.* New York: Wiley, 1976.

Schank, R. C., & Abelson, R. P. *Scripts, plans, goals and understanding: An inquiry into human knowledge structures.* Hillsdale, N.J.: Lawrence Erlbaum Associates, 1977.

Tannen, D. What's in a frame?: surface evidence for underlying expectations. This volume.

Weiner, S. L., & Goodenough, D. R. A move toward a psychology of conversation. In R. Freedle (Ed.), *Discourse production and comprehension.* Norwood, N.J.: Ablex Publ. Corp., 1977.

Werner, O. Pragmatics and ethnoscience. *Anthropological linguistics,* 1966, *8,* 42–65.

8 Social Foundations of Language[1]

Elinor Ochs
University of Southern California

I. THE COGNITIVE BIAS IN LANGUAGE STUDIES

A particular bias has marked research on language in this country. If we look over the major research on language since the 1930's, we will see that the bulk of this research examines the relation between *language, on the one hand, and cognitive or conceptual structures, on the other.* Depending on the view put forward, language is frequently seen as a response to, an expression of, a consequence of, or a determiner of the structure of thought of a speaker.

It is tempting to locate the interest in cognitive dimensions of language in this country to the emergence of the Transformational Generative Paradigm and Chomsky's claim that linguistics ought to consider itself a branch of cognitive psychology (1966, 1975). The Chomskian framework certainly made the relation between language and mental operations an object of intense discussion. The interest generated is at least partly responsible for the rapid growth of *psycholinguistics* as an established research concern.

However, while it is tempting to attribute the link between cognition and language structure to the transformational paradigm, it is misleading to do so. Consider earlier approaches to language in this country. As any historical account will report (Hymes 1970, Robins 1959, Lyons 1968), linguistic research used to be carried out within a department of anthropology in this country. What kind of anthropology is associated with this period, with

---

[1]Earlier versions of this paper were presented to the Department of Anthropology, Johns Hopkins University, March 1978, and to the California Linguistics Association (Keynote Address), Eighth Annual Conference, May 1978.

researchers such as Boas, Benedict, Sapir and Hoijer? What kind of anthropology is often paraphrased as "American anthropology"? Why *cultural* anthropology, of course! What has distinguished American anthropologists from their European colleagues is their persistent interest in *culture*, where culture is a system of beliefs and knowledge that allows social life to be achieved. Culture is a conceptual organization that gives meaning to behaviors, including language behavior. It has been referred to as the 'cognitive map' (Wallace 1970) of a people, 'the world view' (Redfield 1953, Whorf in Carroll 1956), the 'premises' of a people (Bateson 1958). Working within this framework, linguistically oriented anthropologists have tended to relate language to these maps, world views or premises. In other words, the conceptual or cognitive bias was much in evidence.[2]

From this point of view, there is considerable continuity from the time in which linguistics was seen as a branch of anthropology to the present era. The location of interest in the *conceptual* underpinnings of language has remained. This continuity is reflected in the writings of Chomsky. For example, in *Reflections on Language,* Chomsky has commented,

> One reason for studying language—and for me personally the most compelling reason—is that it is tempting to regard language, in the traditional phrase, as "a mirror of mind"... By studying language we may discover abstract principles that govern its structure and use, principles that are universal by biological necessity and not mere historical accident, that derive from mental characteristics of the species. (1975:4)

In all of these studies, whatever accounting or explaining there is to be done is done in terms of conceptual or cognitive predispositions. The explanation to be given is in terms of mental operations.

In all of these studies, a major dimension of daily life is given little or no recognition at all; that is, the role of *SOCIAL PROCESSES*. In anthropological research, in this country social life is often seen as the stage on which cultural knowledge is displayed.

For example, Sapir, in describing culture, has claimed

> The true locus of culture is in the interaction of specific individuals...
> (1932:516)

---

[2]Hymes (personal communication) points out that there has been a tradition within cultural anthropology of investigating the relation between personality, language and culture. The expressive nature of individuals and their values as shaped by or expressive of their culture has been investigated by Sapir (1927), Kluckhohn (1954) and others (cf. the readings in L. Spier, A. Hallowell, S. Newman (eds.) *Language, Culture and Personality* (1941), Wallace (1970)).

Here social interaction is recognized as *necessary* to culture; but the social interactional process through which cultural knowledge is created and sustained is not *in itself* a major focus of attention (but see Footnote 2). The study of social processes as a *primary* concern is not associated with cultural anthropology, as practiced in this country. Rather it is associated with the disciplines of social anthropology and sociology. Social anthropology has a few outstanding faculties in this country, but is mainly associated with British schools of anthropological research. Sociology is widespread throughout the United States; however, it enjoys considerably less prestige than anthropology, psychology and linguistics within the social sciences. As a broad generalization, one could say that social phenomena have had a hard time getting attention and status in this country.

It is not surprising that linguistics as well should share this same attitude towards social processes. Social factors are rarely viewed as explanations of linguistic phenomena. If there is to be an explanation for some structure within language, the explanation will be in terms of percepts, concepts, attention, memory or other properties of the human mind. Just as cultural anthropology views social life as the environment for culture, so linguistics views social life as the environment of the language. Just as cultural anthropology attends little to the process through which culture is maintained and transformed, so linguistics pays little attention to the social processes through which language is shaped. Hymes has made this point many times in his work (1967, 1970, 1974): "Social variables have played a sporadic role in descriptive linguistics, inasmuch as they have sometimes obtruded themselves in the core of grammar; e.g., respect forms (honorifics) in Korean and Japanese. When not obtrusive, such variables and functions have not been sought out." (1974:74)

It is a commonplace to say that language is a social behavior. But the social quality itself is not seriously examined. If we took a survey of graduate students in linguistics departments in this country, we would probably find that a sizeable number know something about basic Piagetian cognitive theory. At least they probably have heard the name. But how many of these students would know anything about major sociological theoretical approaches? How many would know even the broad outlines of the work of Garfinckel (1967), Goffman (1963), Berger and Luckman (1966), Durkheim (1938), Radcliffe-Brown (1952), Goody (1958)? Few, if any. The social nature of language is simply not a very serious concern.

It is not the case that all linguistic studies ignore social processes, however. Phonological studies, of course, have had a relatively long history of attending to such social dynamics as status, prestige and formality of situation (Labor 1966). Similarly selected studies of the lexicon have been sensitive to the social situation in which language is used (Kay 1970, Fillmore 1971, 1975).

On the other hand, research on the *syntactic structure of language* has all but ignored social considerations. In trying to account for a particular syntactic structure, cognitive rather than social processes are brought to bear. For some researchers, syntax itself is viewed as basically a vehicle for expressing particular propositions or ideas. If we want to understand the syntactic organization of ideas, we should turn to these ideas themselves. Language, in these terms, is responsive to the organization of thought. The choice of one word order over another, one verb voice over another, the sequential order in a clause, all are sensitive to cognitive processes and preferences (Bever 1970, Clark, E. 1971, MacWhinney 1977).

While it is recognized that syntactic structures also convey social meaning, have social functions, the social side of syntax is not a serious influence. While syntactic structure emerges through social interaction in the experience of normal childhood, the *structure* of that interaction is not seen as a serious influence on the *structure* of language. Further, once this period of language development is completed, social interaction is not seen as affecting or shaping adult grammatical patterns. It is as if language needs social nurturing during a critical period, but beyond that point, it stands on its own and is no longer affected by its social environment.

Indeed, social influences are treated as accidental, superfluous and language–specific at best. For example, the linguistic consequences of contact with another society have been documented but these consequences are often treated as "historical accidents" to repeat a phrase from Chomsky (1975:4).[3] Little understood and treated as a marked or unusual state of affairs for a group of speakers, social contact and adaptation is not viewed as a recurrent, and in this sense, natural influence on the syntactic structure of language.

What about the *superfluous* role of the social situation? There is a complementary distribution in the writings of linguists and sociologists on this matter. Most linguistic work, including work within pragmatics, views the information–bearing function of language as primary and the other functions that language can serve as secondary. Hence, such notions as literal and conveyed meaning (Grice 1971, Strawson 1971), locution and illocution (Austin 1962, Searle 1969), where 'locution' is the unmarked and 'illocution' the marked of the terms. If one turns to sociological literature, precisely the opposite orientation is expressed. In these accounts, the use of language to express ideas or new information is not a vital activity of individuals in social interaction. In these accounts, the main business of social interaction is to solidify relationships, manipulate relationships, transform relationships. Social life is a web of rights and obligations that members of a group display and impose on one another. The main work of language is to facilitate this

---

[3]An exception to this generalization is the work of Hoenigswald (1960).

social work. Rather than being superfluous, these social uses of language are essential to interaction itself.

And this brings us to the *scope* of social processes. I mentioned that implicit in linguistic treatments of syntax is the notion that social phenomena are tied to particular languages and particular societies. Given that a major thrust of modern linguistics is the search for universals of language behavior, this would seem to account for the neglect of social influences. A particular social situation might influence a particular language, but we are in the business of finding constraints that cut across groups of speakers and the languages they speak. The question we must address here is whether this association of social with exclusively *local* scope and influence is justifiable. The strong suggestion put forward here is that such an association is not reasonable. It is an association that is a product of non-exposure to sociological research. We can speak of universal social processes as easily as we can speak of universal cognitive processes. For example, social notions such as cooperation, competition, status, power, control, prohibition and sanction are present in social organizations everywhere to varying extents. There are local and global social behaviors just as there are local and global conceptual behaviors. For this reason, social processes ought not to be ruled out as a potential force constraining the grammatical structure of language.

I am in no way advocating that cognitive explanations be disregarded in favor of social explanation. What is advocated is a consideration of both, a recognition that a particular structure in language may be constrained by social and cognitive processes. In certain cases, cognitive accounts may take precedence over social accounts. In other cases, the reverse may hold. The social context may be able to account for phenomena that cognitive accounts can not handle.

II. SOCIAL FOUNDATIONS OF A SYNTACTIC PATTERN: THE CASE OF LEFT-DISLOCATION IN ITALIAN

Word Order

As a trial case for these notions, let us turn to a syntactic structure of great linguistic concern—that of *word order,* in particular the ordering of the major constituents subject, verb and direct object. One of the most well-known linguistic facts is that in the majority of the world's languages, subjects precede direct objects as a basic word order pattern (Greenberg 1966). Languages tend to be SVO, SOV but rarely VOS or OSV, and so on.

Accounts of why these word orders are so prevalent are all cognitive in nature. Several accounts claim that the concepts expressed by subjects have primacy over the concepts expressed by direct objects in the world's languages. The most widespread argument is that subjects usually express agents and actors whereas direct objects express objects undergoing action. The notions of agency and actor are felt to be cognitive more basic. Children acquire these concepts earlier. Further, in actual event time, the speaker may conceptualize or have awareness of the agent or actor before the entity to be acted upon is specified (Bever 1970, Bloom 1970, Brown 1973).

While these accounts provide considerable insight into regularities in word order, they do not account for two facts. First, cognitive explanations such as those just presented do not account for the fact that certain languages do violate this word order preference; for example, Malagasy, which has verb-object-subject as its unmarked word order. The cognitive preference for subject over object or agent over affected object could not be that strong; otherwise, we would not find thousands of speakers violating this preference millions of times throughout their life span.

Second, cognitive explanations cannot account for the appearance of object–subject word orders as *alternative* word orders in languages. In many languages, utterances in which objects precede subject appear very frequently even if they are not the primary word order pattern. Again, the cognitive preference of subject/agent must not be that strong; it does not seem to rule out the reverse word order in most languages.

One might object at this point and comment that the mere appearance of a dispreferred word order does not weaken the claim for cognitive preference. After all, we can imagine that given the right conditions the speaker is allowed to violate a natural encoding strategy. For example, in written communication, many less 'natural' encoding strategies are used by individuals. In English, the written medium provides the right conditions for communicators to use passives, embedded relative clauses and other constructions that are in speaking difficult to process.

Is this what is happening where speakers produce word order sequences in which objects precede subjects? To respond to this question, let us look at the environment in which this word order appears in one language, Italian. The study that I am about to report was conducted by Alessandro Duranti and myself over the past year (Duranti and Ochs, in press). The study examined a particular construction in Italian, that of LEFT-DISLOCATION.

The Scope of Left-Dislocation

Let us first clarify what is meant by the term *left-dislocation*. Originally, the term referred to a transformation in which some constituent of a sentence is moved to the left of a sentence and in its place a pronoun is inserted (Ross 1967). In English, this transformation would produce such sentences as "Freeways I can't stand them," "My car it's out of gas," "Your grandmother I called her this morning," and so on. In these sentences, the lexical items 'freeway,' 'my car' and 'your grandmother' are found to the left or beginning of the utterance and a co-referential pronoun appears subsequently within the utterance.

A major difference exists in the scope of what counts as left-dislocation in English and in Italian; at least in the dialect we have examined, Roman Standard. Whereas in English, subject, direct objects and indirect objects all can be left-dislocated; in Italian as spoken in Rome, subjects cannot be left-dislocated. This is because there are no subject clitic pronouns in Italian and clitic pronouns are used to refer to left-dislocated items. When we make generalizations about left-dislocation in Italian, then, it is to be kept in mind that *overwhelmingly we are talking about constructions in which a direct object or an indirect object precedes a subject constituent.* That is, we are talking about the kind of construction that violates the purported cognitive preference of subject before object.

The Context of Left–Dislocation

Let us consider now the context in which these constructions are found in Italian. As can be immediately seen from the examples provided below, these constructions can be located in everyday spontaneous conversation. In (1), for example, two acquaintances (C and A) are discussing how A manages the cleaning of his clothes and room:

(1) *The Draft*
C: (. . .) cioè c'hai chi ti fa le pulizie inzomma//e:
   that is (you) got who to-you does the cleaning in sho//rt and:
A: No
   devo- cioè per vestiti e cose varie devo andare
   (I) must—that is for clothes and things various (I) must go
   (alla) lavanderia
   (to the) laundry
C: Ho capito ho capito
   (I) have understood (I) have understood
A: Per la stanza me la pulisco da solo
   (as) for the room$_i$ me it$_i$ (I) clean myself
C: (. . .) that is, you have somebody that cleans up for you, in shor//t, and
A: No I must—I mean, for clothes and various things, I must go to the laundromat.
C: I see, I see.
A: As for the room$_i$, I must clean it$_i$ up myself.)

In the course of this discussion, A produces the left-dislocation "Per la stanza me la pulisco da solo." Similarly, in (2), two close friends are discussing the way in which a third friend recurrently manages to foul up everything he touches. One of the speakers (F) introduces an anecdote concerning Roberto's loser status with the left–dislocation "...la più grossa risata ce la siamo fatta co—quando doveva fa' i re(h)e(h)l(h)ly te ricordi?":

(2) *A Friend*

(Andrea and Franco are talking about their friend Roberto and his inability to accomplish something, his 'loser' character.)

F: (...) cioè se tu pensi allo schema suo di vita.
    That is, if you think to the scheme his of life.
    Cioè tutte le cose se so' sempre ripercosse co'
    That is all the things have always repeated with
    le stesse caratteristiche.
    the same characteristics.
    (PAUSE)

?: (Ha fatto)

F: Ma—hh(laugh) a p(h)art(h) e il fatto che la più
    But—besides the fact that the most
    grossa risate ce la siamo fatta co—quando doveva
    big laugh$_i$ us it$_i$ (we) had done with—when (he) had
    fa' i r(h)e(h)l(h)ly te ricordi?//(Laugh)
    to do the rallies (do you) remember?

F: (...) In a few words, if you just think of his way of life. That is, all the things have happened with the same characteristics.
    (PAUSE)

?: (He did/said)

F: But hh besides the fact that the biggest laugh$_i$, we had it$_i$ when he had to go and do the rallies. Do you remember?)

The third example shows a left-dislocation appearing in a lunch time conversation between members of a family. Speaking of noise that bothered them in the middle of the night, the father of the family discusses how this issue applies to him:

(3) *At Dinner*

(Mother, Father and Son have just been discussing noises in the night that woke them up.)

Father: Io— c'è una cosa de bello che—
        I— there's one thing of good that—
        ((0.5))
        Prima d'addormentarme me dà fastidio tutto
        Before falling asleep to-me bothers everything.

Tua madre che russa$_i$ non me ne$_i$ parla' (....)
Your mother that snores$_i$, NEG to me it$_i$ mention
        Father: As for me, there's something good that—
                (0.5)
                Before falling asleep, everything bothers me. Your mother
                who snores$_i$, don't even mention it$_i$ (...)

In the course of this discussion, he uses left–dislocation to provide an example: "Tua madre che russa non me ne parla'."

These examples illustrate not simply one of several environments for left-dislocation; they illustrate the *major* environment for these constructions. Left-dislocation is almost exclusively a conversational construction. It is rarely found in written Italian discourse. In written discourse, it is found only in informal chatty discourse, and even in these contexts it is rare. Furthermore, even in spoken discourse, these constructions tend to be found more often in informal conversation than in formal conversational discourse. The more formal the situation, the more self-conscious the language-users are about their language, the less likely it is that they will use left-dislocated construction.

Here one should see what problems this brings to the argument for a natural preference for subject before direct object. If this were a natural ordering or, rather, if object before subject were an unnatural ordering, we would not expect it to appear more often in relaxed unselfconscious, spontaneous speech than in formal, self-conscious speech or writing. Indeed, it would seem that the more 'natural' the social situation, the more characteristic the object-subject ordering.

Clearly, for these speakers in these situations there is something very natural about putting an affected object before an agent or actor. The naturalness is not a product of some pan-human preference for certain concepts over others; it is a product of a socially-constructed preference. It is natural because it carries out socially appropriate work.

To understand the naturalness of this construction, then, we turn not to the cognitive processes of *individuals,* but to the social processes at work in a particular social context—namely, informal conversational interaction.

Left-Dislocation and Conversational Organization

We start out our analysis, then, with the premise that there is something about the nature of conversation that leads speakers to use left-dislocations. Among the many features of conversation that have been described by Sacks, Schegloff and Jefferson (1974), two are particularly relevant to the construction at hand: *First, in spontaneous conversation, the content of any given turn is not totally specified in advance.* What gets talked about is a co-operatively determined matter, constantly evolving and changing. *Second, in spontaneous conversation, the order in which speakers take their turns is not specified in advance.* The matter of who is to talk next is decided on a turn–by–turn basis.

Turn Content

How are these two features linked to left–dislocation? Let us turn first to the matter of turn content—what gets talked about.

To be a competent conversational partner, a speaker must attend to what is currently under consideration. As a general rule, a speaker must shape her/his talk to the current issue at hand. Not just any conversational contribution is acceptable. One's conversational contribution must be *"warranted" (Jefferson 1978) by the social situation as it has evolved thus far.* Unless the speaker indicates otherwise, there is an expectation that one's utterances will be on-topic (Grice 1975).

We suggest that this expectation, this obligation, affects word order. Specifically, we suggest *that speakers use starting points of utterances to display that the contribution is warranted.* That is, the starting point is used to legitimize the turn.

There are two major ways in which left-dislocated items display this warranted status: First, they are typically *illustrations* or *examples* of some general concern under consideration. For example, in (1) the general concern is the cleaning of the household. The left-dislocation introduces one example or item, la stanza (the room) that is part of his concern. In example (2) the general concern is with the way in which a mutual friend (Roberto) is a loser. Again, the left-dislocation introduces an illustration of this concern. The speaker brings up a particular event, the car rallies, in which Roberto displayed his character. Similarly, example (3) brings up "tua madre che russa" (your mother who snores) as an instance of the general topic, things that bother them in the night.

A second way in which left-dislocated items are tied to current concerns is through *repetition.* The left–dislocated item is relevant to or warranted by prior talk because it has appeared in the immediately prior talk. Examples (4) and (5) illustrate this type of link with prior talk.

(4) *Complementation Seminar*

(Members of the seminar have been discussing verbs that can take complements. They are presently discussing the verb 'fuggire'.)

A: (...) 'fuggire da:l far qualcosa' Non mi sembra-non mi
'escape from doing something NEG to-me seems NEG to-me
//sembra// un buon italiano.
seems a good Italian.

F: No.
No.

V: (Ce l'avresti con)   '*ri*fuggi //re'
((You) would have it with)   'rifuggire' (+re-escape)

L: Rifuggire //e

A: (//)

F: Ri—ri

'rifuggire! già // ce l'abbiamo.
"re-escape$_i$, already us[1] it$_i$ (we) have

A: Allora niente 'fuggire'.
Then nothing 'escape'.

A: (...) 'fuggire da far qualcosa', it doesn't seem//
to me like good Italian

F: No.

V: (You would have it with) 'rifuggi //re'

L: rifuggi//re

A: (//)

F: Ri-ri-ri-rifuggire$_i$ we //already have it$_i$

A: Then no 'fuggire'.)

(5) *Complementation Seminar*

V: Ma. Non so. Io l'ho eliminato. Però. Non so. Ci sarebbe
But. NEG (I)know. I it have eliminated. But. NEG(I)know. There
anche 'struggersi'. Non lo so. Ma mi sembra di no.
also "consume oneself". NEG(I)know. But to-me seems of not.
(PAUSE)

V: "Si strugge per diventare- per essere: 'che ne so io
"(He) consumes himself to become — to be — 'what can say I
//'nominato'
'nominated'.

F: Questo$_i$ lo$_i$ usi solo te.
This$_i$ it$_i$ (you) use only you.
((Laugh))

        (V: But — I don't know. I have eliminated it. Though.
           I don't know, there is also 'struggersi'. I don't know. But it doesn't sound
           like it.
           (Pause)

> V: 'He consumes himself to become — to — what can I say// 'nominated'
> F: This$_i$ only you use it$_i$.
>   (Laugh)   )

In example (4), the same lexical item has appeared in the left-dislocation and in the prior discourse (rifuggire). In example (5), the pronoun *Questo* (this) is used to refer to an immediately prior referent. This type of linkage in which the left-dislocated item appears in the immediately prior talk is relatively uncommon in our corpus, accounting for less than a third of the constructions, only 20%, (5) of left-dislocated nouns, 37.5% (6) of left-dislocated pronouns.

The main point for both of these cases is that the left-dislocated item is placed in initial position *not because some inherent semantic property (such as agency) gives it a preferred status, but because the conversational history of an interaction has given it a preferred status.* The initial position of clauses or utterances are reserved for socially warranted items and if a non-agent, non-human item is nonetheless directly warranted, it will precede other items.

Turn Order

We mentioned that there are two features of conversation that 'word order' is sensitive to. Let us turn our attention to the second of these, the local determination of *turn order*.

As there is no prescribed order of turn-taking, no order that has been fixed in advance, who is to take the next turn is negotiated on a turn-by-turn basis. We would like to suggest here that the use of a socially warranted item in initial position not only legitimizes the content of a speaker's talk, *it legitimizes his taking the turn in the first place.* Using a socially warranted item to begin an utterance is a way of displaying that one has the right to take the next turn, to occupy the floor.

That this is the case for middle class American Anglos has been demonstrated by Jefferson in a study of on and off the point utterances (1978). She found that off-the-point utterances get cut off much more often than utterances that appear to be more directly on-topic. If you want to get a hold of the floor and keep that hold on the floor, then selection of a highly warranted starting point is a good strategy.

Word order, we suggest, is sensitive to these situational demands. Left-dislocation, in particular, appears to be part of a floor-seeking and floor-holding strategy. For example, if we look at where left-dislocations appear with respect to turn margins, we find that, compared with ordinary subject predicate constructions, left-dislocations have a high occurrence in *turn-initial position*. Left-dislocations appear over twice as often in turn-initial position as ordinary subject-verb constructions (LD: 49.9% (21)/SV: 21.5%

(36) in turn-initial position). These figures suggest that left-dislocation may be designed to take the floor.

Indeed, left-dislocations appear to be linked to *competition for the floor*. For example, 64% (12) of the turn-initial left-dislocations actually overlap (interrupt) with immediately prior turns. Further, left-dislocations seem to increase with the number of speakers. Three-party or multi-party conversations have more LDs than 2-party conversations in our data. Finally, LDs appear more frequently where competing assessments are being made. For example, during a linguistics seminar on complementation, left-dislocations were used to display judgments of grammaticality, judgments as to whether particular constructions should be considered, and so on.

In summary, we find that word order, in particular the initial position of utterance, is sensitive to social interaction in two ways. First, word order is *shaped by social interaction,* in the sense that the initial item should be socially warranted. Second, word order is a *shaper of subsequent social interaction.* The initial item in an utterance can determine who will speak next, who will occupy the next turn. These functions of word order can be as important and in some cases, more important than the function of encoding inherently salient information.

III.

The goal of this paper was to give greater status to social processes as constraints on grammatical structure and to simply bring to the attention of the linguistic community the historical neglect of these processes in this country. Goffman in 1964 made the same point to cultural anthropologists in an article entitled "The Neglected Situation." Unfortunately, nearly fifteen years later, the status of social processes remains almost unchanged. It is important to change this state of affairs, to stop treating the social situation in which language is used as a "country cousin." "Your social situation is not your country cousin," Goffman and a score of other sociologists have been telling us. It is a highly complex phenomenon and demands more than a passing acquaintance.

REFERENCES

Austin, J. L. *How to do things with words.* Harvard Univ. William James Lectures. Oxford: Oxford Univ. Press, 1955.

Bateson, G. *Naven,* 2nd Edition. Stanford: Stanford Univ. Press, 1958.

Berger, P., & Luckmann, T. *Social construction of reality.* New York: Doubleday, 1966.

Bever, T. G. The cognitive basis for linguistic structures. In J. R. Hayes (Ed.), *Cognition and the development of language.* New York: John Wiley & Sons, 1970, pp. 279–352.

Bloom, L. *Language development: Form and function in emerging grammar.* MIT Research Monograph 59, Cambridge, Mass.

Brown, R. *A first language: The early states.* Cambridge: Harvard University Press, 1973.

Carroll, J. B. (Ed.). *Language, thought, and reality: Selected writings of Benjamin Lee Whorf.* Cambridge: MIT Technology Press, 1956.

Chomsky, N. *Cartesian linguistics.* New York: Harper & Row, 1966.

Chomsky, N. *Reflections on language.* New York: Pantheon Books, 1975.

Clark, E. On the acquisition of 'before' and 'after'. *Journal of Verbal Learning and Verbal Behavior,* 1971, *10,* 266–275.

Duranti, A. & Ochs, E. Left-dislocation in Italian conversation. In T. Givón (Ed.), *Syntax and semantics,* Vol. 12, *Discourse and syntax.* New York: Academic Press, in press.

Durkeim, E. *The rules of sociological method.* New York: Free Press, 1938.

Fillmore, C. *Lectures on Deixis.* Given at University of California at Santa Cruz, 1971.

Fillmore, C. Pragmatics and the description of discourse. *Berkeley studies in syntax and semantics,* Vol. 1, 1975, pp. 1–25.

Garfinkel, H. *Studies in ethnomethodology.* Englewood Cliffs, N.J.: Prentice-Hall, 1967.

Goffman, E. *Behavior in public places.* New York: Free Press, 1963.

Goffman, E. The neglected situation. *American Anthropologist,* Vol. 66, special issue, 1964.

Goody, J. (Ed.). *The developmental cycle in domestic groups.* Cambridge Papers in Social Anthropology, No. 1. London: Cambridge University Press, 1958.

Greenberg, J. Some universals of grammar with particular reference to the order of meaningful elements. In J. Greenberg (Ed.), *Universals of language.* Cambridge, Mass.: MIT Press, 1966, pp. 58–90.

Grice, H. P. Utterer's meaning, sentence-meaning, and word-meaning. In J. R. Searle (Ed.), *The philosophy of language.* London: Oxford Univ. Press, 1971, pp. 54–71.

Grice, H. P. William James Lectures, Harvard Univ., 1967. Published in part as "Logic and conversation" in P. Cole & J. L. Morgan (Eds.), *Syntax and semantics,* Vol. 3, *Speech acts.* New York: Academic Press, 1975.

Hoenigswald, H. *Language change and linguistic reconstruction.* Chicago: Univ. of Chicago Press, 1960.

Hymes, D. Models of the interaction of language and social setting. *Journal of Social Issues,* 1967, *23*(2), 8–28.

Hymes, D. Linguistic method in ethnography: Its development in the United States. In P. L. Garvin (Ed.), *Method and theory in linguistics.* The Hague: Mouton, 1970, pp. 249–325.

Hymes, D. *Foundations of sociolinguistics: An ethnographic approach.* Philadelphia: Univ. of Pennsylvania, 1974.

Jefferson, G. Sequential aspects of story-telling in conversation. In J. Schenkein (Ed.), *Studies in the organization of conversational interaction.* New York: Academic Press, 1978.

Kay, P. Some theoretical implications of ethnographic semantics. In *Current directions in anthropology, Bulletin of the American Anthropological Association,* 1970, 3:3 (Part 2), pp. 19–35.

Kluckhohn, C. Culture and behavior. In G. Lindzey (Ed.), *Handbook of social psychology.* Cambridge: Addison-Wesley, 1954.

Labov, W. *The social stratification of English in New York City.* Washington, D.C.: Center for Applied Linguistics, 1966.

Lyons, J. *Introduction to theoretical linguistics.* Cambridge: Cambridge Univ. Press, 1968.

MacWhinney, B. Starting points. *Language,* 1977, *53,* 152–168.

Radcliffe-Brown, A. R. *Structure and function in primitive society.* London: Cohen and West, 1952.

Redfield, R. *The primitive world and its transformation.* Ithaca: Cornell Univ. Press, 1953.

Robins, R. H. Linguistics and anthropology. *Man,* 1959, *59,* 175–179.

Ross, J. *Constraints on variables in syntax.* Unpublished doctoral dissertation, MIT, 1967.

Sacks, H., Schegloff, E., & Jefferson, G. A simplest systematics of the organization of turn-taking for conversation. *Language,* 1974, *50,* 696–735.

Sapir, E. Speech as a personality trait. *American Journal of Sociology,* 1927, *32,* 893–905.

Sapir, E. Cultural anthropology and psychiatry. *Journal of Abnormal and Social Psychology,* 1932, *27,* 229–242 (SWES 509–521).

Searle, J. *Speech acts.* Cambridge: Cambridge University Press, 1969.

Spier, L., Hallowell, A., & Newman, S. (Eds.). *Language, culture and personality: Essays in memory of Edward Sapir.* Menasha, Wisc.: Banta, 1941.

Strawson, P. F. Intention and convention in speech acts. In J. Searle (Ed.), *The philosophy of language.* London: Oxford University Press, 1971, pp. 23–39.

Wallace, A. *Culture and personality,* 2nd ed. New York: Random House, 1970.

9 Modes of Thinking and Ways of Speaking: Culture and Logic Reconsidered

Sylvia Scribner
The Rockefeller University

> Our attitude towards what we listen to is
> determined by our habits. We expect things to
> be said in the way in which we are accustomed
> to talk ourselves: things that are said some
> other way do not seem the same at all but seem
> rather incomprehensible... Thus, one needs
> already to have been educated in the way to
> approach each subject.
> —Aristotle, Book II, *Metaphysics*

Of the many issues relating to culture and thought that have been a matter of scholarly concern in the last century, the question of whether industrialized and traditional people share the same logical processes has provoked the most bitter controversy.

Initially centered within sociology and anthropology, the debate has largely shifted to the psychological arena. Here it has taken its most prominent form in the clash over proper interpretation of cross-cultural Piagetian experiments on logical competencies: Do they, or do they not, demonstrate the universality of logical structures of intelligence? (For a historical review of theoretical positions on cultural differences and logical thinking, see Cole & Scribner, 1974. Dasen, 1974, provides a summary and analysis of cross-cultural Piagetian research.)

In the last few years, quite a different line of psychological evidence has become available. Following a time-honored tradition in psychological laboratories (see Woodworth, 1938), a number of cross-cultural investigators have made use of syllogisms and other formal logic problems as tools for studying processes of inference in verbal thinking.

While still in its early stages, this work has produced a coherent body of findings which suggest the fruitfulness of a new strategy in the pursuit of cultural influences on logical processes—a strategy uniting the psychological study of thinking processes with the ethnographic study of ways of speaking.

This paper reviews the principal findings of this research and offers a first, speculative framework for their interpretation. We begin with a brief description of the studies that furnish the data base for the discussion, while Aristotle, the inventor of the syllogism and the analyst of discourse, waits in the wings.

CROSS-CULTURAL STUDIES ON VERBAL REASONING

Verbal logic problems were first used to investigate cultural influences on reasoning by the Soviet psychologist Luria (1971, 1976) and his colleagues in studies conducted in 1931–32 in remote regions of Uzbekistan, Central Asia. Inspired by Vygotsky's theory of mental development which holds that the specific characteristics of complex intellectual processes are determined by conditions of social life and practical activity, these psychologists sought to determine whether the social and economic reforms introduced in Uzbekistan after the revolution had effected changes in the perceptual and cognitive skills of the local people.

To investigate reasoning, Luria prepared simple syllogisms and used them in a semi-experimental, semi-interview format with four basic populations, differing in the extent to which they participated in modern social institutions: nonliterate Muslim women in remote villages who were not engaged in productive activity; nonliterate men in the same villages who carried on traditional modes of farming; young activists involved in collective farming, some of whom had minimal literacy training; women enrolled in courses at teacher training schools. Marked differences in performance between the "traditional" and "modern" groups (described below) were taken as confirmation of Vygotsky's theory.

Some decades later, Cole, Gay, Glick, & Sharp (1971) incorporated verbal logic problems in their extensive series of studies on learning and thinking among the Kpelle, a rice-farming tribal people in Liberia, West Africa. To determine the specific situational and experiential features affecting performance, they used a wide variety of problem materials (sentential and syllogistic problems), tasks (drawing conclusions or judging validity), and settings (individual interviews and group discussions). Comparative populations were nonliterate men and women in traditional occupations and young people with varying amounts of education in the English curricula of government and mission schools. Their finding of what appeared to be massive "error" on the part of traditional populations prompted Scribner (1975) to undertake a series of recall studies among the Kpelle and Vai (a neighboring people), seeking to test the hypothesis that failure to integrate and retain the information in the problem was the source of apparent "nonlogical" performance.

In an attempt to further specify the effects of particular cultural factors on performance, Sharp & Cole (1975) replicated the Kpelle studies among Mayan-speaking and Spanish-speaking villagers in the Yucatan, Mexico. Comparison groups were rural and semi-urban, schooled and nonschooled adult and child populations. Finally, Cole and Scribner administered a set of syllogisms to a sample of 750 Vai adults as part of a project to investigate the cognitive consequences of literacy (the Vai Literacy Project is briefly described in Scribner & Cole, 1974).

The type of problem material used in these studies is illustrated in Table 1.

Considering the diversity of people, settings, tasks, and materials covered in these studies and of the special problems of "nonreplicability" in cross-cultural research, the consistency of basic findings is impressive. Not only are quantitative results strikingly uniform from study to study, but certain

TABLE 1
Representative Problems in Cross-Cultural Studies on Verbal Reasoning

Central Asia

Cotton grows where it is hot and humid.
In the village it is hot and humid.
Does cotton grow there or not?

In the far north all bears are white.
Novaya Zemyla is in the far north.
What colors are the bears there?

West Africa

All people who own houses pay house tax.
Boima does not pay a house tax.
Does he own a house?

Some of the people we know are not in school.
All of the people we know are in Liberia.
Are all of the people in Liberia in schools?

Mexico

A dog and a horse are always together.
The horse is here now.
Where do you think the dog might be now?

So that Jose can carry corn from his farm to the town, he needs a cart and a horse.
He has the horse but doesn't have the cart.
Can Jose carry his corn from his farm?

qualitative aspects of performance are so similar that it is often difficult to distinguish the translated interview protocol of an Uzbekistanian from that of a Vai—cultural and geographical distance notwithstanding.

Performance consistency with respect to problem solution is displayed in Table 2, which summarizes findings in simplified form.[1] (Luria's studies are omitted, since his method, adapted to each individual respondent, does not yield a tally of scores.) Basic comparisons are made with respect to the contrast feature of schooling/no schooling, the only characteristic of populations that was systematically investigated across studies. Two studies of U.S. schoolchildren are included to extend the range of comparisons. In several Yucatecan studies, social conditions made it possible to vary age and schooling independently and these studies are indicated by asterisks.

Taken as a group, these studies appear to support a number of generalizations.

1. *In all cultures,* populations designated as traditional or nonliterate have just somewhat better than a chance solution rate across all types of problem material. (In the majority of studies cited, subjects were confronted with a two-choice judgment decision so that the 50% level may be taken as a crude indicator of chance.) Absolute levels vary with tasks and materials.

2. *Within each culture* there is a large discrepancy in performance between schooled and nonschooled. The major jump seems to occur at levels of education as low as two to three years of school (Luria also reports "educational effects" with minimal literacy training), and there is continued improvement at the second school and college level.

3. With schooling, there is little *between-culture* variation in performance for the cultures studied. Grade, rather than society, is most determinative of performance. The two studies of U.S. elementary school children included in the table show the consistency of the grade level/performance relationship.

A significant finding, not represented in the summary statistics of Table 2, is that there was considerable diversity of performance among nonliterate

---

[1]Although data in Table 2 restrict within-culture comparisons to schooled and nonschooled populations, there is considerable diversity of performance among nonliterate adults that appears related to such social factors as the modernity of the village in which people live (Sharp & Cole, 1975) or whether they are engaged in cash occupations (Scribner, 1974). Interpretations of performance become complex because we are not dealing with a homogenous mass of "nonliterate Vai" or "nonliterate Kpelle." We do not yet have systematic comparative data for groups distinguished by characteristics other than schooling; nor is it clear which are the most important characteristics to consider. Since it is illusory to pursue a "representative" nonliterate performance, we will follow the strategy of focusing on extreme cases to bring out those features of performance that are not encountered in research with school-educated subjects in industrial nations.

TABLE 2
Summary of Cross-Cultural Studies. Percent of Correct Answers to Verbal
Logic Problems

	Nonschooled		Schooled	
Cole, Gay, Glick, & Sharp (Kpelle)				
Study 3	35		91	(High School)
Study 4	61		100	(High School)
Study 5	65			
	*64	(10–14 years)	*82	(10–14 years, 2nd–3rd grade)
			*89	(10–14 years, 4th–6th grade)
Scribner (Kpelle)				
Study 1	63		83	(Jr. High)
Study 2	62			
Scribner (Vai)	52			
Cole & Scribner (Vai)	69		87	(All grades)
Sharp & Cole (Yucatecans)	*45	(Mayan traditional town)	*73	(3rd-grade education)
	*62	(Mayan transitional town)	*76	(4th-grade education)
			55	(1st–2nd grade)
			78	(4th–6th grade)
			97	(Secondary school)
Scribner, Orasanu, Lazarov, Woodring (United States)				
Study 1			74	(2nd grade)
			77	(5th grade)
Study 2			72	(2nd grade)
			74	(5th grade)

[a]Age-controlled studies are indicated by *.

adults. Accuracy of solution varied from problem to problem (consult Cole et al., 1971; Scribner, 1975; and Sharp & Cole, 1975, for detailed problem analyses) and from population to population. These diversities constitute an important line of evidence for the argument developed in this paper. (See discussion below on empiric bias.) Nonetheless, the overall level of performance of nonschooled traditional people and the within-culture differences in performance between schooled and nonschooled groups suggest that logic problems pose special difficulties for traditional nonliterate people. Uniformities in patterns *across* cultures indicate that the source of these difficulties is not likely to reside in aspects of culture that are unique to any one of the given cultures.

LOGICAL THINKING VERSUS LOGICAL ERROR

Is the source of difficulty in these problems the fact that traditional people do not reason logically?

Even minimal familiarity with daily life in these communities makes such a conclusion untenable with respect to everyday thinking. Levy-Bruhl (1966), who first formulated the notion of a different logic characterizing primitive thought, specifically exempted the sphere of practical activity from this generalization.

Is it then the case that traditional people do not apply their logical skills to *verbal* material?

Internal evidence from the experimental situation argues against such a notion. Many of the nonliterate people demonstrated in the course of the interviews that they were perfectly capable of valid inferential reasoning with information presented in the verbal mode.

This is well illustrated in the following protocol from a Kpelle farmer:

Experimenter: If Sumo or Saki drinks palm wine, the Town Chief gets vexed. Sumo is not drinking palm wine. Saki is drinking palm wine. Is the Town Chief vexed?

Subject: People do not get vexed with two persons.

E: (Repeats the problem.)

S: The Town Chief was not vexed on that day.

E: The Town Chief was not vexed? What is the reason?

S: The reason is that he doesn't love Sumo.

E: He doesn't love Sumo? Go on with the reason.

S: The reason is that Sumo's drinking is a hard time. That is why when he drinks palm wine, the Town Chief gets vexed. But sometimes when Saki drinks palm juice he will not give a hard time to people. He goes to lie down to sleep. At that rate people do not get vexed with him. But people who drink and go about fighting—the Town Chief cannot love them in the town.

While this man's answer is "wrong" as far as the experimental problem is concerned, it is the outcome of an elegant piece of logical reasoning from new evidence. We can easily see this by recasting his statements into more traditional syllogistic form:

Sumo's drinking gives people a hard time. (Explicit premise)
Saki's drinking does not give people a hard time. (Explicit premise)
People do not get vexed when they are not given a hard time. (Explicit premise)
The Town Chief is a person. (Implicit premise)
Therefore, the Town Chief is not vexed at Saki. (Conclusion)

This is not an isolated example. Scribner (unpublished notes) analyzed interviews with eight adults in one of the Cole et al. studies, each of whom had received at least three problems to solve. Wherever there was sufficient information to reconstruct the chain of reasoning leading to the answer it was found to follow logically from the evidence used by the subject.

The critical factors is that the "evidence used by the subject," in many cases (as in the illustration given above), bore little resemblance to the evidence supplied in the experimental problem. Cole et al. (1971) concluded that "The subjects were (or seem to have been) responding to conventional situations in which their past experience dictated the answer . . . In short, it appears that the particular verbal context and content dictate the response rather than the arbitrarily imposed relations among the elements in the problem" (p. 188).

Luria had earlier reported the same tendency for Uzbekistanians to respond in terms of direct personal experience. By manipulating the content of the problems, however, he demonstrated that where the subject matter was related to practical *knowledge* but did not deal with already known *facts,* responses were not merely verbalizations of conventional answers but were new conclusions reached through step-by-step reasoning from the problem premises. "Reasoning and deduction . . . follow well-known rules . . . subjects make excellent judgements about facts without displaying any deviation from the 'rules' and revealing a great deal of worldly intelligence" (Luria, 1976, p. 114).

These observations make it clear that inferences about a generalized incapacity of traditional people to reason logically are unwarranted. Moreover, they suggest that any inference about reasoning abilities of members of a traditional culture requires some specification of what they are reasoning *about*. Are subjects making their judgments on the basis of assertions made in the problem statements or are they drawing upon real world knowledge to generate conclusions? Is the *functional* evidence (the information actually used by the subject) the same or different from the *formal* evidence (the information supplied in the premises)? Fortunately, there are data which help us identify the functional evidence used in problem solutions; an examination of the nature of this evidence deepens our understanding of the factors affecting performance on logic problems.

EMPIRIC VERSUS THEORETIC EXPLANATIONS

In some studies, subjects were asked not only to draw conclusions but to justify or explain their answers as well. Scribner took these explanations as indicators of whether subjects were responding to the information contained in the problem or to information external to it. All statements that *explicitly* related the conclusion to the problem premises were coded as "theoretic"; all statements justifying the conclusion on the basis of what the subject knew or believed to be true, and nonresponsive replies, were classified as "empiric." Examples of each will clarify the distinction.

The problem is:

All people who own houses pay a house tax.
Boima does not pay a house tax.
Does Boima own a house?

A theoretic justification: "If you say Boima does not pay a house tax, he cannot own a house." An empiric justification: "Boima does not have money to pay a house tax."

Table 3 presents the proportion of theoretic explanations given by the principal comparative groups in four studies. Population differences here are even more marked than those relating to solution rates, and again the

TABLE 3
Percent of Theoretic Reasons for Problem Answers

	Nonschooled	Schooled	
Africa and Mexico			
Scribner (Kpelle)	22.3	75.0	(Students, Jr. High School)
Scribner (Vai)	8.3	—	
Cole & Scribner (Vai)	29.5^a	72.2^a	(Adults, all grades)
Sharp & Cole (Yucatecans)			
Mayan, traditional town	43.0	75.9	(Mestizo adults, grades 1–6)
Mayan, transitional town	58.5	46.5	(2nd-grade children)
		80.8	(4th–6th grade children)
		97.4	(Secondary school children)
United States			
Scribner, Orasanu, Lazarov, Woodring			
Study 1		77.6	(2nd-grade children)
		93.2	(5th-grade children)
Study 2		76.0	(2nd-grade children)
		95.1	(5th-grade children)

^{a}Sample from survey

dimension of schooling/nonschooling serves as a significant discriminator. Nonschooled villagers overwhelmingly support their answers by appeals to fact, belief, or opinion. With comparable consistency, schooled groups adopt a theoretic approach to the task; even seven-year-old second-graders in school systems known for emphasizing rote learning rather than the development of critical thinking tend to refer to what the problems *say* when asked to account for their answers. These data not only corroborate anecdotal reports of the several investigators, but document the pervasiveness of villagers' resort to the concrete example or particular circumstance. This appeal to real world knowledge and experience, which for the time being we will call "empiric bias," is the single most prominent characteristic of villagers' performance and merits detailed analysis.

WHAT IS EMPIRIC BIAS? SOME EXAMPLES

As ordinarily used in studies on reasoning, empiric bias refers to the subtle effects of problem content which "seduce" the reasoner from the formal task; it operates as a "distractor." In the cross-cultural research reported here such distracting effects are also found, but among some traditional groups empiric bias takes a new form: it operates as an "organizer," characterizing the individual's entire mode of engagement with the material.

In the extreme, such bias is shown in the refusal of some individuals to engage in the reasoning task at all, on the grounds that the problems presented are, *in principle,* unanswerable. This is illustrated in the following protocol of a nonliterate Kpelle farmer who has been presented with a description of this word game and shown how to solve a practice problem by "listening to the words and taking them to be true" (a colloquial Kpelle expression). The problem:

> All Kpelle men are rice farmers. Mr. Smith is not a rice farmer. Is he a Kpelle man?

The subject replies:

S: I don't know the man in person. I have not laid eyes on the man himself.

E: Just think about the statement.

S: If I know him in person, I can answer that question, but since I do not know him in person I cannot answer that question.

E: Try and answer from your Kpelle sense.

S: If you know a person, if a question comes up about him you are able to answer. But if you do not know the person, if a question comes up about him, it's hard for you to answer it.

This man firmly rejects the possibility of coming to a conclusion on the basis of propositions which make assertions about matters on which he has no personal information. He is not distinguishing between the process of drawing conclusions from statements asserting relationships and the process of evaluating information. At the same time, the protocol illustrates that his failure to grasp the nature of this reasoning task should not be confused with failure to adopt a hypothetical attitude. In fact, on several occasions this Kpelle man reasoned hypothetically (i.e., from a conditional statement) in his exposition of why he *could not* answer the question ("If you know a person...you are able to answer..."), but his hypothetical reasoning was within the empiric mode. One might say he was reasoning hypothetically about the *actual* while denying the possibility of reasoning hypothetically about the *postulated*.

Luria's (1976) transcripts have many such examples drawn from interviews with nonliterate Uzbekistanian women, who seem to have been the most isolated of the groups worked with thus far. To the problem: "In the far north all bears are white; Novaya Zemyla is in the far north. What color are the bears there?" the women often suggested, "You should ask the people who have been there and seen them."; "We always speak of only what we see; we don't talk about what we haven't seen."

These represent the extreme examples and were only occasionally encountered in contemporary studies, but no similar cases, to our knowledge, have been reported outside of the cross-cultural literature.

For the majority of traditional adults, empiric bias entered the problem solution process primarily as selector and editor of the "evidence." Personal knowledge and experience were used as (1) the criterion for acceptance or rejection of particular information conveyed in the premises, (2) the source of new information from which to derive a conclusion, (3) verification of a conclusion reached through use of problem information. These functions are illustrated in the protocols on the facing page from Vai respondents, all adult men and women without schooling.

For populations at the extreme end of formal education and/or modernity, theoretic approaches may be an all-or-none matter; at the extreme of rural isolation (as among Luria's Muslim women) empiric approaches may be all-or-none. In the present analysis, formal evidence in the problem controls performance of the schooled groups. The nonschooled groups show no such homogeneity: some respondents appear at either end of the spectrum, handling all problems empirically or, in fewer numbers, all theoretically. The great majority are mixed moders, relying now on the formal information in the problem, now on evidence external to it. Adoption of a particular mode is influenced in varying degrees by specific features of the material, especially the factual status of the information supplied in the premises. Several problems in the Vai research evoked empiric responses from more than 75% of respondents while others drew such responses from only 30% of the

Problem	Answer and Explanation
Rejection of problem information	
(1) All women who live in Monrovia are married. Kemu is not married. Does she live in Monrovia?	Yes. Monrovia is not for any one kind of people, so Kemu came to live there. (denial of first premise)
(2) Some government officials are wealthy. All wealthy men are powerful. Are some government officials powerful?	No. Because all government officials are wealthy, but not all wealthy people have power. (denial of second premise)
Importing new evidence	
(3) All people who own houses pay house tax. Boima does not pay a house tax. Does he own a house?	Yes. Boima has a house but he is exempted from paying house tax. The government appointed Boima to collect house tax so they exempted him from paying house tax. (discussion indicated that this was exception proving the rule that all people pay house tax.)
Verifying a conclusion	
Problem (3) above.	No. If he has a house, he would pay the government tax *as required by the Liberian government* (factual corroboration)
(4) Some of the people we know are not in school. All of the people we know are in Liberia. Are all of the people in Liberia in school?	No. Because you said you know some people who do not go to school and *myself know a lot of them too.* (Corroboration of the formal evidence by personal experience)
(5) All schools in Vai land are in a town. I know a school in Vai land. Is it in a town?	Yes. All schools are in a town. A school *should* be for the *fact human beings are attending it so it can't be built in the bush.* (Corroboration by common sense)

sample. The fact that most nonliterate individuals respond theoretically to at least one problem demonstrates that while their approach to the task is dominated by empiric bias, it is not wholly controlled by it.

EMPIRIC VERSUS THEORETIC EXPLANATIONS AND WRONG ANSWERS

The presence of within-subject as well as between-group variability in empiric and theoretic-based answers raises a critical possibility. If we separate out the problems in which individuals used evidence contained in the premises, as indicated by their theoretical justifications, we should expect to find a high proportion of correct answers. Indeed, theoretical responses should *invariably* be associated with correct responses, provided the subject is able to

TABLE 4
Type of Reason and Error in Problem Solution

	Proportion Theoretic Reasons with Wrong Answers	Proportion Empiric Reasons with Wrong Answers
Sharp & Cole, 1975 (Mexico)		
Mayan, traditional	.02	.21
Mayan, transitional	.01	.15
Mestizo adults (elementary school)	(<.01)	.08
2nd-grade children	.01	.18
4th–6th-grade children	.02	.09
Secondary school students	(<.01)	.00
Scribner & Cole, 1975 (Africa)		
Vai adults	.01	.42

meet the logical demands of the problem. If people are making judgments on the basis of their own experience, however, as evidenced by empiric justifications, their conclusions could be either correct or incorrect, depending on the factual status of the information given in the problem.

To test this line of reasoning, we made a detailed problem-by-problem analysis of the relationship between explanations and answers for the first 100 respondents in a village picked at random from the current Vai survey study. This was a heterogeneous sample in which the majority of respondents were nonliterate, but it included some men literate in the indigenous Vai script and several individuals who had attended English school. Of the 600 cases (100 subjects times six syllogistic problems) there are 171 wrong answers, *but not a single case in which a theoretic reason coexists with a wrong answer* (see Table 4).[2]

To determine the generality of this relationship for logic problems of a different type and for members of another culture, a similar analysis was made for the Sharp–Cole studies. Although, as we have seen, the distribution of empiric and theoretical explanations differs markedly from one group to another, the relationship between theoretical justifications and correct answers is robust. Summing across populations as well as problems, of 233 wrong answers to problems, only 17 are associated with theoretic reasons.

Not only is this relationship constant across groups, but it holds for *any given individual* within every population group: traditional men and women who give theoretical reasons on particular problems produce the logically correct answers on these problems, even though all their other answers may be wrong.

---

[2]Two problems were eliminated from this analysis because the translated material was not sufficiently clear for coding purposes.

Considering that coding was performed on English translations and that it imposed a forced choice allowing for no third category of "doubtfuls," the virtual absence of error when individuals respond to the terms of the problem is an exciting finding.

While theoretic reasons almost always predict accuracy, empiric reasons, as we conjectured, were used to justify right as well as wrong answers. In some problems, the validly correct conclusions coincided with facts that would be known through direct personal experience, e.g., conclusions such as "Not everyone in Liberia goes to school," derived from the premises "Some of the people we know are not in school" and "All of the people we know are in Liberia." Correct answers to these problems could either represent reasoning about familiar situations or merely the person's assent to a true fact of life. In the absence of extended discussion with the subject, we cannot tell which process was involved. In contrast, other problems contained one or more premises that denied a commonly accepted truth, thus setting the valid problem conclusion into opposition with experienced reality. One problem in the Vai research asserted the "absurd" proposition that "All women who live in Monrovia [the capital city of Liberia] are married," the second proposition stated that "Kemu is not married," and the question asked, "Does Kemu live in Monrovia?" Respondents working from real life knowledge-acquaintance with a particular Kemu, for example, or from the known fact that there *are* married women in Monrovia—could arrive at an incorrect answer through logical reasoning.

Thus, while correctness or incorrectness of answers associated with empiric reasons is moot with respect to the logicality of the reasoning processes involved, the association of correct answers with theoretic explanations supports an inference of logicality. The significant comparative conclusion is that, in those instances in which they deal with the problem as a formal "theoretical" one, nonschooled nonliterate traditional men and women display exactly the same logicality as adults and children exposed to Western-type schooling. In the sample at hand, when they are "theoretical," they are virtually never wrong.

This evidence, of course, does not rule out the possibility of error attributable to reasoning processes or other sources. It is well known (Wason & Johnson-Laird, 1972; Henle, 1962) that even test-sophisticated U.S. and British university students err on logic problems, depending on their structural complexity, content, and linguistic features. The present conclusion holds only for the problems used in the two studies analyzed, and the degree of complexity they represent; it may be that the problem sample was weighted toward the structurally simple, easy end of the spectrum. These data are also restricted in that they apply only to members of two cultural groups, and do not include the Kpelle and Uzbekistanian populations with whom early studies were conducted. Further research specifically directed at hypotheses about the relationship between empiric approaches and error is needed to test the generality and limits of this association for both problems and populations.

Nonetheless, the constancy of the relationship between theoretic approaches and accurate solutions represents the strongest evidence to date that traditional people can and do engage in valid deductive reasoning on verbal logic problems, provided they put brackets around what they know to be true and confine their reasoning to the terms of the problems.

More often than not, traditional villagers fail to do just that, under conditions and procedures in which educated subjects almost always do just that. It appears characteristic for villagers to approach informally "as a matter of course" a task that students approach formally "as a matter of course." Those living in the most rural and isolated towns bring to the artibrary problems of the experiment a reasoning system, at play in everyday life, in which inference is intricately interwoven with evaluation and interpretation of semantic information; others, adopting a formal mode for some problems tend to lapse into the semantic-evaluative approach to other problems. Performance on the formal task is rarely free from intrusions of real world knowledge.

The question originally motivating the research—What is the relation between cultural influences and verbal reasoning?—involves us in the exploration of another: What is the relation between cultural experiences and empiric bias? How do we pin down the specific activities within a given cultural milieu that contribute to a "break" between empiric approaches to everyday problems and theoretic approaches to problems whose subject matter does not "count"?

EMPIRIC BIAS: TASK DEPENDENT?

Before turning to some hypotheses suggested in the ethnographic literature, we would like to examine another set of cross-cultural experimental data involving somewhat different operations with syllogisms. Scribner (1975) conducted several studies among the Kpelle and Vai in which she asked subjects to *repeat* the syllogisms after they were read, or to *recall* them after they had been solved.[3] Results from these studies help us determine whether

---

[3]The notion of using recall to tap subjects' understanding of the problem was suggested by Luria's (1971) observation that Uzbekistanians who had difficulty in solving the problems also had difficulty in repeating them. Luria's (1977) full report has since become available. His syllogistic material was simpler than that used here because he followed the ordinary language practice of using implied universals and pronominals, thus avoiding confusing repetition of terms. Nevertheless, recall by his nonliterate subjects was similar in many respects to recall among the Kpelle and Vai. The more recent studies, though, seem to have produced a wider range of performance; in some cases, recall by nonliterate adults approximated that of students.

TABLE 5
Percent of Problems with Accurately Recalled Premises (Kpelle)[a]

	Both Premises	One Premise	No Premise
Kpelle villagers (N = 87)	24.1	39.1	36.8
Kpelle students (N = 93)	48.4	31.2	20.4
U.S. students (N = 90)	69.5	26.3	4.2

[a]Data presented are from subjects' second recall involving repetition of problems immediately after they were read.

the phenomenon of empiric bias in the reasoning experiments was a function of the specific task demands set in those experiments. We know that, at least in some of the cultures studied, disputation and riddling are common forms of verbal exchange. It may be that the experimental situation conveyed to the subjects the implied expectation that cleverness—"good argumentation"—was called for, and thus encouraged the production of culturally-valued types of proof. No such expectation is implied, however, when subjects are asked to repeat as accurately as possible exactly what they have heard. In Scribner's initial studies conducted among the Kpelle, subjects were asked to repeat each syllogism on two occasions: once after having answered and explained it, and a second time, immediately after hearing the problem repeated. In follow-up studies among the Vai, additional groups were added in which the only task was to repeat the syllogism in its entirety or sentence-by-sentence. In the one-sentence-at-a-time procedure, repetition was almost perfect, indicating that the surface structure of individual propositions did not pose any special encoding problems. In the other experimental conditions recall errors were similar to those among the Kpelle (results are presented in Table 5) and the discussion will be based on the Kpelle data.

Recall was scored for preservation of meaning rather than verbatim accuracy; lexical substitutions, omissions, and changes in word order that did not change the meaning were scored as accurate. Even on this basis, recall of the problem as a whole was highly fragmentary; in only a small number of cases did villagers reproduce the sense of the problem as such. Information was omitted or transformed in such a way that implicative relationships were destroyed and questions posed that did not follow from what had gone before. A Kpelle farmer attempts to recall:

Problem: All the stores in Kpelleland are in a town. Mr. Ukatu's store is in Kpelleland. Is Mr. Ukatu's store in a town?
First repeat:
You told me Mr. Ukatu came from his home and built his store in the Kpelleland. Then you asked me, is it in a town?

> Second repeat: (immediately after hearing problem reread)
> All stores are in the land. Mr. Ukatu's store is the one in Kpelleland.
> Is it in the town?

In the first repetition the subject has assimilated the problem to a narrative form. He imported new information pertaining to a personally known Mr. Ukatu ("came from his home and built his store") but omitted the major premise entirely. In the second reptition, the surface form more closely approximates the syllogism, but the major proposition—that all stores in Kpelleland are built in towns—is still omitted. In each case, the question: Is Mr. Ukatus's store in town? does not follow from the information reproduced and appears only as a question of fact, unrelated to the preceding material.

The most common classes of error included changes or omissions in quantifiers that converted generalizing statements into particular statements of fact, omission of entire premises, and displacement of terms. These changes in many instances had the effect of "destroying the syllogism as a unified system" (Luria, 1976) and replacing it with a series of discrete statements that shared the same topic but were not logically related to each other.

In a number of recall reproductions the hypothetical or theoretical status of the problem was converted to a factual status. "Remembering" new information from personal experience was one form this conversion took; another was the rephrasing of the problem question such that it referred, not to the antecedent information, but to matters of belief or fact: "Do you *think* he can be a bachelor?" "Why is it Mr. Zerby *cannot* make rice farm?" "Then, Mr. Ukatu's store, do you *know* it is in town?" "*For what reason do you think* any of them can be a bachelor?" "All the people in Liberia, do you *believe* they are in schools?"

Replication recall studies with Kpelle and U.S. students showed, as did the problem-solving studies, both commonalities and differences with the villagers. Again, magnitude of error was considerably greater for unschooled villagers than for either student group. Educated subjects, both African and American, resembled villagers in that their most common form of error was confusion of quantifiers, and, like the villagers, they sometimes omitted entire premises and switched terms from one premise to another. The one class of errors students did not make was conversion to the factual. Even when their problem repetitions were inaccurate with respect to the originals, students almost invariably preserved their hypothetical status.

It appears that among population groups for whom logical relations do not control problem-solving in the experimental situation, such relations often fail to control memory as well. The dominance of an empiric approach to problem-solving is thus not necessarily a reflection of the fact that individuals are required to draw or justify conclusions. The recall data, taken together with evidence from earlier studies, suggests that more general processes of understanding the material may underlie both recall and solution.

In what follows, we will sketch one approach to the special characteristics of formal problems and what may be involved in understanding them. This approach is not in any way dictated by the evidence at hand, but it is offered as one framework within which to search for the relationship between culture and the formal approach to problem-solving.

SCHEMAS AND GENRES

Bransford's (Bransford, Barclay, & Franks, 1972) and Barclay's (1973) theory of comprehension and sentence memory provides a starting point for the integration of recall and problem-solving findings. They maintain that, with the exception of the special case in which individuals are required to memorize the literal wording of sentences, memory for connected discourse is an active constructive process of comprehension. Comprehension involves relating or integrating the information presented in the individual sentences and assimilating it to existing lexical and nonlexical knowledge schemas. They have demonstrated experimentally that, as an outcome of these processes, memory for information in connected sentences may be richer than the original material—incorporating additional conceptual information from the schemas into which the material was assimilated.

Data from recall studies with syllogisms illustrate the converse case: memory for these connected sentences not only failed to incorporate new logical inferences but often failed to preserve the logical and conceptual information in the original. In Bransford–Barclay terms, this may be interpreted as an indication that the material was not integrated and assimilated to preexisting schemas.

This raises a general question: what are (how can we conceive the nature of) the preexisting schemas into which verbal logic problems can be assimilated? If the information they contain is completely congruent with practical knowledge, their assimilation could follow the course of comprehension of other forms of connected discourse. (Recall Luria's excellent results with material involving practical knowledge but not directly related to people's own personal experiences). If the relations the problems express are arbitrary, though, not consonant with, or in opposition to, accumulated knowledge, their assimilation into preexisting knowledge schemas may militate *against,* rather than facilitate, comprehension, recall, and problem-solving.[4] Such

---

[4]It is interesting in this connection that in Barclay's early experiments (1973) in which he used sentences expressing a set of *arbitrary* relationships (an ordered spatial array of animals, for example), he instructed his subject in the "comprehension" condition to *construct* a mental array to help them remember. "Assimilation to existing schema" clearly did not apply to artificial material of this type.

assimilation would manifest itself in "empiric bias," as preexisting schemas become the field of operation for remembering and reasoning activities. For a formal or theoretic approach to be maintained, and operations restricted to the arbitrary terms of the problems, the schema to which the material is assimilated must be a schema based on relationships rather than subject matter.

In addition to the concept of schemas, the general interpretive framework we would like to develop makes use of another analytic category, that of genre. Hymes (1974) has proposed that *genres* and *performances* be considered basic categories for the study of ways of speaking in different speech communities. As he uses the term, *genre* refers to stylistic structures or organized verbal forms with a beginning and an end "and a pattern to what comes between" (p. 442). Greetings, farewells, riddles, proverbs, prayers are among well-known elementary genres, and tales and myths representative of complex genres. *Performances* refers to the use of genres in particular contexts. Both genres and performances may vary from one speech community to another, and the relationship between them may vary as well: certain genres in certain communities may be context-bound while in others they range over diverse events and situations.

Let us entertain the proposition that verbal logic problems (along with other "formal problems" which we shall not attempt to specify at this point) constitute a specialized language genre that stands apart from other genres in ways that may be difficult to define with consensus but are readily recognizable (just as poetry may be distinguished from prose by readers who may never exactly agree on what poetry "is").

It is, of course, true that people do not "speak in syllogisms" in any community we know of, but we have good authority for considering logic problems a specialized form of discourse. In one of his definitions of a syllogism, Aristotle referred to it as "discourse in which certain things being stated, something other than what is stated follows of necessity from their being so" (*Prior Analytics,* quoted in Jager, 1964, p. 14). Or, again, he defined the component parts of the syllogism as premises, each of which is a "form of speech which affirms or denies something" and is itself composed of terms which predicate something of something else (Bochenski, 1970, p. 45). Aristotle is here developing new terminology ("premises," "terms") to talk about a language function that has hitherto not been isolated from the other functions in which it is ordinarily embedded. As Bochenski points out, new technical terminology was required to convey the distinction between two customarily related, but conceptually independent, aspects of sentences—the truth value they express (dependent on subject matter) and the relations authorizing necessary inferences that they express and that are independent of subject matter.

In ordinary discourse, these aspects interpenetrate. Discourse that uses language only or primarily to convey necessary relations between propositions constitutes what we have been calling the "logical genre." In its focus on topic-neutral relations rather than topic-bound content, the logical genre stands in contrast to other genres, both formal and informal (see Bricker, 1974, for an analysis of formal and informal Mayan speech genres).

With these constructs—*schema, genre, performance*—we can suggest an interpretation for the findings of both the memory and reasoning studies.

Through experience with the genre (a socially evolved language structure) individuals develop a cognitive schema through which they assimilate increasingly varied and more complex examples of the genre. They will "remember" the form of a problem (the general relationship between premises) even when they forget the particular subjects and predicates used. In a reasoning task, they will "grasp" an example (e.g., approach every logic problem formally) even though they may not be able on any particular occasion, with any particular material, to handle successfully its particular content—the inferential relationships the problem expresses.

An example from memory research makes this point more concretely. In societies in which narrative is a developed genre, recall of "stories" will be facilitated by their assimilation to the narrative structure. This structure confers "sense" on the presented material and serves as a guide to the retention and retrieval of the specific informational content in the given example. The narrative, like the formal problem, may be considered a socially evolved genre that individuals in varying degrees, depending on their own personal life experiences, acquire or, in Vygotsky's terms, internalize. Like narrative, when the formal problem's structure is internalized, it helps to make sense of the material presented and serves as a device that guides and constrains remembering and reasoning.

In the studies we have reviewed, there were some individuals who seem not to have developed the requisite schema for handling the type of discourse represented in the logic problem. They denied the sense of the question or failed to retain the logical system in their recall reproductions. The overwhelming bulk of respondents in all cultural groups, however, showed some grasp of the genre. For most nonschooled adults this was a transient phenomenon. Several possibilities exist here. Schemas may not be generalized across all content and may be more vulnerable to certain subject matters than others. Alternatively, or concurrently, the experimental or interview context may not have provided the appropriate cues to elicit the desired performance—use of the logical genre (cf. Hymes, 1974).

We know very little about the social conditions which give rise to the logical genre, how cultures define the occasions for its use, through what experiences individuals acquire its schema. Within Western academic institutions, examples of the genre are not uncommon. Verbal arithmetic problems would seem to fall into the class of problems whose content is arbitrary and whose meaning resides in the relationships expressed. If the teacher presents a problem: "Johnny has one red apple and Mary has one red apple, how many apples do Johnny and Mary have altogether?" it won't do for a child to look around the room to see who else may have an apple or to question whether apples are really red. An empiric approach to the verbal problem will not earn a passing grade. Specialized studies—algebra, geometry, chemistry—and other fields that use technical notational systems may be considered to present "arbitrary problems" in the sense that the problems derive from a system outside the learner's own personal experience and must be taken in their own terms. It would be interesting to examine school curricula to find to what extent students must learn to work with other verbal problems that represent the genre of logical discourse.

More challenging is the question of what activities outside of school, and especially what activities in traditional cultures might give rise to this form of discourse. Ryle (1963) has made the provocative suggestion that the "logical idiom" arises when societies face pressures for "special kinds of talk," especially involving commercial transactions, contracts and treaties, legal and administrative services. To our knowledge, no researches in the ethnography of speaking have yet identified and analyzed examples of this genre, but it appears to be an important direction in which to carry studies of specialized language functions.

For the psychologist, the leading developmental question becomes that of specifying under what circumstances and as a result of what experiences individuals in a culture possessing this genre internalize it as a schema available for cognitive activities. The leading functional question becomes that of specifying the experimental conditions, as well as everyday conditions, under which a given example of this form of discourse is assimilated in the logical schema.

ACKNOWLEDGMENTS

Preparation of this paper was assisted by Ford Foundation Grant 740-0255 and National Institute of Medical Sciences Grant GM 16735. Ongoing research among the Vai is supported by the Ford Foundation. I want to thank Michael Cole, Ray McDermott, and Judith Orasanu for their careful reading of an early draft of this paper and for their many wise comments, only some of which I was able to assimilate into my schemas. I am solely responsible for the method of analysis and interpretive framework presented.

REFERENCES

Barclay, J. R. The role of comprehension in remembering sentences. *Cognitive Psychology,* 1973, *4,* 229–254.
Bochenski, I. M. *A history of formal logic.* 2nd edition. Notre Dame, Indiana: University of Notre Dame Press, 1970.

Bransford, J. D., Barclay, J. R., & Franks, J. J. Sentence memory: a constructive versus interpretive approach. *Cognitive Psychology,* 1972, *3,* 193–209.

Bricker, V. R. The ethnographic context of some traditional Mayan speech genres. In R. Bauman, & J. Scherzer (Eds.), *Explorations in the ethnography of speaking.* London: Cambridge University Press, 1974.

Cole, M., Gay, J., Glick, J., & Sharp, D. *Cultural context of learning and thinking.* New York: Basic Books, 1971.

Cole, M., & Scribner, S. *Culture and thought.* New York: Wiley, 1974.

Dasen, P. R. Cross-cultural Piagetian research: a summary. In J. W. Berry & P. R. Dasen (Eds.), *Culture and cognition: readings in cross-cultural psychology.* London: Methuen, 1974.

Henle, M. On the relation between logic and thinking. *Psychological Review,* 1962, *69,* 366–378.

Hymes, D. Ways of speaking. In R. Bauman & J. Sherzer (Eds.), *Explorations in the ethnography of speaking.* London: Cambridge University Press, 1974.

Jager, R. *Essays in logic.* Englewood Cliffs, N.J.: Prentice-Hall, 1963.

Levy-Bruhl, L. *How natives think* (1910). New York: Washington Square Press, 1966.

Luria, A. R. Towards the problem of the historical nature of psychological processes. *International Journal of Psychology,* 1971, *6,* 259–272.

Luria, A. R. *Cognitive development. Its cultural and social foundations.* Cambridge: Harvard University Press, 1976.

Ryle, G. Formal and informal logic. In R. Jager, *Essays in logic.* Englewood Cliffs, N.J.: Prentice-Hall, 1963.

Scribner, S. Developmental aspects of categorized recall in a West African society. *Cognitive Psychology,* 1974, *6,* 475–494.

Scribner, S., & Cole, M. Research program on Vai literacy and its cognitive consequences. *Cross-cultural psychology newsletter,* 1974, *8,* 2–4.

Scribner, S. Recall of classical syllogisms: a cross-cultural investigation of error on logical problems. In R. J. Falmagne (Ed.), *Reasoning: representation and process.* Hillsdale, N.J.: Lawrence Erlbaum Associates, 1975.

Sharp, D. W., & Cole, M. The influence of educational experience on the development of cognitive skills as measured in formal tests and experiments. Final Report to Office of Education. New York: Rockefeller University, 1975. (mimeo, 87 pp.)

Vygotsky, L. *Mind in society.* (Cole, M., John-Steiner, V., Scribner, S., Souberman, E., Eds.). Cambridge: Harvard University Press, 1978.

Wason, P. C., & Johnson-Laird, P. N. *Psychology of reasoning: structure and content.* Cambridge: Harvard University Press, 1972.

Woodworth, R. S. *Experimental psychology.* New York: Holt, 1938.

10 Repetition in the Non-Native Acquisition of Discourse: Its Relation to Text Unification and Conversational Structure*

Deborah Keller-Cohen
University of Michigan

INTRODUCTION

In recent years the process of nonnative language acquisition has come to be an increasingly frequent topic of investigation. The focus of many of these studies has been intrasentential phenomena, in particular the acquisition of various grammatical morphemes (Cancino, Rosansky & Schumann, 1974; Dulay & Burt, 1973, 1974). How the nonnative child comes to communicate effectively and meaningfully through the development of different conversational rules has rarely been examined. As discussed elsewhere (Keller-Cohen, in press (a)), the purposes for which a child uses language and the rules governing its use are in some sense more relevant than other phenomena to questions of acquiring competence in a second language. This position is in agreement with Hymes (1972), who argues that command of a language involves more than knowledge of grammaticality.

> Recall that one is concerned to explain how a child comes rapidly to be able to produce and understand (in principle) any and all of the grammatical sentences of a language. Consider now a child with just that ability. A child who might produce any sentence whatever—such a child would be likely to be institutionalized; even more so if not only sentences, but also speech or silence was random, unpredictable.... We have then to account for the fact that a normal child acquires knowledge of sentences, not only as grammatical, but also as appropriate. He or she acquires competence as to when to speak, when not, and as to what to talk about with whom, when, where, in what manner. In short, a child becomes able to accomplish a repertoire of speech acts, to take part in speech events, and to evaluate their accomplishment by others. (p. 277)

This paper reports the status of our investigation of nonnative children's acquisition of conversational competence. A theme central to our investigation is the child's construction of rules of conversation in his second language.

The nonnative child of 4 or 5 years is confronted with the enormous task of determining what alternations in the second language are relevant for the construction of rules of conversation in that new code. Having had several years experience with one language, he has certain resources to draw on to assist him in developing conversational skills. These linguistic resources include:

1. *Knowledge of form-function covariance.* The child learning a second language has already determined that different linguistic forms in his native language communicate the same function and that the same linguistic forms can be used to convey different functions. For example, Dore (1977) reports this type of alternation for children's responses to questions in their use of the same form to answer different types of questions while at the same time using different forms to respond to the same question.

2. *Knowledge of the relationship between addressee variables and form-function covariance.* Research on the child's use of different speech styles to talk to speakers of different ages (Gelman & Shatz, 1975; Sachs & Devin, 1976) indicates that by 4 or 5 years the young child adjusts his speech in particular ways according to the age of the co-present speaker.

3. *Juxtaposition of old and new information.* During the first few years of language acquisition, the child learns to exploit the devices available in his native language to contrast old and new information. This development begins quite early. Greenfield and Smith (1976) found that children's single word utterances tended to encode new information, aspects of the environment undergoing change, rather than old information. The expression of old or shared information appears to be a somewhat later development (Bloom, Rocissano, & Hood, 1976).

4. *Knowledge of conversational features.* As the result of several years of experience with one language, the nonnative child's conversation in his first language displays knowledge of the following features:

(a) *Turn-taking.* He alternates his speech with that of other speakers; he does not, in general, speak at the same time as a co-present speaker. This can be seen, for example, in the work of Keenan (1974b) and Scollon (1976). Similarly, in his first language, the nonnative child uses and responds to turn-allocation techniques like questions. This is indicated by the first language acquisition research of Ervin-Tripp (1974), Dore (1977), and Garvey (1977).

(b) *Relevance.* He has learned some things about making his utterances relevant to those of another speaker. In a longitudinal study of four children from 21 to 36 months, Bloom, Rocissano, and Hood (1976) report a developmental increase in the frequency of contingent speech, i.e., utterances by the child that share the same topic with the preceding adult utterance and add new information.

The developments described above touch on some of the more important acquisitions that the nonnative child brings to the task of learning a second language. We believed that the speech of the second language learners would exhibit certain basic features of conversation given their experience with another language. For example, we expected to find general features of turn-taking like the alternation of speakers and the presence of some form of turn-allocation devices. In addition, we anticipated attempts by the child to make his speech relevant to that of the adult's. It was not known whether the nonnative child's knowledge of one language would mean the rapid acquisition of the necessary tools in the second language. It was expected, however, that he would be more attentive to linguistic contrasts given native language hypotheses to draw on.

This chapter examines the relation between repetition and devices that are used to construct conversation. Repetition has been viewed in a variety of ways in the past: as an attempt to approximate a model; as a means for the acquisition of vocabulary; and as a cover-term for structurally similar speech productions that serve a range of communicative functions (requesting, agreeing, etc.). The research reported here considers repetition in a new light, both in its relation to processes that create a cohesive conversation and in relation to mechanisms that allocate turns in a conversation. Hence, repetition is viewed against a larger background consisting of the materials that knit together a conversation (cohesion) and those that move the flow of speech along (turn allocators).

Utterances across speakers can be related in numerous ways and there is considerable disagreement over the range and domain of such devices (Johnson & Bayless, 1976). Part I of this chapter explores repetition and lexical cohesion, two devices that serve to unify utterances in a conversation, linguistic mechanisms that the child in this case uses to link up her utterances with those of another speaker. These are cohesion creating devices, linguistic tools that create textual unity. While textual unity can be found in both written and spoken texts produced by one or many speakers, our discussion is limited to repetition and lexical cohesion in dialogue.

This chapter also examines rules of conversation that govern the flow of speech between speakers, particularly mechanisms that allocate turns in a conversation. In our view the rules that govern turn allocation are part of a larger set of rules that regulate the structure[1] of conversational flow. Part II

---

[1]Halliday and Hasan (1976) present a view of text unification that treats cohesion as a semantic notion that operates above the sentential level, and structure as an intrasentential relation. Structure is used in this chapter to refer to the sequential organization of speech in a conversation. No position is taken here with respect to Halliday and Hasan's distinction. (However, see Johnson and Bayless, 1976, for arguments against the Hallidayan contrast.)

considers the interrelations among repetition and mechanisms that allocate turns in conversation. These include both attention-directing devices (e.g., "look," "see") and information-seeking devices (e.g., questions). The analyses presented here do not attempt to exhaustively treat either discourse cohesion or the regulation of the flow of conversation. Instead, we attempt to suggest ways in which these phenomena are related and to indicate the direction that future research might take.

PART I

It has often been observed that in the course of learning language children frequently reproduce all or part of a prior utterance. This utterance may have been produced by the same speaker with or without other utterances intervening. Spontaneous reproduction of a co-present speaker's utterance has variously been referred to as imitation (Baldwin, 1895; Bloom, Hood, & Lightbown, 1974; Ervin-Tripp, 1973; Scollon, 1976), echoic utterances (Nakanishi & Owada, 1973), and repetition (Keenan, 1977). Spontaneous reproduction of one's own speech has been termed repetition (Scollon, 1976) and self-repetition (Garnica & Edwards, 1975; Keller-Cohen & Gracey, 1976). The purpose of reproductive or imitative language behavior has often been viewed as rehearsal or practice of the speech productions of another speaker, the end result apparently being to learn the imitated form(s) (Baldwin, 1895; Preyer, 1888; Sully, 1896; Stern, 1924).

In more recent years it has generally been agreed that while imitation is probably involved in the process of language aquisition it does not sufficiently explain how a child learns to communicate verbally with members of his environment. For example, Ervin-Tripp (1973) investigated the language development of five children approximately 2 years old. She compared rules formulated to describe word order in the children's spontaneous utterances with those describing imitative utterances. With the exception of one child, she found that the same rules described both utterance types. Similarly, Kemp and Dale (1973) examined grammatical features in both spontaneous and imitative utterances of 30 children and discovered no difference between utterance types. Their finding thus agrees with that of Ervin-Tripp (1973), that "there is not a shred of evidence supporting a view that progress toward adult norms of grammar arises merely from practice in overt imitation of adult sentences" (p. 397).

While these studies concluded that imitation could not be a major impetus in language development, they left unexplored the nature of its contribution. Bloom, Hood, and Lightbown (1974) investigated imitative and spontaneous utterances from six children during the period in which their MLU increased from 1.0 to 2.0. Three of the children were found to be low-frequency imitators (15% of total utterances). The three remaining children were high-frequency imitators (30% or more of total utterances). Bloom et al. found that there were marked contrasts between the spontaneous and imitative utterances of the high-frequency imitators.[2] There was a consistent tendency for lexical items and grammatical forms to distinguish imitative from spontaneous speech for these children. In addition, the MLU of their imitative utterances was equal to or exceeded that of spontaneous utterances. As the authors indicate, these findings do not conflict with those of Ervin-Tripp since she compared word order in spontaneous and imitative utterances, and did not examine the lexical and grammatical features of these utterances. Moerk (1977) has similarly found that imitation serves as a testing ground for new constructions during their early stages of acquisition.

In contrast to previous studies, Keenan (1974a; 1977) approached repetition in terms of the communicative functions that it can serve. She argued that essential facts about the process of acquiring a language are ignored if the communicative intentions expressed by repetition are not considered. Drawing on data from twin boys, Keenan (1977) found that repetition served the functions of agreement, self-informing, querying, counterclaiming, and the like.[3] She suggests that Bloom's high-frequency imitators may simply be carrying out certain communicative intentions using repetition, while the low-frequency imitators might be expressing these same functions with other devices.[4]

On the basis of previous research we believed that nonnative children would use repetition as a means of creating cohesion in conversation.

---

[2]The proportion of imitative utterances in one of the high-frequency imitator's speech (Kathryn) fell to .11 in the second sample. Her first sample, however, was similar to that of the high-frequency imitators.

[3]In Keenan's data many of the communicative functions reported were expressed by repetition with prosodic change. The imitations reported in Bloom et al. and Ervin-Tripp apparently excluded by definition repetitions with intonational change. It remains to be seen whether the functions of repetition without prosodic change are as readily determinable. Our data (See Table 1) indicate that the frequency of repetition with prosodic change is far below that without prosodic change.

[4]If this observation is correct one might expect a difference between the children in the proportion of repetitions with prosodic change, since as indicated above this type of repetition expressed numerous discourse functions. As Table 1 indicates, Toko and Maija differed strikingly in the frequency with which they used repetition with prosodic change. Bloom (1970) and Bloom, Lightbown, and Hood (1975) found that children acquired expression of certain notions about the world in similar developmental orders; however, they expressed them through different formal devices. This leads us to suspect that Toko used repetition with prosodic change to express those communicative functions. This would tend to support Keenan's (1975b) claim that "it may be the case that 'imitators' are not in fact imitating and that all of these children do similar communicative work; they simply differ in the formal devices used to carry out this work."

However, it was expected that repetition would be a less productive (hence less frequent) means of unifying texts for the second-language-learning child since he could indentify other means based on observations made during learning his first language. This is examined in Part I.

In addition, it seemed that the frequency of repetition might be inversely related to the use of turn-allocation devices since repetition does not directly select the next speaker. That is, while a repetition occupies a turn in the stream of conversation, it does not exert pressure on the other participant to take a turn talking. While it was expected that this same pattern would be found in first language acquisition, the existing literature has not addressed this question. This is examined in Part II.

Subjects and Methods

The subjects in the present investigation are females who were living in this country while their fathers were graduate students or visiting scholars at the University of Michigan. The first child, Toko, a native Japanese speaker, was 5 years 6 months when our investigation began. She had been in the United States 5 months prior to our contact with her. The second child, Maija, a native Finnish speaker, was 4 years 3 months at the onset of the study and had been here for 3 months. While two additional subjects, a Japanese speaker and a Swiss German speaker, were participants in the study, discussion of their development is not included here.

The children were videotaped nearly every week for one-half hour in a structured play setting interacting with a native English speaking graduate student investigator. A different graduate student was assigned to each child and the adult interacted with the same child throughout the duration of the investigation. The type of interaction between the child and adult in our study can be characterized by what Goffman (1963) has called *focused interaction,* "the kind of interaction that occurs when persons gather close together and openly cooperate to sustain a single focus of attention, typically by taking turns in talking" (p. 24).

The development of discourse skills is examined here in terms of adult–child interaction because evidence suggested that the relations that a child comes to acquire within his own utterances may first arise between his utterances and those of the adult (Keenan, Schieffelin, & Platt, 1976; Shugar, 1975). This observation is related to Scollon's report (1976) that sentence construction grows out of sequential utterances in discourse (vertical constructions). Hence, it seemed that examination of adult–child interaction would provide particularly revealing insights into developments that will occur later within the child's own speech.

The period of development examined here is equivalent in gross terms to Brown's Late Stage I through Late Stage III or the beginnings of Stage IV.

During the eight months of our investigation, Toko's MLU increased from 1.8 to 2.7. Maija's rose to a point slightly beyond Toko's, from 1.7 to 3.1. Their type-token ratios increased from .44 to .62 for Toko and to .66 for Maija. While there are certainly questions to be raised about the informativeness of the MLU and the type-token ratio for nonnative children, these indices enable us to compare their progress in language development in a very general way with first-language learners.[5] In general, both children developed increased linguistic abilities in English as is demonstrated by their production of longer and more diverse utterances.

Repetition and Text Unification

Repetition.   Repetition is defined here as the reproduction of all or part of a preceding adult utterance (1 and 2).

(1) Adult: You know what? We have bone.

Toko: we have a bone/

(Playing with Fisher-Price dolls)

(2) Adult: Daddy wants to go to work.

Can he get out?

(Maija shakes head)

Adult: No?

Maija: daddy/

Initially our analyses dealt with repetitions that were not accompanied by prosodic change. In order to permit comparisons with Bloom, Hood, and Lightbown (1974), we considered an utterance to be a repetition if no more than five utterances intervened between the adult's and the child's utterance. One could certainly argue that the five utterance limit is arbitrary, but we were initially interested in obtaining comparable data.

Table 1 presents the types and tokens of total utterances and repetitions for the two children. Table 2 presents the proportion of repetition types and tokens in Toko's and Maija's monthly samples. The proportion of repetitions in Toko's utterance tokens ranged from 9 to 2% and in Maija's from 6 to 1%. Toko repeated significantly more often than Maija (correlated) $t(7) = 2.75$, $p < .025$. The frequency of repetition in their speech was far below that in the child–child interaction reported in Keenan (1977); the proportion of repetition in their speech was similar to Bloom's subjects who imitated

---

[5]For discussion of the limitations of the MLU as a reliable measure of language development see Crystal (1974).

TABLE 1
Types and Tokens of Total Utterances and Repetitions[a,b]

	Number of Sessions	Utterance Types	Repetition Types	Repetition with Prosodic Change Types	Utterance Tokens[c]	Repetition Tokens	Repetition with Prosodic Change Tokens
TOKO							
Nov.	3	220	26	8	480	32	10
Dec.	2	191	14	7	474	15	8
Jan.	2	122	9	1	282	9	1
Feb.	3	142	26	9	345	28	9
Mar.	4	510	51	15	933	61	16
Apr.	4	658	30	10	1042	33	10
May	2	428	5	2	683	12	2
June	3	492	19	9	825	21	9
MAIJA							
Nov.	2	57	6	0	113	7	0
Dec.	2	123	8	0	267	9	0
Jan.	2	215	13	2	506	16	2
Feb.	4	634	13	0	1200	14	0
Mar.	3	478	11	0	800	12	0
Apr.	5	819	11	0	1233	11	0
May	1	226	2	1	374	2	1
June	4	815	18	1	1309	18	1

[a]The actual volume of speech produced by the children was greater than seen in these figures which represent only those utterances that were fully intelligible.

[b]The rightmost column in this table includes repetitions with all types of prosodic change (rising intonation, falling intonation, "counting" intonation, "surprise" intonation).

[c]The figures correct an earlier version of this chapter.

TABLE 2
Proportion of Repetitions in Total Utterances

	Proportion of Repetition Types	Proportion of Repetition Tokens
TOKO		
Nov.	.12	.08
Dec.	.07	.03
Jan.	.07	.04
Feb.	.18	.09
Mar.	.10	.07
Apr.	.05	.03
May	.01	.02
June	.04	.03
MAIJA		
Nov.	.10	.06
Dec.	.07	.04
Jan.	.06	.03
Feb.	.02	.01
Mar.	.02	.02
Apr.	.01	.01
May	.001	.01
June	.02	.01

infrequently.[6] It is not surprising that repeating a preceding utterance might be a less productive means of creating cohesion in second-language conversation if one considers that the nonnative child has had experience with a broad range of such devices in her native language.

Since the frequency of repetition accounted for only a small proportion of Maija's and Toko's speech, it seemed reasonable to explore what other kinds of cohesive relations existed between their utterances and those of the adults'. The range of potential relations was narrowed by the decision to consider only those that obtained between *adjacent* utterances. A child's utterance that *immediately followed* an adult's utterance was considered to be adjacent to that utterance (3b, 4b)

    (3a) Adult: There's a baby.

                            (3b) Toko: yeah, monkey's baby/

    (4a) Adult: What about the mailman's house?

                                   (4b) Maija: is fire/

---

[6]Both our data and Bloom's consist of adult–child interactions. The proportion of repetition in our data is considerably less than that reported in Keenan. However, since her data are of child–child interactions, the two samples are not comparable.

Adjacent utterances were examined because it seemed likely that children initially employ cohesion-creating devices that relate their utterance to an immediately preceding utterance. In the early stages of language devleopment, reliance on more recent conversational information, i.e., on immediately prior speech, would be a necessary accommodation to the rapid and frequent exchange of information. Adjacent utterances might therefore be a fruitful area for investigating the ontogenesis of cohesion-creating relations. It was expected that the proportion of child utterances adjacent to adult speech would increase as the children acquired means for relating their utterances to that of the adult. In addition, a leveling off was expected to follow the increase as the children became able to elaborate on their own speech.

It was necessary to establish the frequency of adjacent utterances in order to determine the proportion of speech to be considered in subsequent analyses. To investigate the extent of adjacency, we sampled 100 consecutive utterances per child per session across the 8-month period.[7,8] The proportion of adjacent utterances is described in Table 3.

The children did not differ significantly in the proportion of adjacency in their speech over the eight months (correlated) $t(7) = 1.07$. There was a tendency in both girl's data for the proportion of adjacency to rise and level off. The peak was reached in February in Toko's speech and March in Maija's. Over the eight months the change in proportion of adjacency was significant for Toko, $\chi^2(7) = 14.63$, $p < .05$ but nonsignificant for Maija, $\chi^2(7) = 6.31$. Since the highest proportion of adjacency (.75) and the June proportion (.63) were identical for both children, the significant difference found in Toko's speech appears to be due to the low proportions during the first three months (November, December, and January).

---

[7]The 100-utterance sample size was selected because 100 utterances was the minimum number of total utterances per session. The exception to this was Maija's November data in which only 55 utterances/session were available. This was due to the large proportion of unintelligible utterances in those sessions (as much as 50%).

[8]Three sessions in each of the children's data included interactions with peer native English speaking playmates with sporadic adult participation. Because of the difficulty in obtaining 100 consecutive utterances of adult–adult interaction, these sessions were excluded from the adjacency and cohesion analyses only. A revised version of relevant portions of Table 1 for those three months is presented below.

	Number of sessions	Utterances tokens
TOKO		
March	3	748
April	3	826
May	1	385
MAIJA		
March	2	599
April	4	949
June	3	1175

TABLE 3
Adjacency, Repetition, and Lexical Cohesion

	Proportion of Adjacent Utterances	Proportion of Lexical Cohesion in Adjacent Utterances[a]	Proportion of Repetition in Adjacent Utterances
TOKO			
Nov.	.45	.13	.11
Dec.	.53	.13	.06
Jan.	.41	.05	.12
Feb.	.75	.06	.12
Mar.	.63	.13	.06
Apr.	.63	.19	.08
May	.56	.16	.03
June	.63	.15	.08
MAIJA			
Nov.	.57	.04	.09
Dec.	.58	.02	.08
Jan.	.68	.08	.06
Feb.	.61	.07	.02
Mar.	.75	.11	.02
Apr.	.64	.06	.01
May	.51	.14	.02
June	.63	.12	.02

[a]This excludes repetitions in adjacent utterances.

Taken together, the general absence of difference between the children in the frequency of adjacent utterances and the relative stability in the proportion of adjacency suggest that the second-language-learning child may adapt some rules from her first language in constructing conversation in her second language. One might suspect that certain kinds of rules like adjacency (a manifestation of turn-taking) are likely to be generalized from the first to second language because of their pervasiveness, whereas the actual devices employed to link utterances in a conversation differ more between languages. Further research will be needed before we can be certain of the extent to which rules of constructing conversation in the first language are evident in second-language productions.

The following section examines one type of text-unifying relation that appears in adjacent utterances, lexical cohesion.

Lexical Cohesion. Perhaps the earliest and most well-known discussion of cohesion appears in the work of Halliday (1964, 1967; Halliday & Hasan, 1976). Halliday was concerned with determining how a speaker of English differentiates a series of unrelated sentences (or utterances) from those that form a text, a unified whole. He basically claims that the presence of devices that relate one sentence with one or more sentences signal the native speaker that the sentences are unified. One such set of devices are those that create cohesion. "Cohesion occurs where the interpretation of some element in the discourse is dependent on that of another. The one presupposes the other, in the sense that it cannot be effectively decoded—except by recourse to it." (Halliday & Hasan, 1976, p. 4). Cohesion is an important phenomenon to examine in the acquisition of language since it allows us to see how a child learns not only to make his speech relevant to the context, in general, but to the linguistic context of other speakers in particular.

While cohesion is created through the use of many devices (ellipsis, anaphora, substitution, and lexical cohesion among others) our investigation was confined to lexical cohesion. As proposed in Halliday and Hasan (1976), lexical cohesion is the creation of text unification through the type of vocabulary chosen. Repetition of a lexical item (5), synonymy (6), and superordinacy (7) are a few examples.

(5) The small car has four *wheels*. Each *wheel* is mounted on a large axle.

(6) The *painting* won first prize. The *drawing* depicted an old farmhouse.

(7) The *chocolate* was kept in a small dish on the table. He kept it there because he liked *sweets* so much.

Lexical cohesion was selected for investigation because it is closely related to repetition. Whereas repetition includes the reproduction of all or part of a prior utterance, lexical cohesion includes repetition plus the addition of new material. Our analysis of lexical cohesion is narrower than Halliday's.[9] Although Halliday includes relations like synonymy and superordinacy, we included only those adjacent child utterances that contained the same word or coreferent. Morphologically variant forms of a word were also included as in *break–broke, Mommy–Mommy's*. Examples of lexical cohesion by category type in the children's data appear below.

Nominal

     (Adult and child are playing store)
(8) Adult: How about some *milk?*

                                   Maija: now I take it *milk/*

     (Playing with dolls in toy cars)
(9) Adult: (Laughing) That's a little car isn't it?

                                      Toko: toy *car/*

---

[9]More complex relations like synonymy and superordinancy were not examined here. Our initial analyses suggested they were rarely present.

Morphological variant

> (Adult is trying to understand
> Toko's explanation of her
> friend's name)

(10) Adult: *Adrian* what?

> Toko: Adrian's friend is Erin/

Pronominal identity

> (Adult and Maija are playing
> with Fisher-Price toy cars)

(11) Adult: Uh-huh. Ok. (picking
up car) Whose car is
this, I wonder?

> Maija: *this* is house car/

Pronominal coreference

> (Adult just drew a picture
> of a snake)

(1) Adult: (Wiggling her fingers
across floor at Maija)
(It's a *snake*.

> Maija: what *her* doing/

Because lexical cohesion is structurally related to repetition, we predicted that Toko's data would contain a higher proportion of lexical cohesion than Maija's.

Table 3 presents the proportion of lexical cohesion and repetition in adjacent utterances. Toko used both lexical cohesion and repetition in adjacent utterances significantly more often than did Maija (correlated) $t(7) = 2.27$, $p < .05$, (correlated) $t(7) = 3.15$, $p < .01$, respectively. The difference between the children in the frequency of repetition in adjacent utterances is a function of the difference between them in repetition in all utterances.

The view one gets of the development of cohesion becomes clearer if repetition and lexical cohesion are examined together. When a child repeats a prior utterance (without any prosodic change) he is producing an utterance that derives some of its meaning from a prior utterance, in this case the adult's. In this sense, repetition is the basis for lexical cohesion. Repetition is limited in its contribution to cohesion in that it creates only one cohesive tie with a prior utterance, derived from the reproduction of prior lexical items. One area in the development of discourse must therefore be growth in the number and diversity of cohesion creating devices. With a wider range of devices available, those acquired earlier may not be employed as frequently. Hence it was expected that repetition would decline slightly over time as lexical cohesion increased.

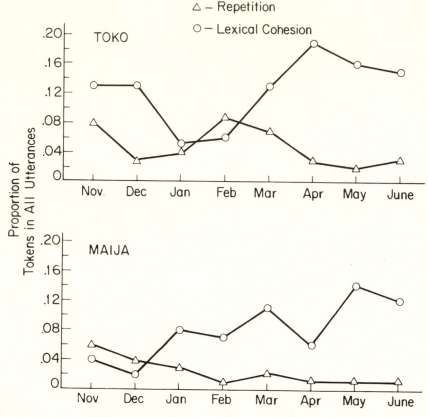

FIG. 1.   Proportions of repetition and lexical cohesion.

Figure 1 describes the relationship between lexical cohesion and repetition. In the children's data the proportion of repetition tended to decrease over time. While lexical cohesion was unstable in Toko's speech during the first three months, it rose and leveled off from February to June. Lexical cohesion rose more consistently in Maija's speech from 2 to 4% in November–December to 12 to 14% in May–June. What emerges in Maija's speech is a system of cohesion that gradually expands to include lexical cohesion. Hence, whereas Maija repeated a prior utterance in the earlier months, she was able both to incorporate and elaborate on a prior utterance in the later months. There is no apparent explanation for the fluctuation in the first three months of Toko's speech. From February through June, however, lexical cohesion and repetition do follow the predicted pattern with repetition falling and lexical cohesion rising. Hence, the frequency of repetition appears to decline as lexical cohesion becomes a more fully developed system. Although the proportion of these devices is small, the direction rather than the size of the proportion is important here.

The children were similar in that their speech exhibited the properties of repetition and lexical cohesion. In addition, there was similarity between the children in the relationship between these devices, with the tendency for repetition to decline and lexical cohesion to rise. However, the children were different in the extent to which they employed these cohesion-creating mechanisms with Toko's speech exhibiting significantly more repetition and lexical cohesion. It was suspected that this level of difference between the children would be related both to the proportion of utterances devoted to turn allocation and the type of utterances selected to allocate turns. The reasons for anticipating these relationships are elaborated in Part II.

PART II

In the Introduction we argued that acquiring conversational skills includes (at least) learning to relate your utterances to those of another speaker (cohesion) and developing the ability to move the flow of speech along. Learning to take one's turn and acquiring different means of expressing the content of a turn are also integral parts of acquiring conversational skills. A speaker's turn in conversation has at least the following characteristics: (1) It is a socially cooperative act in that it is an occasion for participating in conversation. (2) It is informationally relevant. "It is an event that occurs with respect to other conversational events, takes them into account, builds on or alters them in methodical ways" (Speier, 1972, p. 402). (3) It creates the opportunity for further conversation. It contributes sufficient information to the dialogue to enable the other participant to continue. A turn that is a repetition is conversationally cooperative in that it is an act of participation in the conversation. Since repetition is one way of taking one's turn in conversation, it signals the speaker that the hearer is still participating in the exchange of speech. Likewise, it is relevant in that it acknowledges that the hearer, in this case the child, has paid attention to the speaker's utterance to the extent that she is able to incorporate all or part of it into her turn at speaking. No claim is made here regarding the extent of the hearer's comprehension of what she repeats. Rather, it is argued that the hearer has processed the acoustic signal of the speaker sufficiently to repeat some portion of it.

In general, however, repetition without prosodic change does not directly allocate the turn to the next speaker. That is, while a repetition without prosodic change constitutes a turn in conversation, it does not require a subsequent response from the other speaker the way a question does. Hence, while it displays feature (3) above, it does not provide new information.

Figure 2 below illustrates this point. Using Schegloff (1972) as our point of departure, part (1) of Fig. 2 represents the sequencing of turns in a conversation between two speakers, *a,* and *b.* The conversation is underway, the assignment of roles, *a* first speaker, *b* second speaker, will not be discussed here. This diagram simply conveys the underlying pattern of alternation of speech between two speakers. For purposes of this discussion *a* represents the adult and *b* the child.

Part (2) of Fig. 2 characterizes a somewhat idealized conversational exchange. In a_1 the adult makes a contribution to the conversation that either directly requires a response from *b* as in a question–answer sequence, or provides enough new information for *b* to build on. These relationships are represented by an arrow (↓). In b_1 the child responds in such a way that the conversation is returned to the adult. Among other things, this can be accomplished by asking a question in response to a question (13) (Schegloff's insertion sequence, 1972) or by providing sufficient new information that enables the adult to continue the conversation (14).

(13)   X: Are you coming tonight?
        Y: Can I bring a guest?
        X: Sure.
        Y: I'll be there.

(Schegloff, 1972)

(14) Adult: When are your mommy's
              parents coming to visit?

                                        Toko: mom/no she's n·
                                              that parents not
                                              coming/

        Adult: Never?
        (shaking head)   Toko: she's not coming/

Part (3) of Fig. 2 displays two effects that a repetition without prosodic change can have on a conversation. In the left column, the child's repetition (*b*) does not provide new information; it does not extend the contribution in

(1)	*a*	(2)	a_1	(3)	a_1	*a*
	b		↓		↓	↓
	a		b_1		*b*	b_1
	b		↓			
			a_2		a_2	b_2
			↓			
			b_2			

FIG. 2.   Turn-allocation sequences.

a's turn[10]; *a* must therefore extend the conversation if it is to move forward. The absence of an arrow between *b* and a_2 represents *b*'s failure and *a*'s subsequent attempt to extend the conversation. An example of this is (15).

(15) Adult: You know what? We
have a bone.

Toko: we have bone/

Adult: We have bones for
the dog and we have
a cat.

That *b*'s repetition does not add new information should not be taken to mean that it serves no function in the dialogue. Indeed *b*'s repetition might be interpreted as agreeing with *a*'s assertion. Yet it does not contribute information sufficient for *a* to comment on. Hence, the job of moving the conversation along falls on *a*.

In the right-hand column of Fig. 2, part (3), *b*'s repetition also fails to provide adequate new information. However in this case *a* does not extend the conversation, but rather *b* moves off in a new direction with a second comment on her own. Example (16) illustrates this type of sequence.

(Toko, playing with dollhouse, puts doll in chimney)
(16) Adult: That's the chimney.

Toko: chimney/

(trying to put doll through
window of dollhouse,
laughing)

Toko: no:/

Part (3) of Fig. 2 then presents a picture of repetition without prosodic change as a means of affiliation, a technique for making your speech relevant. Furthermore it captures the burden that such a turn places on subsequent turns insofar as it contributes no new information.

A repetition without prosodic change does not directly allocate the turn to the next speaker as does a question. It is commonly agreed that question–answer (QA) sequences are effective means of allocating turns (current speaker selecting next speaker). They are a subset of sequential units in conversation termed *adjacency pairs* (Schegloff & Sacks, 1973) or *conversational tying procedures* (Speier, 1972). They exert pressure on the other participant to take a turn in a more direct manner than does an

---

[10]See Keller-Cohen and Gracey (in press) for further discussion of this idea.

assertion. In contrast to simple repetition, repetition with rising intonation is effective in allocating turns. Repetition with rising intonation is a subset of QA sequences and is related to contingent queries (Garvey, 1977) in that it questions a prior utterance by using a portion of that utterance and adding question intonation. Examples (17) and (18) illustrate repetition with rising intonation.

(17) Adult: We have big crayons,
             if you like the big
             ones better.

                                        Toko: big crayon ↑/

       Adult   Yeah, let's use those.

                                        Toko: big crayon/ ---/

(18) Adult: I'm gonna make a duck.

                                        Toko: [do:wk] ↑ /

       Adult: Duck.

                                        Toko: duck!/duck ↑/

       Adult: Mm-hm. Do you know
              what a duck is?

Both Toko and Maija used repetition although Toko's speech exhibited significantly more repetition. Hence, it was expected that Toko's speech would contain more repetition with rising intonation.

Table 4 compares repetitions with rising intonation in both children's data. The hypothesis that Toko would use repetition with rising intonation for turn allocation more often than Maija is clearly borne out by the data. Over the eight months of our investigation, Maija *never* used repetition with rising intonation while the proportion of this utterance type in Toko's speech ranged from .002 to .02. The fact that these proportions are small does not

TABLE 4
Frequency and Proportion of Repetition with Rising Intonation

| | Toko | | Maija |
	Frequency	Proportion in Total Utterances	Frequency
Nov.	9	.02	0
Dec.	6	.01	0
Jan.	1	.004	0
Feb.	4	.01	0
Mar.	15	.02	0
Apr.	8	.007	0
May	2	.002	0
June	5	.006	0

diminish the difference between the two children. The small size of these proportions does suggest, however, that other means of turn allocation must have been used.

As discussed above, effective techniques for turn allocation are those that create the greatest pressure on the conversation, e.g., QA sequences or summons–answer sequences (X: Jack. Y: Yes?).[11] Another way of thinking about these devices is that they unambiguously require a response, although not necessarily selecting a particular speaker to make that response. QA sequences may allocate a turn without allocating it *to* someone, while summons–answer sequences by definition call on a specific person to respond (Sacks, Schegloff, & Jefferson, 1974).

In order to further compare Toko and Maija, we examined their use of those conversational devices that most clearly return the conversational ball (Fillmore, 1973) to the co-present speaker. These devices include Wh-Questions, Yes–No Questions, Utterances with rising intonation (excluding repetitions with rising intonation),[12] *What* with rising intonation, Attention Directors (*look, see*), and Vocatives. Table 5 describes these results. In both sets of data the proportion of Wh-Questions tends to rise although this trend is more apparent in Maija's speech. Using a correlated t-test, Maija was found to use significantly more Wh-Questions than Toko, $t(7) = 2.07, p < .05$. No difference was found between the children in the frequency of their use of Yes–No Questions, $t(7) = -1.32$. Utterances with rising intonation were used significantly more often by Toko, (correlated) $t(7) = -4.78, p < .005$. Maija used the Attention Directors *look, lookit, lookat,* and *see* significantly more often than Toko (correlated) $t(7) = 2.75, p < .025$. No difference was found to exist between the children in the proportion of the vocative in their speech. This last result is not surprising since the adult and the child were the only participants present in a relatively confined quiet area, a room in a university building; hence, the use of the vocatives was rarely called for. Although the proportions are small, .4 to 1% of Toko's utterances contained *What*! whereas none of Maija's did.

As discussed above, repetition without prosodic change is a less effective means of turn allocation than QA sequences or Attention Directors because it does not directly pass the conversation back to the other speaker. Hence, it was expected that repetition might be inversely related to turn allocation. In order to explore this relationship repetition was compared with the turn allocators (Wh-Q, Y/N-Q, *What* with rising intonation, Utterances with rising intonation, excluding repetition with rising intonation, and Attention

---

[11] See Schegloff (1972) for a discussion of speaker assignment in conversational beginnings.

[12] Well-formed Y/N Questions contain rising intonation. Here utterances with rising intonation included those that were not fully formed Y/N Questions (no subject-auxiliary inversion, phrases, single words).

TABLE 5
Device for Turn Allocation[a,b]

	Wh-Ques.	Y/N-Ques.	Rising Intonation	*Look See*	Vocative	What↑
TOKO						
Nov.	.004	—	.02	—	—	—
Dec.	.02	—	.07	—	.04	.004
Jan.	.03	—	.04	.004	.004	.004
Feb.	.07	—	.009	—	—	—
Mar.	.09	.008	.02	.005	.001	—
Apr.	.04	.007	.03	—	—	.01
May	.07	.008	.04	.001	.001	.004
June	.03	.02	.05	.007	—	.007
MAIJA						
Nov.	.04	—	—	.01	—	—
Dec.	.04	—	.01	.01	—	—
Jan.	.09	—	—	.004	—	—
Feb.	.07	—	.001	.03	—	—
Mar.	.08	.01	.01	.08	.003	—
Apr.	.12	.005	.004	.08	.01	—
May	.06	—	.002	.07	.008	—
June	.10	.001	.003	.03	—	—

[a]Proportion in total utterances.

[b]Utterances falling under more than one category (such as *see*↑) have been included in the figures for both categories. These double-coded utterances constitute 1% (Maija) and 3% (Toko) of the turn allocators in this table.

Directors) in both children's data. Since the turn allocators include a larger number of phenomena, it is the direction rather than the amount of change across months that should be considered.

Examination of between-month shifts in Toko's data reveals that, in general, repetition and turn allocation were inversely related. The March–April shift is the exception since there was a drop in repetition and turn allocation. A similar pattern is seen in Maija's speech with repetition and turn alocation inversely related. The April–May and May–June shifts in Maija's speech are neutral with respect to our hypothesis since the proportion of repetition remained stable. In sum, then, the children were similar in that the proportion of repetition was inversely related to the proportion of devices that sequentially organize conversation. They differed in their choice of turn-allocating mechanisms—Maija using Wh-Questions and Attention Directors; Toko using rising intonation. This suggests that to the extent that repetition and turn allocation are present in the child's speech, they may reflect competing conversational pressures.

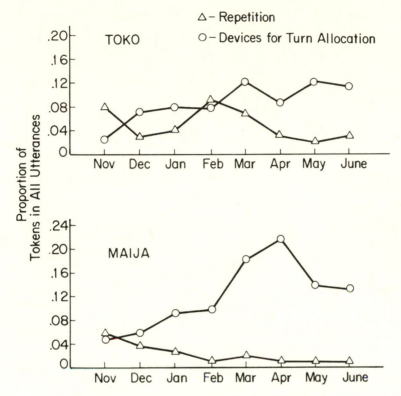

FIG. 3.   Proportions of repetition and devices for turn allocation.

CONCLUSION

This chapter has reported a view of repetition that considers it both in relation to processes that weave together conversation (cohesion-creating devices) and mechanisms that regulate the flow of speech between speakers (turn-allocating devices). The discussion below examines some implications for the study of conversational competence in general and child second-language learning in particular.

The following picture emerges when repetition is considered against the background of conversational structure. The child learning to construct conversation is faced with a myriad of considerations that must be taken into account in order for the conversation to be meaningful, relevant, and appropriate. In the early stages of language development, the child may begin establishing linguistic links to other speaker's utterances by manipulating prior text (Shugar, 1975), that is, by exploiting contributions from the speech of the co-present speaker. To the extent to which prior text is a source of data for the language-learning child, repetition is a logical device to employ in the creation of cohesion. As the child comes to have greater resources, prior utterances shift from serving as a foundation for speech to functioning as a stimulus for further speech. Whereas in earlier stages the child occasionally recaptures all or part of a prior utterance, at a later time he *incorporates* the other's speech, building on what has gone before. The slight decrease in repetition and increase in lexical cohesion suggest such a pattern of discourse. Bloom, Rocissano, and Hood (1976) report similar findings. In examining native language development, they report that there was an increase over time in the proportion of child utterances that incorporate part of the prior adult utterance and added new information.

The incorporation of a prior utterance is one means of making your utterance relevant. Repetition is an obvious device for making one's comments relevant since it allows the speaker to stay on the same topic. Since a second-language-learning child already knows that one rule of conversation is "say something relevant" (Hatch, 1976) it is not surprising that repetition is chosen to help meet this end. A partial explanation for the low proportion of repetitions in Toko's and Maija's speech is the presence of alternative means for making their utterances relevant. Lexical cohesion (*Repeat/Add* in Bloom, Rocissano, and Hood) is another means of achieving conversational relevance. What other devices are employed to create cohesive, relevant utterances is not yet known. Further investigation ought to be directed toward determining what these devices are and whether they are used similarly in first- and second-language acquisition. A further problem will be to determine whether similar devices serve the same functions across language-learning situations. For example, in second-language acquisition repetition may be used more often to achieve relevance to another's utterance than in first-language acquisition since the nonnative child already recognizes that relevance is an essential feature of conversation. This is not to deny the other functions that repetition serves (Keenan, 1977); rather it is argued that at least in the early stages of second-language learning, certain features of conversation may be considered more essential than others.[13]

Arguing that repetition is conversationally cooperative but not effective in allocating next speaker, we found that repetition and turn allocation tended

---

[13]Our analyses also indicate that repetition is very frequently used in service of the acquisition of lexical items, i.e., as a vehicle for rehearsal.

(19)
  Adult: m-hm.

  Adult: 's called a huskie.

    Toko: this is dog↑/

    Toko: oh/

    Toko: huskie/

to be inversely related. The children were similar in that the proportion of utterances with turn allocators increased over time; they differed in the extent to which each device was employed. Since the proportion of utterances that contained turn-allocating devices was small, further research is necessary before more definitive statements can be made about the acquisition of mechanisms that regulate the flow of speech between speakers.

Our analyses thus far indicate that the children displayed different discourse styles. This is not surprising since it has been noted elsewhere (Bloom, Lightbown, & Hood, 1975) that children may use different linguistic devices to express similar semantic relations (Nelson, 1975). The child learns that while the structure of conversation exhibits certain requisite features (Sacks et al., 1974), the manner of expressing these characteristics is somewhat flexible.

Both children used all devices investigated with the exception of repetition with rising intonation and *what*↑ which were absent in Maija's data. It would seem that to some extent, the children have acquired different forms of expression for the same functions. For example, whereas Maija might use a Wh-Q to request information, Toko is more likely to use a statement with rising intonation. Despite this difference, Toko does use Wh-Q and Maija does select statements with rising intonation on occasion. What we have found then is a difference in the extent to which each child selects among a variety of communicative devices.

In more general terms, Toko selected repetition-related strategies to create both cohesive utterances and to allocate turns. This might be characterized as a lexically-based conversational strategy. In addition, she has clearly learned to use prosodic variation to communicate different functions. For each device that carried with it prosodic features different from declarative intonation[14] (slight word final fall). i.e., repetition with rising intonation, *what*↑, and utterances with rising intonation[15], Toko's speech exhibited a significantly higher proportion of utterances. Her style of turn allocation appears to be one which displays a general sensitivity to the internal composition of utterances. This can be seen for example, in her awareness of phonological contrasts in English. Her data contain numerous examples of repair sequences with phonological repairs, while Maija's contained few. One such sequence is presented below.

---

[14] We also found that Toko's speech contained a higher proportion of repetitions with other types of prosodic change, e.g., surprise intonation, falling intonation, etc.

[15] The absence of utterances with rising intonation in Maija's speech must be due in part to generalizations she has made on the basis of her native language. Finnish is unique in its absence of rising intonation in questions. For a detailed discussion of these issues see Keller-Cohen (1977, in press (b)).

(Adult and Toko are playing with
toy dogs. Toko is pretending they are
at Disney World but adult does not understand)

(20) Adult: Why are you, why are
you doing this?

Toko: playing this [wIz]
[dInyi wərd]/

Adult: (not understanding)
[dɛnyi wor]?

Toko: [dInyi wərs]/ this
[wIs] [dInyi wərt]
and thi- this wIz
Disney [wərld]

Adult: (laughing) What's
that? [dInyi wərt]?

Toko: [dinyi wərlt]
[dIhnñi wərt

Adult: [dInyi wərt]? (laugh)
Ah what is that?
[dɛnyi→ wərt]

Toko: [dɛ] [dIcni wərs]

Adult: Ess--.

Toko: ess·s Frorida/

Adult: Oh Florida! Oh!
Disney World! (laugh)
Oh yeah! Woo!
(continues)

In contrast to Toko, Maija seems to concentrate on conversational frames, first working on the outlines of dialogue. The difference between the children in the proportion of utterances that contain routines further suggests that contrast. Maija's speech tended to contain more social routines (*hello, please, thank you*) than did Toko's.

The picture we have of the different discourse styles in Toko's and Maija's speech is reminiscent of the referential-social expressive contrast reported by Nelson (1973) for early lexical development. While the pattern of differences between the children is not absolute, taken together they do suggest differential approaches to the task of acquiring conversational skills. Some children may attend to the larger frames in conversation acquiring a wide variety of such frames, while others may concentrate more on elaborating the internal structure of a limited number of frames. Whether the type of discourse style is related to other domains in language is not yet known.[16] It is

---

[16]See Keller-Cohen (1977) for a discussion of this issue.

clear that research into the development of second language discourse is handicapped by inadequate models of adult discourse and by the absence of more extensive descriptions of conversation in first language acquisition. As our knowledge of these areas is expanded, it will become more apparent what similarities and differences exist between first- and second-language acquisition. Our current findings suggest that further investigation of language development will require sensitive examination of the subtleties exhibited in the use of conversation.

ACKNOWLEDGMENTS

This research was supported by the English Language Institute, University of Michigan and by Rackham Faculty Research Grants 387105 and 387188 from the Horace H. Rackham Graduate School, University of Michigan. We appreciate the comments of Lois Bloom and Roy Freedle on an earlier version of this paper.

REFERENCES

Baldwin, J. M. *Mental development in the child and the race: Methods and processes.* New York: Macmillan, 1895.

Bloom, L. *Language development: form and function in emerging grammars.* Cambridge, Mass.: M.I.T. Press, 1970.

Bloom, L. *One word at a time.* The Hague: Mouton, 1973.

Bloom, L., Hood, L., & Lightbown, P. Imitation in language development: If, when, and why. *Cognitive Psychology,* 1974, *6,* 380–420.

Bloom, L., Lightbown, P., & Hood, L. Structure and variation in child language. *Monographs of the Society for Research in Child Development,* 1975, *40,* (Serial No. 160).

Bloom, L., Rocissano, L., & Hood, L. Adult–child discourse: Developmental interaction between information processing and linguistic knowledge. *Cognitive Psychology,* 1976, *8,* 521–552.

Cancino, H., Rosansky, E., & Schumann, J. Testing hypotheses about second language acquisition: The copula and negative in three subjects. *Working Papers in Bilingualism,* 1974, *3,* 80–96.

Crystal, D. Review of a first language by R. Brown. *Journal of Child Language,* 1974, *1,* 289–306.

Dore, J. Oh them sheriff: A pragmatic analysis of children's responses to questions. In C. Mitchell-Kernan & S. Ervin-Tripp (Eds.), *Child discourse.* New York: Academic Press, 1977, 139–163.

Dulay, H., & Burt, M. Should we teach children syntax? *Language Learning,* 1973, *23,* 245–258.

Dulay, H., & Burt, M. Natural sequences in child second language acquisition. *Language Learning,* 1974, *24,* 37–53.

Ervin-Tripp, S. Imitation and structural change in children's language. In C. Ferguson & D. Slobin (Eds.), *Studies of child language development.* New York: Holt, Rinehart & Winston, 1973, Pp. 391–406. (Originally published, 1964).

Ervin-Tripp, S. The comprehension and production of requests by children. *Papers and Reports on Child Language Development,* 1974, *8,* 188–196.

Fillmore, C. Deixis, I. Unpublished lectures, delivered at the University of California, Santa Cruz, 1973.

Garnica, O., & Edwards, M. *Phonological variation in children's speech: The trade-off phenomena.* Paper presented at the Fourth International Congress of Applied Linguistics, Stuttgart, August 1975.

Garvey, C. The contingent query: a dependent act in conversation. In M. Lewis & L. Rosenblum (Eds.), *Interaction, conversation, and the development of language.* New York: Wiley, 1977, Pp. 63–93.

Gelman, R., & Shatz, M. Appropriate speech adjustments: The operation of conversational constraints on talk to two year olds. In M. Lewis & L. Rosenblum (Eds.), *Interaction, conversation and the development of language.* New York: Wiley, 1977, Pp. 27–61.

Goffman, E. *Behavior in public places.* New York: Free Press, 1963.

Greenfield, P., & Smith, J. *The structure of communication in early language development.* New York: Academic Press, 1976.

Hagen, J., Jongeward, R., & Kail, R. Cognitive perspectives on the development of memory. In H. W. Reese (Ed.), *Advances in child development and behavior,* Vol. 10. New York: Academic Press, 1975.

Halliday, M. A. K. Descriptive linguistics in literary studies. In G. I. Duthie (Ed.), *English studies today,* 3rd series, Edinburgh: Edinburgh University Press, 1964, Pp. 25–39.

Halliday, M. A. K. The linguistic study of literary texts. In S. Chatman & S. Levin (Eds.), *Essays on the language of literature.* Boston, Mass.: Houghton Mifflin, 1967, Pp. 217–230.

Halliday, M. A. K., & Hasan, R. *Cohesion in English.* London: Longman, 1976.

Hatch, E. Discourse analysis and second language acquisition. Unpublished manuscript, Department of TEFL, UCLA, 1976.

Hymes, D. On communicative competence. (Originally published 1966.) Reprinted in J. B. Pride & J. Holmes (Eds.), *Sociolinguistics: Selected readings.* Baltimore: Penguin, 1972. Pp. 268–293.

Johnson, L., & Bayless, R. Cohesion in a discourse-based linguistic theory. Unpublished manuscript, Department of Linguistics, University of Michigan, April 1976.

Keenan, E. O. *Again and again: The pragmatics of imitation in child language.* Paper presented at the Meeting of the American Anthropological Association, Mexico City, November 1974. (a)

Keenan, E. O. Conversational competence in children. *Journal of Child Language,* 1974, *1,* 163–183. (b)

Keenan, E. O. Evolving discourse—The next step. *Papers and Reports on Child Language Development,* 1975, *10,* 80–88.

Keenan, E. O. Making it last: Repetition in children's discourse. In S. Ervin-Tripp & C. Mitchell Kernan (Eds.), *Child discourse.* New York: Academic Press, 1977, Pp. 125–138.

Keenan, E. O., Schieffelin, B., & Platt, M. Propositions across speakers and utterances. *Papers and Reports on Child Language Development,* 1976, *12,* 127–143.

Keller-Cohen, D. *Variation in the non-native child's acquisition of conversational competence.* Paper presented at N-WAVE VI, Washington, D.C., October 1977.

Keller-Cohen, D. Developmental psycholinguistics. In R. Shuy (Ed.), *Building a research agenda on bilingual education.* Arlington: Center for Applied Linguistics, in press. (a)

Keller-Cohen, D. Systematicity and variation in the nonnative child's acquisition of conversation. *Language Learning,* in press. (b)

Keller-Cohen, D., & Gracey, C. A. Repetition and the non-native acquisition of discourse. Unpublished manuscript, University of Michigan, April 1976.

Keller-Cohen, D., & Gracey, C. A. Learning to say no: Functional negation in discourse. In O. Garnica & M. King (Eds.), *Language, children and society.* Oxford: Pergamon, in press.

Kemp, J., & Dale, P. *Spontaneous imitations and free speech: A developmental comparison.* Paper presented at the Biennial Meeting of the SRCD, Philadelphia, April 1973.

Moerk, E. L. Processes and productions of imitation: Additional evidence that imitation is progressive. *Journal of Psycholinguistic Research.* 1977, *6,*(3), 187–202.

Nakanishi, Y., & Owada, K. Echoic utterances of children between the ages of one and three years. *Journal of Verbal Learning and Verbal Behavior,* 1973, *12,* 658–665.

Nelson, K. Structure and strategy in learning to talk. *Monographs of the Society for Research in Child Development,* 1973, *38* 1-2, (Serial No. 149).

Nelson, K. Individual differences in early semantic and syntactic development. In D. Aaronson & R. Rieber (Eds.), *Developmental psycholinguistics and communication disorders. Annals of the New York Academy of Sciences,* 1975, *263,* 132–139.

Preyer, W. *The mind of the child.* Leipzig: Fernav, 1888.

Sachs, J., & Devin, J. Young children's use of age-appropriate speech styles in social interaction and role-playing. *Journal of Child Language,* 1976, *3,* 81–98.

Sacks, H., Schegloff, E., & Jefferson, G. A simple systematics for the organization of turn-taking for conversation. *Language,* 1974, *50,* 696–735.

Schegloff,, E. A. Sequencing in conversational openings. In J. Gumperz & D. Hymes (Eds.), *Directions in sociolingusitics.* New York: Holt, Rinehart & Winston, 1972. Pp. 346–380.

Schegloff, E., & Sacks, H. Opening up closings. *Semiotica,* 1973, *8,* 289–237.

Scollon, R. *Conversations with a one year old: A case study of the developmental foundation of syntax.* Honolulu: University of Hawaii Press, 1976.

Shatz, M., & Gelman, R. The development of communication skills: Modifications in the speech of young children as a function of listener. *Monographs of the Society for Research in Child Development,* 1973, *38* (5, Serial No. 152).

Shugar, G. W. *Text analysis as an approach to the study of early linguistic operations.* Paper presented at the Third International Child Language Symposium, London, September 1975.

Speier, M. Some conversational problems for interactional analysis. In D. Sudnow (Ed.), *Studies in social interaction.* New York: Free Press 1972. Pp. 397–427.

Stern, W. *Psychology of early childhood up to the sixth year of age.* New York: Holt, 1924.

Sully, J. *Studies of childhood.* New York: Appleton, 1896.

11 The Role of Adults' Requests for Clarification in the Language Development of Children*

Louise J. Cherry
University of Wisconsin, Madison

The purpose of this chapter is to examine the role of adults' requests for clarification in the child's process of language development. Conversations between adults and children are situations when children use language for the purpose of communication. Participation in conversation involves assuming the alternating roles of speaker and listener. There is a constant effort between speakers and listeners to maintain conversation by clarifying misunderstandings and by resolving ambiguities. The request for clarification functions to indicate that the speaker has failed to communicate. The speaker can provide clarification so that the conversation can continue. There has been no previous investigation of adults' differential use of various forms of the request for clarification, children's differential responses, and the relationship of both of these to children's level of language development. This chapter presents a model of the request for clarification and offers examples of this language function from adult-child conversations. The chapter reviews other investigators' models of similar sequences, including the role of the sequence in stimulating the child's process of language development.

THE REQUEST FOR CLARIFICATION

The request for clarification is a conversational device which functions to allow either speaker to bring a misunderstanding in the conversation to the attention of the other. Misunderstandings can be inferred from the

---

*A preliminary report on some of the data presented in this paper was given at the Fourth Annual Colloquium on New Ways of Analyzing Variation in Language, Georgetown University, School of Languages and Linguistics, Washington, D.C. 1975.

occurrence of clarification questions but are not limited to them. Questions such as "Huh?" "What?" "Wha' dija say?" "It's what?" indicate that the conversation has broken down, since one of the speakers does not understand what the other has said. Once the speaker becomes aware of the misunderstanding, that speaker may attempt to repair it. The use of the request for clarification sequence can thus have the effect of clarifying what was misunderstood so that the speakers can resume their conversation. The request for clarification accomplishes two functions in adult–child conversation in addition to the general function of allowing misunderstanding in the conversation to be resolved. The child is made aware of the success or failure of his/her communicative performance, and the sequence also encourages the child to participate appropriately in conversation. For example, the adult's acknowledgment of a child's answer may serve as a reinforcement for the child's answering in this communicative situation. In addition, different types of requests for clarification encourage different types of responses.

Requests for clarification are a subset of all requests. A request whose referent is the preceding utterance of the other speaker is a request for clarification. Neither the topic nor the turn-taking sequence is changed because of the occurrence of the request for clarification sequence, since the context for the request is the prior linguistic context. The request for clarification sequence consists of (a) an *initial utterance* (first speaker), (b) a *request for clarification* (second speaker), (c) an appropriate response, an *answer* (first speaker), (d) an optional *acknowledgment* of the answer (second speaker).

There are two types of request for clarification depending on the kind of information requested: those which request that the first speaker repeat his initial utterance, such as "Whad' ja say?" and "Hmm?", and those which request that the first speaker confirm or deny the second speaker's repetition or reformulation of the first speaker's initial utterance, such as "you say you're 28?" In examining the use of requests for clarification by preschool teachers to children aged 2 to 4 years,[1] the author identified three types in which the adult requests that the child *repeat* the original utterance by using interrogative words, phrases, expressions, or gestures, including: (a) lexical forms such as "What?" "What did you say?" (b) nonlexical forms such as "Huh?" "Hmm?" or (c) nonverbal forms such as cupping the hand over the ear and bending toward the other speaker. The author also identified three types of requests for clarification in which the adult requests that the child *confirm* the adult's rendition of the child's utterance by using a request which is (a) a repetition of the complete initial utterance or some part of it; (b) a repetition of the initial utterance with expansion, expressing in syntactically complete

---

[1]The examples used in the following discussion are from conversations between preschool teachers and children (Cherry, 1975) and mothers and children (Cherry & Lewis, 1976).

form the meaning of the first speaker's utterance as the second speaker understands it (after Cazden, 1972), or (c) a repetition of the initial utterance with reformulation due to changes of person. Figure 1 illustrates the types of requests for clarification.

The repetition request for clarification. The *repetition* request for clarification is a request by the adult for a repetition of the child's entire utterance by using an interrogative word, phrase, expression, or gesture. Often, this request is prompted by the child's failure to articulate clearly. Both lexical forms such as "what" and nonlexical forms such as "huh" appear, and all are characterized by rising intonation.

Example 1:   (Child is pointing to a toy)
    Child: Goes inside?
    Adult: Hmm?
    Child: Goes inside?
    Adult: Yeah, it goes inside.

In using *repetition* questions, adults inform their children that the acoustic signal is deficient and thus encourage children to repeat the initial utterance with sharper articulation. *Repetition* requests can also function to prompt paraphrase and elaboration as in the following example, but rarely do so for children of 2 and 3 years:

Example 2:   (Child is holding a "Raggedy Ann" doll)
    Child: Pocke?
    Adult: What?
    Child: Where's Raggedy's pocket?
    Adult: There it is.

The confirmation request for clarification.   The *confirmation* request for clarification is a request by the adult for a confirmation from the child of the adult's repetition of the child's preceding utterance. The adult repeats some part or the entire utterance with rising intonation.

Example 3:   (Child is holding a toy airplane)
    Child: It's broken.
    Adult: It's broken?
    Child: Yes.
    Adult: That's too bad.

Confirmation clarification requests function as a request for confirmation concerning the adult's repetition of the child's utterance. By repeating the

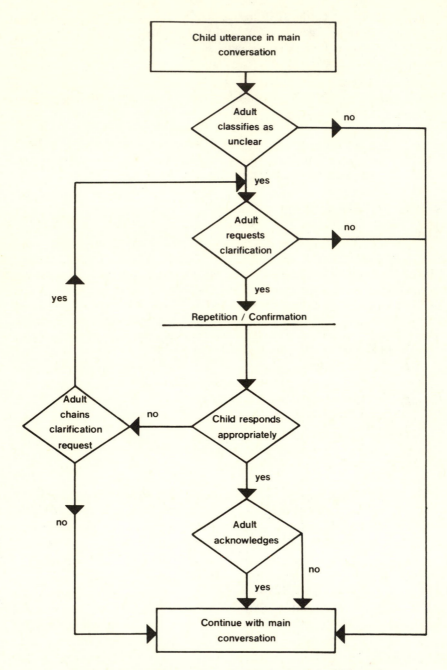

FIG. 1.   The types of requests for clarification in adult–child speech.

child's utterance, the adult requests confirmation on the accuracy of her/his perception and/or comprehension of that utterance. Some *confirmations* involve a reformulation of the child's initial utterance for "speaker-based" adjustments, including changes in pronoun form or verb form due to changes of person. For example, in the following interchange the adult uses a reformulated *confirmation* clarification request and makes the adjustment for first and second person pronoun and verb forms:

Example 4:   (Child is playing with clay at a table with the teacher)
           Child: I'm making a pie-ee.
           Adult: You're making a pie?
           Child: Yeah.
           Adult: Oh, how nice.

There is some evidence that the acquisition of the pronoun system is not complete until children reach the latter stages of language development (Ervin-Tripp, 1977). Children do not use deictic pronouns involving first and third person transformations until stage III, or deictic pronouns involving second person transformation until stage IV. It is expected that reformulated *confirmation* questions would be more difficult for a child who is in the earlier stages of language development than for children who have reached the latter stages.

Some *confirmation* clarification requests involve the adult's expansion of the child's preceding utterance by adding missing grammatical elements. This request is also produced with a rising intonation. The child's utterance which precipitates the adult's expansion is incomplete in its syntactic form. As a result, the utterance may be further incomplete in its propositional content. The adult provides a syntactically expanded version of her interpretation of the child's utterance, as in the following example:

Example 5:   (Child is pointing to his shoes, which are on the floor)
           Child: On.
           Adult: You want your shoes on?
           Child: Yes.
           Adult: I'm glad.

In using the expansion *confirmation* question, adults may demonstrate speaker-based adjustments as in the reformualted *confirmation* questions, but most importantly, this type of sequence provides syntactically correct for what the adult believes the child meant in his initial utterance. In conversation, expansions function as requests for information on the accuracy of the listener's interpretation of the speaker's intended proposition. The young child is limited to the amount of information he can organize and incorporate into any one utterance. The semantic expression of the child's message often suffers due to the absence of some critical aspect, and it is left up to the linguistically sophisticated adult to supply the missing elements with which efficient messages are constructed.

Chaining of clarification questions.   In some cases the adult's first attempt at requesting clarification may fail to induce the child to provide the appropriate response, and the adult may continue to attempt to have the child provide an utterance which the adult can understand. This device is referred to as *chaining*. In the following example, the adult uses a *repetition* clarification request, and when that fails to completely clarify what the child said, the adult uses a reformulated *confirmation* request:

Example 6:   (Adult has come over to the child who is playing with clay)
Child: I made a mink cake.
Adult: What?
Child: A mink cake.
Adult: A mint cake?
Child: Yeah.
Adult: (nods head in acknowledgment)

In the following example, a series of *confirmation* clarification requests are used by the adult until the clarification is achieved and the interaction can continue:

Example 7:   (Child and adult sitting on the floor surrounded with toys)
Child: What are they?
Adult: What are they?
Child: What are they?
Adult: What are they called?
Child: Called.
Adult: Those are called?
Child: Toys.
Adult: And what are these? (pointing to other toys)

Inappropriate responses to the clarification question.   In situations in which the child does not provide appropriate responses to the clarification request, several kinds of responses can occur. The adult may assume that her request has received an implied confirmation, in the case of the *confirmation* request, or the adult may "guess" what the child said on the basis of nonverbal contextual cues. In these cases, the adult may comment on the topic of the clarification request or else make additional requests for information which is related to the topic. In both situations, the adult has attempted to continue the conversation: she is doing the work of conversational maintenance for both the child and herself. In using requests for information, the adult attempts to have her child verbally respond and thus continue the conversation. The following sequences are examples of adults' attempts to continue the conversation through commenting and questioning:

Example 8:   (Child is holding a piece of chalk in front of the blackboard)
        Child: Heidi eat chalk.
        Adult: Eat chalk?
                   No.
                   Don't eat the chalk.
                   You write with the chalk.
                   There. (adult writes the child's name on the board)
                   See?
                   What does that say?
Example 9:   (Child has just returned from the other classroom and approaches the teacher)
        Child: Toys.
        Adult: Toys?
                   What kind of toys were there?
                   What did you find down there?
Example 10: (Child has written something on the blackboard)
        Child: Dubbydee.
        Adult: Dubbydee?
                   Double-U?
                   Is that a double-U?

Figure 2 illustrates the model of the request for clarification sequence discussed here.

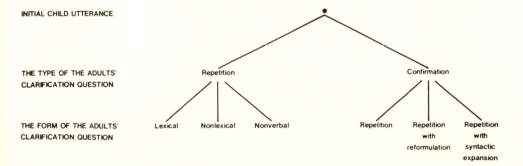

FIG. 2.   The request for clarification sequence.

REVIEW OF OTHER WORK ON
THE REQUEST FOR CLARIFICATION

Several investigators have developed models of the request for clarification. Some of these models are similar to the model presented here, while some of the models differ. Requests for clarification may refer primarily to semantic ambiguities so that the response (if appropriate) introduces new information. In addition, some of the models make distinctions of form that are not made by the model presented here.

Brown (1968) has suggested that forms of interaction involving the use of the "occasional question" may be grammatically instructive for the child. Occasional questions differ from other types of questions since they require that a Wh-word occur in the exact sentence location as the referent in the answer. For example, in the following occasional question "John will read *what*?" and answer "John will read *the book*?' both "what" and "the book" are located at the end of the sentence, while the normal question form is "What is John reading?" Brown has identified four interaction patterns involving the use of the occasional question: (1) "say again"; (2) "say constituent again"; (3) "constituent prompt"; (4) "supply antecedent." He suggests that although the first pattern, including, for example, an initial child utterance, mother's use of "what," followed by the child's repetition of his utterance, has no clear instructional function, it may be a necessary preliminary step to the second pattern. In the second pattern, "say constituent again," the mother finds only part of the child's utterance unintelligible or unclear and repeats what she understood by substituting the unintelligible constituent with a Wh-word. Brown argues that this kind of interchange teaches the membership of the noun phrase constituent. Members are whatever can be replaced by a "what" in the sentence. In the third pattern, the "constituent prompt," the mother first asks a normal question such as "What do you want?" and the child does not reply. The mother then reformulates the question as an occasional question,"You want what?" and is thus attempting to prompt the child into answering. Brown sees this type of exchange as teaching the equivalence of normal and occasional forms. In the fourth pattern, "supply antecedent, "the child's initial utterance contains an unspecified constituent such as the pronoun "it." The mother is unsure of the referent for the pronoun so she repeats the remainder of the child's utterance, substituting a Wh-word for the pronoun, as in "You want what?" The child can then follow with the response "Milk." This pattern teaches defining the pronoun as well as demonstrating that a Wh-word can replace a pronoun and effectively elicit the referent. Occasional questions were used by the three mothers in Brown's longitudinal study at the rate of 2% for Adam's mother, and 1% each for Eve's and Sara's mothers. Brown concludes that parents may be using occasional questions as prompts and probes because they have a strong concern to communicate with their child. Brown's model makes distinctions among *repetition*-type clarification requests in terms of formal aspects.

Holzman (1972) defined an "interrogative in which what is questioned is not in the vocalization" in her analysis of mother–child speech. All of the mothers in this study used interrogatives such as "huh" and "what" when there was a communication failure between mother and child, such as when the mother was unsure of what the child said. Holzman observed that the frequency of mothers' use of this particular kind of clarification request declined between the two- to four-morpheme period, and she claims this is a result of the children's improving communication skills. This type of clarification request is the same as the *repetition* clarification request presented in the present model.

Moerk (1972) defined a "reaffirm correctness of understanding of constituent" sequence in which the mother has an idea of what the child initially said and seeks confirmation of her formulation of the child's utterance. For example, the child initially says "I made it break"; the mother follows with "You made it break?" and the child can confirm or deny the mother's utterance. This type of clarification request is the same as the *confirmation* clarification question presented in our model.

Clarification requests are subsumed within Garvey's (1977) category of "contingent queries." Contingent queries are used to communicate a request for information to a listener. Garvey differentiates between solicited and unsolicited contingent queries. When understanding fails to be communicated, unsolicited queries serve to correct or adjust the information required by a speaker in order to respond appropriately. Solicited queries serve the function of assuring attention or participation in the conversation. Garvey's model of the contingent query sequence consists of three parts: an initial utterance which is the occasion for the query, the query, and the reply to the query. Queries exercise both selectivity and determining functions with respect to the initial utterance. Selectivity functions focus on different aspects of the initial utterances including specific, in which the query selects a particular aspect of the initial utterance; nonspecific, in which the query does not select any particular aspect of the initial utterance, but the entire utterance itself; and potential, in which the query selects some missing aspect from the surface form of the initial utterance. Determining functions require a particular type of reply from the speaker of the initial utterance including a repetition, a confirmation, a specification, or an elaboration. Garvey investigated the use of contingent queries among 3½-year-old children, and found that these children seem to have learned how to participate appropriately in the contingent query sequence. While Garvey's "nonspecific repetition query" is similar to the *repetition* clarification question presented in our model, the contingent query is broader than the clarification question presented in this paper. Garvey's model allows clarification of semantic ambiguity and further elaboration of the topic with new information.

In Jefferson's (1972) "misapprehension sequence" a hearer informs the speaker of a communication failure. The speaker is then constrained to clarify what he said. Jefferson argues that misapprehension sequences are governed by the rule: "... if a statement is made and is followed by a demonstration/assertion that a hearer did not understand, then the one who made the statement may/must provide a clarification" (p. 305). She has postulated a three-part conversational sequence: an initial statement, the misapprehension, and the clarification response. The misapprehension is often conveyed by what Jefferson refers to as the "question-repeat," an interrogative utterance produced by a speaker to indicate his failure to understand the ongoing talk. The "question-repeat" is similar to the clarification question presented in this paper, but Jefferson's misapprehension sequence, like Garvey's, also allows the further elaboration of the topic through new information. Table 1 provides a comparison of the models reviewed here. None of these models of the clarification request combines the study of adults' differential use of the types of clarification requests, children's responses to these requests, and adults' differential follow-ups to children's responses. The present model allows such comparisons to be made, thus enabling the examination of the effect of such interactional sequences on the language development of children. The author has argued elsewhere that the interactions which involve the child as a participant in conversation, where he assumes the alternating roles of speaker and listener, serve as the richest source of experience from which the child can test, modify, and create the rules of language structure and use (Cherry, 1978).

THE ROLE OF ADULTS' REQUESTS FOR CLARIFICATION FOR THE CHILD'S LANGUAGE DEVELOPMENT PROCESS

A basic assumption of a sociocognitive approach to language development is that adults use strategies of requesting information from children which maximize the probability that the child will respond appropriately (Cherry, 1978). With respect to clarification requests, it is expected that adults use different strategies for requesting clarification from children of different levels of language development, enabling children to be roughly equally successful in responding appropriately to these requests. The clarification requests which demand that the child confirm the adult's formulation of the child's initial utterance are cognitively more difficult for the child than is the *repetition* request, which simply demands that the child imitate what he just

TABLE 1
Models of the Request for Clarification

Investigator	Request for Clarification	Categories	Examples
Cherry (24–48 months)	Clarification question	Repetition	"Huh?"
		Confirmation	"You're making a pie?"
Brown (1968) (18–49 months)	Occasional question	Say again	"What?"
		Say constituent again	"You want what?"
		Constituent prompt	"What do you want?"—"You want what?"
		Supply antecedent	(pronoun referent)—"You want what?"
Holzman (1972) (18–49 months)	Interrogative in which what is questioned is not in the verbalization	Interrogative in which what is questioned is not in the verbalization	"Huh?"
Garvey (1977) (38–49 months)	Unsolicited contingent query	Nonspecific repetition	"What?"
		specific repetition	"A what?"
		specific confirmation	"He does?"
		specific specification	"Which one?"
		specific elaboration	"Where?"
Jefferson (1972) (adults)	Misapprehension sequence	Question-repeat	"Who?"
Moerk (1972) (20–60 months)	Reaffirm correctness of understanding of constituent	Reaffirm correctness of understanding of constituent	"You want toast?"

said. The child is required to make a judgment in the former case, while in the latter case, the child repeats the original utterance. It is expected that adults use *repetition* requests with children in the early stages of language development. In contrast, it is expected that adults will use predominantly *confirmation* requests with children at the higher levels of language development. Children at different levels of development have varying success at providing appropriate responses, or answers, to adults' requests for clarification. All children should be able to answer *repetition* questions since children imitate their own utterances at a very early age (Keenan, 1974).

Children should be able to confirm adults' *confirmation* reqests without reformulation for speaker changes before they will be able to confirm reformulated requests since these requests involve knowledge of the pronoun and verb inflectional systems which are not known until later stages of development. In some situations in which the child does not provide the appropriate response to an adult question, it is expected that the adult will attempt to maintain the conversation by assuming an affirmative answer and then either commenting on the topic or else questioning the child further on the topic.

Empirical evidence of adults' use of clarification questions to children. Adults' use of clarification questions was examined using a body of data obtained from four preschool teachers and their thirty-seven students who ranged in age from 2½ to 4 years; and twelve mothers and their 2 year-old children.[2] Requests for clarification were identified and coded according to the categories of *repetition* and *confirmation*; appropriate responses or answers and inappropriate responses which included nonresponses; acknowledgments; and chaining of requests. Reliabilities were calculated for these categories as percentage agreements between the author and a research assistant who each coded two transcripts, and the mean percentage agreement was 87%. Contextual notes made during the data collection were used during coding when this information clarified a particular coding category. Conditional probability scores were calculated for each adult–child dyad in each measure. The adult's use of clarification requests was scored as the proportion of all the adult's requests (requests for information) that were clarification requests. The adult's use of each clarification request was scored as the proportion of all clarification requests that were of this particular type. The child's use of answers was scored as the proportion of all the adult's clarification requests that were answered appropriately by the child. The adult's use of acknowledgments was scored as the proportion of all the child's appropriate answers that were verbally acknowledged by the adult.

The analysis showed that 9% of all teachers' utterances and 9% of all mothers' utterances were requests for clarification. Table 2 shows the proportion of different types of requests and the probabilities of children responding appropriately. The children's level of language development was calculated according to mean length of utterance (Brown, 1973). Correlations were computed between the request and response scores and mean length of utterance, and two-tailed *t*-tests were performed to test the significance of the difference.

The *confirmation* requests were the most frequent type of clarification requests in teacher–child conversations, accounting for 76% of all clarifica-

---

[2]This is a reanalysis of the data collected in Cherry (1975) and Cherry and Lewis (1976).

TABLE 2
The Use of the Request for Clarification in Adult–Child Conversations

Type of Request	Proportion of Adult's Requests for Clarification		Probability of Child's Answering Request for Clarification	
	Teacher–Child	Mother–Child	Teacher–Child	Mother–Child
All requests for clarification	.27	.28	.49	.43
Repetitions	.23	.28	.43	.52
Confirmations	.76	.66	.53	.40

tion requests. Teachers' use of clarification requests overall and use of different types of requests were unrelated to the children's level of language development as was the children's overall level of answering. In cases of children's inappropriate nonresponses, teachers attempted to maintain the conversation by commenting on the topic or questioning in the *confirmation* request sequences 79% of the time and rarely in the *repetition* sequences. Children's probability of answering clarification requests was relatively constant for different types of requests. *Confirmation* requests were also the most frequent types of clarification requests in mother–child conversations, accounting for 66% of all clarification requests. Mothers' overall use of clarification requests was unrelated to the children's level of language development, but use of different types of clarification requests was related to the children's level of language development. Mothers used fewer *repetition* clarification requests with children of higher mean length of utterance ($r = -.55$, $p \leq .05$) but used more *confirmation* requests with children of higher mean length of utterance ($r = .63, p \leq .05$). There was no relationship between children's answering and their level of language development overall for clarification requests or for any particular type of request with the exception of the trend of the positive relationship between answering *confirmation* requests and children's level of language development ($r = .22$, NS). In cases of children's inappropriate nonresponses, mothers also attempted to maintain the conversation by questioning or commenting on the topic in the *confirmation* request sequence 74% of the time, and rarely in the *repetition* request.

In conclusion, these cross-sectional observations of adults' conversations with young children provide evidence that adults adjust the form of clarification requests to the children's level of language development. One result of this adult behavior is that children who are in the process of acquiring the grammar of their native language are roughly equally successful in responding appropriately to these requests. Adults' use of the request for clarification provides the child with the information that his/her utterance has failed to communicate effectively, and thereby encourages the child to reformulate the utterance or confirm the adults' reformulation of it. Direct information about language production and the immediate opportunity to produce language may be important experiences for children in the early stages of languge development (Cherry, 1978). Further research which addresses the effect of participation in such sequences on children's language development is necessary.

ACKNOWLEDGMENTS

The author is grateful to Roy O. Freedle for helpful comments on an earlier version of this paper and to Jane Leifer for assistance in data analysis. Support of this work was provided by an NIMH postdoctoral fellowship (MH #08260).

REFERENCES

Brown, R. The development of Wh questions in child speech. *Journal of Verbal Learning and Verbal Behavior,* 1968 *7,* 279–90.

Brown, R. *A first language: The early stages.* Cambridge: Harvard University Press, 1973.

Cazden, C. *Child language and education.* New York: Holt, Rinehart, & Winston, 1972.

Cherry, L. The preschool teacher–child dyad: sex differences in verbal interaction. *Child Development,* 1975, *46,* 532–6.

Cherry, L. A sociocognitive approach to language development and its implications for education. In O. Garnica, & M. King, (Eds.), *Language, children and society,* New York: Pergammon Press, 1978.

Cherry, L., & Lewis, M. Mothers and two-year olds: a study of sex-differentiated aspects of verbal interaction. *Developmental Psychology,* 1976, *12*(4), 228–82.

Ervin-Tripp, S. Early discourse: some questions about questions. To appear in M. Lewis & L. Rosenblum (Eds.), *Interaction, conversation, and the development of language: The origins of behavior, Volume V.* New York: Wiley, 1977.

Garvey, C. Contingent queries. In M. Lewis & L. Rosenblum (Eds.), Interaction, conversation, and the development of language: the origins of behavior, Volume V, New York: Wiley, 1977.

Grice, P. Logic and conversation. Unpublished manuscript, 1968.

Holzman, M. The use of interrogative forms in the verbal interaction of three mothers and their children. *Journal of Psycholinguistic Research,* 1972, *1*(4), 311–36.

Jefferson, G. Side sequences. In D. Sudnow (Ed.), *Studies in social interaction.* New York: Free Press, 1972. Pp. 294–339.

Keenan, E. Conversational competence in children. *Journal of Child Language,* 1974, *1,* 163–83.

Moerk, E. Principles of interaction in language learning. *Merrill-Palmer Quarterly,* 1972, *18*(3), 229–57.

12

The Effects of Staging on Recall from Prose

P. Clements
Cornell University*

Staging is a dimension of prose structure which identifies the relative prominence given to various segments of prose discourse.

Evidence is adduced to show that staging significantly affects recall from prose. The findings reported have interest for both psycholinguistic theory and educational practice.

With respect to psycholinguistic theory, it is shown that staging is an important factor in language production and reception processes. Thus an understanding of staging is essential in studying the cognitive processes which accompany language use. Furthermore, staging is not only of interest in its own right, but will be a useful tool in the design of experiments in related areas.

With respect to educational practice there are two obvious applications of staging analyses. One is in the writing of educational materials. The work reported here shows how to determine, by means of linguistic analysis, which aspects of a message have been given maximum prominence. A corollary of this is that a method is provided for ensuring that the most crucial aspects of a message are indeed given maximum prominence. A second application is in the teaching of written expression. An important writing skill is that of ensuring that the form of a message reflects the relative importance of its components.

There are three major sections in this chapter. The first presents the necessary theoretical background, the second reviews the experimental findings, and the final brief section is devoted to summary and concluding comments.

---

*Present address: Western Australian Institute of Technology.

DISCOURSE ANALYSIS AND STAGING

The problem of finding rich enough ways to characterize the semantic relations underlying discourse has received renewed interest by psychologists in recent years. Among the more prominent contributors to this field have been Schank (1972), Crothers (1975), Kintsch (1974), and Frederiksen (1975). Grimes (1975), a linguist, has provided some interesting new perspectives on this problem.

Grimes' Analysis of Discourse

Grimes has posed himself two basic questions. The first he shares with the other authors cited above. How best can one characterize the basic meaning of a prose message? The second reflects a more linguistic orientation—How does the surface structure of prose guide a reader to the organization of the message? Pursuit of these questions has led Grimes to suggest that prose may be characterized in terms of three basic dimensions—content, cohesion, and staging.

With respect to content, Grimes uses a case grammar as the basic semantic component. In addition, he has posited "rhetorical predicates" which serve to link the case segments together. For example, two sentences (analyzed in terms of case relations) may be linked by a simple conjunction, or by a cause–effect relationship. etc. The units I have termed "case segments" are in fact propositions—simple or complex. Thus the rhetorical predicates serve as a higher order organizational system linking propositions together.

At the sentence level, Grimes' analysis is similar to Frederiksen's in that both use case systems (though Frederiksen had developed systems of stative relations which in Grimes' analysis would be assigned to the "patient" case role). Beyond the sentence level, both Grimes and Frederiksen have sought to characterize the ways in which propositions may be connected. At this between-sentence level, Frederiksen has provided a more fine-grained semantic analysis than has Grimes. Grimes' analysis at this level reflects both semantic distinctions and surface organizational properties of text. More recently, Grimes (personal communication) has come to regard surface organizational features as belonging to the staging dimension.

The second dimension of prose which Grimes identifies is cohesion. This has to do with the way a speaker or writer attempts to relate what he is saying to the knowledge he presupposes in his audience and to the connections he wishes his audience to make. Some of the linguistic phenomena which Grimes sees as part of this dimension are linking devices such as anaphora, cataphora, and chaining and linking. As an example of linking, a speaker might tell a story by saying, "The oarsmen climbed into the boat. When they were all on board they began to row. After they had been rowing for a short while..." In this style of storytelling each sentence begins with an explicit recapitulation of part of the previous sentence. An alternative way of telling a story would be to say..." Then... and then... After this...". Yet again, one might expect his audience to understand an intended temporal sequence with less explicit help. Other linguistic phenomena which affect the cohesive structure of prose are placement of intonation, and lexical choices related to focus and presupposition.

Thus the basic notion of cohesion is that a speaker or writer can vary the manner in which he uses linguistic devices to bind segments of a discourse together.

The third prose dimension which Grimes identifies is staging. It is this dimension of prose structure that is of primary interest in the research reported here.

The notion of staging depends primarily on three linguistic intuitions, two of which have been around for some time. In recent papers Halliday (1974) and Daneš (1974) have suggested that the theme/rheme distinction and the new information/given information distinction are important determinants of prose structure. According to Daneš, these two distinctions can be traced back to a 1939 paper by Mathesius. The third linguistic intuition is Grimes' idea (unpublished manuscript) that these two distinctions might be combined to yield a hierarchical structure. Height in this structure would indicate the degree of prominence given to particular parts of a message.

In Grimes' terminology, each simple sentence and clause may be divided into topic and comment (theme and rheme). In a simple sentence the topic consists of all the words preceding the main verb and the comment consists of the remainder.[1] In general, the topic is what is fronted. Consider, for example, the sentences:

(1a) Man's greatest problem is pollution.
(1b) Pollution is man's greatest problem.

In (1a) the topic is "Man's greatest problem" whereas in (1b) the topic is "pollution." The *topic* announces what the speaker is talking about and the *comment* recounts what he says about it. The topic thus indicates the speaker's perspective for that segment of the communication. Consider the different perspectives in:

(2a) John seduced Mary.
(2b) Mary was seduced by John.

---

[1]It is sometimes difficult to tell where a topic ends. Some linguists have proposed theme–interlude–rheme because of this indeterminancy.

Throughout a discourse each topic may be identified as new (if it is being introduced for the first time) or old (if it has been previously mentioned in an earlier topic or comment).

The basic principle by which Grimes orders *topics* hierarchically for English is that an old topic retains the level of its previous mention, while a new topic is placed one level below the preceding topic unless it is coordinated with an earlier topic. In general, each *comment* is considered to have the same level in the hierarchy as the topic to which it is attached. Thus, all the information in a text is ordered hierarchically on the basis of the topic pattern.

A more detailed account of staging follows, but first I would like to indicate the direction the argument will take.

Additional Perspectives on Staging

Thus far, I have characterized staging as a set of rules for the analysis of prose. I shall continue in that vein throughout much of the discussion, for ease of communication. It is important to notice, however, that staging can more helpfully be viewed as a set of decisions made by the speaker or writer and communicated to the hearer or reader. (Henceforth I shall speak only of writers and readers, since the studies reported are concerned with reading.) In speaking of decisions made by writers and readers, there is no implication that such decisions are necessarily conscious. The reader of this work will correctly understand my claim if he translates "decisions" into "production or reception rules having psychological reality but not necessarily being above the threshold of awareness."

It would seem that in producing prose discourse a writer must go through several layers of decisions. For example, he must decide what knowledge he wishes to presuppose in his audience and thus what part of the intended message requires explicit communication. He must determine how the message is to be staged. The end result of a writer's decisions is the surface form of the discourse. Any of these decisions may be conscious or unconscious. With respect to staging, for example, writers often make a conscious attempt to present material with appropriate emphases and perspectives. It is quite likely however that staging is sometimes determined primarily by the form in which the ideas to be expressed are stored in the writer's memory. That is, some staging decisions may follow automatically from an author's own perspective.

With respect to the role of staging in the production of text, two points are worthy of note. First, every message is necessarily staged in some way. Topics are chosen and some organization—helpful or otherwise—is imposed on the text by the author. Therefore, if Grimes' analysis of staging has psychological substance (and evidence will be adduced to show that it does) staging must be regarded as a necessary component in a model of discourse production. Second, once staging decisions are made, the number of surface syntactic options is sharply reduced. For example, a staging decision might guarantee that the passive voice will be used for a given sentence. This assumes, of course, that staging decisions govern surface syntactic choices and not vice versa. Nonetheless this would seem the most plausible hypothesis with which to begin.

Turning now to the reception process, we may ask how staging affects the reader. Evidence will be presented to show that staging significantly affects what is remembered from the reading of prose. Thus it will be argued that staging is also an essential component in a reception model.

If the above claims can be substantiated, it follows that staging must be an essential component in a performance theory of semantics. Since an analysis of staging makes it possible to predict which components of a message have the lowest probability of recall, it also makes it possible to predict that certain inferences, for example, have a low probability of being made. At a practical level, this means that studies of semantic variables in prose must control staging if the results are to be interpretable.

Overall, staging may be seen as a set of rules which operate on the semantic base of a message in discourse production and which exert a high level of control over the reception process. Staging rules thus provide part of the story about how deep structure is mapped into surface structure and vice versa. Grimes has therefore identified an important component of prose structure which has not been dealt with by the more psychologically oriented authors. In relation to the work of Schank, Kintsch, and Frederiksen, Grimes' analysis of staging provides one component of the required mapping between the base and surface structures.

Staging Rules

The basic rules have already been mentioned. They are:

(i) *Topic rule:* Identify the topic of each clause and simple sentence.
(ii) *Old/new rule:* Decide whether the topic is new (never previously mentioned) or old (mentioned in an earlier topic or comment). If new, assign it one level below the previous topic. If old, assign it the same level as its first mention.
(iii) *Coordination rule*: If a topic is coordinated with an earlier topic or comment, assign it the same level as that earlier topic or comment.

These rules require further discussion and modification, but first let us apply them to a piece of simple prose. Consider the following example:

Grapes for wine-making require a temperate climate but table grapes flourish in warmer climates. California provides the climatic range needed for both kinds of grapes. Californian vineyards produce high quality wines but some regions of California are too warm for wine-producing grapes. Warmer climates produce grapes with a high sugar content. Such grapes are good to eat but are not ideal for wine making.

The staging structure of this passage is shown in the Table 1. There are four comments which should be made about this example. (1) The "signal" column shows the basis on which the hierarchical level is assigned. Level is shown by the number of asterisks preceding the topic. No asterisks means that the topic (and its comment) are at the highest level in the structure, one asterisk means one level down, etc. (2) The first topic is at the highest level by definition. If the passage had had a title, the title would have been the first topic. (3) Toward the end of the passage, "warmer climates" is "old" because it occurred in the comment of the second topic. "Such grapes" is "old" because it is referentially the same as "grapes with a high sugar content" from the previous comment. (4) The "marker" column shows when explicit linguistic signals are used. (Typically these occur in coordination and subordination.) Additional staging rules are as follows:

(iv) *Subordination rule 1:* Topics of embedded sentences or subordinate clauses are assigned one level below the topic of the sentence in which they are embedded or to which they are subordinated.

TABLE 1
Staging Chart—First Example

Signal	Marker	Topic	Comment
Start		Grapes for winemaking	require a temperate climate.
Coord	but	table grapes	flourish in warmer climates.
New		*California[a]	provides the climatic range needed for both kinds of grapes.
New		**Californian vineyards	produce high quality wine.
Coord	but	**some regions of California	are too warm for wine-producing grapes.
Old		Warmer climates	produce grapes with a high sugar content.
Old		Such grapes	are good to eat.
Coord	but	(such grapes)	are not ideal for wine-making.

[a]Asterisks are explained in the text.

(v) *Subordination rule 2:* New topics which follow an embedded sentence or subordinate clause, are assigned one level below the last unembedded or unsubordinated topic (unless otherwise coordinated).

(vi) *Minimum depth rule:* An old topic is never placed lower in the hierarchy than it would be placed if it were a new topic.

Suppose, for example, that a topic were first introduced low in the staging hierarchy, say five levels down from the first topic. If it were later reintroduced immediately following a top level topic, what level should it then take? According to the old/new rule, it should stay at level 5; but the minimum depth rule overrides this and requires that our topic be placed only one level below its predecessor.

(vii) *Explicit precedence rule:* Explicit signals always take precedence over implied signals.

Signals may be explicit or implicit. The old/new distinction for example is usually not made explicit. Coordination is sometimes made explicit by markers such as *and, but, however, therefore, nonetheless.* On the other hand a coordinating signal is implied if a new topic is the answer to a previous question, if it contrasts with an earlier topic, or if it is otherwise anticipated by an earlier topic.

(viii) *Conflict rule:* In cases of conflict, the higher numbered rule always takes precedence over the lower numbered rule.

Some Problems

While the rules given for determining staging levels are clear-cut, problems can arise in making some of the necessary discriminations. In particular, there are problems associated with identifying the topic of a sentence, distinguishing old from new information, deciding when topics are coordinated, and knowing how to treat subordination. These four areas will be discussed in turn.

Topic Identification

While it is easy to identify the topic of sentences having subject–verb–object form, other constructions present some difficulty. In particular sentences with cleft or pseudocleft constructions present problems which Grimes (1975) has discussed in some detail. Some such constructions are sufficiently rare in written prose that understanding their role in staging is not urgent for psycholinguistic purposes. There are three constructions, however, which are quite common and for which at least interim solutions must be found.

Topics not directly associated with a verb. The first of these types typically contains locative or temporal information in topic position. Consider the following examples:

(3a) In Florida, the beaches are often crowded.
(3b) The beaches in Florida are often crowded.
(3c) The beaches are often crowded in Florida.

The topic of (3c) is "The beaches" and of (3b) "The beaches in Florida," but what of (3a)? Here, the locative information has been fronted and presumably has topic status. But then what of "the beaches," for this seems to be the topic of the segment "the beaches are often crowded"? Furthermore, (3a) must surely be distinguished from (3b) because the topic of (3b) delineates a set of beaches whereas (3a) gives greater focus to the locative information.

The solution I have adopted is to regard (3a) as having two topics. The first topic is "In Florida" and the comment attached is "The beaches are often crowded." This latter segment is then divided into topic "the beaches" and comment "are often crowded." I represent this in a staging chart as shown in Table 2.

The signal *new.nv* shows that the topic is new and is not associated directly with a verb (nv = no verb). The signal *new.v* shows that the level of this topic is determined by the previous one and that it is associated directly with a verb. Where a topic occurs in a staging chart without an associated comment, this shows that the following topic–comment combination is all in fact the "missing" comment. The reason for not placing the second topic one level down in the hierarchy is that comments are considered to share the same level as the topics with which they are associated. Hence, in (3a) above, "the beaches are often crowded" must all share the same level as "In Florida." Thus the difference between (3a) and (3c) is that "In Florida" is given topic status in (3a), while the status of "the beaches" is left unchanged.

The level of the first topic in such constructions depends on its status as new, old, or coordinated. (Such constructions are frequently used to

TABLE 2
Staging Chart—NV Construction

Signal	Marker	Topic	Comment
New.nv		In Florida	
New.v		the beaches	are often crowded.

coordinate segments of information.) Thus possible signals are *new.nv*, *old.nv*, and *coord.nv*, followed by *new.v*, *old.v*, and *coord.v*, respectively.

I refer to this construction as the "no-verb construction" since it occurs not only in locative constructions but also in temporal constructions (as in "Before World War II,...") and in metaphorical equivalents (as in "In our desire to help people change,..." or "In the world of the birdwatchers,...").

The solution adopted for constructions of this kind represents an hypothesis which needs further investigation. Usually, temporal and conditional clauses are treated as subordinate. The hypothesis embodied in the analysis proposed above is that such clauses have a level setting effect when they come first.

Extraposed questions.   The second kind of problem construction is illustrated by the following examples.

(4a) It is clear that he doesn't agree with me.
(5a) It was strange for John to leave early.
(6a) It seems that that tightwad left without paying.

A common feature of these constructions is that they all supply answers to extraposed questions. These questions are:

(4b) What is clear?
(5b) What is strange?
(6b) What seems (to be the case)?

Sentences (4a) and (5a) assert that given events are "clear" and "strange," respectively. Sentence (6a) typically means that an event is thought ("seems") to have occurred (though with appropriate intonation it may be taken to assert the occurrence of an event). Thus, in these three cases an event is recounted and something is asserted about the event. The assertion about the event is fronted, and thus given topic status, while the event may also be divided into topic and comment. Thus I have analyzed such constructions as shown in Table 3.

In Table 3, *ex* stands for "extraposed question" and *ans.ex* stands for "answer to extraposed question." In each case, both topics are at the same level because all of what follows the first topic may be regarded as the comment attached to that topic (i.e., the answer to the extraposed question). The level of each topic pair is determined by the first member of the pair.

As in the previous section, the analysis is offered as an hypothesis rather than an assertion.

TABLE 3
Staging Chart—Extraposed Questions

Signal	Marker	Topic	Comment
New.ex		It is clear	
Ans.ex	that	he	doesn't agree with me.
New.ex		It was strange	
Ans.ex	for	John	to leave early.
New.ex		It seems	
Ans.ex	that	that tightwad	left without paying.

Sentences without comments.   Consider the following examples:

(7a) It was a sunny day.

(8a) It is raining.

Such constructions are used to point to events or states without mentioning objects, actors, or other concepts in relation to the event or state. Such a move is impossible in English without the use of a dummy "it." Thus, in these cases, each entire sentence is viewed as a topic.

Overview.   The lengthy explanations in this section have been an attempt to explain and partially justify the method used in this study. It remains to be pointed out that the decisions reached in this section would typically have very little effect on the overall staging hierarchy of a passage unless the problem constructions identified were used repeatedly.

The Old/New Distinction

There are two problems associated with this distinction. One is the occasional difficulty of distinguishing old from new information. The second is that of identifying the range of influence of old topics.

Distinguishing old from new information.   In many cases the distinction between old information and new information presents no problems. Sometimes, however, the reader's judgment is called into play. An author may speak in one place, for example, of "psychosurgery" and in another place of "psychosurgical methods." The criterion question is whether or not the author intends a distinction. If the two forms are used simply to alleviate repetition of the same word or phrase, then the two forms count as the same and the second occurrence is old. If, on the other hand, the author makes a distinction between a global notion of "psychosurgery" (in the context perhaps of its history, methods, outcomes, value, etc.) and specific "psychosurgical methods," then the two forms count as different and the second occurrence is new. In spoken discourse, the speaker's intonation usually reveals his intentions. The trick in good writing is to force the right intonation.

It is important to notice that the distinction hinges on the way the author uses words, not on conceptual analysis. With respect to the example in the previous paragraph, for instance, it may plausibly be argued that psychosurgery *is* a set of methods. Such a claim, however, is irrelevant to the old/new question.

Unfortunately, no clear-cut rules can be offered here. In analyzing staging patterns, the investigator must sometimes use his judgment about intonation patterns and context to decide whether an author intends a distinction. As a guiding principle, however, if no plausible evidence for a distinction can be found, the default decision should be "old." The reason for this is that classifying topics as old tends to reduce the depth of the staging hierarchy. Where real doubt exists it seems better to err in the direction of under-estimating staging differences since this at least avoids the problem of testing spurious distinctions.

Range of influence of old topics.   The problem here is that it is necessary to allow for the occasional introduction of old high level topics at a level below that of first mention. I suspect that the coordination and subordination rules (which take precedence over the old/new rule) are generally able to handle this, but occasional ambiguities may arise. Systems of headings and subheadings prevent these ambiguities, which is precisely the advantage in using such systems. In very long discourses, such as in books, explicit signaling of the top levels of the staging system is essential if readers are to find their way.

Paragraphing provides a guide in that topics within a paragraph cannot be placed at a higher level than the first topic of that paragraph. No additional staging rule is required for this, however, because paragraphing simply provides a guide to coordination. Similarly, the level of the first topic of a paragraph depends on its coordination with the first topics in other paragraphs. For example, imagine a short discourse comparing the political systems of Russia and China. Suppose that the first five paragraphs were devoted to Russia and the next five to China. In this case, the first topic of paragraph six would usually be at the same staging level as the first topic of paragraph one, by virtue of contrastive coordination. On the other hand, the level of first topics in other paragraphs would depend on more local coordination.

Ambiguity in staging might arise when it is unclear whether an author, in introducing an old topic, intends to return to the old topic or to treat it as subordinate to more recent topics. For the investigator analyzing staging, this is a problem of implied coordination.

In general, then, I have regarded the problem of range of influence of old topics as a problem of implied coordination. Further work is needed to see whether some better approach is possible.

Coordination

At the between-sentence level, two kinds of problem can arise. First, when explicit coordinators are used, there may sometimes be room for doubt about what is to be coordinated with what, even though there is no doubt that some level of coordination is intended. As an example of how such a problem might arise, authors sometimes use *therefore* in a context which makes it difficult to decide whether the sentence which follows is to be coordinated with the immediately preceding sentence, or with some larger or earlier segment of the text.

Secondly, when no explicit signals are used it may be difficul to decide whether the new topic is intended to coordinate with an earlier one by virtue of contrast or anticipation, or not. For example, if an author devoted a paragraph to discussing "the rich" and then introduced "the poor," this would clearly count as implied coordination unless the author defeated this by some means such as introducing "the poor" in a subordinate clause. As an example of coordination by anticipation consider the following:

> The winter rush was occasioned by a sighting. Within minutes of the sighting, word was spread far and wide by early-morning telephone calls. Dozens of bird watching enthusiasts flocked to the scene. A Ross's gull had been sighted.

In the last sentence of the above passage "A Ross's gull" is certainly a new topic. But it is coordinated with the first sentence (in my judgment) because the author sets up a clear expectation of some such announcement.

The resolution of difficulties where they arise must be left to the investigator's judgment. Once again, I can offer no clear rules, but my preferred default option is to assume no implied coordination unless a plausible case can be made to the contrary. My reason for this is that if a researcher, after careful thought, is still unsure about a possibly implied coordination, then it is probably unlikely that many readers will treat the topics concerned as coordinated.

At the within-sentence level, *and* and *but* are treated as coordinators. A problem arises, however, in knowing whether other connectives at this level serve to subordinate clauses. This leads us to the last of our problem areas.

Subordination

From a syntactic point of view, certain clauses have traditionally been regarded as subordinate. In the analysis of staging which I have used, I have placed the topic of subordinate clauses and embedded sentences one level below the sentences in which they are subordinated or embedded. Since new topics are always placed one level below the last unembedded or unsubordinated sentence or clause, subordination has scarcely any effect on the overall staging levels of a passage. Nonetheless, it is of interest to ask how subordination relates to staging.

There are two distinct problems with respect to subordination.

First, there is the problem of distinguishing subordination from coordination. Furthermore, it is important to be clear that we are only concerned with subordination in a syntactic sense and not, for example, in a set-theoretic sense.

In company with most linguists, Grimes regards *and* and *but* as *coordinators*. His list of *subordinators* includes relativizers (*who, which, that, where, when*) and complementizers (*for, to, that*) and other subordinators (*because, while, in order to, except, until*). Unfortunately, this list is not universally agreed upon. For example Dik (1968), who has written extensively on the subject, regards *for* as a coordinator but *because* as a subordinator.

Thus one problem in the area of subordination is finding adequate criteria for the phenomenon.

Second, even given adequate criteria, there is the question of whether syntactic subordination also signals staging subordination.

Because of the uncertainties about subordination, one of the experiments reported in the next section has been devoted to an examination of the psychological evidence with respect to subordination, and the closely related phenomenon of sentence embedding, as they affect staging.

Overview of Staging

In order to help the reader clarify the rules for staging, they are presented in a flow chart (Fig. 1).

The extended discussion has been provided in an attempt to render the method of analysis sufficiently unambiguous for any interested investigator to implement the same analysis. Further illustration of the method is provided by the charts depicting the staging analysis of one of the passages used in the experiments reported later in this chapter.

The experimental evidence which follows not only demonstrates that the phenomenon is worthy of study, but also shows that it is important to control for staging in studies of semantic variables in prose.

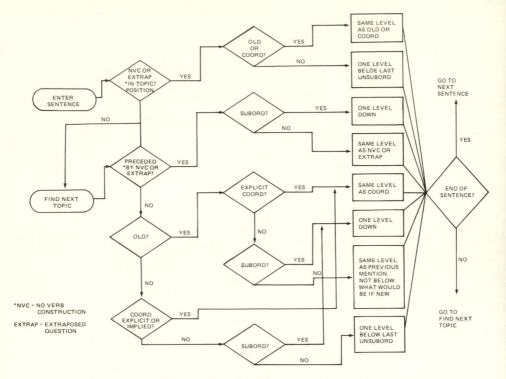

FIG. 1. Flow chart of staging rules.

With respect to some of the detailed problems discussed, three further comments are offered.

First, the problems that arise are by no means so frequent or difficult as to be intractable. Although I have been familiar with Professor Grimes' work for little more than a year, he and I have had very good agreement on independent staging analyses of the same passage.

Second, from a practical research point of view, it is obviously desirable to write passages that avoid the major bugs in the system.

Finally, passages which present problems for staging analysis may often be characterized, for independent reasons, as poorly written. What else can one say about a passage in which it is impossible to decide whether or not an author intends to coordinate two segments or whether a new term is meant to contrast with an earlier term rather than simply avoid repetition? I tremble to make this point, since staging analyses of some of my own prose have made me aware of the problems a reader would face. Perhaps staging analysis will be taken up by journal editors as an objective tool to justify their intuitive reactions! Certainly, the notion of staging has something to offer teachers of written expression.

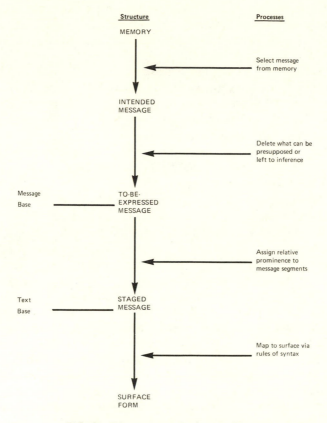

FIG. 2. Discourse production model.

A Discourse Production Model

One way to conceive of components of text structure is to consider how they might arise in the production of text. Figure 2 presents a tentative model for this.[2]

According to this model, a writer first selects from memory some message he wishes to communicate. Typically there is much he can assume that the reader will understand by way of shared context and reasonable inferences. Thus not all of the message is actually expressed. The to-be-expressed message is therefore the semantic base for what is actually expressed. This is

[2]I am indebted to Professors Carl Frederiksen and George McConkie for ideas on this approach.

what I call the *message base*. The message base is the same as content in Grimes' analysis. It is important to distinguish this level from the intended message level, since it is precisely the writer's selection of what to express that on occasion leads to a breakdown in communication. The writer may be mistaken in assuming certain knowledge or expectations in his readers. Given the message base (to-be-expressed message) the information is then staged in some way. This means that certain parts of the message base are selected as topics, and that statements are arranged in a way which determines the level of prominence given to each part of the message. The staged message is what I call the text base, because it contains all the information necessary for derivation of the surface text. Finally, the rules of syntax are applied to yield a surface form of the text.

This model has, I believe, some heuristic value, though it may also be misleading. Two problems in particular deserve comment.

The first problem has to do with lexicalization of the message. If Schank is right to demand a conceptual base, at what point are words introduced? Indeed, is there a single place in this system where lexicalization occurs? When writing prose we frequently begin wtih certain words and then change our minds and select others. Such changes of mind may sometimes reflect changes in what we intend to communicate, but on other occasions our purpose is to make the intended message clearer. This latter possibility argues in favor of Schank's view and also suggests that lexicalization of parts of a message can sometimes take place quite late in discourse production.

The second problem has to do with the place of staging. It may be that certain staging decisions are implicit in selecting the intended message. On the other hand, we sometimes rearrange texts precisely to alter the pattern of emphases. Perhaps topicalization (what one is talking about) is decided at an earlier level than sequencing and chunking (which may both be consequences of staging decisions), in which case staging should not be regarded as a unified set of decisions which all occur together.

Despite these problems, there are two claims implicit in this model that I wish to affirm. The first claim is that staging decisions, however they occur, are prior to surface syntactic choices. This claim is made on the basis of plausibility. The effect of staging is to determine levels of prominence for parts of a message. It would seem odd indeed to suggest that syntactic decisions should be allowed to restrict staging decisions. Furthermore staging provides a theoretical answer to the question of why certain surface forms are chosen over others. Indeed, it might turn out that staging removes all remaining syntactic decisions. In this case, a grammar to convert the staged message to surface form would consist of mapping rules.

The second claim I wish to make is that a message base as depicted by this model may be staged in a variety of ways. In this sense, staging necessarily follows determination of the to-be-expressed message. That is, determination of the message base is logically prior to staging, whether or not it is psychologically prior. The production model was, of course, intended as a tentative basis for a psychological model—not a logical one. Thus, the problems discussed above are not to be dismissed. From a psychological viewpoint, the model is no doubt a gross oversimplification. Nonetheless one can represent a message base in terms of a set of propositions and their interrelations. Such a base may then be staged in a variety of ways, and it is helpful to distinguish the before-staging and after-staging forms of a message.

In the research presented here I have represented the message base using Frederiksen's (1975) system. The main reason for choosing this form of representation is that it is well developed for purposes of scoring recall protocols, yet it is not unreasonable for discussing mappings to language. Since the study is concerned with the question of recall differences between groups, any well developed representation would probably suffice to test the question statistically. It is not essential for this research that the representation of the message base be theoretically optimal. Thus Frederiksen's system was used for pragmatic reasons, and not in rejection of Schank's hypothesis. Frederiksen's system is better adapted for scoring protocols than is Schank's, and of the systems which match lexical entries to concepts, I believe Frederiksen's to be the best developed by a good margin.

Discourse Reception Processes

The major question in the research reported here is what effect staging has on the reader. Thus this research is concerned with the role of staging in the reception of information.

In the experimental section, evidence is adduced to show that staging does indeed regulate the acquisition of information in most situations. Nonetheless, there are at least two circumstances in which one would not expect staging to affect recall. One such situation is when the task is to read and criticize an author's viewpoint. In this case, at least part of what one tries to do is ignore the way the author has set up the relative emphases of information (i.e., one tries deliberately to overcome the influence of staging). Another such situation is when one has heightened interest or very strong feelings about some part of the total message. In this case one is apt to block out the staging the author gives without any conscious effort. (Professor Grimes once remarked to me that academics who disagree with a writer's viewpoint can be remarkably adept at missing the main point of his communication!)

Thus I view staging as a system which regulates the acquisition of information unless some higher level of control prevents this.

EXPERIMENTAL EVIDENCE

Orientation to Experiments

Research Paradigm

Throughout the experiments to be described, a total of five pairs of passages were used. The members of each pair had identical content but different staging. Thus each pair of passages could be viewed as two versions of a single passage.

Within each pair of passages certain chunks of information were staged higher in one version than the other. Subjects were assigned randomly to read one of the two versions. The hypothesis was that recall of a given information chunk would be better following reading of the version in which it was staged high.

It is important to notice that the basic hypothesis is that a given chunk of information is better recalled if it is staged high than if it is staged low. This is not the same as the hypothesis that within a given version, information staged high is recalled better than information staged low. Furthermore, there is strong reason for not testing this latter hypothesis, since a result in either direction would be inconclusive. If, within a version, information chunks high in the staging structure were recalled better than information chunks staged low, one could not be sure whether this was due to staging differences or content differences between the chunks. Equally, if no difference was found this would not guarantee that staging had no effect, since it is known that staging is not the only factor that influences recall from reading.

The experimental paradigm used in the present study permits a clear test of the staging hypothesis. The test is always for recall differences on identical information chunks. Furthermore, the information chunks are always embedded in exactly the same semantic contexts, because the content is the same for both versions of each passage. Therefore only staging differences could account for recall differences.

Basic Experimental Questions

Does staging influence recall? The first experiment used two pairs of passages to see whether staging differences would affect recall.

If staging affects recall, is the effect on input, retrieval, or both? Subjects were given probes (some in question form, some in incomplete sentence form) after they had written their recalls. This was done in all the experiments in which recall data were collected. It was considered that should recall effects remain undiminished after an attempt to elicit all the information subjects could remember, recall differences would probably be due to differences in the information subjects had stored in memory. In particular, it is always possible that what subjects write in free recalls reflects not only what they can remember, but also some selection of what they remember based on what seems most salient to them. The probes were used to see whether this kind of retrieval selection could explain differences which might arise in free recall.

Inability to recall information with the help of probes does not guarantee that such information has not been stored in memory, though this was considered the most plausible explanation in the context of the exeriments to be reported.

If staging affects recall, what is the mechanism?   One possibility here is that readers assign varying degrees of importance to statements on the basis of staging. To check this, subjects were asked to rate statements from the passages they read for their importance in the passage. This was done in all of the recall experiments.

The question is whether or not readers are able to identify the patterns of prominence set up by the staging. If so, then recall differences due to staging might result from the reader's conscious direction of his attention during reading. If, on the other hand, readers are unable to identify the staging pattern, then some different explanation must be sought.

If staging affects recall, do all the features of staging analysis contribute to this?   Staging analysis depends on three main components: (i) the old/new rule and coordination, (ii) embedding and subordination, and (iii) topicalization.

The second experiment was designed to see whether staging effects on recall would occur if staging differences depended exclusively on the old/new rule. To test this, two versions of a passage were used in which the topics of all sentences were the same in both versions and in which no staging differences were introduced by means of varied subordination or coordination. Thus all staging differences depended on the old/new rule.

The third experiment was designed to test the effect of subordination. Two versions of a passage were used in which some statements were subordinated in one version but not in the other. Once again probes and ratings were included.

Does staging affect speed of retrieval?   The fourth experiment was designed to test the effects of staging on retrieval by using reaction time data.

Scoring Method

The data base.   As mentioned previously, Frederiksen's (1975) system was used to represent the semantic content of the passages. Charts were prepared which depicted the semantic structures of the chunks to be scored.

Readers are referred to Frederiksen's paper for a full description of his method. A brief example is provided below to illustrate the method. In Frederiksen's system, the sentence *Susie tickled Ralph with a feather* would be represented as:

agent   dative
(Susie) $--\rightarrow$ (tickle) $\begin{array}{l} \ulcorner-------------\rightarrow\text{(Ralph)} \\ \llcorner-----\underline{\text{instrument}}\rightarrow\text{(feather)} \end{array}$

Thus, the system represents propositions as slots connected by labeled relations. I have here ignored determination, quantification, tense, and aspect in order to keep the example simple. In this example, then, Susie is the agent of the action "tickle," Ralph is the recipient ("dative") and a feather is the instrument.

There are seven score points in this example—four slots and three relations. If a subject's recall said *Someone tickled Ralph with a feather,* then the first slot would not be scored but the remaining six data points would be, because the recall says that some agent tickled Ralph with a feather.

Given the recall *Susie tickled Ralph for fun,* then the first five data points would be scored, but not the last two because no mention is made of a feather or of any instrument.

In the present study, a separate semantic structure chart was prepared for every subject recall. Those elements which were present in a recall were marked on the subject's chart for that passage. The number of data points present in each information chunk were then tallied for each subject. Thus each subject was given a score for each chunk he or she recalled.

It was necessary to develop some specific scoring rules to cope with cases where fragments of propositions were recalled—particularly when the semantic structure contained two or more propositions that were very similar in meaning. The rules developed were as follows:

1. Propositions were not scored if the recall contained a substitute main verb unless the substitute was a close synonym.

2. Where two or more propositions had a common segment one of them was scored only if the feature which distinguished it from the others was present in the recall. Fragments which did not contain the critical difference were scored in a predetermined place in the structure.

3. Fragments of propositions were not scored unless at least one of the main actors or concepts was present in the recall. (In event propositions, either the instigator or the recipient of the action had to be present in the recall. In stative propositions, one of the first two concepts and the correct relation had both to be present in the recall.)

Scores.   Three scores were developed for each subject on each information chunk.

1. *Free recall score.* This was the number of data points present in the subject's free recall for a given chunk of information.

2. *Cued recall score.* This was the free recall score for a subject on a given chunk plus any additional data points the subject gained in response to the probes. Thus the cued recall score for a subject on a given information chunk was always equal to or greater than the free recall score.

3. *Rating score.* Ratings for each item were on a three-point scale and responses were scored 0, 1, or 2. More than one item was rated for each chunk and the rating score of a subject for a chunk was the sum of the relevant item scores.

Scoring Reliability

A sample of recalls containing 18 information chunks was rescored by another investigator trained in the use of Frederiksen's method. This investigator was unaware of the direction of the hypotheses and of any of the experimental details.

There are two measures of agreement that may be considered. One is the number of data points on which both scorers agreed. The other is the correlation between raters for scores on each chunk. It is the latter measure which is crucial for this study, but the former more detailed comparison may be of interest to investigators who plan more fine-grained semantic analyses than the between-chunk comparisons used in this study.

In the 18 information chunks that were rescored there were 762 data points. There was agreement on 721 of these and disagreement on 41. Thus there was agreement on 94.6% of the data points. This yields a phi correlation of .87 based on a two-way contingency table showing the number of points scored as present or absent from recalls by each rater. While this may seem a disappointingly low reliability coefficient, the reader should not overlook the fact that it is based on a much more searching comparison than has traditionally been reported for recall scoring procedures. Two further observations are worth reporting.

First, of the 41 points on which there was disagreement, approximately one-third were acknowledged by one or other scorer to be scoring mistakes. It is very difficult to score consistently at such detailed level and this suggests that in studies aimed at fine-grained semantic analyses all recall protocols should be scored independently by at least two scorers. This would reduce unreliability due to avoidable human error.

Second, the disagreements that scorers were unwilling to acknowledge as errors were, without exception, disagreements about fragments of propositions. That is, there were disagreements about statements in the recalls which represented only part of the information in any given proposition in the data base. Disagreement was sometimes about where best to represent the fragment in the base and sometimes about how best to interpret the information in the recall without making unwarranted, if low-level, inferences. These disagreements reflect, at least in part, the fact that it is not always possible to determine with certainty what a writer intends to convey. Thus these disagreements should not be seen as a weakness in the scoring system. Rather, they show that the scoring system is sensitive enough to pick up real problems in language use. The best way to resolve difficulties of this sort will obviously depend on the questions of primary interest to the scholar conducting research.

Turning now to the measure of most interest for this study, the between-scorer product moment correlation for chunk scores was +.95. This shows that despite occasional disagreement over detail, the scores determined for chunks of information in this study are highly reliable. Since all of the comparisons in the study are between mean scores for chunks of information, it is clear that confidence in the reliability of the findings is fully justified.

Statistical Analyses

Experimental designs varied from experiment to experiment and will be discussed as appropriate.

Throughout the study, recall differences were tested using the Mann-Whitney U test, to avoid the assumption that the relevant population data were normally distributed. One-tailed tests were used because the direction of the effect was predicted by the hypotheses. Most of the sample distributions were negatively skewed, a situation which makes it desirable to avoid the assumption of normality when one-tailed tests are performed.

Notwithstanding the foregoing, t tests are fairly robust and departures from normality often make little difference. The results of t tests are presented in addition to Mann-Whitney U tests and it can be seen that while specific probabilities vary between tests, the nature of the findings is not affected by the choice of test.

First Experiment

Purpose

The aims of this experiment were to discover:

1. Whether the probability of recalling certain information in free recall is higher when that information is staged higher in the passage,
2. whether the probability of recalling certain information in cued recall is higher when that information is staged higher in the passage,
3. whether the probability of recalling certain information in cued recall varies, depending on whether probes are in question or incomplete sentence form,
4. whether ratings of the importance of certain chunks of information are higher when that information is staged higher in the passage.

Subjects

Two groups of subjects participated in this experiment. The first group was comprised of students taking an introductory psychology course at Cornell University. There were 24 subjects (12 males and 12 females) in this sample.

The second group was comprised of high school students who had just completed their junior year at high school and who had come to Cornell for a special summer program. These students were also taking an introductory psychology course. There were 32 subjects (16 males and 16 females) in this sample.

Passages

Two pairs of passages were used in this experiment. The first pair (Passages Nos. 1 and 2) was about the sighting of a rare bird. The second pair (Passages Nos. 3 and 4) was about psychosurgery. In the first two passages there were four information chunks of interest (labeled A, B, C, D) and in the second pair there were two such chunks (labeled E, F).

The staging charts for Passages 1 and 2 are shown in Tables 4 and 5. Semantic structure charts for the information chunks that were scored are in Table 6.

Procedure

Each subject read two passages, one from each pair. The instructions appeared on a cover sheet and are reproduced below.

TABLE 4

STAGING CHART - PASSAGE 1

SIGNAL	MARKER	TOPIC	COMMENT
START		OUR NOTIONS OF NORMALITY	DEPEND TO A LARGE EXTENT ON THE GROUPS
SUBORD	(TO WHICH)	* TO WHICH	WE BELONG
COORD	AND	* TO WHOSE VALUES	WE ARE COMMITTED
COORD	THEREFORE	THE BEHAVIOUR OF ADHERENTS OF STRONG SPECIAL-INTEREST GROUPS SUCH AS BIRD WATCHING ENTHUSIASTS	SEEMS TO BE A LITTLE ECCENTRIC SOMETIMES TO THOSE
SUBORD	(WHO)	* WHO	ARE OUTSIDERS.
NEW.NV		* AT SOUTH SALISBURY, MASSACHUSETTS,	
SUBORD	WHERE	** THE MERRIMACK RIVER	FLOWS INTO THE ATLANTIC
NEW.V		* THE MARSHES AND BEACHES	HAVE BECOME POPULAR HAUNTS FOR BIRDWATCHERS.
NEW		** BONAPARTE'S GULLS AND LESSER GREBES	ARE REGULAR INHABITANTS OF THE AREA.
OLD		* SOUTH SALISBURY	ALSO HOUSES AN AMUSEMENT AND BEACH RESORT
SUBORD	(TO WHICH)	** TO WHICH	VISITORS FLOCK IN SUMMER,
COORD	BUT	** THE TOWNSPEOPLE	WERE RECENTLY SURPRISED BY A RUSH OF WINTER VISITORS.
OLD		BIRD WATCHING	IS NOT A WIDESPREAD OBSESSION
COORD	BUT	ITS DEVOTEES	ARE WILLING TO GO TO GREAT LENGTHS TO SIGHT A RARE BIRD.
OLD		* THE WINTER RUSH	WAS OCCASIONED BY A SIGHTING.
COORD .NV		* WITHIN MINUTES OF THE SIGHTING	
COORD .V		* WORD	WAS SPREAD FAR AND WIDE BY TELEPHONE CALLS IN THE EARLY HOURS OF THE MORNING
COORD		* A ROSS'S GULL	HAS BEEN SIGHTED.
OLD		* THE ROSS'S GULL	IS A SMALL GRAY-WINGED SEAGULL WITH ROSY CHEST MARKING, A WEDGE-SHAPED TAIL, RED FEET AND, IN SUMMER, A BLACK COLLAR.

Type	Connector	Constituent	Text
OLD		* IT	IS A NATIVE OF THE ARCTIC AND BREEDS IN NORTHWESTERN SIBERIA.
SUBORD	ALTHOUGH	** IT	HAS SOMETIMES BEEN SEEN OFF POINT BARROW, ALASKA,
OLD		* IT	IS RARELY SEEN EVEN IN ITS OWN HABITAT.
NEW.NV		* ON RECEIVING TELEPHONE CALLS	BEGAN LEAVING THEIR HOMES AT TWO O'CLOCK IN THE MORNING AND
NEW.V		* BIRDWATCHERS	TRAVELLED THROUGH THE NIGHT FROM AS FAR AWAY AS NEW YORK CITY TO TAKE UP THEIR WATCHES IN THE COLD DAYBREAK.
OLD		* MANY	FORSOOK THEIR JOBS FOR THE DAY.
COORD		* THE LENGTHS TO WHICH BIRD WATCHERS GO IN THE HOPE OF GLIMPSING A RARE BIRD	WAS CERTAINLY SURPRISING TO ONE LOCAL POLICEMAN
SUBORD	(WHO)	* WHO	REMARKED THAT HAD HE SEEN THE BIRD HE WOULD HAVE TOLD NO-ONE.
COORD.NV	(HOWEVER)	* IN THE WORLD OF THE BIRDWATCHERS, HOWEVER	WAS THE SIGHTING OF A TUFTED DUCK
COORD.V		* AN ADDED BONUS FOR THE DAY	IS ALSO A RARE BIRD AND NORMALLY NATIVE TO EUROPE.
SUBORD	(WHICH)	** WHICH	HAS BEEN DEVOTED TO DEMONSTRATING THE PREDICTABILITY OF BIRDS' WHEREABOUTS.
NEW		** MUCH OF THE LITERATURE IN ORNITHOLOGY	
COORD.NV	(HOWEVER)	** AS IN ANY SCIENCE, HOWEVER	SOMETIMES FAIL
COORD.V		** PREDICTIONS	
COORD	AND	** BIRDS SUCH AS THE ROSS'S GULL AND TUFTED DUCK	ARE FOUND IN THE MOST UNEXPECTED LOCATIONS.
OLD		** SUCH EVENTS	MAKE SCIENTIFIC HISTORY.

TABLE 5

STAGING CHART – PASSAGE 2

SIGNAL	MARKER	TOPIC	COMMENT
START		MUCH OF THE LITERATURE IN ORNITHOLOGY	HAS BEEN DEVOTED TO DEMONSTRATING THE PREDICTABILITY OF BIRDS' WHEREABOUTS.
COORD .NV	(HOWEVER)	AS IN ANY SCIENCE, HOWEVER	
COORD .V		PREDICTIONS	SOMETIMES FAIL
COORD	AND	BIRDS SUCH AS THE ROSS'S GULL AND TUFTED DUCK	ARE FOUND IN THE MOST UNEXPECTED LOCATIONS.
OLD		SUCH EVENTS	MAKE SCIENTIFIC HISTORY.
NEW		* SOUTH SALISBURY, MASSACHUSETTS	HOUSES AN AMUSEMENT AND BEACH RESORT
SUBORD	(TO WHICH)	** TO WHICH	VISITORS FLOCK IN SUMMER,
COORD	BUT	** THE TOWNSPEOPLE	WERE RECENTLY SURPRISED BY A RUSH OF WINTER VISITORS.
OLD		** THE WINTER RUSH	WAS OCCASIONED BY A SIGHTING.
COORD .NV		** WITHIN MINUTES OF THE SIGHTING	
COORD .V		** WORD	WAS SPREAD FAR AND WIDE BY TELEPHONE CALLS IN THE EARLY HOURS OF THE MORNING.
OLD		A ROSS'S GULL	HAD BEEN SIGHTED.
OLD		THE ROSS'S GULL	IS A SMALL GRAY-WINGED SEAGULL WITH ROSY CHEST MARKING, A WEDGE-SHAPED TAIL, RED FEET AND, IN SUMMER, A BLACK COLLAR.
OLD		IT	IS A NATIVE OF THE ARCTIC AND BREEDS IN NORTHWESTERN SIBERIA.
SUBORD	ALTHOUGH	* IT	HAS SOMETIMES BEEN SEEN OFF POINT BARROW, ALASKA,
OLD		IT	IS RARELY SEEN EVEN IN ITS OWN HABITAT.

NEW	* BONAPARTE'S GULLS AND LESSER GREBES	ARE REGULAR INHABITANTS OF THE SOUTH SALISBURY AREA.
NEW	** THE MERRIMACK RIVER	FLOWS INTO THE ATLANTIC AT SOUTH SALISBURY
SUBORD (WHOSE)	*** WHOSE MARSHES AND BEACHES	HAVE BECOME POPULAR HAUNTS FOR BIRDWATCHERS.
COORD .NV	** ON RECEIVING TELEPHONE CALLS	
COORD .V	** BIRDWATCHERS	BEGAN LEAVING THEIR HOMES AT TWO O'CLOCK IN THE MORNING
COORD AND	**	TRAVELLED THROUGH THE NIGHT FROM AS FAR AWAY AS NEW YORK CITY TO TAKE THEIR WATCHES IN THE COLD DAYBREAK.
OLD	** MANY	FORSOOK THEIR JOBS FOR THE DAY.
NEW	*** THE LENGTHS TO WHICH BIRDWATCHERS GO IN THE HOPE OF GLIMPSING A RARE BIRD	WAS CERTAINLY SURPRISING TO ONE LOCAL POLICEMAN
SUBORD (WHO)	**** WHO	REMARKED THAT HAD HE SEEN THE BIRD HE WOULD HAVE TOLD NO-ONE.
COORD .NV	** IN THE WORLD OF THE BIRDWATCHERS, HOWEVER	
(HOWEVER) COORD .V	** AN ADDED BONUS FOR THE DAY	WAS THE SIGHTING OF ANOTHER BIRD.
OLD	A TUFTED DUCK	WAS SIGHTED.
OLD	THE TUFTED DUCK	IS ALSO A RARE BIRD AND NORMALLY NATIVE TO EUROPE.
OLD-SUBORD ALTHOUGH	** BIRD WATCHING	IS NOT A WIDESPREAD OBSESSION
OLD	* ITS DEVOTEES	ARE WILLING TO GO TO GREAT LENGTHS TO SIGHT A RARE BIRD.
NEW	** OUR NOTIONS OF NORMALITY	DEPEND TO A LARGE EXTENT ON THE GROUPS
SUBORD TO WHICH	*** (GROUPS)	WE BELONG
COORD AND	*** TO WHOSE VALUES	WE ARE COMMITTED
COORD THEREFORE	** THE BEHAVIOUR OF ADHERENTS OF STRONG SPECIAL-INTEREST GROUPS SUCH AS BIRD WATCHING ENTHUSIASTS	SEEMS TO BE A LITTLE ECCENTRIC SOMETIMES TO THOSE
SUBORD (WHO)	*** WHO	ARE OUTSIDERS.

TABLE 6

SEMANTIC STRUCTURE CHART – PASSAGES 1 & 2

INFORMATION CHUNK A
----

1 ('WE)--PAT->('BELONG.TO)--DAT1->(:GROUPS.1)

2 (:GROUPS.1)--PAT->('HAVE)--THEME2->{'VALUES.1}

3 ('WE)--PAT->('ACCEPT)--THEME2->{'VALUES.1}

4 ('WE)--PAT->('HAVE)--THEME2->{{'NOTIONS}--THEME1->{'NORMALITY}}

5 {{#1}{#2}{#3}}--CAU@QUAL(TO.LARGE.EXTENT)->{#4}

6 (:OUTSIDERS)--PAT@ASP(ITER)->('THINK)--THEME2->
                              {(:ADHERENTS.SSIG)--PAT->('BEHAVE)--MAN->('ECCENTRIC)--EXT1->('A.LITTLE)}

7 {#5}--CAU->{#6}

INFORMATION CHUNK B
----

8 ( )--PAT@T(PAST)ASP(COMP)->('SEE)--DAT2--(:ROSS'S.GULL.1)

9 (:ROSS'S.GULL.2)*<-CAT--(('SEAGULL)--EXT1->('SMALL))
                         /--HASP->('CHEST)--HASP->('MARKING)--EXT1->('ROSY)
                         /--HASP->('FEET)--EXT1->('RED)
                         /--HASP->('TAIL)--CAT.ATT->('WEDGE.SHAPED)
                         /--HASP->('COLLAR)--EXT1->('BLACK)--TEM1->('SUMMER)
                         /--HASP->('WINGS)--EXT1->(GRAY)

10 {'NATIVES.OF.ARCTIC}--CAT->(:ROSS'S.GULL.2)

11 (:ROSS'S.GULL.2)-- PAT->('BREEDS)--LOC22->('N.W.SIBERIA)

12 ( )--PAT@T(PAST)ASP(ITER)->('SEE)*--DAT1->(:ROSS'S.GULL.2)
                         /--LOC22->('OFF.PT.BARROW)--LOC22->('ALASKA)
                         /--MAN.EXT1->('SOMETIMES)

13 ( )--PAT@T(PRES)ASP(ITER)->('SEE)*--DAT1->(:ROSS'S.GULL.2)
                         /--LOC22->('OWN.HABITAT)
                         /--MAN.EXT1->('RARELY)

314

INFORMATION CHUNK C

14 (:BIRDWATCHERS)--AGT@T(PAST)ASP(INCPT)->('MOVE)*--DAT1->('THEMSELVES)
    /--SOURCE->{(:BW)--LOCO3->('IN.HOMES)}
    /--RESULT->{(:BW--LOCO3->('OUTSIDE.HOMES)}
    /--GOAL->{(:BW)--PAT->('WATCH)--TEM1->
                                        ('DAYBREAK)--CAT.ATT->('COLD)

        /--TEMO->(2.A.M.)

15 ('SOME.BW)--AGT@T(PAST)->(MOVE)*--DAT1->('THEMSELVES)
    /--SOURCE->{('SOME.BW)--LOCO2->('NYC)}
    /--RESULT->{(SOME.BW)--LOCO2->('FAR.FROM.NYC)}
    /--TEM11->('THROUGH.NIGHT)

16 ('MANY.BW)--AGT@T(PAST)QUAL(NEG)->('MOVE)*--DAT1->('THEMSELVES)
                        /--RESULT->{('MANY.BW)--LOCO2->('AT.WORK)}
                        /--TEM11->('THROUGH.DAY)

INFORMATION CHUNK D

17 ( )--AGT@T(PAST)ASP(COMP)->( )*--RESULT->{{('LIT.IN.ORNITH.}--HASP->('L.1)--EXT1->('MUCH)}
        /--GOAL->{{L.1 --IPAT->('DEMONSTRATE)--THEME2->
            {( )--PAT@QUAL(CAN)->('PREDICT)--THEME2->{('BIRDS)--LOC22->( )}}}}

18 (:SCIENTISTS)--PAT@ASP(ITER)->('PREDICT)*THEME2->{'UNTRUE.STATE}
                                        /--MAN.EXT1->('SOMETIMES)

19 ( )--AGT@ASP(ITER)- ('FIND)*--DAT1->(:BIRDS.1)
        /--LOC22( )
        /--RESULT->{( )--PAT->('SURPRISED)}

Instructions

1. Read the passage twice at your *normal reading speed.*
2. Record (on the cover sheet) the time spent reading.
3. If you have some background knowledge of the subject of a passage, indicate what (e.g., personal interest, course taken) on the appropriate "Special Knowledge" line.
4. Place the passage in the envelope provided.
5. Write all you can remember of the passage on the yellow sheet.
6. Place the yellow sheet in the envelope provided.
7. Fill in the question blanks *according to what the passage said.*
8. Place the questions in the evelope provided.
9. Rate statements from the passage for their relative importance to the passage. First mark the most important statements, then the least important statements. Rate all others "medium."
10. When you finish, place all materials in the envelope.

Design

Within sex and sample, subjects were assigned randomly to a given version of each passage and to one of the two possible order of presentation conditions.

Hypotheses

Free and cued recall.   The hypothesis was that information is better recalled after reading a passage in which it is staged high than after reading a passage in which it is staged at a lower level. The specific predictions for the information chunks in this experiment are shown in Tables 7 and 8.

Ratings.   There was no strong prior hypothesis with respect of ratings. The ratings were regarded as an exploratory measure.

The weak hypothesis was that if ratings were significantly different between versions of a passage, the direction of the difference should be toward higher ratings when the information was staged higher in the passage.

Results

Passages 1 and 2.   Table 7 presents the Average Free Recall Scores, Average Cued Recall Scores, and Average Rating Scores for each of the four information chunks scored in Passages 1 and 2.

As can be seen, the differences for the Free Recall and Cued Recall Scores were all in the predicted directions, indicating higher levels of recall for the information when it was staged higher in the passage. Several of the differences were statistically significant. This was not true for the Rating

TABLE 7
Free Recall, Cued Recall, and Rating Scores for Passages 1 and 2[a]

Information Chunk	Predicted Direction	Passage 1 Mean	Passage 2 Mean	t	Prob.[b]	Mann Whitney U	Prob.[b]
			Free Recall				
A	1 > 2	11.93	4.89	3.88	< .001	172.5	< .001
B	2 > 1	17.18	17.89	0.21	NS	386	NS
C	1 > 2	16.25	11.50	1.69	< .05	307	< .09
D	2 > 1	2.71	5.82	2.15	< .025	233	< .005
			Cued Recall				
A	1 > 2	15.18	6.18	5.68	< .001	102	< .001
B	2 > 1	20.96	21.82	0.21	NS	383	NS
C	1 > 2	19.32	14.54	1.92	< .05	294.5	< .06
D	2 > 1	4.36	7.71	2.29	< .025	212.5	< .002
			Ratings				
A	1 > 2	2.50	2.75			376.5	NS
B	2 > 1	4.53	4.96			325	NS
C	1 > 2	2.57	2.64			391.5	NS
D	2 > 1	2.21	2.60			216.5	NS

[a]Data combined for two samples of subjects, $n = 56$.
[b]One-tailed.

TABLE 8

Free Recall, Cued Recall, and Rating Scores for Passages 3 and 4[a]

Information Chunk	Predicted Direction	Passage 3 Mean	Passage 4 Mean	t	Prob.[b]	Mann Whitney U	Prob.[b]
			Free Recall				
E	3 > 4	28.25	20.61	1.81	< .05	276	< .03
F	4 > 3	14.96	15.00	0.01	NS	385	NS
			Cued Recall				
E	3 > 4	33.54	26.36	1.42	< .10	289.5	< .05
F	4 > 3	17.43	18.10	0.16	NS	384	NS
			Ratings				
E	3 > 4	10.00	9.60			287	< .05
F	4 > 3	6.28	6.71			343.5	NS

[a]Data combined for two samples of subjects, $n = 56$.
[b]One-tailed.

Scores, however, where all differences were small and two out of four were in the wrong directions. Thus there is no evidence that information staged high in the passage was perceived as being more important by these subjects.

Two of the information chunks, A and D, differed between passages by two levels of staging, while there was only one level of staging difference for chunks B and C. Thus we would expect greater difference in recall between the two passages for chunks A and D than for chunks B and C. The data in Table 2 are also supportive of this expectation, indicating a small recall difference for chunk B and a larger difference for C, but the largest differences for A and D.

Passages 3 and 4.   The results for Passages 3 and 4 on the combined sample are shown in Table 8. All differences were in the predicted directions. The differences for chunk F, however, were small and not statistically significant.

Discussion

Effects of staging on free recall.   Free recall differences were, without exception, in the directions predicted by the hypotheses. Thus, the data provide strong support for the view that information is better recalled when it is staged high in a passage than when it is staged at a lower level.

Acquisition versus retrieval.   The results of the first experiment consistently show that where a staging effect occurred in the free recalls, it remained following probes. These results are consistent with the view that staging has a marked effect on the acquisition of information.

This is to speak of acquisition of information at a fairly crude level. At a more refined level one might ask what features of text are processed to what level of understanding, and for how long given features are available in memory. Nonetheless, first things must come first. It is important to be sure that staging has some effect on acquisition of information before designing research to answer more specific questions about how the effect arises during input processing.

Ratings.   Only four of the six rating differences were in the predicted directions, and of these only one was significant. There is therefore scant evidence for the view that subjects' ratings of importance are determined by the staging structure of a passage.

In addition there was considerable disagreement between subjects in the ratings. Even on chunk E, for which a significant difference in ratings was found, agreement between subjects was low.

This lack of agreement between raters makes one question the value of such ratings in psycholinguistic research. Perhaps ratings of importance are made on the basis of several factors, one of which is staging. In this case the weight of the staging component of the rating decision might vary as a function of the weight of the other factors, none of which has been sorted out yet. In other words, "importance" is not well enough defined in linguistic or semantic terms to constitute a meaningful test.

The matter of ratings is worth further exploration. There is reason to suppose that ratings are not made on a unidimensional basis. Perhaps an approach using multidimensional scaling would bring to light a few underlying dimensions. If so, such results could be useful in further research by providing a means to develop more precise rating systems for use in psycholinguistic research.

Summary

The results of this experiment provide a clear demonstration of the importance of staging in determining what is recalled from prose. Furthermore, they suggest that staging probably has its major influence on the acquisition of information rather than on its retrieval. Finally, the results show that staging differences are not mirrored in readers' judgments of the importance of various segments of text.

The remaining experiments address more specific questions about the influence of staging on recall. They are reported very selectively in order to stay within the editor's space allocation for this chapter. It is anticipated that fuller reports of these experiments will appear in the forthcoming journal *Discourse Processes: a Multidisciplinary Journal* during 1978.

Second Experiment

Purpose

The aim of this experiment was to determine whether staging differences would affect recall when those differences depended solely on the old/new rule.

Subjects

The subjects who participated in this experiment were students enrolled in an introductory educational psychology course at Cortland College of the State University of New York. There were 22 subjects in the sample (12 males, 10 females).

Passages

The passages used were shorter than those used in the first experiment, being only 200 words in length.

Information chunks G, H, and I were staged at different levels in each passage. Staging differences in these passages depended solely on the classification of each topic as old or new.

As in all experiments, both passages had the same content.

Procedure

The procedure was the same as in the first experiment except that in this experiment:

1. each subject read only one passage.
2. subjects only read the passage once,
3. seven days later, without prior warning, subjects were asked to recall freely all they could about the passage they had read. This delayed recall was obtained during a normal class meeting, and thus no subterfuge was required to have the subjects return.

Results

Results of the experiment are shown in Table 9.

Discussion

Grimes' notion that the old/new distinction provides a basis for assigning relative prominence in text is strongly supported by these results.

These results are quite striking considering the small sample size and the brevity of the passages. The complexity of the passages somewhat offset their brevity, however.

Of particular interest in this experiment is the finding that the effects of staging were still quite marked after a seven-day delay. There are two possibilities with respect to this finding. One possibility is that the loss of information over time was independent of staging. In this case the size of the staging effect should remain roughly constant over time. The other possibility is that staging selectively affects the loss of information over time. In this case, the size of the staging effect should increase over time. Inspection of the results in Table 9 shows that for each information chunk, the ratio between means of passages is greater in the delayed condition. Since the total amount recalled in the delayed condition was quite small, however, one must be

TABLE 9

Free Recall, Cued Recall, and Rating Scores for the Second Experiment[a]

Information Chunk	Predicted Direction	Passage 9 Mean	Passage 10 Mean	t	Prob.[b]	Mann Whitney U	Prob.[b]	Ratio	High Mean Low Mean
				Free Recall					
G	9 > 10	9.73	4.27	2.25	<.025	28	<.025		2.28
H	10 > 9	4.09	14.45	2.05	<.05	32	<.05		3.53
I	10 > 9	5.73	10.27	1.28	<.25	39.5	<.20		1.79
				Cued Recall					
G	9 > 10	10.73	5.27	2.08	<.05	29.5	<.025		2.04
H	10 > 9	5.27	14.82	1.77	<.05	36	<.08		2.81
I	10 > 9	6.55	13.36	1.78	<.05	33.5	<.05		2.04
				Delayed Free Recall					
G	9 > 10	3.80	1.60	1.37	<.1	31	<.08		2.38
H	10 > 9	1.10	7.70	1.91	<.05	23.5	<.03		7.00
I	10 > 9	0.20	3.90	1.63	<.1	25	<.03		19.5
				Ratings					
G	9 > 10	4.9	3.8			43	NS		
H	10 > 9	4.2	4.5			49.5	NS		
I	10 > 9	3.8	3.6			51	NS		

[a]Sample 3, *n* = 20 for immediate recall conditions; *n* = for delayed recall.
[b]One-tailed.

cautious in interpreting these results. Nonetheless there is at least some suggestion in the data that staging affects forgetting as well as storage of information.

Third Experiment

Purpose

The aim of this experiment was to discover whether information is less likely to be recalled if it is subordinated in the passage read than if it is not subordinated. Since earlier experiments had shown recall effects due to staging, it was considered that if subordination was part of the staging system, it should similarly affect recall.

Subjects

The subjects who participated in this experiment were students enrolled in an introductory educational course at Cortland College of the State University of New York. There were 20 subjects in the sample (10 males, 10 females). This was a different sample from that used in the second experiment.

Passages

Two passages were used which had not been used in earlier experiments. Each passage contained three subordinated propositions that were not subordinated in the other passage. Thus there was a total of six propositions which occurred in the subordiante position in one passage but not the other. Only one method of subordination was used throughout. In each case the subordinated proposition was doubly embedded. Here is an example:

1. Civilized Oriental peoples can be grouped into four high cultures.
2. The music of these peoples is known as Oriental art music.
*3. Oriental art music should be distinguished from primitive tribal music.

In one version, the asterisked proposition was doubly embedded thus:

Civilized Oriental peoples, whose music is known as Oriental art music, which should be distinguished from primitive tribal music, can be grouped into four high cultures.

The other version simple contained the three separate sentences in the order in which they are numbered above.

Procedure

The procedure was the same as for the second experiment except that there was no delayed recall condition.

The scoring procedure was also the same as in other experiments. The asterisked propositions, which were embedded in one version but not the other, were represented by means of Frederiksen's system. Subjects were therefore assigned a score for each of the six propositions of interest.

Results

Scores were tallied across propositions so that each subject was given a score for subordinated propositions and for unsubordinated propositions. The means of these scores for free recall and cued recall are shown in Table 10. The results in this table indicate that the prediction was borne out. Propositions were better recalled when they were not subordinated than when they were. In the cued recall condition the observed difference was significant using both t test and the Wilcoxon Signed Rank Test for matched pairs.

Discussion

The results of this experiment show that subordination of the type used in the experiment significantly affects recall. These results are consistent with the view that subordination should be included as part of the staging system.

The matter warrants further investigation, however, for a number of reasons. To begin with, there is the question of whether the effect occurred because of double embedding or because relativizers were used at the head of subordinate clauses. Yet again, if the effect only occurs when lead sentences are divided between the beginning and end of complex propositions, then it might be that processing demands, rather than linguistic signals, are the cause. Furthermore, there are questions of whether it makes any difference

TABLE 10
Free and Cued Recall Scores for Third Experiment[a]

Mean Score Subord.	Mean Score Unsubord.	t[b]	Prob.[c]	Wilcoxon[d] Prob.
		Free Recall		
2.9	4.4	.917	NS	NS
		Cued Recall		
3.8	7.6	1.87	< .05	< .04

[a]Sample four. $n = 20$.
[b]t for correlated means.
[c]One-tailed.
[d]Wilcoxon Signed Rank test for matched pairs.

whether subordinate clauses precede or succeed the main clause, whether some linguistic signals and not others produce an effect, and whether the topic of a subordinate clause being old or new makes a difference.

Fourth Experiment

Purpose

Since the earlier experiments had shown that staging influences what is recalled from prose, this experiment was designed to explore the possibility that staging also influences retrieval time. The notion was that staging might affect the way in which memory is accessed, perhaps by determining the entry point for memory search.

This was very much an exploratory experiment and two features of staging were selected for study, making two parts to the experiment.

The aim of the first part was to see whether retrieval cues which are topicalized in the same way as the passage read, lead to shorter retrieval times than cues which contain the same information but different topicalization. Since topics define what one is speaking about, and since staging depends on the pattern of topics in relation to preceding information, it was thought that topics might have special salience in memory.

The aim of the second part was to see whether subordination affects retrieval time. The hypothesis was that retrieval times would be longer for subordinated propositions than for the same propositions when they are not subordinated.

Subjects

The subjects who participated were 32 high school students about to enter their senior year.

Passages

For the topicalization part of the experiment a pair of passages was written concerning an engagement dispute between two people. In one version the male was topicalized throughout and thus became the main character. In the other version the female was topicalized. Changes in topicalization were accomplished by using verbs that did not require the use of the passive voice, to avoid confounding topicalization with the active/passive distinction. An example is:

John gave an engagement ring to Lana.

versus

Lana received an engagement ring from John.

The subordination part of the experiment used the passages from the third experiment.

Equipment

A Digital Equipment Corporation PDP-11 computer, equipped with a real time clock, VT-11 cathode ray tube (CRT), and digital input/output activated by push buttons was used.

Procedure

The basic procedure for each part was to have subjects read a passage twice. Following this, probes were presented on the CRT and subjects were required to respond "true" or "false" by pushing the appropriate button.

Results

The reaction times of interest were those for correct responses to true probes.

Topicalization.   There was a mean reaction time difference of 40 msec in the predicted direction. The mean reaction time was shorter for probes having the same topic as the passage read. This difference was not significant.

Subordination.   There was a mean reaction time difference of almost 200 msec in the predicted direction, with mean response time being longer to probes that had been subordinated in the passage read. This difference was marginally significant ($p < .1$).

Discussion

The major problems in this experiment were the enormous variability in the data (due in part to inadequate training of subjects) and the collection of too few data points for analysis.

Although the evidence from this experiment does not warrant strong conclusions, it does suggest that further investigation of the effects of staging on retrieval might be worthwhile.

SUMMARY AND CONCLUSIONS

As the previous experimental section shows, the data have consistently been as predicted. Thus, there is strong empirical evidence to show that staging has a marked effect on what is recalled from reading.

In this section, the findings of the experiments are reviewed, the possibility of alternative explanations is considered, and some directions for further research are explored.

Does Staging Affect Recall?

The major question posed in this research was whether staging significantly affects what is recalled following reading of prose. Before resting the case with an answer in the affirmative, we must consider two further questions.

Is There an Alternative Explanation for the Results?

Part of the reply to this question is that very great care was taken to vary nothing save the staging between each pair of passages. Passages in each pair had the same content, were matched for number of words to within five words, and even shared the same surface forms to a very large degree. Surface forms were only altered when staging changes required this. Changing the topic of a sentence, for example, alters both the staging and the surface form of that sentence. At the text level, variations in text sequence which were used to alter staging may be regarded as text-level surface changes. What then of alternative explanations?

Since the device of changing topics to vary staging levels was used but twice in this study, we can dismiss considerations of surface structure changes within sentences. Of more interest is the question of text level variations in sequence.

Probably the most obvious rival explanation at this level would be a serial position effect; in fact, I know of no other rival. This would predict that information located at the beginning and end of a passage would be best remembered (due, respectively, to primacy and recency) and information a little after the middle of a passage would be worst remembered.

Fortunately, care was taken in preparing the passages to develop a number of instances in which the prediction from a serial position hypothesis would run counter to the prediction from staging. In Passages 1 and 2 (first experiment) chunk C occupied the same serial position in both passages. Staging was varied by changing the information which preceded this chunk. The serial position prediction in this case would be no recall difference, but there was indeed a difference in the direction predicted by staging. The results on Passages 9 and 10 (second experiments) provide further evidence. There were three information chunks (G, H, and I) and in Passage 10 they occurred in the sequence H, G, I. Inspection of the means for each chunk (Table 9) shows that the differences for Passage 10 are consistent with the serial position hypothesis; but it coincides with the staging hypothesis for this passage. In Passage 9, however, the chunks were in the sequence G, I, H. The serial position effect would predict that recall for chunks G and H be high and

I low. Staging would predict G best, I next, and H worst. As can be seen, the results do indeed follow the staging hypothesis. This is a strong demonstration because it shows that by using staging rules one can set up a passage to mimic the serial position effect or destroy it at will.

A further comment is necessary with respect to the evidence just cited. In an earlier section it was emphasized that a test of staging differences for a given chunk of information between passages (same content, different staging) is not the same as a test of differential recall for different chunks in a given passage (different content, different staging). In particular, it was noted that differences in the latter situation may be due either to staging or to content differences between chunks. This problem need not concern us in the comparisons just made between recalls from Passages 9 and 10, however. The reason is that in this case we are noting the different patterns of relationships between the three chunks in each passage. To the extent that content differences between chunks determined the recall differences between chunks in these passages, the pattern of recalls should be the same for both passages. Thus, if content factors did indeed affect the results, then the demonstration in the previous paragraph is strengthened thereby.

In answer to the question posed at the head of this section, therefore, we have found no better explanation for the results than that provided by the staging hypothesis, and we have been able to dismiss the serial position hypothesis.

Can Special Interest Override Staging Effects?

In an earlier section, I suggested that staging should be viewed as a default option, in the computer programming sense, which regulates the acquisition of information unless some higher level of control overrides this. Such a situation might arise when one deliberately tried to criticize an author's viewpoint, or when one has some special interest in the content. The first experiment provides an example, not previously mentioned, of a situation in which special interest can override staging.

This occurred with females in the first sample on chunk E, Passages 3 and 4. Although the overall staging effects for chunk E were signfiicant in the predicted direction, there was no recall difference for females in the first sample.

As it happens, there is a strong explanation for this. A number of the females in the first sample noted on the cover sheets of their experimental booklets (where "special knowledge" relevant to the passage was sought) that they had recently attended a performance of K. Kesey's play *One Flew over the Cuckoo's Nest*. This play has a strong emotional theme concerned with abuses of psychosurgery. Chunk E in the passages was about the concern of a fictitious Congressman with just such abuses. Thus it is not surprising that his chunk had high salience for these women regardless of the staging.

Thus, there is reason to suppose that special interests on the part of readers can diminish the effects of staging. These departures from recall differences in the directions predicted by the staging hypothesis do not, however, detract from the overall strength of the findings in this study. There are three reasons for this. First, the bulk of the evidence reported still overwhelmingly supports the staging hypothesis. Second, the notion that special interests might diminish recall effects due to staging is not a post hoc notion developed to explain occasional discrepancies. Such possibilities were hypothesized in advance, and not only for cases of special interest on the part of readers. Third, strong evidence has been provided to show that, in the case discussed, the readers concerned did indeed have heightened interest in certain segments of the passages read. This was not a weak supposition of what might have been the case.

Finally a suggestion for further research is inherent in the explanation offered. The research would be to prepare passages with staging differences, and have groups read them under varying task constraints. If the view of staging as a default option is correct, it should be possible to find recall differences due to staging in one sample, and to obliterate staging effects for the same passages in other samples by changing the task requirements. Such experiments would be interesting both with respect to the adequacy of the view of staging presented in this study and with respect to the capability of various groups of readers to overcome the effects of the emphasis patterns imposed by an author.

Reprise

In answer to our question of whether staging affects recall, we can now answer in the affirmative. No better explanation than staging has been found to fit the results and a strong explanation has been provided for the case in which the predictions were not borne out.

Concluding Comments

While it is clear that staging affects recall from prose, further work is needed to identify the precise ways in which staging influences cognitive processes during reading.

The evidence from the studies reported here suggests that staging might influence both acquisition and retrieval processes.

It would be worthwhile to study the effects of staging during reading. In this context one might ask, for example, whether staging influences attention and/or memory load at given points in a message. Eye-tracking could be used to monitor a readers's progress through text and probes interrupting reading could be introduced at selected points. The location and duration of fixations in relation to the staging hierarchy could be examined. Fixation times could perhaps be used as indices of processing load during reading.

The question of just how staging structure influences a reader's processing of a message is worth pursuing, because an adequate theory of reading will obviously need to take account of staging effects.

ACKNOWLEDGMENTS

The research reported here was supported through Grant No. NIE-G-74-0018, Structure and Learning from Natural Prose, from the National Institute of Education. Principal Investigator is Prof. George W. McConkie. This report is based on the author's PhD dissertation presented to the Graduate School, Cornell University, 1976.

REFERENCES

Crothers, E. J. *Paragraph structure description.* Unpublished manuscript, Program on Cognitive Factors in Human Learning and Memory, Report #40, Institute for the Study of Intellectual Behavior, University of Colorado, Boulder, Colorado, May, 1975.

Daneš, F. Functional sentence perspective and the organization of text. In F. Daneš (Ed.), *Papers on functional sentence perspective,* Janua Linguarum Series Minor No. 147. The Hague: Mouton, 1974.

Dik, S. *Co-ordination.* Amsterdam: North Holland, 1968.

Frederiksen, C. H. Representing logical and semantic structure of knowledge acquired from discourse. *Cognitive Psychology,* 1975, *7,* 371–458.

Grimes, J. E. *The thread of discourse.* The Hague: Mouton, 1975.

Halliday, M. A. K. The place of functional sentence perspective in the system of linguistic description, In F. Daneš (Ed.), *Papers on functional sentence perspective.* The Hague: Mouton, 1974.

Kintsch, W. *The representation of meaning in memory.* Hillsdale, N.J.: Lawrence Erlbaum Associates, 1974.

Schank, R. C. Conceptual dependency: A theory of natural language understanding. *Cognitive Psychology,* 1972, *3,* 552–631.

Author Index

Abelson, R., 2, *22*, 121, *135*
Abelson, R. P., 3, 7, *21*, 138, 140, 141, 142, *179, 181*, 201, 202, 203, *206*
Adams, M. J., 10, *21*
Anderson, R. C., 121, *135*, 143, *180, 196*
Austin, J. L., 210, *219*

Baldwin, J. M., 248, *269*
Baratz, J. C., 184, *195*
Barclay, G., 239, *242, 243*
Barr, R., 9, *21*
Bartlett, F. C., 2, *21*, 23, *51*, 53, 54, 72, 98, *119*, 138, 139, 142, *180*
Bateson, G., 138, 141, *180*, 208, *219*
Bayless, R., 247, *270*
Bearison, D. J., 113, *119*
Becker, J. C., 2, *21*
Berger, P., 209, *219*
Berlin, B., 140
Berndt, E. G., 113, *119*
Berndt, T. J., 113, *119*
Bever, T. G., 210, 212, *219*

Bloom, L., 212, *220*, 246, 248, 249, 266, 267, *269*
Bobrow, D. G., 2, 4, 5, 6, *21, 22*, 138, 140, *180*
Bochenski, I. M., 240, *242*
Bower, F. C., 49, *51*
Bransford, J. D., 55, *119*, 143, *180*, 184, *196*, 239, *243*
Bricker, V. R., 241, *243*
Brown, A. L., 53, 54, 73, 99, 117, 118, *119*
Brown, R., 212, *220, 286*
Bruce, B., *206*
Burt, M., 245, *269*

Cancino, H., 245, *269*
Carroll, J. B., 208, *220*
Cattell, J. McK., 10 *21*
Cazden, C., 275, *286*
Chafe, W., 121, 124, *135*, 138, 139, 144, 179, *180*
Chall, J., 9, *21*
Charniak, E., 2, *21*, 139, *180*

Cherry, L., 274, 282, 284, 286, *286*
Chomsky, N., 13, *21*, 207, 210, *220*
Circourel, A. V., 185, *196*
Clark, E., 210, *220*
Clark, H. H., 2, *21*, 24, *51*, 184, *196*
Clements, P., 128, *135*
Colby, B., 56, *119*
Cole, M., 56, *119*, 223, 224, 225, 226, 227, 229, *243*
Craik, F. I. M., 50, *51*
Crothers, E. J., 288, *330*
Crystal, D., 251, *269*

Dale, P., 248, *271*
Daneš, F., 289, *330*
Dasen, P. R., 223, *243*
DeForest, M., 53, 54, *120*
Devin, J., 246, *271*
Dewey, J., 50, *51*
Dik, S., 299, *330*
Doctorow, M., 2, *22*
Dore, J., 246, *269*
Dulay, H., 245, *269*
Duranti, A., 212, *220*
Durkheim, E., 209, *220*

Edwards, M., 248, *270*
Eimas, P. D., 2, 13, *22*
Ervin-Tripp, S., 197, *206*, 246, 248, *269*, 277, *286*

Fillmore, C., 55, *120, 220, 269*, 209, *220*
Fillmore, C. J., 41, *51*, 138, 140, 143, *180*
Flappan, D., 98, *120*
Fraisse, P., 73, 98, *120*
Frake, C. O., 138, 142, *180*
Franks, J. J., 143, *180*, 239, *243*
Frederiksen, C. H., 288, 303, *330*
Freedle, R., 121, 129, 131, 134, *135*, 199, *206*

Garfinkel, H., 185, *196*, 209, *220*
Garnica, O., 248, *270*
Garvey, C., 246, 262, *270*, 281, *286*
Gay, J., 224, 227, 229, *243*
Gelman, R., 246, *270, 271*
Gensler, O., 148, *180*
Glenn, C. G., 32, 35, 46, 49, *51, 52*, 53, 54, 57, 62, 72, 73, 98, 99, *120*, 121, 122, *135*
Glick, J., 224, 227, 229, *243*
Goffman, E., 138, 142, *180*, 209, 219, *220* 250, *270*
Gold, C., 2, 13, *22*
Goldman, A. I., 32, *51*
Goodenough, D. R., 200, 204, *206*
Goody, J., 209, *220*
Gracey, C. A., 248, *270*
Greenberg, J., 211, *220*
Greenfield, P., 246, *270*
Grice, H. P., 210, 215, *220, 286*
Grimes, J., 128, *135*, 288, *330*
Gumperz, J., 142, *180*
Gumperz, J. J., 199, 201, *206*

Hagen, J., *270*
Hall, V. C., 184, *196*
Halliday, M. A. K., 128, 247, 255, 256, *270*, 289, *330*
Hallowell, A., 208, *221*
Hasan, R., 128, 247, 255, 256, *270*
Hatch, E., 266, *270*
Haviland, S. E., 2, *21*, 184, *196*
Head, Sir Henry, 139, *180*
Heider, F., 46, *51*
Henle, M., 235, *243*
Herasimchuck, E., 199, *206*
Hoenigswald, H., 210, *220*
Holzman, M., 281, *286*
Hood, L., 246, 248, 249, 266, 267, *269*
Hymes, D., 138, 141, *180*, 197, *206*, 207, 209, *220*, 240, 241, *243*, 245, *270*

Isaacs, L., 113, *119*

Jager, R., 240, *243*
Jefferson, G., 215, 216, 218, *220, 221,*
    263, 267, *271,* 282, *286*
Jennings, K. H., 185, *196*
Jennings, S. H., M., 185, *196*
Johnson, L., *52,* 247, *270*
Johnson, M. K., 143, *180,* 184, *196*
Johnson, N. S., 32, 36, *51,* 53, 54, *120,*
    121, 122, 123, 131, *135*
Johnson, R., 72, 98, *120*
Johnson-Laird, P. N., 235, *243*
Jongeward, R., *270*

Kail, R., *270*
Kant, E., 2, *21*
Kaplan, R. M., 13, *22*
Kay, P., 140, 209, *220*
Keenan, E. O., 246, 248, 249, 250, 251,
    266, *270,* 282, *286*
Keller-Cohen, D., 245, 248, 267, 268,
    270, 271
Kemp, J., *271*
Kintsch, W., 24, 49, 50, *51,* 53, 54, 55,
    120, 121, *135,* 184, *196,* 288,
    330
Kluckhohn, C., 208, *220*
Kozminsky, E., 49, *51*

Labov, W., 145, 147, 167, 173, *180,*
    194, *196,* 201, *206,* 209, *220*
Lachman, R., 143, *180*
Lakoff, 151, 170, *180*
Lehnert, W., 2, *21*
Levy-Bruhl, L., *243*
Lewis, M., 274, 284, *286*
Lightbown, P., 248, 249, 251, 267, *269*
Lindauer, B., *135*
Lockhart, R. S., 50, *51*
Longacre, R., *135*
Lord, A. B., 56, *120*
Luckmann, T., 209, *219*
Luria, A. R., 224, 232, 236, 238, *243*
Lyons, J., 207, *220*

MacWhinney, B., 210, *220*
Mandel, T. S., 49, *51*
Mandler, J., 121, 122, 123, 131, *135*
Mandler, J. M., 32, 35, 36, *51, 53, 54,*
    120
Maratos, M., 13, *22*
Marcel, T., 13, *22*
Marks, C., 2, *22*
Marslen-Wilson, W., 13, *22*
McCarrell, N. S., 55, 119
Meyer, B. J. F., 41, 43, *51*
Meyer, D. E., 13, *22*
Minsky, M., 2, 4, *22,* 138, 142, *180*
Moerk, E. L., *270,* 281, *286*
Montague, W. F., 121, *135*

Nakanishi, Y., 248, *271*
Nash-Webber, B., 13, *22*
Naus, M., 121, *135*
Nelson, K., 267, 268, *271*
Newell, A., 8, *22*
Newman, S., 208, *221*
Nicholas, D. A., 24, *51*
Nicholas, D. W., 24, *52*
Nix, D. H., 186, *196*
Norman, D., *135*
Norman, D. A., 2, 4, 5, 6, *22,* 138, 140,
    180
Northcutt, N., 183, *196*

Ochs, E., 212, *220*
Omanson, R. C., *52*
Ortony, A., 2, 7, 8, *22,* 143, *180*
Owada, K., 248, *271*

Paris, S., *135*
Paris, S. G., 53, 54, 55, *120*
Pearson, P. D., 2, *22*
Piaget, J., 73, 98, 117, *120,* 122, *135*
Pichert, J. W., *196*
Platt, M., 250, *270*
Pompi, K. F., 143, *180*
Preyer, W., 248, *271*
Propp, V., 56, *120,* 140, *180*

Radcliffe-Brown, A. R., 209, *220*
Redfield, R., 208, *220*
Reicher, G. M., 2, 10, *22*
Rieger, C., 184, *196*
Rieger, C. J., III, 24, 43, *51*
Robins, R. H., 207, *220*
Rocissano, L., 246, 266, *269*
Rosansky, E., 245, *269*
Rosch, E., 140
Ross, J., 212, *220*
Ross, R. N., 138, *180*
Ruddy, M. G., 13, *21*
Rumelhardt, D. E., 2, 5, 7, 8, 13, *22*, 53, 54, 56, 57, 58, 75, *120*, 121, 123, *135*, 138, 140, *181*
Ryle, G., 242, *243*

Sachs, J., 246, *271*
Sacks, H., 215, *221*, 261, 263, 267, *271*
Sapir, E., 208, *221*
Schank, R., *22*, 62, 68, *120*, 121, *135*
Schank, R. C., 2, 3, 23, 46, 50, *51*, 138, 140, 141, 142, *181*, 201, 202, 203, *206*, 288, *330*
Schegloff, E. A., 215, *221*, 260, 261, 263, 267, *271*
Schmidt, C. F., 201, *206*
Schreffelin, B., 250, *270*
Schuberth, R. E., 2, 13, *22*
Schuman, J., 245, *269*
Schutz, A., 183, *196*
Schvaneveldt, R. W., 13, *22*
Schwartz, L., 121, *135*
Scollon, R., 246, *248, 250, 271*
Scribner, S., 223, 225, 226, 227, 229, 236, *243*
Searle, J., 210, *221*
Searle, J. R., *196*
Sharp, D., 224, 227, 229, *243*
Sharp, D. W., 225, 226, 227, *243*
Shatz, M., 246, *270, 271*
Shugar, G. W., 250, 265, *271*
Simon, H. A., 8, *22*

Smith, J., 246, *270*
Speier, M., *271*
Spier, L., 208, *221*
Spiro, R. J., 121, *135*
Stein, N. L., 32, 35, 46, 49, *51, 52,* 53, 54, 57, 62, 72, 73, 99, *120*, 121, 122, *135*
Stern, W., 248, *271*
Stevens, A. L., 13, *22*
Strawson, P. F., 210, *221*
Sully, J., 248, *271*

Tannen, D., 147, 150, 151, 170, *181*, 199, 205, *206*
Thorndyke, P. W., 32, 35, 36, 49, *52, 135*
Trabasso, T., 24, *52*
Tulving, E., 2, 13, *22*
Turner, R. R., 184, *196*
Tyler, L. K., 13, *22*

Vygotsky, L., *243*

Wallace, A., 208, *221*
Wannemacher, J. T., 13, *22*
Wanner, E., 13, *22*
Wason, P. C., 235, *243*
Waugh, N., *135*
Weiner, S. L., 200, 204, *206*
Werner, O., 199, *206*
Wheeler, D. D., 2, 10, *22*
Wittrock, M. C., 2, *22*
Woods, W. A., 13, 14, 15, *22*
Woodworth, R. S., 2, *22*, 223, *243*

Yendovitskaya, T. V., 72, *120*

Subject Index

B

Bilingualism, acquisition, 245–271
Bottom-up processing, 5–7

C

Cognitive science
  and dialogue, 197–206
  and sociolinguistics, 197–206
Cohension of text
  lexical, 255
  repetition, 251
Comprehension, of stories, 23–52;
  53–120, 121–135
Conversational requests, 273–286
Coordination of clauses and staging,
  298
Culture
  and logic, 223–243
  and language, 223–243
  and thinking, 223–243

D

Dialogue, 197–206; 245–271; 273–286
Discourse
  comprehension, 303
  production model, 301–303
  framing of, 193
  staging of, 287–330

E

Event chains, 23–52
Expectations and language, 137–181
Expository grammar, 121–135

F

Frame theory, 137–181
  cultural frame, 183–195
  story-telling frame, 149–150
  semantic frame, 142
  thematic frame, 142

I

Inference, text, 23–52; 117–118; 173; 184
Interactive processing across linguistic levels, 7–22

K

Knowledge activation, 193

L

Language
 acquisition issues, 23–52; 53–120; 121–135; 245–271; 273–286
 norming, 193

N

Narative, 23–52; 53–120; 121–135
Narratives
 grammar, 23–52; 121–135
 production, 118–119
Network, target, 186–188

O

Old/new information and staging, 296–298

P

Participant structure and sociolinguistics, 197–206
Propositions, staging of, 287–330

R

Reading, 7–22; 183–195

S

Schema theory, 1–22; 53–120; 121–135; 137–181; 183–195; 239–242
Scripts, 143
Setting and sociolinguistics, 197–206
Sociolinguistics, 137–181; 197–206; 207–221; 239–242
Syntax bending, 193
Subordination of clauses and staging, 299

T

Text cohesion, 251–259
Top-down processing, 5–7
Topics and sociolinguistics, 197–206
Topics, staging of, 287–330
Transfer of discourse schemata across genre, 121–135
Turn-taking, 246; 273–286